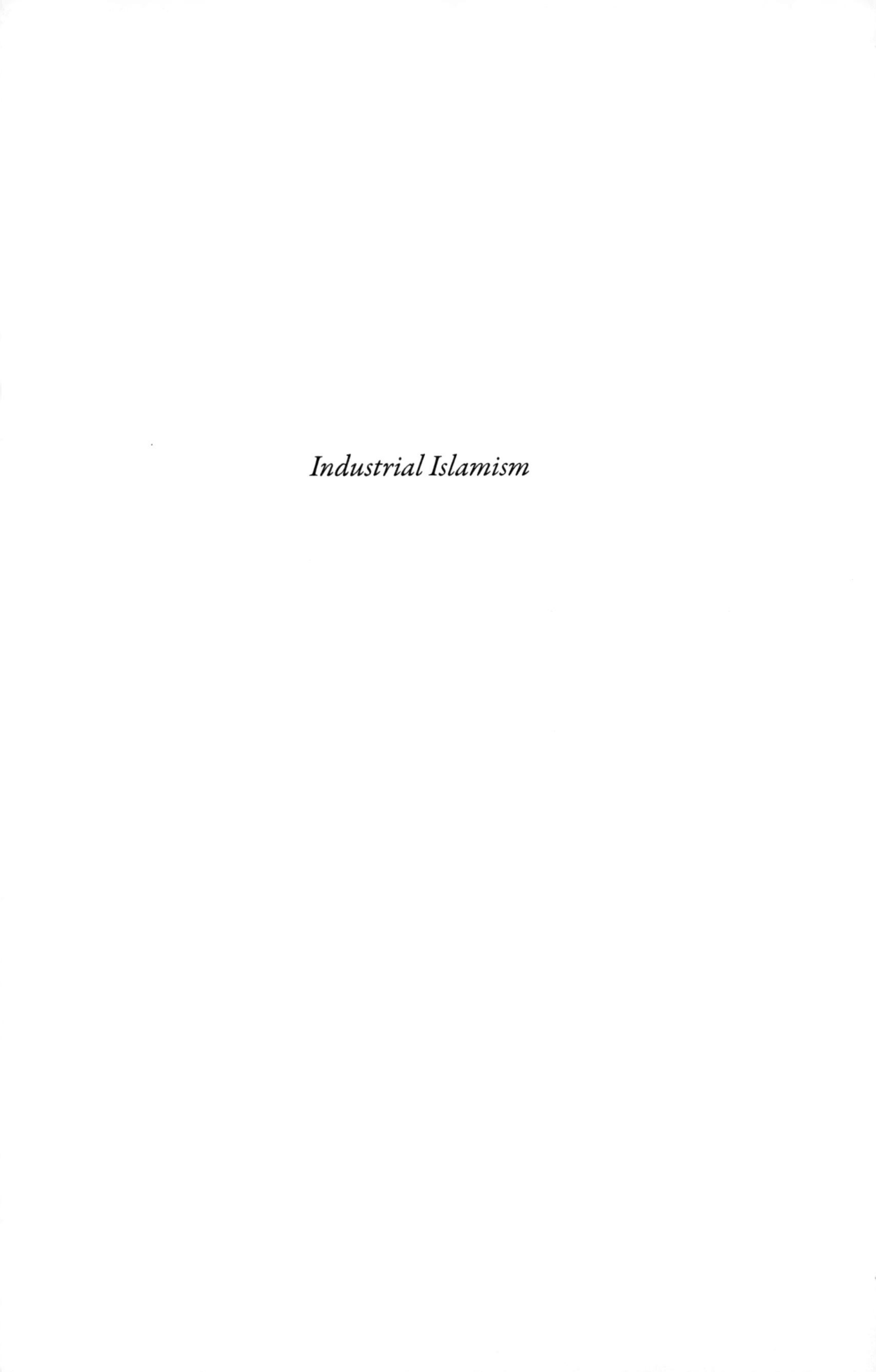

Industrial Islamism

Industrial Islamism

HOW AUTHORITARIAN
MOVEMENTS MOBILIZE WORKERS

Utku Balaban

UNIVERSITY OF CALIFORNIA PRESS

University of California Press
Oakland, California

Suggested citation: Balaban, U. *Industrial Islamism: How Authoritarian Movements Mobilize Workers*. Oakland: University of California Press, 2025.
DOI: https://doi.org/10.1525/luminos.240

Library of Congress Cataloging-in-Publication Data

Names: Balaban, Utku Barış, author.
Title: Industrial Islamism : how authoritarian movements mobilize workers / Utku Balaban.
Description: Oakland, California : University of California Press, [2025] | Includes bibliographical references and index.
Identifiers: LCCN 2024059213 | ISBN 9780520422537 (cloth) | ISBN 9780520389342 (paperback) | ISBN 9780520389359 (ebook)
Subjects: LCSH: Industrialization—Turkey. | Islamic fundamentalism—Political aspects—Turkey. | Authoritarianism—Turkey. | Middle class—Turkey. | Labor movement—Turkey.
Classification: LCC HC495.I52 B35 2025 | DDC 305.5/5309561—dc23/eng/20250417

LC record available at https://lccn.loc.gov/2024059213

GPSR Authorized Representative: Easy Access System Europe,
Mustamäe tee 50, 10621 Tallinn, Estonia, gpsr.requests@easproject.com.

34   33   32   31   30   29   28   27   26   25
10   9   8   7   6   5   4   3   2   1

CONTENTS

ILLUSTRATIONS

FIGURES

MAP

TABLES

ACKNOWLEDGMENTS

I am grateful to the Rosa Luxemburg Foundation, TAREM, the Friedrich Ebert Foundation, the Fernand Braudel Center at Binghamton University, the Migration and Environment Foundation at Koç University, the Social Policy Forum at Boğaziçi University, and the European Commission's Marie Skłodowska-Curie Actions for supporting various research projects between 2007 and 2015. Support from the following organizations and institutions was similarly crucial: Forum Transregionale Studien, IGK Work and Human Life Cycle in Global History at Humboldt University, Cornell University ILR School, Scholars at Risk, Scholars Rescue Fund, The New University in Exile Consortium at the New School, Middle East Studies Association Global Academy, and Eğitim-Sen. Amherst College provided funding to cover the costs of the open access program for this book.

Many have helped me with these research projects, and I am sure I have forgotten to mention some of them here. The Bağcılar Municipality provided the results of the 2006 survey. Bekir Ağırdır's Konda shared their research material. My colleagues at Siyasal Bilgiler Fakültesi and Republican People's Party informed me about the intricacies of politics in Ankara. Neşe Şen and Pelin Tuştaş diligently assisted me with the content analysis about Turkish Muslim orders. My colleagues, who spoke up against the government's military operations against the Kurdish civilians in 2015–16, came to my aid whenever I needed them. My parents and in-laws supported us unconditionally during the turmoil in the late 2010s and early 2020s. My brother helped me catch up on many bits and pieces in the final stages of the manuscript. Without my interlocutors, socialist friends and coworkers such as Ali, Engin, Serkan, and Ufuk, I could not have completed those research projects and updated some of my findings in recent years.

I would also like to thank Latife Akyüz, Aslı Bali, Beth Baron, Lourdes Beneria, Korkut Boratav, Aslı Iğsız, Eileen Kane, Çağlar Keyder, Georges Khalil, Mimi Kirk, Kader Konuk, Risa L. Lieberwitz, Marcel van der Linden, Arien Mack, Paulo Pedroso, Joan Scott, Amy Erica Smith, Judith Tucker, Michael West, and my colleagues at Xavier University for their support at various stages of the project. Richard J. Bernstein, Kiren A. Chaudhry, Donald Quataert, and Benita Roth, whom we lost before I could present them the manuscript, inspired me in distinct ways. Chris Dole, Zeynep Gönen and Thomas Movle provided insightful comments on the final manuscript. The excellent reviews by Christine Philliou and Cihan Tuğal uniquely improved the text.

In particular, I am indebted to Nazan Bedirhanoğlu, my partner, and Judith Friedlander, my mentor. Without their intellectual support, this book would not have become what it is. Needless to say, the mistakes are my own.

Cincinnati
February 7, 2025

The Context

Introduction

DURING THE EARLY 1990S, my family moved out of Ortaköy, a gentrifying lower-middle-class neighborhood along the Bosporus, and into the working-class community of Şirinevler. My new neighborhood, located near Istanbul's main highway, was a gateway to the rest of the city for recently settled working-class families taking root in the European part of Istanbul. The fathers of my new friends worked in construction and in garment sweatshops, one of which was located on the narrow street where we played soccer (see figure 1).

I was not an athletic child, but I enjoyed the game. One day, as I was trying to block my friend Tarık from tackling me, the others stopped to stare silently at a young man we had accidentally hit with our ball as he walked by. Usually, we paid little attention when this happened. The irritated passerby might chase us for fifty yards or so as part of the game.

This time was different. The young man's shocking appearance silenced me as well. He was dressed in a Metallica T-shirt, he had an earring in his left ear, and his long hair flowed to his shoulders. Strolling nonchalantly down the street as if he blended in, it seemed he cared little about causing a scandal, which he certainly knew he was doing. My friends elbowed one another, whispering, "Look at that dude!" I had seen men like him before in Ortaköy, so his looks did not surprise me, but I never expected to see someone like this walking down the streets of working-class Şirinevler, where almost nobody challenged local dress codes.

A moment later, I realized we were not the only ones staring at this strange man. He had also attracted the attention of a group of (male) workers taking a tea and cigarette break outside the garment sweatshop up the street. They

FIGURE 1. The author's childhood street in Şirinevler. Anonymous photographer, December 28, 2023.

had been looking for a distraction during their precious fifteen minutes of freedom from their tedious work routines. This weird-looking creature, with his long hair and curious outfit, fit the bill.

After the stranger turned the corner, we went back to our game. The men at the sweatshop gazed at us and at passersby, no doubt assuming that nothing else interesting would happen before they went back to work. But then another strange man came walking down the street, sporting a long beard, a green overcoat, and a turban; despite his youth, he was also carrying a cane. He looked as if he had leapt off the pages of a picture book of nineteenth-century religious Muslims. I didn't think this second man looked like a local either. Based on the expressions on their faces, the workers at the garment sweatshop seemed as surprised by him as they had by the man with long hair, earring, and Metallica T-shirt.

My father had taken the risk of leaving gentrifying Ortaköy and moving to Şirinevler in the 1990s to open a pub with his brothers and nephews. He had been unable to make ends meet on his meager salary as a teacher, so this opportunity looked promising. I would go to the pub to watch soccer games on TV and help my uncles and cousins serve customers. Even though fights frequently broke out among intoxicated customers, the pub had the feel of a congenial place where men could let off a little steam after the drudgery of their workday routine. This working-class community had become more conservative than it had been in the 1970s, but the Islamists had not yet taken over.

When I began my research in 2008, things looked very different in Şirinevler and neighboring communities. Although the daily routine for sweatshop workers had changed very little, the political allegiances of the workers had been transformed. Şirinevler had become an unrivaled stronghold for Islamists. In this new political and religious climate, my family's pub had been forced out of business. Exorbitant taxes on alcoholic beverages and the growing stigma against alcohol consumption made it impossible for my father and uncles to keep the pub afloat. Furthermore, the workers had much less money than before to spend on recreation.

I realize now that even as a child, I saw changes taking place, especially in the lives of the women in my family. Like my parents, these women had left their homes in rural Turkey for working-class neighborhoods in Istanbul. We came from Kars province, in the northeastern part of the country, one of Turkey's ten poorest provinces.[1] My relatives were pious, but they also loved Mustafa Kemal Atatürk, Turkey's secularist founder, whom they credited with liberating Kars in the 1920s from four decades of Russian occupation. Once the Islamists got a foothold in Şirinevler, they began criticizing secularism. By the 1990s, it had become impossible to proclaim allegiance to Atatürkism and identify as a pious Muslim. What it meant to be pious had changed as well.

In response to these changes, a few female cousins of mine adopted the chador. Their commitment to their new cosmological outlook let them aggressively proselytize other cousins and aunts—with success. They described to my female relatives the same kind of patriarchal bargain Deniz Kandiyoti discussed in her seminal article[2] about why so many Iranian women enthusiastically supported the Islamic revolution. Like their counterparts in Iran, my cousins and aunts accepted "the restriction imposed on them by an Islamic order [in exchange] for the security, stability and presumed respect [the new] order promised them."[3]

First-generation migrant women came to believe their lives had improved in the city. They no longer had to perform heavy farm labor. The meager wages their husbands earned in sweatshops and on construction sites were enough to purchase groceries and rent an apartment with amenities unavailable in their villages. They had little incentive to take jobs in sweatshops alongside their husbands, as they would not earn enough money to change their families' living conditions significantly or improve their social status. In any case, working in a sweatshop was not an option for most: the Turkish government did not provide subsidized or public childcare, so women had to remain home to look after the children.

The self-proclaimed proselytizers of the new Islamist ideology gave women in our family a way to justify and take pride in becoming full-time homemakers. They may have forfeited the dubious privileges they had enjoyed in the old patriarchal order, privileges earned by performing the unforgiving tasks of pastoral life, but they had been emancipated from wage labor in the city. It was not their fault that the rural economy had crumbled in the wake of the neoliberal reforms of the 1980s, forcing their families to move to the cities. They were offered a new bargain, and many of them were ready to take it.

In 1980, a coup had crushed the socialist movement across the country. The coup destroyed the political aspirations of my parents and those of their political comrades. Some of my parents' closest friends, those whom I called "uncle," were killed. Many others were imprisoned, tortured, fired, or blacklisted. Although socialism was no longer a realizable goal for the foreseeable future, I vividly remember how my mother resisted the proselytizers in our family as she tirelessly tried to convince my female cousins and aunts that the ideal of gender equality was something worth salvaging from the political mess after the coup. "Find a job," my mother urged her female relatives, so that they might regain a degree of economic independence from their husbands. Her counsel fell on deaf ears. The proselytizers in our family offered something much more practical: a path that assured our female cousins and aunts of "security, stability, and presumed respect" through a new kind of patriarchy.[4]

Looking back on her inability to convince her female relatives, I realize my mother had been one of the rare achievers in our family. She had one of the highest scores in our poor town on the entrance exams for the all-girls public boarding school that trained future teachers. By eighteen, she had already become a primary school teacher. Her cousins and aunts did not share her experiences and dreams, which may explain why they welcomed the new bargain.

They were not alone. As I was growing up, women across the nation were withdrawing from the labor force in impressive numbers—this, in a country with one of the lowest rates of female labor force participation in the world. In 1991, Turkey's female labor force participation ranked 148th out of 187 nations. By 2000, it had dropped to 169th.[5] Labor economists associate declines of this magnitude with rapid urbanization and illustrate it on a "U-shaped female labor force function"[6]—a model that describes Turkey particularly well. In the 1980s, Turkey experienced record-breaking rates of urbanization.

Islamist ideology provided female proselytizers, like those in my family, with a political and moral justification for this widespread economic trend. With the help of these proselytizers, female homemakers became the most enthusiastic supporters of Islamism at the polls.[7] By the 1990s, this homemaker ideology was extremely influential. It would have a long-lasting impact on gender relations and on the composition of the labor force. With a slowdown in rural-to-urban migration after the 1990s, the rate of female labor force participation increased slightly, but it never caught up with the rate found in other upper-middle-income countries. In 2023, Turkey still ranked 160th out of 185 nations.[8]

The patriarchal new deal set in those years was an indirect but essential component of a new labor regime that left no room for organized labor, collective action, or public services for working mothers. Many of the daughters and granddaughters of my cousins and aunts later wanted to work, yet the cultural milieu was no less conservative, the work conditions were even more severe, and the social policy was designed to keep women at home. They had to stay at home even if they did not want to. They were paying a bill left them by the previous generation of women.

As one of the most formidable successes of the Islamist movement, this patriarchal new deal was mostly invisible in the 1990s, as was the discursive struggle between the proselytizers like my cousins and the high achievers like my mother. The political spectacle that made headlines in the 1990s gave outside observers a very different impression about the growing conservative groundswell: young college students wearing hijabs were denied access to higher education by the secularist political establishment.

Faculty members forced female students to remove their headscarves and interrogated them about whether their families were forcing them to preserve this sartorial practice.

This story was real, as was the suffering of these young women. Their experience, however, was the opposite of what was happening to poor rural migrant women. Having no other option, they embraced a system that protected them from the punishing pressures of the capitalist market by isolating them at home. Young college women from culturally conservative homes wanted to take part in public life as Muslim women and demanded access to privileged public-sector careers, which they ultimately gained. Some came from poor families, but many did not. Either way, very few of them worried about the impact of the new patriarchal bargain on poor migrant women. There was a class difference or a difference regarding the prospects of economic mobility between my cousins and these young female college students. We were told the story of the latter, as though the former was not worth telling.

THE ACTOR

Moving from a lower-middle-class neighborhood to a working-class neighborhood was a big change for me as a child, especially given the Islamist transformation taking place in my new neighborhood and extended family. As I look back on those years, I realize that my experiences motivated and guided this research. This book, based on fifteen years of research, begins in working-class neighborhoods in Istanbul, then moves on to smaller industrializing cities in distant parts of the country, with a brief detour to Addis Ababa, Ethiopia.

My burning quest was to find a more persuasive explanation for why an Islamist transformation had occurred in Turkey. The grand narrative on this subject contradicted what I had experienced or observed through ethnographic research. Using the center-periphery approach to history,[9] most scholars describe the rise of Islamist movements during the twentieth century as the reaction of oppressed subaltern masses to the secularist political establishment. According to this account of the rise of Islamism and its conservative patriarchal values, waves of rural migration brought subaltern members of society to urban centers during the 1970s. They strengthened the ranks of the marginalized in cities; together, they overthrew the secularist elite. This explanation draws, ironically, on Edward Shils's Cold War rhetoric.[10]

Although this grand narrative has appealed to many, it is factually flawed. Islamist values gained influence in working-class neighborhoods during the 1990s, not the 1970s. Although Islamists had been a permanent fixture in Turkish party politics since the 1970s, migrants were not then running to the ballot box to support them. Many working-class communities like Şirinevler remained a "breeding ground" for socialists.[11]

In the 1990s, proselytizers like my female cousins and that mysterious young man with his cane and turban became the most influential voices. Women like my mother were accused of being representatives of "the secularist elite." It mattered little that my mother had grown up in one of the poorest towns of the country and was an unaffiliated socialist.

As I conducted my research, I came to understand a major flaw in this grand narrative. It assumed that rural migrants were a homogeneous mass who rose up with one voice against an almost mystical secularist elite. In this script, proselytizers were regarded as legitimate representatives of this homogeneous mass and key actors in bringing about a patriarchal shift. Lumping the migrants into one ill-defined mass turned key actors into irrelevant details.

One of these key actors was the small entrepreneur, like the man in Şirinevler who owned the sweatshop on the street where I played soccer as a child. He could easily be confused with one of his workers, a mistake he did his best to cultivate, implying by his demeanor that he shared the same destiny as his employees.

The sweatshop owner in Şirinevler was not a diehard Islamist or even a devout Muslim. Yet he tacitly supported Islamist policies and promoted the political agenda of local conservatives. As the employer of the husbands and fathers of my female relatives, he was the enabler of the patriarchal new deal, the one who helped the first of my proselytizing cousins persuade the other women in our family to listen to her and not to my mother. My cousin's victory pulled the prospects of a revival of socialist politics from the equation, so it helped the sweatshop owner intensify his exploitation of his workers and survive ruthless local and global competition.

Sweatshop owners like this man in Şirinevler are not unique to Turkey. People like him exist in every country impacted by the wave of global transformations in industrial relations, known by some as "the second industrial divide"[12] and by others as post-Fordism.[13] The outsourcing of manufacturing

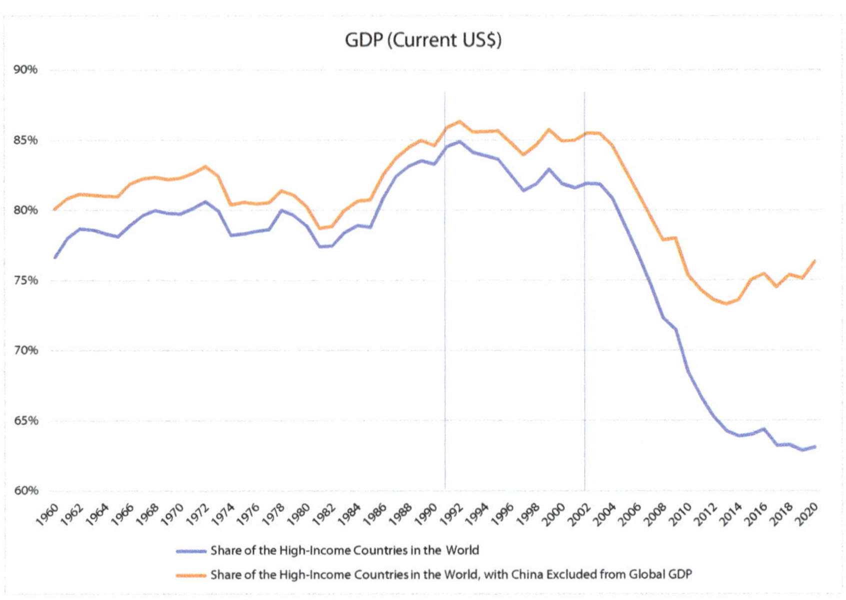

FIGURE 2. High-income countries' share of global GDP (1960–2020). Calculated by the author using the World Bank country indicators.

activities from the North Atlantic to the rest of the world deindustrialized the former and reindustrialized the latter.

With these changes, a new economic actor emerged at the bottom of global commodity chains. This nonmonopoly entrepreneur, often a sweatshop owner like the one in Şirinevler, exploits employees in a desperate effort to survive the pressure of domestic and global competition. According to recent International Labour Organization estimates, roughly four hundred million people—10 percent of the global working population and 15 percent of the global urban working population—are employed in such small and micro-sized industrial enterprises.[14] The owners of these sweatshops are the third biggest employers worldwide, after governments and global corporations.

In other words, the sweatshop owner on my street, together with millions of others, has played a critical role in facilitating a significant shift in the global redistribution of wealth. As this entrepreneurial group reduces the price of manufactured goods for North Atlantic consumers, the gap between high- and low-income countries is narrowing. As shown in figure 2, the share of global gross domestic product (GDP) held by high-income countries rose to around 80 percent in the 1960s and 1970s and to 85 percent in the early 1990s. Then the trend reversed. The share of global

GDP held by high-income countries fell dramatically, from 82 percent in 2002 to 63 percent in 2020.[15]

For the first time since the Industrial Revolution two centuries ago, global inequality is not driven by a growing divide between rich and poor countries.[16] This development coincides with the rise of a new middle class in the non–North Atlantic world, especially in emerging Asian economies.[17] Together, the old and new middle classes account for 15 percent of the world's population. It stands between the richest thousandth of the richest thousandth of the global population, or the monopoly capitalists—who, in 2021, owned approximately $26 trillion, 6 percent of the world's total wealth—and the poorest 84 percent, who own 18 percent of the total wealth and are unable to save enough to provide their children with the basic resources they need for even a modest chance at social advancement.[18]

Industrial Islamism shows how nonmonopoly entrepreneurs in Turkey enabled the rise of Islamism in a nation where, for decades, the government had provided a secular alternative for people living in Muslim-majority countries. These entrepreneurs belong to a hitherto undefined social class, which I call the *faubourgeoisie*. The defining members of this class are small manufacturers, but other nonmonopoly entrepreneurs, those who serve global commodity chains, are also members of the faubourgeoisie. They include shopkeepers, slumlords, and construction contractors who do business with or employ workers.

As I make the case that the faubourgeoisie has played a key role in the rise of the Islamist movement to power, I analyze and compare the relationship of these nonmonopoly entrepreneurs to other major class actors in Turkey: the proletariat, the petty bourgeoisie (professionals, bureaucrats, and scholars), and the bourgeoisie (monopoly capitalists).

Members of the faubourgeoisie are neither monopoly capitalists nor proletarians. Culturally and socially, they look and sound more like workers than like members of any other class, but they are employers, fragile though their economic position may be. As entrepreneurs, they serve a function in the capitalist economy that could be taken over at any time by big corporate structures controlled by the bourgeoisie. To appease monopoly capitalists, members of the faubourgeoisie squeeze what they can out of their workers while trying to protect their interests against the bourgeoisie by supporting Islamic populism. Members of the faubourgeoisie also do not belong to the conventional middle class, the petty bourgeoisie. The interests of those two nonproletarian, nonbourgeois classes often clash, resulting in tension between secularists and Islamists.

The faubourgeoisie decided to support the Islamist movement as a strategy for protecting its place in the global economy by becoming an influential actor in local and national politics, especially after the end of the Cold War. Over 450,000 small and medium manufacturing enterprises, or manufacturing SMEs, employ roughly two-thirds of the manufacturing workers in Turkey. Most of these enterprises are located in working-class neighborhoods like Şirinevler.[19] Because the owners of these manufacturing SMEs work as subsidiaries of global corporations under the control or ownership of the bourgeoisie, they needed the support of a political party to give them some leverage over the wealthiest class in Turkey and their foreign corporate customers. The populist Islamists offered this; in exchange, and with incentives of their own, the faubourgeoisie used its influence to encourage its millions of employees to abandon their socialist leanings and embrace the Islamist narrative instead.

Unlike members of the bourgeoisie, proletariat, or petty bourgeoisie, the faubourgeoisie work directly with the Islamists. As such, they are not merely a faction of the business sector but a separate social class whose own political agenda includes finding an ally to help control the interests of the bourgeoisie. Working hand in hand with the Islamists, the faubourgeoisie helped transform that movement into a dominant political force.

THE ARGUMENTS

In *Industrial Islamism*, I make four arguments to explain how the faubourgeoisie helped the Islamists come to power and transform Turkish politics.

My first argument is that there is a connection between industrialization and Islamization. The rise of Islamism in Turkey conforms to a wider pattern found throughout the Muslim-majority world (MMW). The more industrialized a Muslim-majority country becomes, the more visible the Islamization process, defined as the increasing use of religious motifs in politics. Various forms of mystification have obscured this pattern, such as questionable assertions about Islamism being "a cultural reaction to modernism" or Turkey being "a bridge between the East and the West." Using Turkey as my case study, *Industrial Islamism* offers the first detailed analysis of a Muslim-majority country to clearly connect the rise of Islamism to industrialization in the context of globalization. I argue that the most direct and effective way to understand how these processes intersect is through a class analysis that focuses on the relationship between employers and employees and the historical conditions behind Islamization. Turkey is not an exception within the MMW but is a case illustrative of this connection.

My second argument is that the Turkish Islamists' outstanding political performance can be traced to their strategy of making an alliance with the faubourgeoisie, the key actor in bringing about post–Cold War industrialization in the country. The Islamists have stayed in power in Turkey without interruption longer than other Islamist movements within the MMW, with the single exception of the mullah regime in Iran.[20] It has been a success. Jihadists and dynastic/oligarchic regimes have triumphed elsewhere, but in Turkey Islamism has come to power by nonviolent, democratic means. This story originates in the late 1950s, when Islamists in Turkey first reached out to small manufacturers.

My third argument is that the core motif in the relationship between the Islamists and the working class is domination. Although the Islamists came to power in Turkey by democratic means and their relationship with the working class can be described to a certain degree as clientelism, they developed and used tools honed by what Michel Foucault once called "regimes of domination"[21] to try to mobilize the proletariat on their behalf. Thanks to the Islamists' success at mobilizing the proletariat—with the critical support of the faubourgeoisie—they have been winning national parliamentary and presidential elections since 2002. In the 2010s, the leading Islamist clique purged its major rivals in national politics—the secularists, the Kurdish movement, and another Islamist clique led by cleric Fethullah Gülen—thanks to these regimes of domination.

My fourth argument grounds my analysis in a theory of class formation and of capital accumulation. My analysis of how the faubourgeoisie helped Islamists come to power and transform Turkish politics invites a return to the old debate among Marxist theorists about definitions of "the middle classes." What are commonly referred to as the middle classes are, in fact, "circulation classes." Marxists such as Nicos Poulantzas and Erik O. Wright have described three major circulation classes but failed to relate the formation of these classes to the theory of capital accumulation. In my discussion of the faubourgeoisie, I analyze the formation of the middle classes in relation to the theory of capital accumulation in Turkey, other Muslim-majority countries, and beyond.

This book is divided into three parts: "The Context" (this introduction and chapter 1), "The Alliance in Formation" (chapters 2 and 3), and "The Alliance in Action" (chapters 4–7).

Chapter 1, "Industrial Islamism," analyzes the connection between the Islamization of politics and post–Cold War industrialization across the MMW. It focuses on the changes taking place across three key indicators: the size of the industrial labor force, the volume of capital investment, and the availability of hydrocarbon resources. I relate these indicators to the University of Gothenburg's Varieties of Democracy (V-Dem) dataset,[22] which allowed me to use country experts' opinions about the extent of the Islamization of politics as a quantitative metric. The size of the industrial labor force is closely correlated with V-Dem scores for the Islamization process since the early 1990s, for both individual countries and the MMW in general. If a Muslim-majority country has a relatively large industrial labor force, there is a very good chance it also is assigned a high Islamization score.

I then add the other two indicators to gain a better understanding of the defining character of the Islamization process in individual countries. In countries where none of these factors are large, the Islamization process is weak. Countries at the other end of the spectrum, those with an abundance of capital and hydrocarbon resources, tend to develop dynastic regimes—the Islamization process in these countries is led by the political establishments of those regimes rather than by independent political movements. The jihadist movements have been particularly successful in countries with substantial oil and natural gas reserves but without significant capital investment. Nonviolent or nonjihadist Islamist movements have effectively challenged the political establishments in countries that have a large industrial labor force, receive significant capital investment, and lack significant hydrocarbon resources. Turkey has what I call a *movement-led regime.*

The model proposed in chapter 1, though simple, is very successful at predicting the extent of the Islamization process and the key actors behind this process in individual countries. The model also offers a good explanation for outliers, many of which (such as Somalia and Afghanistan) had a socialist past. Tunisia resembles Turkey according to the indicators under examination, but unlike in Turkey, Tunisia's Islamists were contained by the secularist establishment thanks to the strength of organized labor until very recently. The quantitative and historical material reveals that the strength of organized labor in countries that have adopted an extensive export-oriented growth model since the 1970s is the key factor that determines the chances of Islamist movements. Where Islamists are strong, organized labor is suppressed. Where organized labor is strong, Islamists have less chance to come to power.

Chapter 2, "The Islamists," and chapter 3, "The Islamists and the Faubourgeoisie," focus on how Islamists became successful in Turkey, which was once regarded as the most secular of the Muslim-majority countries. Chapter 2 begins by correcting the historical record about the rise of Islamism in Turkey. Due to the pervasive effect of Orientalism, practically everyone who writes on the subject feels obliged to trace the story back to something or someone in the nineteenth century or before. Islamists support and enjoy these efforts because they give legitimacy to the idea that Islamists represent the subaltern masses confronting the alien regime of secularist republicans.

I argue that the rise of today's Islamist movements does not have roots in a distant past. I trace its origins to the 1960s, when Islamism emerged as part of a political movement that sought an alliance with small-time manufacturers. Under the leadership of Necmettin Erbakan, a mechanical engineer, they championed an industrialization strategy that favored small manufacturers over a small number of big industrialists who had been acting as the *compradors* of US-based capital at the time. A few years later, after the bloody 1980 coup, Turgut Özal, an electrical engineer, passed neoliberal reforms that turned these small manufacturers into the strongest actors in the Turkish economy. Özal was a member of Erbakan's Islamist party in the 1970s. He also had the support of the secularist junta, which embraced his export-oriented reforms. He personified a tacit agreement between the secularists and the Islamists about the new antilabor political and economic transformation of the country.

Thanks to Özal's export-oriented growth policies, these small manufacturers had gained a prominent position in the Turkish economy by the 1990s. Erbakan's decades-long strategy had apparently paid off. The bitter irony was that the pious small manufacturers active in the Islamist party supported Tayyip Erdoğan, now the president of the country, who ultimately expelled Erbakan from politics.

Chapter 3 describes how these small manufacturers, the faubourgeoisie, were recruited to support the Islamist movement. Erbakan's decision in the 1970s to ally himself with these small manufacturers was astute and pragmatic. No other political party at the time had reached out to the faubourgeoisie. But why did this class support the Islamists with increasing enthusiasm over the next twenty years? This chapter describes how the Islamists offered a comprehensive portfolio to members of the faubourgeoisie to ensure the support of both the pious and more secular members of this class.

Three major actors within the Islamist movement organized the campaign: the political cadre, the business community, and the religious orders. The political cadre offered the faubourgeoisie subsidized credit to let this class have relative autonomy from the bourgeoisie. With this goal in mind, members of the Islamist business community played a critical role in the 1990s, transforming the Islamist party into what it is now by helping the faubourgeoisie define itself as a class deeply embedded in the Islamist narrative. The religious orders denigrated the labor of workers and assigned a higher social-spiritual status to the faubourgeoisie.

Chapter 4, "The Faubourgeoisie and the Proletariat," and chapter 5, "The Proletariat," draw on ethnographic research I conducted in 2008. During that year, I worked as an unskilled laborer in four garment facilities in the very center of the largest working-class region of the country, Bağcılar—a district just a few miles away from my childhood neighborhood, Şirinevler. I lived in the district and had previously worked there as a grassroots organizer for one of Turkey's socialist parties. This experience convinced me that the relationship between the Islamists and their constituency was characterized by domination, not cultural affinity or clientelist bargains. Through my fieldwork, I identified three regimes of domination exerted over the workers in the neighborhood by local members of the faubourgeois-Islamist elite.

Workers were under constant surveillance by members of the local elite to minimize their political autonomy. The pressure of the local elite took on a scopophobic form. I call this the *gaze regime*. Workers also faced political isolation. My experiences in 2008 showed me how working in a sweatshop cut my coworkers off from organizing politically. The constant fear of unemployment due to the erratic nature of the global commodity chains compounded the problem and persuaded the workers to be exceptionally docile. The drudgery of work, precarious employment, and identity-based segmentation of workers are the pillars of this *labor regime*.

The third regime of domination is the *hygiene regime*. Even though few of them were active followers of the movement, many of my coworkers were receptive to the messages of the religious orders. I sensed that this was in part a response to the drudgery of their work and how it isolated them from politics. The religious stories circulated by self-proclaimed proselytizers provided my coworkers with an escape from the capitalist labor process. Defining symbolic purity as the spiritual goal of Muslims, the religious orders provided my coworkers with guidance about community norms and gave them limited but practical tools to shield themselves from the pressure of the local elite. The narrative was also fine tuned so that their class-related anger was directed from their employers to "the secularists" or "the Europeans," whom my coworkers saw as the real enemy. This boundary-making process helped their employers present themselves as allies of their workers.

Chapter 6, "Rifts and Authoritarianism," discusses the implications of the previous two chapters for the rifts between the ruling clique of Islamists under the leadership of Erdoğan and the three other major political actors in the 2010s: the secularists, a rival Islamist clique led by Gülen, and the Kurdish movement. In each rift, the faubourgeoisie played a key role. The Erdoğan clique owed its victory in the first rift to the reluctance of the secularists to intervene in the relations between the proletariat and the faubourgeoisie because those relations were the source of the secularists' economic and cultural privileges as well. The tensions between the faubourgeoisie and the Gülenist big businesses over industrial relations helped the Erdoğan clique muster the support of the former and purge the Gülenists. The peace negotiations with the Kurdish movement had the potential to undermine the political unity of the Turkish and Kurdish faubourgeoisie under the ideological canopy of Islamism, and a stronger Kurdish faubourgeoisie could have posed a threat to the left-oriented leadership within the Kurdish movement. The negotiations failed in the mid-2010s, with dramatic consequences for Kurdish politicians and civilians.

In chapter 7, "The Theory," I ground the research material from previous chapters in a theoretical framework about class formation in the post–Cold War period that can be used for future research in Turkey and other countries. My theoretical observations focus on four patterns of class formation that have taken shape since the 1990s. First, a new middle class has emerged in non–North Atlantic countries. Inspired by the French historian Henri Pirenne's description of the rise of new groups of merchants and artisans on the outskirts, or the faubourgs, of flourishing cities in eleventh-century Europe, I argue that a significant portion of this new middle class in "the global faubourgs" of the world economy are members of what I call the faubourgeoisie. Second, the ensuing change in the global composition of the middle class is prone to political tensions. Professionals, scholars, and bureaucrats are losing prestige and status, and nonmonopoly entrepreneurs are playing a more visible role in politics and authoritarian movements like Islamism, provoking conflicts between themselves and the traditional middle class (the petty bourgeoisie). Third, these changes are happening at the expense of the working class, which suffers from a growing split between their productivity and income. Fourth, the proportion of capital owned and controlled by monopoly capitalists or the bourgeoisie has grown considerably since the end of the Cold War.

I argue that these patterns can be combined into a unified theory of class formation with the help of Marx's paradigm described in *Capital*. The story of the Islamist movement in Turkey and the Islamization process in the MMW offers a new perspective about the notion of middle class, which has been a theoretical riddle for Marxists and non-Marxists for over a century. The key to this puzzle (and my contribution to the theory of class formation) is in what Marx called "the circulation of surplus value." Analysis of the appropriation and production of surplus value as the two other processes of capital accumulation reveals the position of the nonproletarian and nonbourgeois social classes in wealth distribution and their motives in the capitalist labor process. Analysis of the circulation process identifies three middle classes and their functions in the accumulation process. The petty bourgeoisie and the faubourgeoisie, the first two of these social classes, played a significant role in Turkish politics. The third social class of corporate executives, which I call the *technocracy*, has been similarly critical in the foundation of the new global political economic order after the Cold War. This framework is informed by the recent history of class formation in the Turkish case. It presents a new way of understanding the rise of authoritarian movements around the world, including in the North Atlantic.

The analytical focus of this book flows from chapter to chapter. It begins at a global level and moves through the national and city levels before settling in neighborhoods in chapters 4 and 5. As it does so, it shifts from statistical and historical data to original ethnographic field research and content analysis. Theory becomes more abstract as the story lays the ground for chapter 7's presentation of the relationship between class formation and capital accumulation. Relationships become more complex as the book progresses, with each new actor presented in relation to those who have already entered the stage.

To compose this fugue of setting, theory, and actors, I draw upon data from the World Bank, the International Labour Organization, the International Monetary Fund, the Turkish Statistical Institute, the University of

Gothenburg, and others. Data also come from various field projects, including the one I conducted in 2007 and 2008 in Istanbul, where I was employed as an unskilled worker in four garment factories, and the pilot project I conducted in 2010 in Addis Ababa, Ethiopia. In 2012–15, I conducted over 140 in-depth interviews with businesspeople, policymakers, representatives of civil society organizations, and workers in Denizli, Gaziantep, and Kayseri, three of the fastest-industrializing cities of the country in those years. My data also include content analysis of the narratives of Muslim religious orders in Turkey over recent decades.

ONE

Industrial Islamism

ISLAMIZATION AND INDUSTRIALIZATION

The Key on the Table

IN 2008, AS PART OF MY RESEARCH for this book, I worked as an unskilled worker in four garment plants in Bağcılar, a district in the greater Istanbul area. Bağcılar bordered my childhood neighborhood, Şirinevler, and at the time was the largest working-class district in all of Turkey. On Sundays, I would join my fellow workers at their favorite coffeehouse, where, on their days off, men—and men only—hung out and played cards. Our group consisted of young workers like myself, shopkeepers, and a few pensioners. At first, I assumed we all were of modest means and belonged to the same social class. But there were differences among us. Early on, for example, I noticed that several members of our crowd had bigger-than-life personalities. One man stood out over all the rest. Not only was he louder, but he was also a bit better dressed and played cards a little more aggressively. Occasionally, he ordered tea for everyone at the card table. This gesture of apparent generosity was also aggressive, because he knew perfectly well that nobody would be able to reciprocate. To drive the point home, the man marked his superiority by ostentatiously leaving the key to his fancy car on the table for everyone to see, as if to say, "Don't forget, I am richer than you. In no way are we equals."

I later learned that this show-off belonged to the neighborhood's elite of sweatshop owners, contractors, and slumlords. As such, he was the direct beneficiary of the sweat and toil of members of the working class, the one who got the first cut of the value of what his companions at the card table produced every day of the week except on their "lazy Sundays off." They may have all lived in Bağcılar and socialized in the same coffeehouse, but such congenial details did not obscure the hard reality of their class differences. These differences made an impact on almost everything, including whose views prevailed when they talked about politics while playing cards. With few exceptions, the rich man's opinions mattered more than those of the others. This was not an incidental detail for me. If I wanted to understand the dynamics involved in the growing relationship between Islamization and industrialization, I would have to recognize who was who. Just because everyone used the same cultural codes and socialized in public spaces together, they did not necessarily all belong to the same social class.

Despite being an ethnographer who thought he understood the dynamics of local-level politics in Bağcılar, I had difficulty identifying the socioeconomic position of this man. To others, he was clearly the boss, the entrepreneur who employed as many as four dozen workers, some of whom may have been the very same people with whom he played cards on Sunday. It took significant time and effort for me to formulate the kind of "thick description"[1] that would let me see this power dynamic. I failed at first to see that this man was playing a critical role in a much broader and hitherto unidentified connection. The remarkable post–Cold War industrialization process, which this man and millions of others like him in Turkey and other Muslim-majority countries, or the Muslim-majority world (MMW), made possible, has been closely associated with the growing use of religious motifs in politics. I call this "the Islamization process."

Between 1990 and 2020, the share of manufacturing and construction in total value added, for example, grew by over 30 percent in the MMW. Thanks to this, the MMW's share of manufacturing and construction in the global economy grew by 2.4 times.[2] Taken together as a meta-region, these fifty countries are now at least as industrialized as most other parts of the world. Analysts regularly acknowledge that the extraction of hydrocarbon resources shaped the politics of the Gulf region in the postwar period.[3] They also write repeatedly that many of these countries have implemented market-friendly reforms since the 1980s that favor an export-led growth strategy.[4] Nevertheless, "systematic empirical evidence regarding the consequences of industrial policy is rare if not nonexistent" in reports published about the Middle East and North Africa (MENA).[5] Similarly, "too often political scientists do not recognize the importance of labor and industrial relations in shaping the policies and capacity of [individual MENA countries], and vice versa."[6] They say almost nothing about any relationship these changes might have had with the simultaneous Islamization of Muslim-majority countries.

Since the 1990s, Islamization, whether initiated by the opposition or by those in power, has been the defining feature of MMW politics. Even in countries like Egypt and Bangladesh, secular rulers use religious motifs to consolidate their position in politics. According to the University of Gothenburg's Varieties of Democracy (V-Dem) dataset,[7] on which I relied for this chapter, 65 percent of the governments of forty-seven Muslim-majority countries espoused a religious ideology in 1991.[8] The percentage has grown at a galloping pace, reaching 78 percent in 2020. Not only is this figure the highest since 1945, but the trend has been rising without interruption since 1990, which had not been the case. Moreover, as industrialization and Islamization have increased, socialism and the policies socialists introduced have lost their appeal.

As I show later in this chapter, not only do these trends in industrialization and Islamization meaningfully correlate with each other, but an assessment of major industrial dynamics also let me develop a typology of political regimes that has strong predictive power. Depending on the configuration of industrial labor, capital investment, and hydrocarbon sources, dynastic regimes, jihadists, and nonviolent political movements prevailed in different Muslim-majority countries. Given this connection, anything related to industrialization should be a major topic in studies of politics and social life in the MMW. But it is not.

The Connection

Given the lack of attention, I first examined the relationship between industrialization and Islamization to see whether this was an illusion or real. To address this, I used indicators in the V-Dem dataset that measure the relative strength of religious "regime support groups" (*v2regsupgroups*) and religious "regime opposition groups" (*v2regoppgroups*) in national politics.[9] I then used the mean values for both groups as a primary composite proxy indicator of Islamization and called those values the "political religiosity scores." These steps were necessary to avoid overemphasizing the role of those who are in power or in the opposition. The conclusions I drew from this analysis reflect my reading of the scores of these two individual indicators. I used the share of the industrial labor force in total employment as the first and main measure of industrialization.

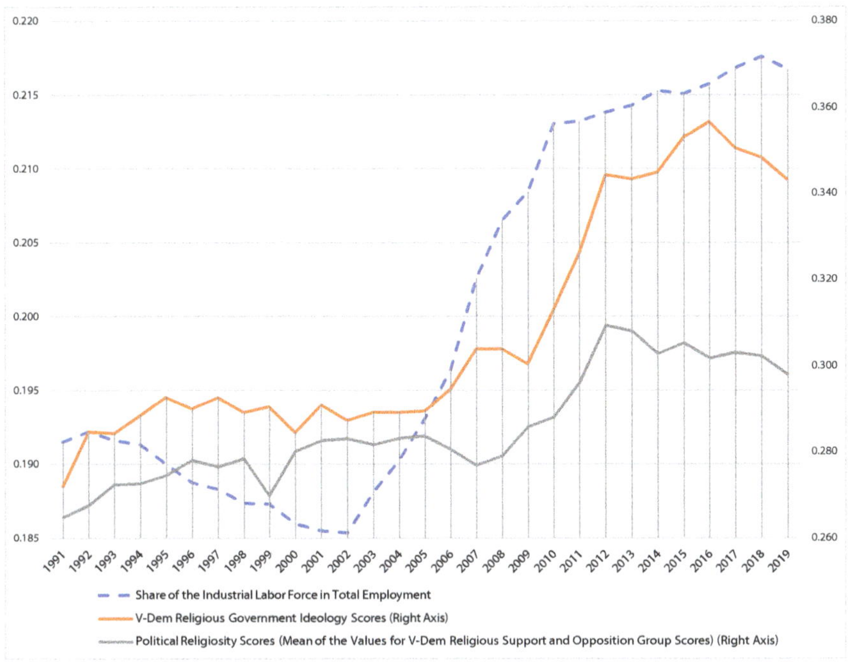

FIGURE 3. Political religiosity and relative size of the industrial labor force (1991–2019). Calculated by the author using the V-Dem and ILO country indicators.

When I cross-correlated the 1991–2019 country averages for this last indicator with V-Dem's 1991–2019 country averages for religious government ideology and political religiosity respectively, the resulting values came to 0.92 and 0.85. In other words, the growth and decline patterns of the relative size of the industrial labor force in the Muslim-majority countries overlapped with V-Dem's political religiosity and religious government ideology scores with statistically significant values.[10] This is shown in figure 3.

This high correlation between the rates of Islamization and industrialization holds at the country level as well. As figure 4 illustrates, the relative size of the industrial labor force is a good estimator for the level of religiosity in the domestic politics of Muslim-majority countries. Spearman's rho of the average rankings of the Muslim-majority countries for their political religiosity scores and the share of their industrial labor force within their total employment for every year between 1991 and 2019 is 0.46 ($p < 0.01$). Its value would be 0.77 ($p < 0.01$) if Somalia, Mali, Azerbaijan, Turkmenistan, Tunisia, and Algeria were omitted as the outliers in their geographic regions and 0.68 ($p < 0.01$) if Albania, Bosnia and Herzegovina,

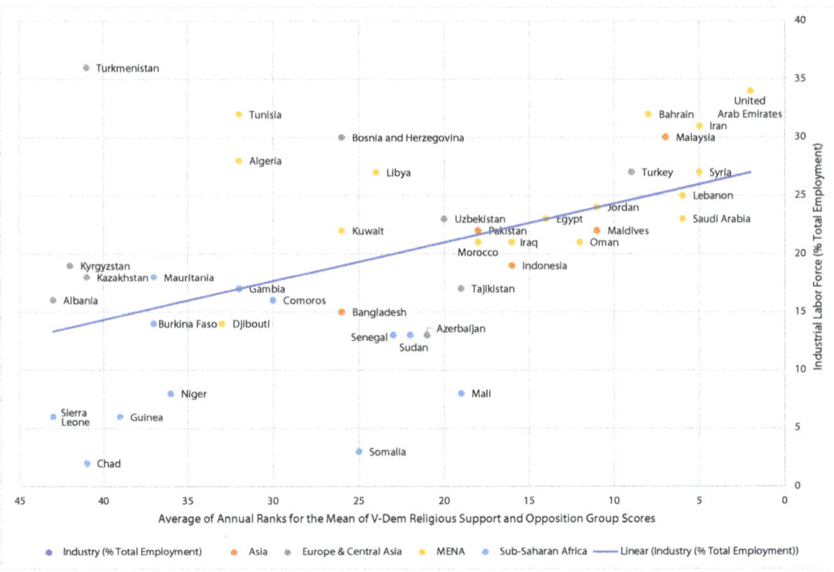

FIGURE 4. Political religiosity and industrial labor force (1991–2019 average). Calculated by the author using the V-Dem and ILO country indicators.

and the former members of the Soviet Union were omitted as diverging from the Cold War industrialization experience of other Muslim-majority countries. Furthermore, again except for these Eastern Bloc countries, each geographic region has a pattern similar to the general one: the larger the portion of the industrial labor force in total employment, the higher the political religiosity rankings and scores.

ISLAMIZATION IN THE MUSLIM-MAJORITY WORLD

Countries and Clusters

I used these correlations to construct a typology of Muslim-majority countries that would allow me to compare the rates of industrialization and Islamization in those countries. In addition to comparing the relative size of the industrial labor force, I also compared the relative abundance of natural resource rents and gross fixed capital formation as a share of gross domestic product (GDP), both of which served as proxy indicators to identify the relationship of land and capital, the other two factors of production, to the Islamization process.[11] I used each indicator in three independent two-step cluster analyses. Each calculation yielded two clusters, so there are eight country clusters in all.

The upper part of table 1 shows the averages for each indicator in the eight country clusters for 1991–2019. The lower part shows the average country scores for the same indicators over the same years. The overall trends suggest three important conclusions, two of which I address in the next section. First, the share of industrial labor in total employment helps one make a rough prediction about the political religiosity scores or rankings of 79 percent of the forty-two Muslim-majority countries in table 1. This ratio increases to 85 percent if the former socialist countries in Europe and Central Asia are omitted. Second, gross fixed capital formation is a better predictor of the level of political religiosity in Muslim-majority countries with a large industrial labor force than the relative size of natural resource rents as a share of GDP. In this category, those with relatively high political religiosity scores tend to have smaller gross fixed capital formation, and the relationship between natural resource rents and political religiosity is less clear. Third, the relative size of natural resource rents as a share of GDP is a better predictor of the level of political religiosity in Muslim-majority countries with a relatively small industrial labor force than gross fixed capital formation. Political religiosity scores are negatively associated with the volume of natural resources in this country cluster.

The correlations provided in table 1 allow one to predict, for four of five Muslim-majority countries in this dataset (or five of six if Eastern Bloc countries are omitted), whether a country will have an above- or below-average political religiosity score simply by looking at the average of the relative size of its industrial labor force over these three decades. The Islamization process generally takes a nonviolent path in countries that receive significant investment. In the absence of a large industrial workforce, Islamization is negatively linked to hydrocarbon resources. In other words, the share of industrial labor in total employment serves as a better predictor of the Islamization process than the volume of natural resources.

Understanding all these correlations is important because the MMW is a major site for the global industrial workforce. In 2019, MENA, for instance, had the largest ratio of industrial workers to total employment (27 percent) among the seven world regions defined by the World Bank. To put this into perspective, the figure for the same year was 23 percent for the global economy and 20 percent for North America.[12] In other words, if one uses the relative size of the industrial labor force as the main indicator of the level of

TABLE 1 Political religiosity and factors of production (1991–2019 country averages)

	Clusters							
Industrial labor force (% total employment)	*High (27%)*				*Low (13%)*			
Gross fixed capital formation (% GDP)	Low (17%)		High (27%)		Low (18%)	High (27%)	High (25%)	Low (%16)
Natural resource rents (% GDP)	Low (6%)	High (36%)	Low (1%)	High (27%)	Low (5%)		High (19%)	
Industrial labor force (% total employment)	24	27	26	27	13	16	11	4
Gross fixed capital formation (% GDP)	18	15	26	26	18	27	25	16
Natural resource rents (% GDP)	6	36	1	27	5	5	21	15
Average of the mean of religious regime support and opposition group scores	0.44	0.43	0.38	0.37	0.22	0.17	0.13	0.12

Countries							
High-Low-Low	*High-Low-High*	*High-High-Low*	*High-High-High*	*Low-Low-Low*	*Low-High-Low*	*Low-High-High*	*Low-Low-High*
Syria (4/30/8/6) – (27/18/6)	UAE (2/6/12/1) – (34/21/20)	Lebanon (6/24/9/8) – (25/25/0)	Iran (5/1/1/35) – (31/29/25)	Mali (19/35/24/10) – (08/19/6)	Indonesia (16/26/19/14) – (19/28/7)	Azerbaijan (21/34/18/17) – (13/27/28)	Somalia (24/21/27/15) – (03/14/21)
Egypt (15/33/30/4) – (23/19/9)	Iraq (16/16/13/18) – (21/10/46)	Turkey (9/17/7/20) – (27/25/0)	Saudi Arabia (6/1/4/13) – (23/21/36)	Tajikistan (20/33/31/8) – (17/21/1)	Sudan (22/5/22/16) – (13/23/8)	Kazakhstan (41/35/32/37) – (18/23/18)	Guinea (39/35/26/38) – (06/21/15)
Pakistan (18/16/16/19) – (22/16/1)	Libya (24/20/31/9) – (27/16/41)	Jordan (11/26/23/5) – (24/24/1)	Malaysia (6/19/2/25) – (30/28/11)	Senegal (23/31/14/29) – (13/20/3)	Bangladesh (26/25/20/28) – (15/25/1)	Chad (41/11/29/37) – (02/23/19)	Sierra Leone (42/35/32/38) – (06/12/12)
		Maldives (11/7/7/20) – (22/38/0)	Bahrain (8/14/15/8) – (32/23/19)	Comoros (30/14/21/31) – (16/16/2)	Djibouti (33/32/27/36) – (14/28/1)		
		Morocco (18/6/16/15) – (21/28/2)	Oman (12/17/4/29) – (21/24/36)	The Gambia (32/17/31/22) – (17/13/4)	Mauritania (37/13/32/29) – (18/37/12)		
		Bosnia (26/17/10/37) – (3/25/2)	Uzbekistan (20/35/32/6) – (23/24/16)	Niger (36/35/19/38) – (08/19/8)	Kyrgyzstan (42/32/30/38) – (19/22/4)		
		Tunisia (32/26/27/27) – (32/23/4)	Kuwait (26/22/19/24) – (22/22/43)	Burkina Faso (37/35/31/31) – (14/19/9)	Albania (42/35/32/38) – (16/26/2)		
			Algeria (32/30/32/21) – (28/30/22)				
			Turkmenistan (41/35/27/38) – (36/35/39)				

SOURCE: ILO, World Bank, and V-Dem.

NOTE: Political religiosity scores are the mean of V-Dem's religious regime support and opposition group scores (v2regsupgroups 7 & v2regoppgroups_7). For countries, indicators for the values in parentheses are as follows: (political religiosity rank/religious government ideology rank/political support group rank/political opposition group rank)—(industrial labor force (% of total employment)/gross fixed capital formation (% of GDP)/natural resources rents (% of GDP)).

industrial development, the MMW comprises one of the most industrialized meta-regions in the world.

The growing share of the MMW in industrial output is coupled with a parallel process: labor-intensive industries have increased their share of employment at the expense of resource- and capital-intensive industries. The largest manufacturing employers in the MMW over the past three decades have been the food and beverage, textile, garment, and metal industries.[13] The clothing industry recorded the highest growth rate over that period. Between 1963 and 1990, the output of this industry in the MMW accounted for only 2 percent of global apparel production, while the corresponding figure for 1991–2018 was around 14 percent. There is a similar growth pattern in sectors such as food, beverages, and metals over the same period. In contrast, the nonmetallic mineral extraction/processing, chemical and chemical products, and rubber and plastic products sectors, all of which heavily use petroleum and its byproducts, have accounted for about 18 percent of total manufacturing employment since the early 1990s, and their employment growth has declined sharply over the past three decades. These figures point to the role of Islamic motifs in the political control of the growing number of industrial workers in the MMW. Next, I took a closer look at the relationship of these indicators to the prevailing political regimes in the MMW.

Dynasties, Movements, and Jihadists

Although the size of the industrial labor force is a good predictor of political religiosity, capital investment sheds light on a salient characteristic of the political regimes in each country. If the Muslim-majority countries are reclustered according to their average gross fixed capital formation from 1991 to 2019, four trends emerge, as table 2 illustrates. First, countries that receive a higher volume of fixed capital formation in relation to their GDP are the ones where dynastic regimes and strong Islamist movements emerge. In contrast to this meta-cluster, clusters I–IV in table 2, other countries have either stronger jihadist movements or significantly lower political religiosity scores. Substantial fixed capital investment is associated with the Islamization of politics under dynastic regimes and nonviolent Islamist movements, and violent movements in countries with substantial fixed capital investment generally do not pose a challenge to the existing political establishment.

Second, the rentier state thesis,[14] according to which the presence of extensive hydrocarbon resources is associated with the presence of dynastic regimes in Muslim-majority countries that receive extensive fixed capital investment, is confirmed with two specifications. First, dynasties have a better chance of survival if those hydrocarbon resources are coupled with sizable capital investment: jihadists succeeded in dethroning Muammar Qaddafi in Libya, which has substantial hydrocarbon resources and a low share of fixed investment in GDP. Second, countries with small hydrocarbon resources and significant fixed investment, such as Turkey, Indonesia, and Tunisia, have strong Islamist movements but no dynastic regimes as of yet.

Third, among countries with substantial fixed capital investment, those with large numbers of industrial workers tend to have higher political religiosity scores. For example, among hydrocarbon-rich Muslim-majority countries, Azerbaijan and Kazakhstan have relatively small industrial workforces, and Saudi Arabia and Iran are the opposite. Although the regimes in these four countries are dynastic or oligarchic, the first two are relatively secular and the latter two are theocratic. Among the hydrocarbon-poor Muslim-majority countries, Islamist movements have challenged or overthrown the political establishment in countries with larger industrial workforces, such as Turkey, Lebanon, and Tunisia. In turn, Islamist movements in countries with low hydrocarbon resources and small industrial workforces either have reconciled with the existing political establishment, as in Indonesia, or have been kept in check by the political establishment, as in Bangladesh.

Finally, the Islamization process has had little impact in countries with low values on all three indicators (industrial workforce, capital investment, and hydrocarbon resources). Senegal, for example, has been widely hailed as having succeeded in integrating its Islamists into the political system.[15] This integration overlaps with the "failure" of Senegal's integration into industrial capitalism. Even the prominent jihadist groups active in some of the countries under this category (Azawad and Boko Haram) have had limited success and only for a short time.[16]

As shown in figure 5, political regimes in Muslim-majority countries can be divided into four categories based on the three indicators I have used. Muslim-majority countries that have less industrial labor and less capital investment follow two patterns. Those without rich hydrocarbon resources have generally skipped the Islamization process of the past three decades. I call these countries the *rural regimes*. However, when such countries have rich hydrocarbon resources, jihadist movements have emerged

TABLE 2 Political regimes and factors of production (1991–2019 country averages)

				Clusters				
	I	*II*	*III*	*IV*	*V*	*VI*	*VII*	*VIII*
Industrial labor force (% total employment)	High (27%)	Low (13%)	High (27%)	Low (13%)	High (27%)		Low (13%)	
Gross fixed capital formation (% GDP)	High (27%)				Low (17%)			
Natural resource rents (% GDP)	High (23%)		Low (3%)		Low (6%)	High (36%)	High (19%)	Low (5%)
Industrial labor force (% total employment)	27	11	26	16	24	27	4	13
Gross fixed capital formation (% GDP)	26	25	26	27	18	15	16	18
Natural resource rents (% GDP)	27	21	1	5	6	36	15	5
Political religiosity score	0.37	0.13	0.38	0.17	0.44	0.43	0.12	0.22

	Dynasties	Dynasties <=> Movements	Movements		Movements <=> Jihadists	Jihadists		Rural Islam
Countries	Iran (5/1/1/35) – (31/29/25)	Azerbaijan (21/34/18/17) – (13/27/28)	Lebanon (6/24/9/8) – (25/25/0)	Indonesia (16/26/19/14) – (19/28/7)	Syria (4/30/8/6) – (27/18/6)	UAE (2/6/12/1) – (34/21/20)	Somalia (24/21/27/15) – (03/14/21)	Mali (19/35/24/10) – (08/19/6)
	Saudi Arabia (6/1/4/13) – (23/21/36)	Kazakhstan (41/35/32/37) – (18/23/18)	Turkey (9/17/7/20) – (27/25/0)	Sudan (22/5/22/16) – (13/23/8)	Egypt (15/33/30/4) – (23/19/9)	Iraq (16/16/13/18) – (21/10/46)	Guinea (39/35/26/38) – (06/21/15)	Tajikistan (20/33/31/8) – (17/21/1)
	Malaysia (6/19/2/25) – (30/28/11)	Chad (41/11/29/37) – (02/23/19)	Jordan (11/26/23/5) – (24/24/1)	Bangladesh (26/25/20/28) – (15/25/1)	Pakistan (18/16/16/19) – (22/16/1)	Libya (24/20/31/9) – (27/16/41)	Sierra Leone (42/35/32/38) – (06/12/12)	Senegal (23/31/14/29) – (13/20/3)
	Bahrain (8/14/15/8) – (32/23/19)		Maldives (11/7/7/20) – (22/38/0)	Djibouti (33/32/27/36) – (14/28/1)				Comoros (30/14/21/31) – (16/16/2)
	Oman (12/17/4/29) – (21/24/36)		Morocco (18/6/16/15) – (21/28/2)	Mauritania (37/13/32/29) – (18/37/12)				The Gambia (32/17/31/22) – (17/13/4)
	Uzbekistan (20/35/32/6) – (23/24/16)		Bosnia (26/17/10/37) – (3/25/2)	Kyrgyzstan (42/32/30/38) – (19/22/4)				Niger (36/35/19/38) – (08/19/8)
	Kuwait (26/22/19/24) – (22/22/43)		Tunisia (32/26/27/27) – (32/23/4)	Albania (42/35/32/38) – (16/26/2)				Burkina Faso (37/35/31/31) – (14/19/9)
	Algeria (32/30/32/21) – (28/30/22)							
	Turkmenistan (41/35/27/38) – (36/35/39)							

SOURCE: ILO, World Bank, and V-Dem.

NOTE: Political religiosity scores are the mean of V-Dem's religious regime support and opposition group scores (v2regsupgroups 7 & v2regoppgroups_7). For countries, indicators for the values in parentheses are as follows: (political religiosity rank/religious government ideology rank/political support group rank/political opposition group rank)—(industrial labor force (% of total employment)/gross fixed capital formation (% of GDP)/natural resource rents (% of GDP)).

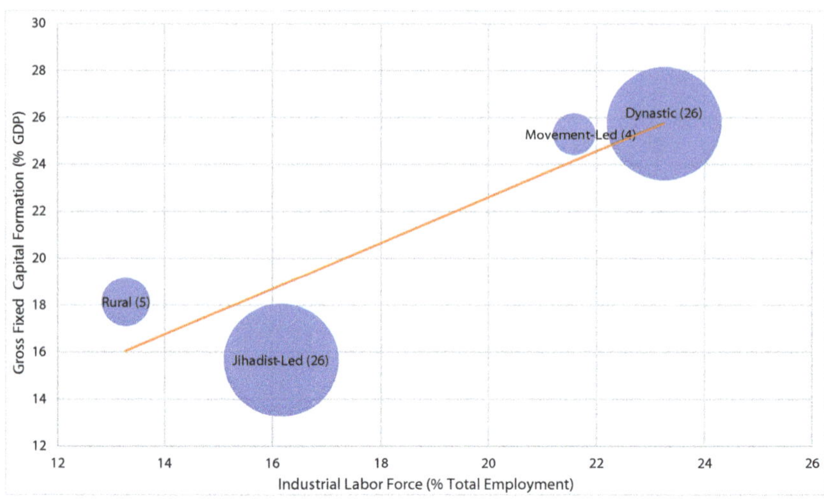

FIGURE 5. Political regimes and factor endowments (1990–2019 country averages). Dynastic regimes are clusters 1 and 2 ($n = 12$); movement-led regimes are clusters 3, 4, and 5 ($n = 17$); jihadist-led regimes are clusters 6 and 7 ($n = 6$); and rural regimes are in cluster 8 ($n = 7$). Calculated by the author using the V-Dem and World Bank country indicators. The size of the dots for each country category indicates the average size of total natural resource rents (in parentheses) as a share of GDP.

as formidable challengers to the political establishment. Regardless of whether these jihadist regimes have been successful, I call the regimes in these countries *jihadist-led* because the impact of these movements on political dynamics is consequential. Other Muslim-majority countries receive significant capital investment and have relatively large industrial workforces. Within this broader category, those with significant hydrocarbon resources have (Islamist or secularist) "dynastic regimes." In those without such resources, nonjihadist Islamist movements actively negotiate with, challenge, and sometimes even overthrow the political establishment, as in Turkey. In other words, nonjihadist Islamist movements have a chance only under a specific combination of these three factors that leads to what I call *movement-led regimes.*

Movement-led regimes fit one of the four main patterns of industrial development, each of which sits on an identifiable position in a respective spectrum of Islamization processes. Each pattern is associated with different forms and degrees of global industrial linkages, ranging from the mere supply of national hydrocarbon resources to manufacturing industries in the North Atlantic, as in Iraq and Libya, to complex subsidiary relationships within global industrial commodity chains, as in Turkey and Indonesia. The rest of this chapter focuses on these countries.

Historical Patterns

This simple model offers an explanation for why most of its outliers are within the Soviet zone of influence. There are not only cases like relatively secular Turkmenistan, with high proletarianization, natural resource, and investment scores, but also cases like Tajikistan, with a much smaller industrial labor force and fixed investment coupled with higher political religiosity scores. The post–Cold War era for these countries did not coincide with the collapse of a capitalist development regime, but with that of a noncapitalist regime. Thus, the historical dynamics and social actors that established the connection between industrialization and Islamization in other Muslim-majority countries were largely irrelevant to or absent from countries under Soviet influence.

This idea broadly applies to Afghanistan and Somalia as well, the two other outliers to the model. Based on the three indicators, these countries fit the rural regimes, which typically have low political religiosity scores, yet both have been a hotbed for the jihadist groups for multiple decades. These cases stand out as major exceptions to my model, yet I need to underline that their socialist governments, albeit weak and brief, distinguished these countries from the rural regimes that have similar political economic characteristics.

Afghanistan was the final battleground of the Cold War, as the United States began to support the jihadists against the socialist government and the Soviet Union decided to invade the country.[17] It is remarkable that Afghanistan is widely regarded by the international community as the typical case for understanding the defining elements of the Islamization of politics even though it does not offer any vantage point for reading the political dynamics in countries with or without similar political economic characteristics. The general perception of Islamism and the Islamization of politics is framed by a perspective that regards exceptional cases like Afghanistan as the ideal types and disregards typical cases like Turkey as anomalies. Thus, this section looks at the last category of Muslim-majority countries, to which Turkey belongs. About two-thirds of the population in the MMW lives under what I call movement-led regimes. Movement-led Muslim-majority countries and dynastic regimes have the highest scores on the KOF Swiss Economic Institute's various globalization measures, including strong urban centers that promote economic, trade, and political globalization; rural regimes have the lowest scores.[18] The Islamization of politics in these countries is not some almost mystical trend of religious revival but is illustrative of those global patterns.

In these countries, nonjihadist Islamist movements and parties have a significant role in politics. There are similarities to how these movements participate in their putatively democratic states. For example, the stands they take in their ideological pronouncements concerning economic policy and other financial matters are similar, as are the relationships they have to the military and civilian political establishments. These mobilizations take place in Muslim-majority countries that do not have significant hydrocarbon reserves but receive considerable capital investment or have a large industrial labor force. These countries serve as intellectual centers for Islamist activities that may spread to other Muslim-majority countries. The movements in these countries have also often drawn inspiration from the ideologies of other political movements, such as nationalism and, in fewer cases, socialism.

Notwithstanding these similarities, Islamist movements have had varying degrees of success in national politics. Those different outcomes are closely related to their idiosyncratic political and economic development over three successive historical phases after their independence from colonial rule in the twentieth century.

In the first phase, founding figures such as Sheikh Mujib, Mustafa Kemal Atatürk, Gamal Abdel Nasser, Muhammad Ali Jinnah, Sukarno, and Habib Bourguiba played major roles in the decolonization process during different decades of the twentieth century. They implemented various forms of development-oriented growth and redistribution policies based on import-substituting industrialization.[19]

Having ended colonial rule or a monarchical dynasty, these nationalist leaders had a firm grip on power and did not have to share it with the Islamists. Nevertheless, except for socialist Mujib, who was assassinated shortly after Bangladesh's War of Independence, in which West Pakistan actively allied itself with the Islamists, the early leaders of the nations in this cluster cooperated to varying degrees with Islamist movements and with the religious members of their own cadres in the name of their common anticolonial cause.[20]

After this first phase, the founding cadres gave way to a second generation of leaders who broke away from developmentalism. The developmentalist policies of the previous generation had different degrees of success and underwent various forms of crisis.[21] Thus, Anwar Sadat in Egypt, Suharto in Indonesia, Ziaur Rahman in Bangladesh, Zia-ul-Haq in Pakistan, and Kenan Evren in Turkey all sought alliances with Islamists—even when the Islamists refused to join an official coalition—to gain support for their post-development economic agenda. In exchange for the Islamists helping defuse possible upheavals among the working class, the ruling parties made concessions to the religious extremists. Two factors played an important role in the formation of these alliances. First, the new leaders needed to secure their positions vis-à-vis their political rivals within the ruling elite who insisted on preserving the developmentalist framework. This required finding allies elsewhere, and the marginalized Islamists served that purpose well. Second, the Islamists could help suppress the opposition coming from the left. Socialists, vocal opponents of moving away from developmentalist growth strategies, were even more threatening than opponents within the ruling elite.

Suharto's strategy in Indonesia is a good example of how these second-generation leaders sought an alliance with the Islamists to consolidate their position. Suharto waged a double war to consolidate his position. His first war was against the communists. In 1965, the Communist Party of Indonesia (PKI) had 3.5 million members, making it the largest in the world after the Soviet Union and China. Together with its affiliated organizations, the party had around twenty million followers. In alliance with the Santri and Nahdlatul Ulama, an orthodox Sunni Islamic organization established in the 1920s, Suharto initiated an unofficial military campaign against the communists and their supporters, some of whom came from the heterodox Muslim Abangan. The politicide led to the murder of about one million unarmed civilians and the imprisonment and torture of many millions more for years.[22]

Suharto began his second war, against Sino-Indonesian entrepreneurs, in the mid-1970s with the *asas pemerataan* (foundation for equal distribution) plan under his New Order. An expanded version of the SME-friendly Benteng program launched in the 1950s, the plan gave priority to small Muslim government contractors over their Chinese counterparts in public works and rural development projects. Suharto's plan envisioned a close patronage relationship between these Muslim contractors and his government.[23] The *asas pemerataan* plan complemented the massacre of the communists with the help of the Islamists so that Suharto could eliminate the remnants of Sukarno's vision of Indonesia as a secular egalitarian country.

In the third phase, the Islamists began to flex their muscles and turned against the pro-market generation of leaders, posing a serious threat and, in some cases, eventually taking over. Since 1980, the Islamists have used three strategies to achieve their goal, with different levels of success. As I show in later chapters, the Islamists in Turkey used one strategy: taking over by gradually purging older members of the political establishment.

The second strategy was to support the economic agenda of the old establishment and let them remain in power over the economy and politics in the postdevelopment era. Egypt is an outstanding example,[24] thanks to Sadat's decision in the 1970s to implement limited pro-market reforms. Even after Sadat was assassinated in 1981 by Islamists, the ruling elite stayed in power under Hosni Mubarak, who continued the strategy of limited pro-market reforms. In 1985, Mubarak concluded an agreement with the International Monetary Fund (IMF) that contained contradictory elements such as the expansion of proprietary rights for foreign companies while providing an exemption from subsidies for strategic commodities such as grain, sugar, and cotton. The Islamists cooperated because Mubarak selectively accommodated moderate Islamists within his political agenda[25] by giving them seats in Parliament[26] and making sure the legislature passed pro-Islamic laws such as the 1985 Personal Status Law.[27] Thanks to Mubarak's pro-market stance and accommodating attitude toward Islamism, political analysts expected a massive wave of privatization to take place in the late 1990s after a more comprehensive structural adjustment program came into effect in 1991.[28] This agonizingly slow process was postponed by a food crisis in 2008.[29] Only in 2022 did the Egyptian government negotiate a new privatization plan with the IMF to "double the private sector's share in its economy."[30] Under the same limited, market-friendly reform strategy, the military elite in Egypt managed to create a new regime-loyal class of businessmen, ironically with the help of the same IMF-driven reforms.[31]

Unlike in Indonesia, where Islamist movements are fragmented, the Muslim Brotherhood in Egypt developed into the dominant Islamist movement. It swung back and forth politically, presenting itself sometimes as a threatening oppositional force and at other times as a willing collaborator. Despite pressure from Nasser's government, the Brotherhood sided with the Free Officers' developmentalist agenda, but then went on to support Sadat's pro-market reforms, known as *infitah*, allying themselves with the new president and his attack against the remaining socialist elements and other pro-Nasser actors in Egyptian politics.[32] In exchange, the Sadat regime reversed Nasser's repressive policies against Islamism and rejuvenated the Muslim Brotherhood,[33] tacitly allowing it to operate extensive charity networks that mitigated the negative effects of the new pro-market reforms.

While the Muslim Brotherhood's influence among the working class continued to grow after World War II, the movement remained primarily an organization of professionals, civil servants, and students.[34] As free-market reforms began to undermine their economic status, the interests of these now poorer educated members of the Brotherhood began to diverge from the interests of the increasingly wealthy entrepreneurial members who held most of the leadership positions in the organization. This divergence of interests played a role in temporarily splitting the Brotherhood into factions, one of which, the Gama'a al-Islamiyya, is believed to have assassinated Sadat and indirectly played a role in stalling economic liberalization for another decade.[35] By the first decade of the twenty-first century, a reunified Brotherhood was mobilizing against Egypt's political elite and its dominating military arm, but in ways that advanced their common economic agenda during the Arab Spring and resulted in the downfall of the Brotherhood.

At first, although the Muslim Brotherhood monopolized the Arab Spring protests, the movement did the government's bidding by contributing to the disenfranchisement of organized labor and preventing the formation of a common political platform among the protesters. After the fall of Mubarak, this lack of a common political agenda led to the demobilization of the protesters[36] and paved the way for a new dictatorship to take control under Abdel Fattah Saeed Hussein Khalil el-Sisi, the former head of the Egyptian state's military intelligence service.

In countries like Egypt and Turkey, secular political elites faced serious threats from Islamist movements. They either gave in to the Islamists' demands entirely or found ways to stay in power while accommodating them. In other Muslim-majority nations, the Islamists succeeded by using a third strategy that did not involve building a strong and united Islamist movement. In Bangladesh, for example, Islamist parties have a limited voter base, but they succeed by becoming indispensable to non-Islamic parties that need their vote in Parliament. Sheikh Hasina, Mujib's daughter and chairperson of the non-Islamist (and supposedly left-leaning) Avami League, bowed to the demands of the Islamist Bangladesh Khelafat Majlis and legalized "the right to issue fatwas, impose a ban on enacting any law that goes against

Quranic values, initiate steps for proper implementation of the initiative for government recognition of the degrees awarded by Qwami madrasahs, and ban criticism of the Prophet Muhammad, or in other words, introduce a blasphemy law."[37] Positioning themselves as the "kingmaker,"[38] the weak Islamist parties only lend their vote after other parties agree to adopt aspects of their political agenda.

In Indonesia, Islamist parties control up to 40 percent of the vote, but political dissension has made it impossible, since the days of New Order, for them to form a united block.[39] Nevertheless, Nahdlatul Ulama and Muhammadiyah, the largest Islamic organizations in Indonesia (and probably the world), insert Islamist policies into the political agenda of non-Islamist parties that desperately need their votes. The resulting Islamization process stems from initiatives introduced by non-Islamist parties, which rationalize undermining the civil liberties of the nation's citizens by claiming they are doing it in the name of "God-pleasing nationalism."[40]

In the first decade of the 2000s, a considerable number of pro-sharia laws were passed in Indonesian districts where non-Islamist nationalist parties have had a majority. The same pattern exists at the national level, particularly with legislation introduced by Golkar and the Democratic Party (PD).[41] Although the new legislation respects Islamic law, it also restricts civil liberties in the everyday lives of Indonesian citizens. Some of these laws had less to do with sharia than with dismantling progressive public policies.[42] Sharia, in other words, served as a shield for undermining the country's democratic traditions.

One reason Islamist movements in Indonesia remain or want to remain fragmented is to advance their political and religious agenda more effectively. In the current political climate, the dividing line between Islamist and non-Islamist parties has become blurred, making it increasingly unnecessary for authentic Islamist parties to rise up against their political opponents in what has become a semi-Islamist political establishment. In these circumstances, Islamists simply delegate decision-making and its associated political risks to non-Islamist parties such as Golkar or PD[43] and let them turn Indonesia into an Islamist nation.

The common feature of policymaking in these countries after the first generation of leadership was an incomplete neoliberalization characterized by the political establishment's efforts to limit privatization and slow down urbanization. In Egypt, the military-political establishment discouraged fixed capital investment. The reforms under Suharto in Indonesia and both the Avami League and the BNP in Bangladesh did not trigger significant rural-to-urban migration and limited the transformative effect of these reforms on the industrialization process. Incomplete neoliberalization empowered these leaders in different ways and enabled them to advance their own Islamization process to ally with, use, or disempower the Islamists.

This brief assessment shows the close relationship between the overall performance and strategies of individual Islamist movements and the idiosyncratic historical factors that have facilitated or disrupted the transition from import-substituting developmentalist policies to export-led growth policies in Muslim-majority countries. In this respect, Turkey is an instructive example of how a broader process of neoliberalization could help Islamists slowly replace the old political elite while holding on to its economic agenda. The next question is whether these historical factors can be used to identify quantifiable criteria for a more formal account of the nexus between neoliberal industrialization and Islamization.

Varieties of Industrial Islamism

In this subsection, I take a closer look at the Islamization and industrialization processes in the MMW, focusing on investment, export volume, and the political power of the working class in the most populous Muslim-majority countries: Bangladesh, Egypt, Indonesia, Pakistan, and Turkey. These countries account for approximately 54 percent of the total population of the MMW and 86 percent of the total population of those with movement-led regimes. They also account for 44 percent of the MMW's total GDP and 89 percent of the total GDP of those with movement-led regimes in 2019. Thus, they are representative examples of the countries in their clusters and account for about half of the MMW's labor and capital. Even though Tunisia is not one of the most populous Muslim-majority countries, I included it in this discussion; this country challenges the general model that the more advanced a country's industrial development, the stronger its tendency toward Islamization. The reasons Tunisia defies the general pattern strengthen my argument: if export-oriented industrialization policies are extensive, then stronger organized labor means weaker Islamist movements.

I use different metrics in this subsection. Hydrocarbon resources are not a major source of income for any of these countries, so I skip that indicator.

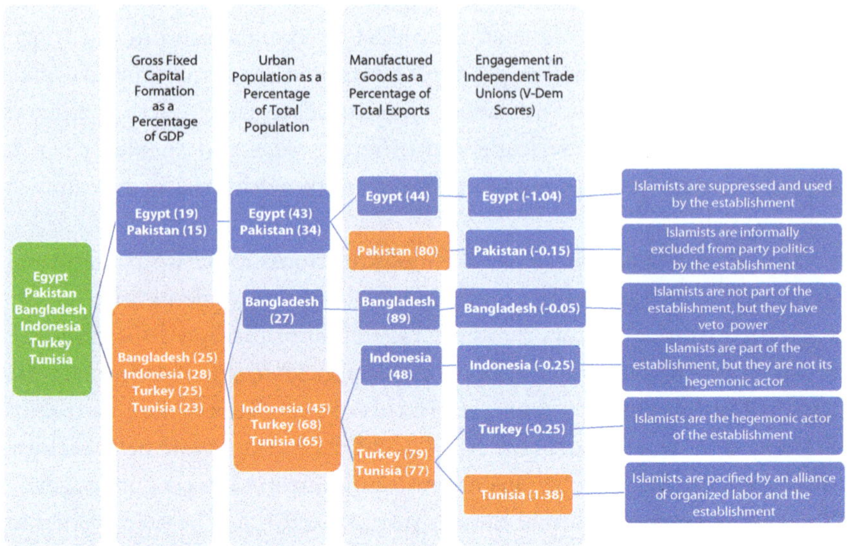

FIGURE 6. Islamization and industrialization in the most populous Muslim-majority countries and Tunisia (1990–2021 average). Calculated by the author using the V-Dem and World Bank country indicators.

I keep gross fixed capital formation because it is sufficiently robust to see the broad differences in political patterns within this group. I substitute three new indicators for the share of the industrial labor force because that indicator does not vary much among the countries in this group. The three new indicators (urbanization rate, the share of manufactured goods in total exports, and engagement in independent trade unions) allow me to identify the broad contours of the political and employment conditions of the working class. As figure 6 summarizes, this comparative exercise reveals similarities and differences between Turkish Islamists and their counterparts in other populous Muslim-majority countries.

First, the values for private fixed investment in Indonesia and Turkey, where Islamist parties and leaders participated in or led national governments, are much higher than in Bangladesh, Egypt, Pakistan, or Tunisia. Islamist movements were either excluded from power sharing—as in Egypt, Pakistan, and Tunisia—or were unsuccessful at the ballot box, as in Bangladesh. The lowest private fixed investment scores are in Egypt and Pakistan, where the role of the military in politics was not challenged as much as in the other four countries.

Second, there are clear differences in the growth patterns of these countries' export volumes. The share of exports in Egypt's GDP is about the same today as it was in the 1960s. The share of exports in Pakistan's GDP has fallen steadily since 1993, from 15 percent to less than 10 percent. Similarly, the share of exports in Indonesia's GDP peaked in the 1990s and then fell from 50 percent to 20 percent in the following two decades. On the other hand, the export volumes of Bangladesh, Turkey, and Tunisia have increased steadily since the 1980s, although exports still account for a small share of Bangladesh's GDP. Except for Tunisia, where things have recently been changing, there is a clear association between the stability and pace of growth in export volume and the ability of Islamist movements to challenge the political establishment. Similarly, the share of manufactured goods in total exports is much lower in Egypt, where the military directly governs the state, than in Pakistan, where the military still has to work with civilian politicians to legitimize its influence over politics. Indonesia has a lower value for this indicator than Turkey and Tunisia, where Islamist movements act as a unified political force.

Third, the more urbanized these countries are, the more likely it is that elections are held regularly and that nonviolent Islamist movements will be strongly represented at the ballot box. Tunisia and Turkey have relatively high urbanization (69 percent and 76 percent respectively in 2019). Indonesia's urbanization has increased dramatically since the 1990s, with 66 percent of the population now living in urban areas. Bangladesh (37 percent), Egypt (43 percent), and Pakistan (37 percent) had lower urbanization in 2019. Egypt's urbanization has remained virtually the same over the past three decades, and Pakistan's has only increased by 23 percent over the same period.

Countries with over 40 percent of the population living in rural areas pose unique challenges to Islamist movements and the political establishment. The pressure on Islamist movements to appeal to both urban and rural constituencies may explain the fragmentation of Islamist parties in Indonesia, where they must appeal to voters in Java and Sumatra, the two most industrialized and urbanized regions of the country, and to the 44 percent of its citizenry scattered throughout the extensive rural areas of the archipelago.[44] Large rural populations are associated either with relatively weak Islamist movements that oppose the (military-backed) political establishment, as in Pakistan and Egypt, or with non-Islamist political parties, as in Bangladesh and Indonesia.

Fourth, the right of workers to join independent trade unions is severely restricted in each of these countries. Unionization is the indicator that best explains why Tunisia is different from the other countries in this group. Among them, Egypt has the lowest V-Dem "engagement in independent trade unions" indicator averages for 1990–2019, followed by Turkey, Indonesia, Pakistan, and Bangladesh. This is hardly surprising. Egypt never had independent trade unions. Suharto in Indonesia and the military junta in Turkey crushed theirs, in the mid-1960s and early 1980s respectively. In Pakistan, the military establishment's fierce opposition to pro-Soviet India limited trade unionism and any other rights that smacked of socialism. Only Bangladesh still pays lip service to socialism in its constitution, a pale reminder of the spirit of Mujib's original text but hardly an uplifting detail considering how workers' actual rights to engage in independent trade unions have declined over the years. Comparing 1990–2009 with 2010–19, the rights of workers to engage in independent trade unions declined the most in Bangladesh, followed by Indonesia, where the labor force as a percentage of total employment has grown the fastest of these six countries. In other words, the two countries in this cluster with the most competitive democratic party systems, Bangladesh and Indonesia, are where workers experienced the most significant deterioration in their basic collective rights.

Ultimately, in Egypt, Islamists are suppressed and used by the establishment. In Pakistan, Islamists are informally excluded from party politics by the establishment. In Bangladesh, Islamists are not part of the establishment, but they have veto power. In Indonesia, Islamists are part of the establishment, but they are not its hegemonic actor. In Turkey, Islamists are the hegemonic actor of the establishment. In Tunisia, Islamists are pacified by an alliance of organized labor and the establishment.

Class Actors

This discussion illustrates two interconnected factors that facilitate or disrupt the strategies of Islamist movements in major Muslim-majority countries with few hydrocarbon resources. First, if the country went through substantial neoliberal reforms in previous decades that boosted capital investment, triggered rural-to-urban migration, and facilitated export-oriented manufacturing industries, there is a good chance that the Islamists tend to act in unison, adopt a nonviolent strategy, and successfully challenge the political establishment. In Egypt, where the conditions for export-oriented industrialization are the least favorable, the military establishment has suppressed the Islamists. In Turkey, where export-oriented industrialization has become the main engine of growth, the Islamists are the new establishment. Indonesia had until recently failed to boost its manufactured goods exports, so its Islamist movements, despite the strength of its religious orders, remained secondary players. Nonetheless, they have taken a path similar to that of the Turkish Islamists as export-oriented manufacturing industries have grown in recent years. The more favorable conditions are for export-oriented industrialization, the more likely it is that Islamists participate in politics, either as influential parties that can impose their will on the government by threatening to block legislation or as the new dominant party that has replaced the old political establishment.

Second, a major attack on organized labor and socialists by the more secular political establishment helps Islamist movements. Tunisia is a particularly representative case, as it has gone through an export-oriented industrialization process yet kept the Islamists at bay. This country does not fit my model in that it has developed a substantial export-oriented industrial base but its Islamist movement failed to take over the government using democratic means. The Tunisian case is special from an industrialization perspective due to the political strength of its industrial working class: 32 percent of strikes and lockouts between 1990 and 2018 in the sixteen Muslim-majority countries in the corresponding ILO database took place in Tunisia.[45] This is a deviation from the general trend: strikes have declined in the five most populous Muslim-majority countries since the 1970s. Turkey and Egypt are interesting in this respect. In Egypt, the peak number of strikes and lockouts in one year since 1973 was only ten, in 1976. In Turkey, the peak year since 1969 was 1990, when 458 strikes and lockouts were recorded as public employees and workers resisted privatization policies. The corresponding figure in 2018 was only twelve. Between 1992 and 2018, an average of thirty-five strikes and lockouts were recorded in the ILO dataset for Turkey; this drops to twenty-three per year since the Islamist Justice and Development Party (AKP) came to power in Turkey in 2002. In other words, Egypt and Turkey, like others in this dataset but not Tunisia, have been strike-free countries for many decades. Furthermore, Tunisia had a unionization rate of 38 percent in 2019, significantly higher than any other country discussed in the previous subsection.[46] The Arab Spring was successful only in Tunisia, with the overthrow of Ben Ali.[47] The resistance of grassroots trade unionists to the earlier decision of the Tunisian General Trade Union to ally with Ennahda during the Jasmine Revolution prevented Rachid Ghannouchi from forming an Ennahda-centered coalition afterward.[48]

In other words, unlike Bangladesh and Indonesia, where export-oriented industrialization was accompanied by increasing pressure on workers' rights, Tunisia shows how a different combination of the scope of export-oriented industrialization and the political power of organized labor yielded a different political outcome. Tunisia coupled an extensive export-oriented industrialization process with a strong labor movement. Popular protests overthrew the dictator, yet the Islamists failed to defeat the old establishment. In many other countries, organized labor is not a major actor in politics and export-oriented industrialization has remained limited, an outcome I called "incomplete neoliberalization" above. Egypt is the ideal case for this second category: here too, the Islamists failed to become the dominant actor in politics. A third category is extensive export-oriented industrialization coupled with the defeat of organized labor. This broadly describes the situation in Turkey, and the rest of this book is about this case.

The fourth combination, limited export-oriented industrialization and strong organized labor, applies to one country: Iran. Besides Turkey, Iran is the only case where Islamization largely took place under an Islamist government that replaced the existing regime and managed to preserve the country's relatively modern state structure. According to Peter Mandaville, Iran is the third major Islamic state to have emerged, after Saudi Arabia and Pakistan.[49] If the success of the Islamist movement in Turkey is generally regarded as exceptional because of the legacy of its secularist institutions, the success of its counterpart in Iran also poses a challenge to dominant perspectives like Mandaville's. Iran is the only hydrocarbon-rich country where an Islamist movement achieved sustainable success against the political establishment.

What distinguishes Iran from most other Muslim-majority countries is its relatively successful nonsocialist industrialization experience before 1979. Unlike the oil monarchies in the Gulf region, which adopted consequential industrialization strategies in recent decades, Iranian industrialization took place long before the 1990s and followed a developmentalist rather than neoliberal mindset. Before 1979, Iran was the most industrialized of the Muslim-majority countries other than Turkey in terms of manufacturing output. Its share of industrial workers in total employment increased from 21 percent in 1962 to 33 percent in 1978.[50] The idiosyncratic conditions of Iran's development-oriented industrialization facilitated, or at least did not prevent, regime change.

Shah Mohammad Reza Pahlavi's insistence on holding on to his failing developmentalist industrialization policies in the 1970s was a poor strategic decision in that it empowered antiregime forces, including the Islamists and the socialists. The economic crisis in that decade, caused in large part by these policies, made the regime an easy target for the grievances of an increasingly desperate working class. Had Pahlavi chosen instead to liberalize Iran's economy, even just a little, and incorporated some religious motifs into the government's official ideology as Sadat did in Egypt, the Pahlavi regime might have found allies among the merchants in Tahranian Bazaar (and even the mullahs) and presented itself as the guardian of religion against infidel organized labor.

However, Pahlavi chose not to take that path, and the Islamists co-opted the grievances of the growing industrial working class. They later established an even more repressive regime than Pahlavi's to control the working class. In 2021, industrial employment as a share of total employment in Iran was the fourth largest among all Muslim-majority countries and the first among Muslim-majority countries with a population of more than five million.[51] The Islamists effectively killed the unions. Iran was the first country to introduce industrial Islamism.

Iran's Islamic revolution started with the overthrow of Pahlavi in 1979. Turkey's own Islamic revolution started with a coup in 1980. I attribute both of these upheavals to the failure of their countries' economic policies, the magnitude of which was as dramatic as the success they had previously enjoyed. As Iran and Turkey's developmentalist industrialization policies began to fail, opportunities opened for Islamists. Pahlavi responded by refusing to liberalize the economy or incorporate any religious symbols into his regime, opening the way for the Islamists to not only topple his regime but also eradicate Iran's socialist and working-class movements.[52]

In Turkey, which had been facing a growing threat of revolutionary socialist movements since the early 1970s, the military collaborated with the country's conservative government to establish a tacit alliance with the Islamists. Together, they engineered a coup in 1980 that not only eliminated any threat from socialist movements but also rebuilt the economy with export-led industrialization policies. By the 1990s, the Islamists had peacefully taken the reins of government through a democratic electoral process.

Unlike in Turkey, the Islamists in Iran could not have embraced an export-oriented industrialization strategy even if they had wanted to, because the US imposed an economic embargo on the new regime in an effort to crush it.[53] Unfazed by the embargo, the mullahs simply continued the Pahlavi regime's developmentalist industrialization strategies and diversified Iran's industrial base as much as possible beyond hydrocarbon-related economic activities.[54] The remarkable success of the developmentalist model in its early stages and its drastic failure in its later stages led to fundamental political changes in Iran after 1979 and economic changes in Turkey after 1980. In both cases, the Islamists benefited.

In sum, the strength of the organized labor movement vis-à-vis the non-Islamist political establishment has been the major political condition determining the chances of Islamist movements in the Muslim-majority countries. This is unsurprising: the growth of the industrial working class became one of the prominent features of the MMW's economic transformation in the post–Cold War period. The total number of industrial workers in the MMW doubled between 1991 and 2021, outpacing population growth by 14 percent, while industry's share of total employment in the MMW increased by 24 percent over the same period. The MMW's share of the global industrial workforce increased by 50 percent between 1991 and 2021, from 12 percent to 18 percent.[55]

These figures also illuminate why the Islamization process was coupled with the industrialization process in the post–Cold War era. According to a 2019 International Trade Union Confederation report, MENA is "the worst region in the world for workers." What is more, 89 percent of the Muslim-majority countries studied in that report (thirty-one of thirty-five) either do not provide any guarantee of workers' rights—as in Bangladesh, Egypt, Indonesia, Iran, and Turkey—or systematically violate their putative rights as in Pakistan and Tunisia.[56] There is no reason to believe that the other twelve Muslim-majority countries perform any better than those examined in this report. Their political regimes do not even bother to compile reliable data on labor rights violations or allow others to do it for them.

Islamization overlaps with industrialization not because Islamists support workers' rights but because socialists were eliminated either during the Islamists' takeover, as in Iran, or before their involvement in the political establishment, as in most Muslim-majority countries, including Turkey and Indonesia. V-Dem scores for religious opposition in forty-seven Muslim-majority countries show a low but negative correlation with worker unionization scores over the period 1990–2019 (-0.266, $p < 0.01$).

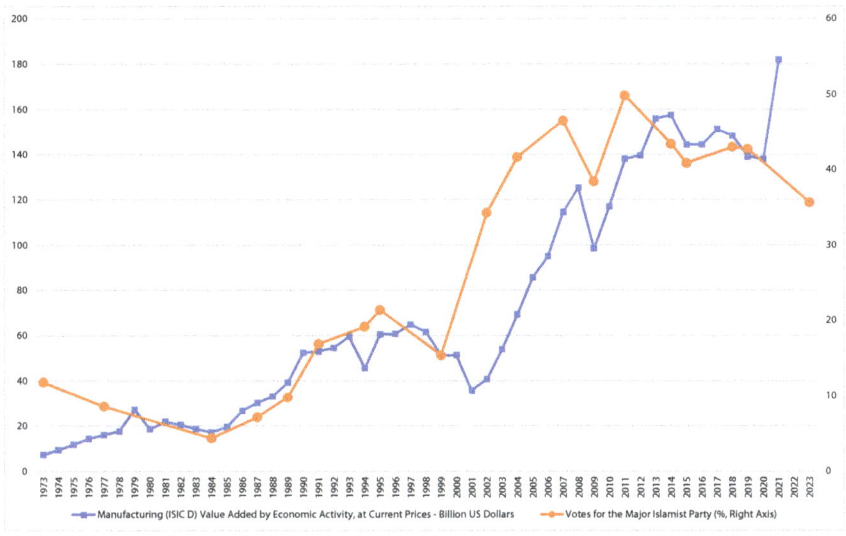

FIGURE 7. Industrial development and electoral support for Islamists (1973–2023). Calculated by the author using the UN Stat and Turkish Supreme Election Council data.

THE TURKISH CASE: INDUSTRIAL GROWTH, SWEATSHOPS, AND ELECTIONS

In this section, I focus on two issues to relate the discussion in previous sections to Turkey. The first is whether the MMW-wide industrialization-Islamization connection applies to Turkey. As figure 7 shows, since the early 1980s, Turkey's manufacturing value added has coincided almost perfectly with the vote shares of the main Islamist parties. When one value falls, so does the other; when one rises, so does the other. Furthermore, the relationship between industrial growth and vote shares among the leading parties in elections applies only to the Islamist parties between 1973 and 2023.[57] In addition to the astonishing extent of this exclusive overlap, this intersection is curious for three reasons.

First, the performance of Islamists in government cannot explain the intersection because the link between industrialization and Islamization existed long before the Islamists came to power in 2002. The Islamists saw a significant increase in their vote share while Turkey's manufacturing sector tripled in value added between 1983 and 1995. During that period, however, they were in opposition.

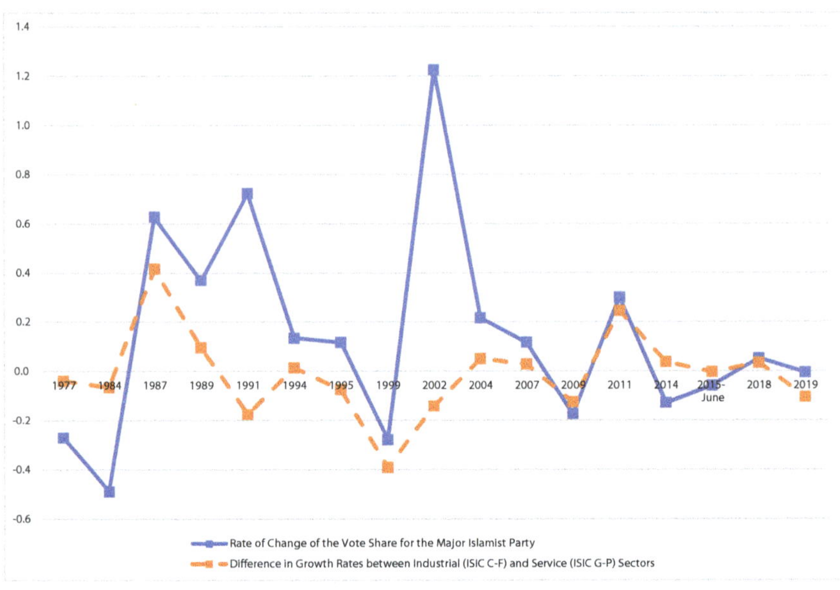

FIGURE 8. Islamists' electoral performance and the relative growth of industrial sectors (1973–2019). Calculated by the author using the UN Stat and Turkish Supreme Election Council data.

Second, although Islamists made their debut in party politics in the 1970s, the vote share of modern Turkey's first Islamist party taking part in elections, the National Salvation Party, declined steadily between 1973 and 1985. The Islamists were unable to surpass their 1973 vote share of 12 percent until 1991, and this only through electoral alliance with ultranationalists. The biggest jump in their vote share was in 2001. If the Turkish electorate had an innate tendency to vote for Islamists, this tendency had three decades to manifest at the ballot box.

Third, the Islamists' vote share was exclusively related to industrial growth rather than to general economic growth and decline. The dotted line in figure 8 illustrates the difference between the growth rates of value added in industrial sectors and all nonagricultural service sectors between election years. The solid line illustrates the rate of change in the vote share of the largest Islamist party between these elections. If the growth in industrial value added since the previous election year is greater than the growth in value added in the services sector, the dotted line is positive.[58] As figure 8 shows, the Islamist vote share increases when the growth rate of value added in industry is higher than the growth rate of value added in the service sector; otherwise, it falls. This relationship holds for fourteen of the seventeen

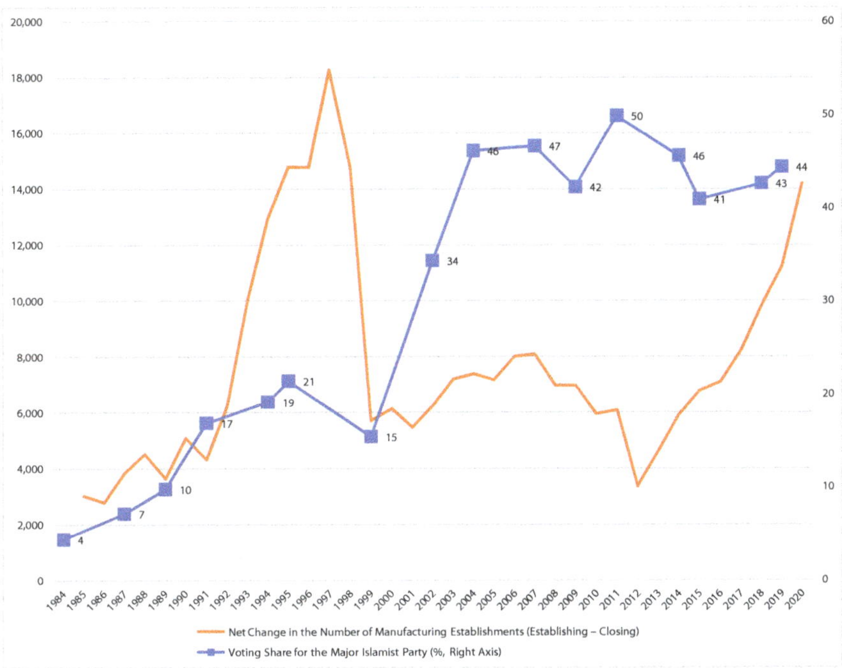

FIGURE 9. Manufacturing enterprises and Islamist votes (1984–2020). Calculated by the author using the Turkish Statistical Institute data.

elections between 1973 and 2019, and the general trend in the graph shows an almost perfect overlap.

The second issue is that the Turkish case reveals a key dynamic in the combination of extensive export-oriented industrialization and weak organized labor: the explosive growth of small and medium manufacturing enterprises (manufacturing SMEs) since the 1990s. Figure 9 shows three aspects of this dynamic. First, the boom in manufacturing output and the number of SMEs in the 1990s preceded the Islamists' first one-party government in 2002. Second, the number of SMEs in the manufacturing sector continued growing in the following decade, albeit more slowly. In the 1990s, the average annual net growth of the manufacturing sector was around ten thousand SMEs; the corresponding average in the first decade of the 2000s was sixty-five hundred. The low point was in 2012, when the difference between new and closed manufacturing firms fell to around three thousand. The AKP lost its majority in Parliament for the first time in 2015 after winning several elections since 2002. Third, since 2013 there has been an increase in the number of new manufacturing SMEs, a trend similar to the 1990s. During this period, despite years of economic stagnation, rampant corruption, and multiple political crises, the Islamists managed to retain a large part of their vote share and, to the surprise of many observers, win the 2023 elections. I will return to this in chapter 6.

CIVILIZATIONAL HISTORIES

These observations point to a complex relationship that demands explanation. On one hand, like in Indonesia and unlike in Tunisia, the source of the collapse of organized labor in Turkey was the bloody 1980 coup. On the other hand, manufacturing sweatshops made unionization more difficult and kept labor politically weak. The Islamists have benefited from industrial growth, though this pattern was already emerging before they came to power. Since the 1990s, the greater the share of small producers in manufacturing, the stronger the Islamists performed at the ballot box. This connection draws attention to the history of the relationship between these small manufacturers and the Islamists.

In some ways, the Turkish Islamists are the most successful among all Muslim-majority countries. They came to power through elections, have remained in control, and have ousted members of the old secularist political establishment. Since 2002, they have reshaped the state apparatus without dismantling it. I attribute this remarkable success to two factors. The first is export-oriented industrialization characterized by extensive private fixed investment, a large industrial workforce, a high urbanization rate, and substantial manufacturing output and exports. The second is the purge or co-optation of organized labor by the non-Islamist political establishment. The first factor turned small manufacturers into a major economic interest, and the second factor made possible an alliance between these entrepreneurs and the Islamists that prevented the rejuvenation of organized labor after the purge.

These observations similarly recalibrate the consensus that Islamic revival was a product of or reaction to the gradual incorporation of the MMW into capitalist relations of production.[59] In countries that provide less critical inputs to the global economy (e.g., agricultural products), the Islamization process is weaker. Islamization has not only a global character but an industrial one, be it through hydrocarbon resources or manufactured goods.

Moreover, the more an Islamist movement can use post–Cold War industrialization to its advantage, the more likely it is to reshape or even dethrone the older political establishment. The more an Islamist movement aligns its ideology, organizational structure, and political alliances with the dynamics of its host country's post–Cold War industrialization strategy, the stronger it becomes in national politics.

Industrial globalization is not just a condition imposed on Islamist movements. The reaction of these movements to this process has become one of its constitutive elements. What granted Islamist movements this capacity was, as in the Turkish case, their alliance with the owners of a swiftly growing number of SMEs. This was coupled with the institutional collapse of organized labor and the socialist movement and often violent political interference by the pre-Islamist establishment, as in the 1980 coup in Turkey or Suharto's politicide in Indonesia. Whether that alliance comes to fruition depends on the political history of individual countries. In Turkey, it did. The topic of the next chapter is the historical conditions framing this alliance between the Islamists and those small manufacturers in Turkey.

PART TWO

The Alliance in Formation

TWO

The Islamists

THE BIRTH OF THE MOVEMENT

The Origins of the Movement

The previous chapter related post–Cold War industrialization to the political performance of the Islamist movements in the Muslim-majority world at large. The Turkish case directs attention to the role of the small manufacturers in this connection. Here and in the following chapter, I discuss the historical relationship between the Islamists and the small manufacturers since the late 1950s. Two factors suggest why the second half of the twentieth century was the foundational period for Islamist movements in Turkey.

First, there was not much in the nineteenth-century history of the Ottoman Empire (or earlier) that Islamists could base their movement on. The process of secularization began during the imperial era. The idea that an Islamic revival could bring the empire back to its glory days faded during the nineteenth-century reform movements under two progressive sultans, Selim III and Mahmut II, and the conservative Abdülhamit II.

During a brief constitutional period following a 1908 coup by relatively secular officers, the imperial Islamic refounders were on their own. From the coup until 1918, thirteen parties were founded alongside the ruling Committee for Union and Progress (Ittihad-ı Terakki). Only one of these thirteen, Ittihad-ı Muhammedi, had a clear Islamist agenda. Apart from its alleged involvement in a rebellion against the junta in 1909, which became known as the 31 March Incident, that party was politically ineffective and ideologically uninspiring.[1]

The Islamic revivalists had a similarly limited influence on the outcome of the Turkish War of Independence in the early 1920s. They did not organize an effective resistance movement against the Christian occupiers, and some of them even took up arms against the resistance led by Mustafa Kemal. But only four of the fifteen substantial armed clashes between the Kemalists and these non-Kemalist militias during the allied invasion were due to a religious agenda.[2] The rest took place with actors that had a monarchist, Kurdish separatist, or pro-Bolshevik agenda. The most destructive internal struggle between local groups during the War of Independence was between the nationalist-secularist Kemalists and the militias of Çerkez Ethem, who was closer to the Bolsheviks than to the monarchists or religious fundamentalists.[3]

Furthermore, apart from Konya, the Muslim fundamentalists did not rise up against the Kemalists in any major city of the remaining fragments of the empire. All the uprisings in the first decades of the republic were by Kurdish clans with a separatist agenda, except for the Nestorian rebellion of 1924 and the Islamist fundamentalist rebellion of 1930 in Menemen. Both of these had a religious character, but they did not pose a fundamental challenge to the new regime, which quickly suppressed them.[4]

The weakness of the imperial Islamic revivalist movement during the constitutional period and the occupation cannot be explained by the supposedly strident secularism of the Kemalists, because the Islamist movement had lost power long before the Kemalists proclaimed the republic. They were not weak because the Kemalists crushed them; rather, the Kemalists easily sidelined them because they were weak.

The second reason to focus on the Cold War era when discussing the rise of the Islamist movement in Turkey is the gradual co-optation of pious political cadres and Islamic scholars in the new regime. The Kemalist regime endeavored to adopt older religious political practices, which later helped pious Muslims trace their political and ideological roots to the imperial regime. The republican regime's Directorate of Religious Affairs (Diyanet) had surprising parallels to the religious leadership (*ulama*) recognized and protected by the older regime.[5]

This co-optation strategy transformed the religious orders (*tariqas*). The success of the republican regime strategy underlines the importance of state support for these groups' activities during the imperial period. When this support ran out, many of them simply disbanded. The few resilient ones had to make their way to the establishment, and to do so they had to reshape their recruitment strategies and the profile of their followers. According to Bernard Lewis, a modest economic interest saved the religious orders in the

1950s from complete dissolution: "One of the strongest elements supporting the revival is the class known in Turkey as the *esnaf*—the artisans and small shopkeepers in the towns. . . . The merchant class is interested in any additional form of insurance against Communism, and has a tradition of pious observance, at least in the provinces."[6]

This merchant class was one of the economic beneficiaries of the Korean War, which overlapped with Lewis's observations in Turkey.[7] As it would again in the 1990s, integration into the global economy directly benefited small capital owners and indirectly benefited the burgeoning Islamist movement by increasing support for the religious orders, which Lewis interpreted as a form of Islamic revival. However, the support of artisans and shopkeepers, who were the predecessors of the manufacturing SME owners of the 1990s, was not enough to revive the old value system. Rather, the religious orders had to adapt to the new value system and seek state patronage to be politically successful.

In this new context, religious leaders such as Said Nurs-i[8] of the later Nurcu movement and Abdülaziz Bekine[9] of the later İskenderpaşa/Gümüşhanevi Dergahı worked out a new strategy to expand their influence in the state bureaucracy. The founders of the modern Islamist movement came from this new cadre of young state bureaucrats and scholars such as Necmettin Erbakan, Temel Karamollaoğlu, Korkut Özal, and his older brother and the eighth president of Turkey, Turgut Özal. They had no difficulty obtaining key positions in the state bureaucracy and public universities that oversaw industrialization efforts during the 1960s. The prestige of their positions in government agencies gave them the legitimacy to advance the network of their religious order within the state. The first political cadre of Turkish Islamism was pro-industrialization state bureaucrats, not the leadership of the religious orders.

Erbakan

An Engineer or a Commander of Jihad? Within this cadre, Erbakan stood out as the first leader of Islamist party politics.[10] He chose small businessmen as strategic allies of the still immature Islamist movement, defined them as pioneers of the glorious history of Muslim Turks, and created the programmatic basis for the alliance between the Islamists and these small businessmen.

Erbakan came from a pious family, but his father, a judge of the republican regime, did not raise him as a rebel against the new secular order. He joined Abdülaziz Bekkine's religious circle at the İskenderpaşa Mosque in Istanbul's

Fatih district in 1946 after enrolling at Istanbul Technical University.[11] His relationship with Bekkine and Bekkine's successor, Zahid Kotku, was close, but his connection to the İskenderpaşa Order was not one of unconditional submission to the religious leadership. Similarly, both Bekkine and Kotku thought Erbakan could be a great asset to their political agenda.[12] The İskenderpaşa Order was one of the most influential Sunni religious orders at the time, so this relationship was beneficial for both sides.

Erbakan's studies in West Germany in 1951 were a formative experience, as he had the opportunity to see the wonders of postwar German industrialization. In his letters to Kotku, he expressed his fascination that the German model could create a new civilization.[13] These observations coincided with the economic policy perspective of the İskenderpaşa Order in the 1950s: "The Order had always been against the domination of foreigners in domestic markets [and] supported domestic capital against foreign capital, and it took appropriate measures. It set up solidarity funds. [For the Order,] Islam was not just about praying and fasting. Muslims were to take over the production of goods and services on the market. These ideas were initially adopted by shopkeepers and merchants and found a growing following."[14]

For Erbakan, Islam was the moral element of his vision of industrialization, and industrialization was the practical element of Kotku's vision of Islamization. Despite this consensus between Kotku and Erbakan, neither had the resources, connections, or resolve to establish a mass Islamist party. Erbakan spent the entire 1960s finding a position for himself as an expert on industrialization within mainstream non-Islamist conservative politics.

With the support of Kotku and his two hundred followers, Erbakan established Gümüş Motor, a factory for the mass production of his prototype five-horsepower engine for agricultural irrigation. The investment raised the eyebrows of right-wing politicians. Prime Minister Adnan Menderes visited the factory when it opened in 1960, praised Erbakan's efforts, and provided foreign currency from state reserves to facilitate the import of intermediate products.[15]

A few months after his visit, low-level officers overthrew Menderes in the first coup of the Turkish Republic, and executed him a year later. This created new opportunities for Erbakan in politics: his schedule in Ankara after the coup was so busy that once, after missing his plane, he jumped on a newspaper van that was on its way from Istanbul to Ankara to reach an important meeting and had a traffic accident that ended in hospitalization.[16] Erbakan was eager to make himself visible in the capital city because the secularist junta continued to show great interest in him. For instance, according to Temel Karamollaoğlu, a confidant of Erbakan and leader of the Islamist Felicity Party, Lieutenant Colonel Mehmet Özgüneş, a member of the junta, expressed his willingness to nominate Erbakan as minister of industry.[17]

The Meeting. The secularist junta seemed to overlook Erbakan's connection to a religious order, and Erbakan did not see any problem with seeking a place for himself within the new hardcore secularist regime. A telling example of Erbakan's close relationship with the secularist establishment was his presentation at a March 4, 1961, cabinet meeting about the feasibility of a domestic automotive industry in Turkey.[18]

The junta cabinet held three meetings that focused on its future industrialization strategy. Erbakan was the only person outside the cabinet who was invited to make a presentation at these meetings. The minutes of the meetings offer fascinating insight into the junta's thinking about the impact of different industrialization strategies on the class structure and elite formation of the country. Cabinet members discussed three broad strategies. The first was to continue Menderes's liberal trade policies. The second was to take protectionist measures to support the existing private large-scale industrial base through partnerships with US corporations. The third was to take alternative protectionist measures to protect and promote small-scale domestic industry. Each strategy, as Mehmet Baydur, the minister of trade, succinctly defined them, benefited three economic interests: importers, assemblers (*montajcılar* or comprador industrialists), and the other industrial sector (*diğer sanayi sektörü*).[19]

The minutes give a strong impression that Erbakan was warmly welcomed at this meeting to help the junta overcome this stalemate. Erbakan's plan would support the small producers, the other industrial sector. Erbakan showed a documentary film about small factories in Turkey, including his own, to convince the cabinet members of the feasibility of his plan to produce cars and trucks in a network of small facilities. According to his plan, small domestic manufacturing companies were able to procure half of the inputs needed to produce the country's first domestic car. A company with thirty thousand small shareholders could be the hub of this supply network for the final assembly of cars and trucks. The only step the government had to take was to provide the first 15 million TL (about $30 million in 2023 dollars) to cover the cost of the prototype.[20] His main point of reference to lend credibility to his ideas was Juscelino Kubitschek, the social democratic president of Brazil, who, Erbakan recounted, hired an engineer who managed to produce 120,000 cars in four years. Brazil exported some of these cars. Low wages contributed to this success, and 95 percent of Volkswagens in the United States were made in Brazil.[21] Erbakan probably identified himself with the nameless engineer in Brazil.

This reference to Brazil irritated one cabinet member, Kemal Kurdaş, who advised the IMF in Latin America after he escaped Turkey because of pressure by the Menderes government in the 1950s: "Brazil was mentioned before. . . . Today, Brazil is governed by a lunatic [referring to Kubitschek]. He established fairy palaces on a red plateau [referring to Brasilia]. The engine industry in Brazil cannot survive without government support. Argentina did the same [and failed]. They imposed tariffs of 700 percent on imported cars, but they still cannot sell their cars. Bribery and all sorts of chicanes corrupted the system. . . . I won't move even one inch before those studies are conducted about the automotive sector."[22]

As the minutes of the next cabinet meeting on the junta's industrial strategy show, Kurdaş's aggressive reaction to Erbakan was related to the similarities and differences between Erbakan's and his visions: at this meeting, which took place three weeks after Erbakan's presentation, Kurdaş enthusiastically proposed the idea of issuing savings bonds (*tasarruf bonosu*) for small investors to finance new joint-stock manufacturing companies and privatize state-owned manufacturing enterprises. In response to the positive comments of Prime Minister Cemal Gürsel, the leader of the junta, he replied: "We will not sell the factories to a gang of capitalists like Ali, Veli and Hasan. We will hand over the factories to the workers."[23] Kurdaş's primary goal (like Erbakan's) was the deconcentration of industrial capital, but the primary clientele of his strategy was the workers, not the nonmonopoly entrepreneurs.

Kurdaş was not the only unimpressed person in the room. Other cabinet members criticized Erbakan's ideas from all possible directions with astonishingly detailed points about foreign currency reserves, previously failed projects, export prospects, coordination among facilities, the lack of backward linkages, and the R&D phase. Erbakan's vision overemphasized engineering-related matters and failed to address other aspects of a much-needed comprehensive industrialization strategy.[24] In the end, Erbakan could not convince the cabinet about the feasibility of his plan. Instead, Şahap Kocatopçu, the minister of industry, who did not attend the meeting, framed the new industrialization strategy that would support the assemblers (*montajcılar* or comprador industrialists) over the importers and small manufacturers (or the other industrial sector). "The other industrial sector" lost the bidding, just like Erbakan.

Disappointments. Erbakan's failure did not have much to do with his close relationship to a religious order, because he was already part of the political establishment. He was involved in the feasibility studies of the domestic automotive industry by the State Planning Organization, the highest technocratic body for industrial policy.[25] He was the chairman of the founding committee of the Ministry of Industry.[26] As mentioned above, he was even considered for the first minister of industry after the coup.[27] His failure was largely a consequence of the weakness of the small producers in the face of the importers and, in particular, the assemblers (or comprador industrialists) as the other two major entrepreneurial groups in the country. In party politics, Süleyman Demirel, his college classmate and a champion of the pro-US big industrial families, became Menderes's successor. The new industrial strategy would favor the comprador industrialists. If we follow the Islamist narrative, this happened because of the support of the Masonic Lodge. Erbakan's Gümüş Motor did not survive the 1960s.

After failing as an industrialist and government bureaucrat, Erbakan focused his energy on the politics of chambers of commerce and industry. In 1967, he was elected secretary general of the Union of Chambers and Commodity Exchanges of Turkey (TOBB), the second highest position of "the highest legal person in Türkiye representing the private sector."[28] Both as the head of the company during the seven-year Gümüş Motor experiment and as the secretary general of TOBB, Erbakan gave lectures to small business owners across the country, starting with the Industrial Congress in 1960[29] and the first Congress of the Automotive Industry in Ankara in 1961.[30] In addition, he worked diligently to create a support base for his future TOBB leadership and channeled TOBB's resources to merchants in the country's provincial cities: "In branches such as Konya [one of the most conservative cities in the country] and Mersin [one of the most liberal cities in the country], he enjoyed the support of the Anatolian capitalists, in contrast to the branches controlled by the big capitalists in Istanbul, Ankara and Izmir. It seems that the industrialists and the merchants were at odds over Erbakan's ideas. Although the industrialists ignored him, the merchants in Anatolia paid tribute to him, adopting and supporting his ideas."[31]

It was not so much their conservative or Islamist worldviews as their hard-to-compromise conflict of interest with big business that led the merchants to support Erbakan's vision. Erbakan was meticulously establishing an Islamist-industrial network throughout the country, a network that did not exist in the last decades of the empire or the first decades of the republic. This was something new, and Erbakan was building it.

Prime Minister Demirel gradually realized that Erbakan was using his position at TOBB to build a political network of these small merchants that could challenge Demirel in party politics.[32] Although initially supportive of his college classmate, Demirel removed Erbakan from this post after Erbakan refused his instruction to grant a loan to an industrialist in Istanbul. This indicated that Erbakan was allocating the financial resources available to TOBB to win the favor of small merchants over big capital in Istanbul. This purge from TOBB did not deter Erbakan from challenging Demirel. After he ran unsuccessfully as a member of Demirel's Justice Party (JP) for a vacant seat in the Senate in the 1968 elections, he was elected to the TOBB's board of directors and then was elected president of TOBB at its twenty-third general assembly in 1969.

Erbakan, as the leader of the future Islamist movement, owed his political career to this election, and the support of small entrepreneurs proved momentous for the result. However, this victory was short lived, as Erbakan was deposed only four months after the election by Demirel himself, who sent police officers to TOBB headquarters. Erbakan locked himself in the office and the police had to break into the room to show him the door.[33] After his last unsuccessful attempt to be elected as a deputy by Demirel's JP in 1969, the turbulent 1960s left Erbakan with no choice but to participate in party politics as the leader of an independent movement, using his credibility among small businessmen as his future constituency. The reluctance of Demirel and his patrons to give Erbakan space within the conservative political elite indirectly framed the future of the Islamist movement.[34]

A New Party

The Foundation. With the support of the İskenderpaşa Order,[35] Erbakan was elected in 1969 as an independent in Konya, a pious and relatively industrialized central Anatolian city that was the only major urban center supporting the fundamentalists against the Kemalist officers during the allied occupation in the early 1920s. His message to his electorate had much to do with his vision of industrialization, which appealed to the city's industrialists and merchants. He told the story of a nameless class struggle between the entrepreneurs of little means and those with big money in Istanbul:

> The economic system serves the big urban merchants, the Anatolian merchant sees himself as a foster child. The lion's share of import quotas is allocated to a handful of urban merchants.... The money in the Anatolian banks is deposited by the Anatolian population, but this money is then lent to the large urban merchants in the form of loans. . . . The Union of Chambers functions completely as an instrument of a comprador-Masonic minority. This huge organization is under the control of the commercial and industrial interests of the compradors. So we said to ourselves, "Let us first get elected to the decision-making body [*idare heyeti*] and turn the Union of Chambers into an organization that serves the interests of Anatolian merchants and industrialists."[36]

Erbakan's success at the ballot box seems to have played a decisive role in the growing consensus between pious establishment politicians and the religious orders that he should be the leader of the National Order Party (NOP), founded in 1970 as the first Islamist party in the republican era. His leadership role in the NOP—and in its successor, the National Salvation Party (NSP)—depended on this consensus. His position in the party was tested several times in the 1970s.

The most sensitive issue for him was the relationship between the religious orders and the party. Erbakan was fighting to consolidate his leadership within the young Islamist movement vis-à-vis the religious orders, including his own İskenderpaşa Order. On the one hand, he wanted to work closely with the followers of the religious orders because he believed their cadres would act with more discipline than independent intellectuals and students. On the other hand, the divisions among the religious orders posed a significant threat to his leadership. At the second congress of the NSP in 1974, for example, Erbakan's team struggled to take control of the party's decision-making bodies. This was not about growing opposition to Erbakan per se, but about the struggle of the religious orders to fill key positions in the party with their supporters. Moreover, the NSP deputies who were close to the orders of Said Nurs-i (the Nurcus) acted as an independent clique within the party.[37] Eventually, the Nurcu deputies resigned from the party during the coalition with the Republican People's Party (RPP), presumably because the NSP agreed that socialist prisoners should benefit from the general amnesty.[38]

Surprisingly, this tension among the religious orders did not strengthen Erbakan's relationship with his İskenderpaşa Order. Rather, he gradually distanced himself from that religious order, even though the support of its leader, Kotku, had helped him early in his political career.[39] Erbakan's increasing independence from individual religious orders was a sign of his growing ability to build an independent following within the party. A simple engineer with a relatively pious lifestyle who could have served successfully (and perhaps even happily) for Kubitschek had he been born on the other shore of the Atlantic, he now called himself "the commander of jihad" (*cihad emri*).[40]

In some ways, unlike in the Islamist parties in Indonesia, which are broadly appendages of Nahdlatul Ulama and Muhammadiyah in national politics, Erbakan's growing hegemony over the embryonic Islamist movement was counterintuitive. He did not initially have strong ties to the most important groups or individuals, except the İskenderpaşa Order. Due to his affiliation with this religious order, he was not in a position to mediate between the different cliques in the young party. Unlike the sheikhs of the religious orders, he had no religious authority.

However, the new movement lacked a coherent and effective doctrine and strategy, as well as unity and cooperation between its various factions. Until Erbakan's entry into national politics, the religious orders used the spoils system to place their supporters in the government bureaucracy but had no long-term strategy on what to do with these new bureaucrats. Lacking a common goal, religious orders and cliques were reluctant to act harmoniously within a united party, as demonstrated by the split between the Nurcus and other Naqshbandi orders within the NSP in the 1970s. It is unclear whether the religious orders in this period contributed to the mobilization strategy of the Islamist movement or harmed it.

The political ideas of pious Muslims were also mainly shaped by conservative nationalists such as Nurettin Topçu, who distrusted industrialization as a corrupting force that could destabilize social harmony in Anatolia's rural communities. Industrialization, Topçu believed, would only accelerate the disintegration of these communities, already underway as a result of urbanization.[41] At this point, the Islamists were not confident that they could thrive among the rural-to-urban migrants in the big cities. Industrialization, they suspected, could further jeopardize their connections to their already tiny electorate.

Erbakan used this ideological, strategic, and organizational vacuum to consolidate his power within the movement and weaken the position of the religious orders within it. When Erbakan rose to become the commander of jihad, he defined his vision of industrialization as an ideological alternative to rural conservatism.

The Political Performance. Rather than trying to alienate them, the political establishment wanted the Islamists to become part of party politics in the 1970s. The military gave a memorandum in 1971 to the civilian government and urged Prime Minister Demirel to resign. Fearing persecution, Erbakan left the country. Just as he had been invited to take part in the industrialization strategy after the 1960 coup, the military made considerable efforts to persuade Erbakan to return to Turkey.[42]

Even more remarkably, despite its declining vote share, the NSP was the most important member of coalition governments in the 1970s.[43] During the first decade of the Islamist movement, from 1969 to 1980, the NSP was part of the government on 32 percent of the days Turkey had an elected government that received parliamentary confidence and a coalition partner on 43 percent of the days Turkey had an elected coalition government that received parliamentary confidence. To put these percentages into perspective, the NSP was the most successful party in terms of days in government, other than the country's two biggest parties, the center-right JP and the center-left RPP.

The Islamists used these cabinet seats effectively. Although they were regularly involved in coalition governments, they underpinned their image as an antiestablishment movement with antisecularist political spectacles and scandals such as the relocation of public sculptures and failed bills to move weekly holidays from Sundays to Fridays and restrict alcohol consumption. They used their control over the ministries to profit from the spoils system and award public contracts to contractors close to them. These practices consolidated the Islamist movement's position in party politics. They now had something to offer college graduates and small producers who were excluded from the spoils system and small public contracts.[44]

In addition to these instrumental steps, the Islamists wanted to distinguish themselves with their alternative industrialization policy. Their main aim was to present themselves as pioneers of industrial development in the name of small producers. An example of this was the NSP's support for the establishment of the State Industrial and Labor Investment Bank during the Thirty-Seventh Interim Government. The aim was to finance multiowner industrial enterprises just like the seventy-five worker-enterprises and public companies that had been established between 1964 and 1972.[45]

Similarly, in 1976, with the financial support of the Ministry of Industry and Technology, which was under the NSP, Erbakan published an industrialization strategy that listed factories that would produce tractor engines, tractors, boilers, truck engines, conveyor elements, heavy equipment, and metal structures in nonmetropolitan cities such as Konya, Yozgat, Nevşehir, Çankırı, and Gerede. Almost daily, Erbakan gave the green light for one of these factories.

The problem was that many of these projects were not in the five-year plan or even in the government program. In one case, it was reported that after breaking ground for a "heavy electronics" factory in a district of Erzurum (Dumlu), Erbakan broke ground for the second unit of this plant in a neighboring district (Pasinler) after that district asked for it incessantly. According to Ali Yaşar Sarıbay, the NSP rejected an early election in 1977 because it assumed that some of these projects would be realized by the next summer and the party could capitalize on its image as an advocate of industrialization.[46] Erbakan and his NSP presented themselves in a large-scale PR campaign as advocates of industrialization that would help provincial towns and small producers.

However, this strategy did not pay off at the ballot box in the 1970s. The NSP, which replaced the NOP on October 11, 1972,[47] received 11.8 percent in the October 1973 elections,[48] but its share of the vote fell to 8.6 percent in the 1977 elections.[49] All three other parties—the center-left RPP, the center-right JP, and the ultranationalist Nationalist Movement Party (NMP)—increased their seats in Parliament. The NSP was not the majority party in any city or district except for some districts in Konya, the stronghold of the movement, and in the Kurdish region.[50] The Islamists would not go above the bar set in 1973 until the 1990s.

Nonetheless, the strategy helped the Islamists consolidate their support among a large "group of provincial Anatolian merchants who had begun to invest in middle-sized industry and were frustrated by government and banking policies that encouraged the concentration of investment in the bigger enterprises of the largest cities."[51] At a broader level, the organizational and ideological transition of the devout Muslims from a loose network of rural conservatives and alienated urban intellectuals into a pro-industrial mass movement in the 1970s was the biggest bet the Islamists made on the fate of the still immature movement. The factor that translated this groundwork into tangible results at the ballot box was the neoliberal reforms that empowered the small producers Erbakan had eagerly courted in the previous two decades. The architect of these reforms was someone Erbakan knew very well: Turgut Özal.

The 1980s: The Bet Paid Off

Özal: A Liberal or an Islamist (or Both)? Even though he enjoyed sipping whiskey after a long day and his wife did not wear a hijab, Özal was an Islamist, or at least as much an Islamist as Erbakan. Like his classmate Erbakan, he began praying regularly after beginning his studies at Istanbul Technical University,[52] and he joined the İskenderpaşa Order during his studies along with Erbakan and his brother Korkut.[53] His connection to the order, like Erbakan's, was more of a conditional relationship than a complete submission to the spiritual leadership. After a remarkable career with different positions at the State Electrical Power Planning Administration, State Planning Organization, World Bank, Sabancı Holding (the second biggest industrial conglomerate of Turkey at that time), and the Turkish Metal Industry Employers' Association, in 1977 he ran in the parliamentary elections for the deputy position as a member of Erbakan's NSP in Izmir, the third biggest city in the country. He was selected to give the propaganda speech on public radio on behalf of the NSP.

Despite his NSP candidacy only two years earlier, Demirel appointed Özal as secretary of state to the prime minister, the highest bureaucratic position in the government, thanks to an exceptionally strong endorsement from the IMF representative for Turkey, Jacques de Groote, who took Özal with him during his visit to Demirel and asked him to commission Özal to draft a strategy to address the immediate foreign exchange shortage. This strategy document became known as the "January 24 Decisions" and provided the blueprint for neoliberal policies after the 1980 coup.

Thus, it was no wonder that he was on the list of Kenan Evren, the staunchly secularist leader of the 1980 junta, for his future cabinet.[54] Evren began working with Özal long before he was appointed as deputy prime minister in the first cabinet after the coup. On September 14, 1980, just two days after the coup, Özal worked with the undersecretary of the Ministry of Finance in the office of Evren's deputy and second in command of the junta, Haydar Saltık, on the details of the closure of the trade unions and political parties.[55]

In addition to Demirel and the IMF, Özal also received support from Vehbi Koç—the richest man in the country, a secularist, and the owner of the largest industrial conglomerate at the time. In his letter to Evren on October 12, 1981, about a year after the coup, Koç underlined that "Turgut Özal is not a genius [*dahi*]. He too can make mistakes. But in these fragile times, he is, among other things, the person who knows our most important issues best."[56]

More interestingly, Özal received a surprising amount of support from Turhan Feyzioğlu,[57] the leader of the right-wing secularist Republican Trust Party. In his memoirs, Evren gave Feyzioğlu unqualified compliments as a true Kemalist for supporting hardcore secularism and rejecting all socialist tendencies as a member of three coalition governments in the 1970s. Evren and other junta members wanted him to become the next prime minister. After reluctantly accepting, he insisted that Özal be minister of state in his cabinet, head the Economic Council, and oversee the implementation of the junta's economic policies. Ironically, the junta decided not to appoint Feyzioğlu as prime minister, but Özal retained his post, thanks to IMF endorsement, with wide-ranging powers and little oversight over his ability to manage the new economy. Like Erbakan in the previous two decades, Özal, a follower of a religious order and a former candidate of the Islamist party, was given the task of framing the country's economic and industrial strategy by the secularist military and bureaucracy.

Özal served as prime minister from 1983 to 1991 and as president until his death in 1993. His policies in the transformative 1980s replaced two key elements of the import substitution model in favor of an export-oriented growth strategy. First, although the new regulations he designed encouraged foreign financial investment to address the chronic lack of capital for small entrepreneurs, the government retained the power to set preferential rates for various groups and used this power to favor manufacturing exporters.[58] Second, agricultural subsidies were cut significantly;[59] both the share of farmers in national income[60] and the share of agriculture in total exports declined in the 1980s.[61] This new policy orientation triggered a massive rural-to-urban migration wave.[62] Between 1980 and 1990, Turkey's urban population grew by 13.4 million, a figure unsurpassed in any other decade before or since. The proportion of the population living in urban areas increased in the 1980s from 44 percent to 60 percent, which corresponds to 36 percent growth in the urbanization rate, the third highest in the world among countries with a population over twenty million, just behind Indonesia (38 percent growth in urbanization rate) and China (37 percent).[63]

As a result of these two policy changes, the overall composition of domestic production changed drastically in just one decade. The share of agriculture in GDP fell from 24.4 percent to 16.4 percent, which corresponds to a 33 percent decline, while the share of industry rose from 20.7 percent to 26.2 percent, which corresponds to 27 percent growth. The share of services, on the other hand, grew only from 54.8 percent to 57.4 percent, which corresponds to 5 percent growth.[64] Özal's policies expanded not only the urban population but also the manufacturing workforce. This growth created a new cadre of small entrepreneurs in manufacturing, a new component of the country's class structure.

The Enclosure of Urban Space. A key factor that turned the rural-to-urban migration and swift industrial growth into a political asset for the Islamists in the 1990s was the commodification of urban land in the metropolitan regions. As millions of rural migrants came to Istanbul and other metropolitan areas during those years, tolerance for squatting quickly faded.

The unspoken aim of these new anti-squatting policies was to launch a construction boom. This paradigm shift favored those who, thanks to earlier amnesty laws, had a legal right to the land they had been occupying as squatters for years and could use their good fortune, with the help of developers, to convert the shacks they had been living in into multistory apartment buildings. For the generations of rural migrants who started coming to the city in the late 1980s, these new policies that criminalized squatters were punishing.[65]

Those who had been able to buy land when it was cheap and those who came to the city early enough to benefit from the collective struggles that defended squatters (often with the help of the socialists) quickly found small contractors who had the capital to replace their one-story shacks with four- to six-story buildings, each of which had eight to eighteen units.[66] The value of these units was split between the landowners and the contractors according to how much each unit cost to build, which depended on the year or season when construction took place. Thanks to this scheme, 80,141 buildings were built in the average year between 1981 and 2001. Between 1964 and 1980, that figure had been only 43,316.[67]

When I was a child in the early 1990s, construction sites for these new buildings were our favorite places to play. The youngest among us, who had never seen a real playground, gravitated to the large piles of sand dumped there so construction workers could make cement on site. We obviously did not understand that rural-to-urban migrant families during the 1980s and

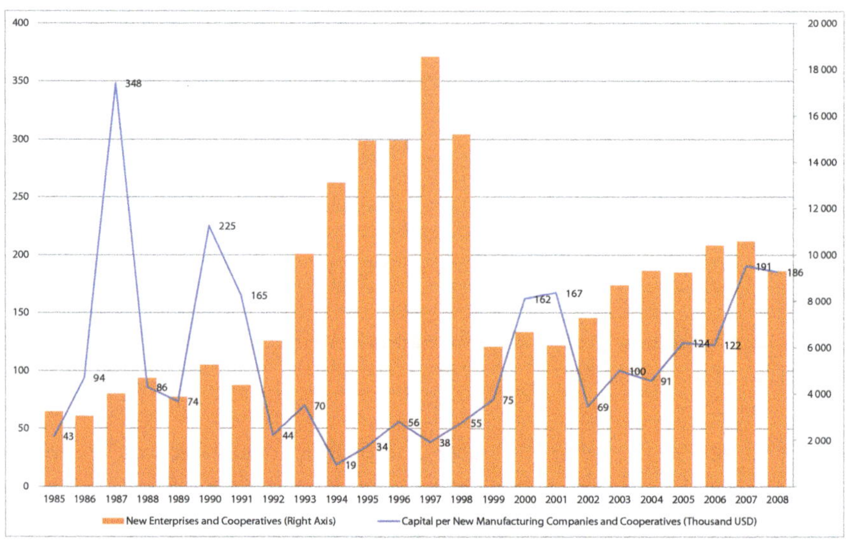

FIGURE 10. Capital per new manufacturing company and cooperative (1985–2008). Calculated by the author using the Turkish Statistical Institute data.

early 1990s were forced to pay high rents to earlier generations of migrants, who had turned the lots of their squatter settlements into multistory apartments on what we considered our temporary playgrounds. We were at the center of an interesting and massive primitive accumulation process through what I have called "the enclosure of urban space."[68]

The dramatic rise in urban sprawl during the last twenty years of the twentieth century was accompanied by a significant change in the industrial ecology of Turkey's manufacturing sector. According to the 1964 industrial census, there were 161,000 manufacturing enterprises in the country.[69] In 1980, the number of enterprises had risen to 186,000. Over those twenty-six years, manufacturing employment increased from 431,000 to 1.3 million.[70] The threefold increase in the work force between 1964 and 1980 was primarily due to the expansion of existing large manufacturing companies. Then, during the 1990s, the number of manufacturing enterprises skyrocketed. The 1992 industrial census still showed only 186,000 manufacturing companies,[71] but in 2002 there were 273,000.[72] As shown in figure 10, between 1993 and 1998, an average of 14,460 new manufacturing companies were founded in Turkey every year, an increase of 47 percent in a single decade.

This numerical growth was so tremendous that if the eighty-seven thousand new businesses had been evenly distributed across all 32,238

FIGURE 11. A readymade garment sweatshop in Gaziosmanpaşa, Istanbul, 2023. Anonymous photographer, December 28, 2023.

neighborhoods in Turkey, there would have been three microenterprises per neighborhood.[73] In fact, of course, these small businesses were disproportionately located in the working-class districts of the country's metropolitan regions. They became an organic element in the socioeconomic life of these poor neighborhoods.

These new businesses became part of a massive and rapidly growing manufacturing sector, but they were hardly factories in the usual sense of the term. The average registered initial capital per company between 1993 and 1998 was $45,000, and the figure for 1994 was only $19,000. For this reason, I often refer to these manufacturing SMEs as "sweatshops." Figure 11 shows a typical sweatshop, barely noticeable on the first floor of a residential building.

The owners of these new sweatshops were a heterogeneous group that included immigrants who had arrived as late as the 1980s and 1990s. Some of these more recent arrivals still had land in their villages, which they used to help raise the $45,000 they needed to open a sweatshop. Others had good relations with fellow immigrants from their hometowns and borrowed the sum from them. Still other families had so many brothers and sisters already working in sweatshops that they were able to save the necessary money in a few years. As for those who had moved to the cities earlier and benefited from the socialists' struggle to protect squatters, they had become slumlords and used the rental income they collected from more recent immigrants to run their own sweatshops. As a result—and the point bears repeating—one way or other, the earlier generation of rural migrants was offloading the conditions of poverty they used to endure onto others, often charging them exorbitant rent for their housing and paying substandard wages. The poverty of earlier generations of migrants was transferred to later migrants, like some of our relatives, in a process Oğuz Işık and Melih Pınarcıoğlu called "poverty in rotation" (*nöbetleşe yoksulluk*) in their study of Sultanbeyli, a working-class Istanbul district that has been a stronghold of the Islamists since the 1990s.[74] This process was the engine of neoliberal industrialization, which produced a new urban elite, the faubourgeoisie.

The 1990s: An Imminent Victory?

The 10 Percent. The new Islamist movement went through three formative processes under Erbakan's leadership in the 1970s. First, the movement emerged as the champion of an alternative industrialization model that favored small producers. Second, the power within the movement shifted from the religious orders and antiurban intellectuals to pro-urban political cadres. Third, the Islamists proved themselves a reliable ally of the secularist establishment in its fight against the socialists. Özal's reforms empowered those small producers, triggered an unprecedented wave of urban migration, and established a new industrial paradigm that rendered the older mobilization strategies of the socialists useless.

Nonetheless, the Islamists had to wait until the mid-1990s to succeed at the ballot box. Even in the 1991 parliamentary elections, the Islamists passed their 1973 vote share only thanks to an election alliance with the ultranationalist Nationalist Labor Party (Milliyetçi Çalışma Partisi). The percentage of Islamist voters in this election was likely the same as in 1973, or maybe even smaller.

In the 1995 parliamentary elections, however, the Islamist Welfare Party (WP) reached 21.4 percent and became the first party. Their vote share was about 10 percent higher than in the 1973 elections, the most rewarding to date for the Islamist party. Election results between 1977 and 1995 leave the strong impression that 10–15 percent of the electorate was ideologically unaffiliated but politically dissatisfied voters. These voters helped the center-left RPP party win 41 percent of the vote in 1977 as it capitalized on the radicalism of the socialist left.[75]

The following three years saw a phenomenal rise in political violence between socialist and ultranationalist factions triggered by the military's illegal anticommunist counterguerrilla branch, which had been set up as part of NATO's Operation Gladio to recruit, fund, and protect ultranationalist militants against socialists. Its goal was to justify the 1980 coup. Once this mission was accomplished, the junta arrested 650,000 people and persecuted another 230,000. About three hundred detainees died in prison, at least 171 as a result of torture, 1.7 million people were blacklisted, and fifty people were executed.[76]

In short, the junta clearly signaled to the Turkish public that the rightwing secularist political establishment would not allow leftist parties to rule the country even if they gained popular and electoral support. After they received this message, that 10 percent distanced itself from the antisystemic left and turned to the antiestablishment right, which Özal and Demirel claimed to represent after the coup. Özal waged a war against the developmentalist bureaucracy, and Demirel was a victim of the 1980 coup. After Özal and Demirel lost their prestige amid the economic and political instability of the 1990s, the Islamists were the next stop for that 10 percent.

In fact, even in the mid-1990s, there were no clear signs at the ballot box that the Islamists were destined to become the country's hegemonic political party. Back then, they were just a contender for the antiestablishment label, like Özal's and Demirel's parties. What turned the tide for the WP was the 1994 municipal elections, when the Islamists won both Istanbul and Ankara, the country's two largest cities, by narrow margins of 3 percent and 0.45 percent, respectively. The Islamists finally succeeded in extending their influence beyond the older and traditionally pious districts in the center of Istanbul such as Fatih and Üsküdar to the emerging working-class districts such as Bağcılar.[77] This result was significant, not only because the Islamists' vote share was growing, but also because it was growing due to the growing new support in the poorer regions of the big cities. As figure 12 illustrates, the Islamists in 1994 succeeded for the first time in achieving a share of the vote in the country's five most industrialized cities (İstanbul, İzmir, Ankara, Bursa, and Kocaeli) above the nationwide share of the total electorate in these cities. In fact, in the five elections between 1987 and 1999, except for 1995, whenever the share of these five cities in the Islamists' nationwide votes grew faster than these cities' share in total population, the Islamists' national vote share also increased, and vice versa.

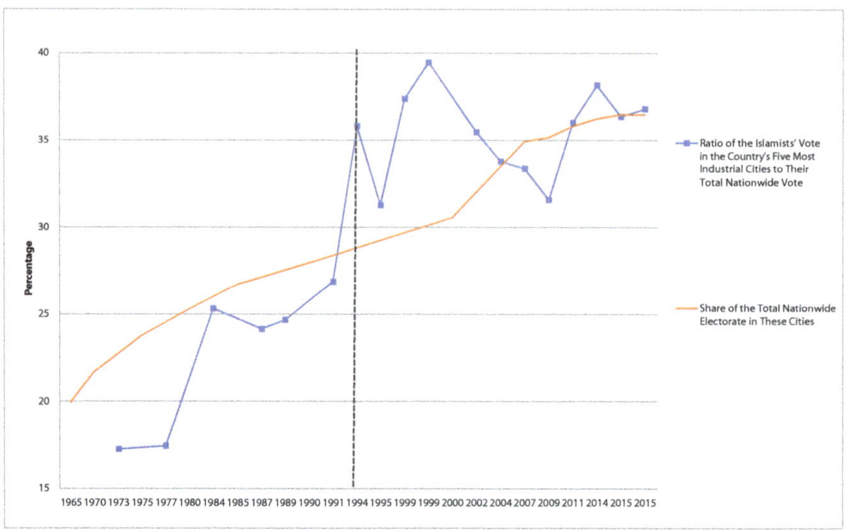

FIGURE 12. Ratio of the Islamists' vote in the country's five most industrial cities to their nationwide vote and the nationwide share of the total electorate in these cities (1973–2015). Calculated by the author using the Turkish Supreme Election Council data.

In other words, the growing electoral base of the Islamists was due to the growing support of rural-to-urban migrants, who did not vote for the Islamists until they moved to the metropolitan areas. The key to the success of the Islamist movement in this decade was not a simple regional shift of the votes from rural areas to metropolitan areas due to the relocation of already pious voters, but a change in the political opinions of those migrants in metropolitan areas to favor the Islamists.

A New Organization

Resources. The Islamists' success in pooling the resources of small manufacturers in their grassroots mobilization activities was a major factor in their electoral success. Starting in the mid-1990s, I can use my observations to support this argument. In those years, the change in the political landscape in the working-class neighborhoods of Istanbul was almost tangible. These neighborhoods were bereft of the political vibrancy of the 1980s.

In Bağcılar, the most populous neighborhood in Istanbul at the time and the site of my yearlong fieldwork in 2008, the long convoys of the two center-right parties, the Motherland Party and the True Path Party, were rare during the 1997 election campaign. People no longer talked about the squabbles between the leaders of these parties, Mesut Yılmaz and Tansu Çiller, who were poor copies of their respective predecessors Özal and Demirel. Politics was now the WP against everyone else. The wealthy members of my extended family preached the merits of Erbakan's brilliant ideas, his truly Muslim values, and his fight against corruption to our poorer relatives.

In addition to this sense of the political milieu that gripped everyone in these neighborhoods, including me as a local, I had the opportunity to make more systematic observations in these neighborhoods shortly after the 2001 crisis and before the 2002 elections that brought the Islamists to power. My colleague Burcu Yakut and I, as research assistants for a United Nations Development Programme project on the impact of this crisis in Istanbul, conducted more than one hundred interviews in different city districts such as Bağcılar, Bakırköy, Büyükçekmece, Eminönü, Esenyurt, Eyüp, Ümraniye, Sultanbeyli, and Zeytinburnu.

What we saw during this project was eye-opening. The crisis had hit the economy hard. The families we spoke to were the poorest of the poor. Some had "flour soup" and onions for dinner, and there were homeless families, a very uncommon phenomenon until this year. Later, on various occasions, we came across several teams bringing furniture to the homes of elderly people and widows. This support had little to do with the immediate crisis of these homeless families, who needed food and shelter, not furniture. This problem did not seem to bother these aid teams. Their primary goal was visibility in the neighborhood, and furniture was a good item for accomplishing this goal.

We decided to find out more about what was really going on. We arranged a meeting with the Deniz Feneri Association, one of the largest Islamist charity organizations at the time.[78] Its main camp in the European part of the city, located in Zeytinburnu, included a two-story hangar with over twenty thousand square feet of floor space, filled with a variety of items—from large sacks of noodles and large containers of cooking oil to assortments of clothing, furniture, and lumber. The room was reminiscent of one of the Salvation Army's storage facilities, only bigger and newer.

The items seemed to be stored randomly in different corners of the hangar. Items with a larger volume, such as sacks or furniture, were stored on the mezzanine, and smaller items were on the second floor. Sensing our confusion, our interlocutor showed us the taxonomy on the computer and the barcodes attached to each item. The apparent chaos was due to the incessant influx of a large amount of donations coming from benevolent businessmen doing business in Istanbul and many other cities around the country.

Indeed, the items in stock reflected the range of what these manufacturing SMEs produced and exported to foreign markets. Many had minor blemishes or were surplus products that were lucky enough to exceed the calculated waste. What lay ahead was probably the largest nongovernmental campaign of patronage of the republican era. It was a museum where all sorts of artifacts of Istanbul's industrial civilization were on display.

No other party or movement had access to such resources. The True Path, Motherland, and Republican People's Parties became parasitic political instruments that benefited from their key position in politics and hid behind the 10 percent threshold that excluded the small parties from Parliament. Their access to the electorate was through TV channels and newspapers controlled by old money, such as the Koç Group, or by the new money of the neoliberal era, such as the Uzan Group. When the 2001 crisis hit the economy, these media outlets and those parasitic parties lost their credibility and could not shape reality for the common people.

Cadres. The money and labor for these operations and the connections to reach the beneficiaries came from the same neighborhoods. It was the time of the Islamist activist. During the same research, we visited one of my cousins, an ardent Islamist who was the *mukhtar* (the elected head of the neighborhood) in Esenler, a working-class district neighboring Bağcılar. Before we took the first sip of our tea, he opened a large map of his neighborhood on the table. An unmistakable fire in his eyes, he tapped his fingers on the corners of the neighborhood's borders and asked me, his voice intense, "Why, *amcaoğlu* [cousin], why? Can't you see how the military messed up the borders of our neighborhood? Because they did not want the true believers [*mümin*] to choose their representatives. We will beat them with Allah's permission."

My cousin was alluding to the obvious gerrymandering that led to nonsensical district boundaries that put more secular and richer neighborhoods together with more pious and poorer ones. As much of a radical as he was, his activism was supported and funded by the same people who helped Islamist civil society organizations like Deniz Feneri thrive. I knew he secured the financial support of another cousin of mine, a relatively well-known and wealthy shopkeeper in Bağcılar whose endorsement was crucial. In a neighborhood of over fifty thousand people, my *mukhtar* cousin needed resources to make himself known to his target audience. The support of my wealthier cousin and his pals was an important asset. Their financial support was an indication that he was an ally of the local elite, a successful player in valence politics.

This connection between resources and cadres came about slowly and gradually in the 1980s. According to Banu Eligür, "there was no popular Islamist mobilization in Turkey [until the 1990s]. Rather, political Islamists were reduced to a marginalized group."[79] Kayhan Delibaş's research in the late 1990s on Islamist mobilization in Ankara, the country's second largest city, similarly confirms my observations and vividly shows the Islamists did not succeed in reaching the urban poor in the 1980s. The situation was exactly the opposite in the 1990s: "Between 1983 and 1991, the WP could not reach the people due to two factors. Firstly, the conformist approach of the party organizations and secondly, the lack of local organizations. From 1991 onwards, the WP expanded its organizational networks both vertically and horizontally."[80]

The Islamists' organizational success during these years combined a persistent grassroots campaign with a relatively decentralized mobilization strategy that granted a high degree of autonomy to local activists and their local funders.[81] About 160,000 village and neighborhood representatives, over ten thousand teachers and propagandists, fifty thousand party leaders, and about two hundred thousand volunteers, including some "economically strong Turkish-European immigrants," were involved to varying degrees in this campaign.[82] According to Delibaş, the Islamist movement in the 1980s and 1990s had a well-disciplined, modern party structure with a limited role for religious orders in the actual mobilization efforts and the cultural identity of party members.[83] Many active members came from the same neighborhoods and districts. The party activists built and controlled an extensive computerized database about the local population. Most activists migrated to Ankara from rural Anatolia at a young age and never left their working-class communities.[84]

Jenny White's ethnography of Ümraniye, then the largest working-class district in the Asian part of Istanbul, attributes this success to the activities of local Islamic charities that established a crucial link, in the 1990s, between the workers and the politically engaged businessmen and industrialists:

> In Ümraniye . . . a number of associations and an Islamic foundation [*vakıf*] . . . worked in tandem with the Welfare Party and the party-led municipality. All claimed autonomy from the municipality and the party, although they cooperated with both. . . . The foundations were run by local businessmen, the cells by neighborhood activists who bridged differences in income, education and even gender. Islamist businessmen donated time and materials, presenting an alternative image of Islamic-based prosperity as a viable

alternative to the secular, Western-style lifestyle that had characterized upward mobility and economic success in the modern republic. . . . These charitable foundations "placed men in jobs found through companies associated with the foundation, through the city government, and by word of mouth through personal connections."[85]

The Islamists were unrivaled in these communities because the socialist left was taken out of the equation by the 1980 coup. As one of Delibaş's interlocutors put it, "No one but us goes around the neighborhoods. . . . Other parties cannot work like us."[86] Similarly, there is virtually no reference to the socialist groups in White's ethnography, even though they had been very active in this district before the 1980 coup.[87]

The socialists of the 1970s were being replaced by new cadres, including ambitious small-town politicians like my *mukhtar* cousin, the followers of religious orders, and determined independent radical activists. This transformation has been well documented in studies of Istanbul's recent political and urban history published in Turkish. Şükrü Aslan documented the purge of socialists from Ümraniye, a working-class Istanbul neighborhood.[88] Sema Erder linked this purge to the transformation of squatter settlements into multistory buildings and the rise of the owners of these buildings as slumlords.[89] Işık and Pınarcıoğlu said this vertical redevelopment reinforced class divisions between slumlords and tenants, early and late migrants, and workers and sweatshop owners.[90]

Finally, Cihan Tuğal's ethnography in Sultanbeyli, the setting of Işık and Pınarcıoğlu's study and located just a few miles east of Ümraniye,[91] provides an excellent description of the internal dynamics of local Islamist mobilization in the early years of the Islamist one-party government. The radical activists were disillusioned with the movement's shift from a utopian perspective of small producers to the cold narrative of unforgiving neoliberalism. Even though they had helped the local elite establish a new regime of political domination in the 1990s in these neighborhoods, they were ultimately marginalized within the movement in the following decade. Many if not most of Tuğal's altruistic Islamist activists would probably have been socialists if they had been born two decades earlier or if the 1980 coup had not triggered a new political economic order.

A New Ally

Formation of an Alliance. While the organizational and financial support of the local businessmen turned the Islamists into the major antiestablishment force in politics in the 1990s, their growing role in the movement recalibrated its ideology along a neoliberal mindset and paved the way for a new political cadre under Tayyip Erdoğan's leadership. The Islamist businessman behind this transformation of the Islamist movement was the voice of the small industrialists, the core of the faubourgeoisie. One business association, Müsiad (Independent Industrialists and Businessmen Association), claimed to represent this persona. Müsiad's story reveals not only the forces behind the adaptation of the Islamist movement to a neoliberal mindset, but also the broad contours of the relationship between the Islamist movement and the faubourgeoisie.

Müsiad was founded in 1990 by young businessmen in their thirties who owned medium-sized manufacturing companies in Istanbul.[92] Even at its founding, it was clear it would be an independent force in politics rather than a mere appendage of the Islamist party. Young, promising Islamist politicians such as Erdoğan, Ali Babacan, and Abdullah Gül were already competing for the support of the organization.[93]

In the official history of the association, its founding members share conflicting accounts of who the patron of the organization truly was. According to Halil Ayan, Erbakan named the association and Erdoğan supported Müsiad in compliance with Erbakan's orders. According to Mehmet Turgut, Erdoğan independently met the prospective founders and assigned them a building in the pious Fatih district of Istanbul for a year to lay the foundation for the association.[94] The tacit competition among the Islamist political leaders to use the inchoate organization as a trump card against each other gave Müsiad some leeway to maintain its autonomy from the movement.

According to Dilek Yankaya's detailed history of the organization, the closest ally of these businessmen was neither Erbakan nor Erdoğan but President Özal. Yankaya argues that Müsiad established a distanced relationship with the Islamists until Özal's death in 1993.[95] The association's relationship with Özal was apparently so close that the very first page in the official history of Müsiad begins with a conversation between the founders of Müsiad and Özal (not Erdoğan or Erbakan) when he received them at the presidential palace in 1992. In strong parallels with Erbakan's rhetoric, Özal advised these young entrepreneurs to act together against monopoly capital: "Children, I see a bright future for this country, not because of us but because of you. . . . Do not be intimidated. They [the big industrialists] have a morally weak foundation. . . . Get your power together, get big. The big fish eats the small fish. If you want to challenge them, you have to grow."[96] Even after

Özal's death, instead of immediately aligning with the Islamist WP, Müsiad tried to maintain its alliance with the center-right Motherland Party and then formed a new alliance with the center-right True Path Party.[97]

Müsiad's initial distance from the Islamist movement probably reflects the founders' efforts to reach out to the nonpious members of the faubourgeoisie. After all, the small industrialists came from all identities and ideologies. For example, small building contractors and sweatshop owners were highly active in the Social Democratic Party.[98] Moreover, Müsiad flourished in the 1990s even without an Islamist government. Small producers had become collectively much more powerful than in the 1970s, not because of Erbakan or the Islamists but because of Özal's reforms.

Thus, as in his relationship with the small industrialists in the 1970s, Erbakan had to make considerable efforts to keep Müsiad as an ally. The short-lived coalition between Erbakan's WP and the center-right True Path Party certainly helped some Müsiad members expand their businesses quickly. Those Müsiad members, accompanied by the prime minister, signed contracts in Muslim-majority countries worth around USD 800 million in 1996.[99]

This was a costly strategy for the Islamists. The WP's willingness to give preference to SMEs in privatization contracts triggered the military memorandum of February 28, 1997, which eventually brought down the coalition government formed by the WP and the center-right True Path Party.[100] Erdoğan described Müsiad rather than his own WP as the real target of the military.[101] This memorandum, commonly referred to as the "postmodern coup," was the only military intervention by the secularist generals that was directed exclusively against Islamists. Erbakan was banned from politics for five years and Erdoğan was sentenced to four months in prison.[102]

Despite these political spectacles, the military targeted the relatively large Islamist industrialists and bypassed the smaller ones,[103] probably because their goal was to disconnect the Islamist movement from the small industrialists, who became indispensable to the postcoup export-led growth paradigm. Representing the small industrialists empowered Müsiad vis-à-vis the Islamist political cadres and helped it act as the kingmaker of the movement against Erbakan and on behalf of Erdoğan.

The Islamist Businessman. In a conversation with Erbakan, Erol Yarar, the first chairman of Müsiad, asked him why the pious business community had not emerged in the 1970s. He received the following response: "Dear Erol, we started this journey with the grocer Mehmet."[104]

The 1970s was the decade of the pious grocers, not the Islamist industrialists. Although Erbakan advocated an Islamic society, his promise to "grocer Mehmets" was to turn them into industrialists. In a sense, he delivered that promise in the 1990s, but the industrialist sons of those grocer Mehmets withdrew their support from Erbakan at the height of the tensions. According to the former deputy of Erbakan's Virtue Party, Mehmet Bekaroğlu, the soured relationship between Müsiad and Erbakan underpinned the proactive role of business groups in the split between Erbakan and the revisionists, including Erdoğan:

> Müsiad or the new business circles known as Anatolian capital were not satisfied with Erbakan. They were dissatisfied with Erbakan's strained relationship with the West and the political establishment, as well as with his economic policies. These nouveau riche made an important contribution to the founding of [Erdoğan's] AKP. In Turkey and similar countries, wealth is still distributed through the government. The government is still an instrument of accumulation/redistribution. The central capital [*merkez sermaye*] of the time excluded Anatolian capital and prevented the latter from receiving a share of what was redistributed by the government. In a way, February 28 was a reflection of this struggle.[105]

Two practical factors pushed the pious nouveau riche from Erbakan to Erdoğan. First, the 1994 local elections helped Erdoğan make his debut in national politics as a candidate who would work closely with small producers.[106] Second, the military memorandum of 1997 discredited Erbakan in the eyes of the pious small businessmen.[107] A third and ideological factor was the dissatisfaction of the small producers with Erbakan's political discourse. Although Erbakan was the architect of the alliance between small producers and the Islamists, his perspective was deeply embedded within a developmentalist and semi-corporatist mindset. The most programmatic, but anachronistic, outcome of his vision was a manifesto drafted in 1985 with the title "The Just Order" (*Adil Düzen*). As I detail in the next chapter, the emphasis on small producers was appealing, yet Müsiad was not satisfied with the doctrine.

Müsiad called for a less programmatic approach based on a free-market model with limited state intervention. Despite his criticism of the current government bureaucracy and his small-government approach, Erbakan's doctrine still made the government too much of a player in the market. For Halil Karaveli, this doctrine ended up "clashing with the evolving interests of the Anatolian business and industrial community, his core constituency, and open[ed] the way for Erdoğan, who wrenched control over the Islamist movement from Erbakan in the late 1990s. . . . [It] was the 'liberal' Erdoğan rather than the statist Erbakan, who answered to the class interests of the Anatolian bourgeoisie in the era of neoliberal globalization."[108]

In the end, the term *Just Order* disappeared from the party's vocabulary in the late 1990s, although party representatives never explained why. Erbakan's preemptive strike against Müsiad and, by proxy, Erdoğan came in the form of an alternative pro-Erbakan business association, Askon, in 1998. However, Askon's project was not as viable as Müsiad's. Unlike Müsiad, its position on exporting manufacturers was unclear. Its leadership had serious internal disputes, even over the location of its headquarters.[109] In the end, Askon failed to absorb Müsiad members.[110]

Meanwhile, Erdoğan built an Istanbul-wide network within the party[111] and provided his allies in this network with public resources under his control as the mayor of Istanbul. Unlike Demirel, Özal, or Erbakan, Erdoğan did not have a strong academic background.[112] He suffered from a problematic family environment and did not or could not develop close relationships with Sunni religious orders or pious intellectuals.[113] He owed his political career to his activism within Erbakan's party. He was not the creator of a new movement but an active cadre politician in a well-established political party. Given his limited skills, expertise, and manners, he knew he had to develop close ties with the business community in Istanbul to consolidate his position within the movement, against not only Erbakan but also other potential candidates of the new Islamist Justice and Development Party (AKP), such as Gül, the eleventh president of Turkey. According to the testimony of an interlocutor in Kayseri who knew Gül personally, as well as many in the pious business community, Gül asked business circles in Istanbul to endorse him for the leadership of the AKP in 2001, but he received the same answer from everyone: "Tayyip knocked on our door before you and we promised him our support."

Ultimately, the pious faubourgeois entrepreneurs from Istanbul organized a nationwide network and created a new, proud narrative for other entrepreneurs within it. They used this network to turn the Islamist movement away from Erbakan's vision, remove him from his own movement, and opt for Erdoğan as the new leader of a new movement.

THREE

The Islamists and the Faubourgeoisie

THE BIG AND THE SMALL

WE HAD WAITED OVER TWO MONTHS for this meeting. Each of us, four economists, a legal scholar, and a sociologist (me), had lost our academic positions a year earlier, in 2016, after we signed a petition to protest the Islamist government's bombing of civilians in Kurdish areas of Turkey. After being fired, we had been blacklisted by the government and had our lives threatened by the leader of a criminal organization. Now we were advising the vice president of Turkey's largest opposition party, the Republican People's Party (RPP), on economic issues, offering suggestions on how to develop strategies that would bring change. The people we were finally going to meet were also eager to strengthen the economy—or so we believed.

We had asked the vice president to arrange a meeting with the economic team of the Turkish Industry and Business Association (Tüsiad), which represented the country's largest industrial conglomerates and played an influential role in the opposition. After warmly welcoming us in a modestly furnished conference room, our hosts invited us to speak. We began with the obvious: the 2018 elections were only a year away, and the Islamist government was using the failed 2016 coup attempt to dismantle what was left of the rule of law in the country. We hoped to persuade Tüsiad that the only way the opposition could beat the Islamists at the polls was by calling for an aggressive redistributive policy. If we succeeded, we knew the RPP would follow suit. This would threaten Islamist party rule for the first time in two decades. The country had stopped serving Tüsiad members' interests as well as those of the working class. We felt that socialist scholars like us should speak directly to representatives of the bourgeoisie and remind them of their long-term class interests.

Tüsiad's chief economist listened respectfully, then raised an objection that in her eyes invalidated the plan. Even if only partially implemented, she warned, our proposal would lead to hyperinflation, which would have a disastrous impact on those who relied on favorable financial conditions for making investments. A member of our team, one of the most respected economists in Turkey, shook his head in frustration. A more vociferous younger colleague could not contain herself and interrupted the chief economist. With all due respect, she countered, Tüsiad's fears about inflation were based on a failed theory. Had the chief economist not seen the International Monetary Fund's updated views on monetary policy?

The chief economist's response could not have been more condescending. We left the building feeling very disappointed. Politicians seeking key positions in the supposedly social democratic RPP needed to gain the tacit endorsement of this powerful body. Our failure to interest Tüsiad in our redistributive program stymied our efforts to influence the electoral strategy of the only opposition party that could replace the Islamists in Turkey. We were not entirely surprised. Much of the profits of the richest Tüsiad families came from loans their banks sold to smaller industrialists; inflation would have wiped this out. They still felt powerful enough to ignore the possibility that the Islamists could cause inflation to skyrocket as well, in order to boost manufacturing exports on behalf of those very same smaller industrialists.

That is precisely what happened after the Islamists won a solid majority in the legislative and presidential elections. By 2021, Turkey had the twelfth highest inflation rate in the world; by 2022, the fifth.[1] Tüsiad's chief economist quit her job and took a position at a London financial institution. In one of her last tweets before abandoning Turkey, she said in response to the new interest rate policy of the Islamist government: "I have nothing more to say."[2]

Others also distanced themselves from Tüsiad after the 2018 elections. None of its billionaire members would agree to serve as president. Although Tüsiad's forty-five hundred members were paying 80 percent of the nation's corporate taxes and most of them were extremely wealthy, only Orhan Turan, the owner of a medium-sized manufacturing company, had the courage to step forward in 2022 and lead this once prestigious association. Turan's factory produced insulation materials for construction projects.

Tüsiad's problem was that the Islamists had decided they no longer
needed the support of the very rich and were allying themselves instead
with small industrialists. They began ridiculing the country's biggest
industrialists in the media. For example, when Turan criticized Tayyip
Erdoğan's monetary policy, which had triggered high inflation in the country, Erdoğan replied:

> You, sir, who are now the head of Tüsiad, you are just an apprentice. How
> dare you think that you can lecture us about our foreign policy [Erdoğan is
> alluding to the monetary policy here]! You haven't even become a journey-
> man yet. Stay in your place! Your overlords [*ağababa*, the former (and richer)
> chairmen of Tüsiad] also thought that they could tell us what to do. As long
> as you act in this way, you can forget about knocking on the door of this
> government. For you only repeat what the RPP tells you to say and we only
> welcome those who stand by our domestic and nationalist interests [*yerli ve
> milli duruş*].[3]

Erdoğan turned his back on the big industrialists and embraced small
entrepreneurs with confidence. Since the 1980s, the global distribution
of income had moved away from the North Atlantic countries. Their big
businesses were now investing in small industrialists in other countries.
A key indicator of this trend is the relative growth rate of larger and smaller
industrial firms.

The Istanbul Chamber of Industry has compiled a list of Turkey's five hundred largest industrial companies since the early 1990s.[4] As figure 13 shows,
these five hundred companies slowly increased their share of the country's
total manufacturing production during the 1990s, while the opposite has
been the case over the past two decades. The share of the largest five hundred
industrial companies fell from 51 percent in 2002 to 13 percent in 2020. The
uninterrupted decline in the share of industrial big business in total industrial employment since the 1990s is a sign of its declining direct involvement
in manufacturing. Moreover, Erdoğan knew that at least half of the revenue
of three of the four richest families in Turkey came from the financial sector, in which he was the single buyer, thanks to his growing control over
the Central Bank.

Erdoğan could insult the richest families in the country because they
were losing influence in the nation's industrial relations even as they continued to accumulate wealth. In 2022, when Erdoğan mocked Tüsiad's new
president, its members owned most of the gas refineries, power plants, heavy
and complex chemical industries, and banks in Turkey. By every measure,

FIGURE 13. Gross value added and workforce, five hundred largest industrial enterprises (1993–2020). Calculated by the author using the Istanbul Chamber of Industry, UN Stat, and Turkish Statistical Institute data.

they were the country's industrialists. But these companies could maintain their profitability only if the small sweatshops in the most remote and poorest neighborhoods of Istanbul and other metropolitan areas continued to employ millions of workers at starvation wages and to consume all that gas, chemicals, and money. Erdoğan was the product of this same process. He relied on hundreds of thousands of owners of manufacturing SMEs and had created a large network of crony capitalists as part of his political clique.[5] As the triumphant president of Turkey who had survived a military coup, he made no secret of the fact that the government was throwing its weight behind the small industrialists, as it had been since the 1970s.

The previous chapter showed that the Islamists had worked to mobilize and ally with small producers since the 1970s. In return, the growing support and economic power of these small producers, the faubourgeoisie, transformed the cadres and ideology of the Islamist movement in the 1990s. The support continued in later years. According to Konda, a respected polling company in Turkey, support for the Islamist AKP by nonmonopoly entrepreneurs—including shopkeepers, artisans, merchants, industrialists, and businesspeople—was an average of 9 percent higher than the share of its votes in seven polls conducted between 2014 and 2021 (except in 2019).[6] Why was Erdoğan so confident about the support of the faubourgeoisie? The answer lies in the relationship of the faubourgeoisie to the tripartite structure that defines the Islamist movement in Turkey: a political cadre, pious small businesspeople, and religious orders.

These three actors' role and weight in the movement has changed since the 1970s. The movement started in the 1970s as the religious orders, especially after the 1960 military coup, placed their technocrat supporters in the bureaucracy. These bureaucrats, who played a key role in Turkey's industrialization policies in those two decades, became the first cadre of the movement in party politics. While this cadre gradually gained its autonomy from the religious orders in the 1970s, the pious business groups increased their influence over the political cadres in the 1990s.

Erdoğan's confidence about continued support by the faubourgeoisie is related to what each actor offers the faubourgeoisie. The political cadre offers cheap credit and subsidies within a broader policy agenda as a safety barrier against monopoly capital. The business community offers an ideology that helps the faubourgeoisie identify itself as a social class and distinguish itself from the two other middle classes, which I called the petty bourgeoisie and the technocracy in this book's introduction. The religious orders offer a moral order that defines the normative terms of the relationship between the faubourgeoisie and the proletariat. In other words, the Islamists present solutions to this social class for its relationships with the bourgeoisie, with the proletariat, and with the middle classes (including itself). The comprehensiveness of this package makes the Islamists the indisputable representative of the faubourgeoisie. Even members of this social class whose lifestyles diverge from the Islamists' tacitly endorse the business environment fostered by Islamist rule.

THE CADRE

Search for an Ally in Politics

The Islamist party appeals to the faubourgeoisie as a guardian against monopoly capital. In 2023, there were 457,870 SMEs and 3,774 large companies active in the Turkish manufacturing sector. The number of manufacturing SMEs has grown by 41 percent since 2010, while the country's population has grown by 17 percent in the same period. Eighty-four percent of these manufacturing SMEs were microenterprises with net turnover or revenue of less than $500,000 and employed fewer than ten people. Another fifty-eight thousand were small manufacturing businesses with net turnover or revenue of less than $5 million and fewer than fifty employees; 14,238 of the manufacturing companies were medium sized, with net turnover or revenues of less than $25 million and fewer than 250 employees.[7] Compared to the four families with wealth over $5 billion (Koç, Sabancı, Şahenk, and Ülker), many owners of large industrial enterprises are small players seeking political support to recalibrate their relations with these families and survive global competition.

SME owners have even more motivation to look for a patron in politics. They have a good reason to worry about the fate of their businesses: SMEs have a short life span. Only 42 percent of the 378,000 SMEs founded in 2015 were still operating in 2020. For every hundred new manufacturing companies founded between 2009 and 2020, eighty-five older companies ceased operations.[8] The main reason for their short life spans is lower profitability than large manufacturing enterprises. During the governments of the Justice and Development Party (AKP) since 2002, large manufacturing companies had an average return on equity of 13.1 percent, according to the Central Bank of Turkey's survey data, while the corresponding figure for medium-sized companies was 7.5 percent, and for small companies 4.5 percent. For 2009–21, the data show a further distinction between small and micro-sized manufacturing companies: the average return on equity for the microenterprises was only 1.4 percent, while that for small and medium manufacturing companies was 6.2 percent and 8.5 percent, respectively. For large manufacturing companies, it was 14 percent.[9]

To put these figures in perspective, the average annual profit per manufacturing enterprise between 2009 and 2021 was $4.8 million for large enterprises, $211,000 for medium enterprises, $27,000 for small enterprises, and only $2,000 for microenterprises.[10] The Central Bank's data are based on these companies' tax returns,[11] so the discrepancy between the actual and reported values is probably greater for SMEs than for large companies. Nevertheless, the figures highlight that owners of small businesses and microenterprises in the manufacturing sector earn about the same as Turkey's physicians and lawyers.

In sum, although the number of companies operating in various manufacturing sectors has grown significantly, many fizzle after a few years. A few lucky ones become medium or even large industrial companies.

The composition of an individual industry may appear to be stable, but over time, new players replace old ones like bubbles in a soda can.

The Narrative

The 1970s. The Islamist parties have addressed these entrepreneurs with a distinct narrative since the 1970s and a composite set of policies since the end of the 1990s. In the 1970s, Necmettin Erbakan's Islamist party indicated that Turkish Islamism would be antilabor, antibureaucracy, and antimonopoly capital. Unionized workers, it said, are "susceptible to [unwanted leftist] political influences"; thus, trade unions should be reformed to "establish solidarity between our workers and employers based on mutual respect, love and conscience."[12] The Islamists' tone about the bureaucracy was similar to the skepticism of US conservatives toward big government. The National Order Party (NOP) promised to "prevent luxury, waste, unnecessary formalities and excessive paperwork in the public service."[13] With this small-government perspective, the Islamists occupied a special position in Turkish politics in the 1970s. None of the major parties, including the center-right Justice Party and the center-left RPP, pursued a similar antibureaucratic agenda.[14]

Erbakan and party documents declared their intention to attack big business on behalf of small producers. In his speech at the first party congress of the NOP, the first Islamist party of the republican period, the first item on Erbakan's list of "structural changes in the economic field" was the replacement of state support for a small group of investors in the private sector with what he called "expansive private sectorism [*yaygın özel sektörcülük*]."[15] The 1973 election manifesto of the National Salvation Party (NSP), the successor to the NOP, pointed out that "a small minority and the government" had taken the initiative in industrialization, which had contributed to regional and status-related (*zümrevi*) inequalities in the country.[16] The RPP favored state-owned enterprises over private investment, while "the Justice Party and other similar parties introduced an unbalanced liberal system that allowed small [privileged] groups [*mahdud zümre*] to make industrial investments."[17]

At the core of the tensions with organized labor, the bureaucracy, and, above all, big business was the question of credit: "Because they have low income, our shopkeepers and artisans should be given interest-free loans. [To this end,] the credit base of the [state-owned] Halk Bankası[18] should be expanded and *big capitalists* should not be allowed to receive loans from this bank."[19] Amid this battle of redistribution, the Islamist parties of the 1970s outlined "anticapitalist . . . expansive private sectorism." In addition to subsidies for bookkeeping costs,[20] export subsidies,[21] abolition of currency quotas,[22] export insurance and credits,[23] and probusiness regional planning,[24] the Islamist movement promised subsidized loans to small producers. The NOP program emphasized the need to eliminate regional inequalities in access to credit.[25] The NSP's 1973 election manifesto expressed its opposition to the policy of granting loans to a limited group (*mahdud zümre*) of big businesses at the expense of the overwhelming majority of the people.[26] Despite the Islamic prohibition of usury (*riba*), that election manifesto promised a "very active capital market."[27] Similarly, the NSP's 1977 election manifesto promised new forms of credit, such as an Islamic shareholding system that would facilitate access to credit for small producers.[28]

On the surface, party documents between 1971 and 1991 emphasized that the Islamists offered an alternative to socialism and capitalism.[29] Despite this, both the NOP and NSP platforms emphasized that private property, inheritance, and free enterprise are alienable rights of individuals.[30] What constitutes the anticapitalism of the Islamists is not their intention to abolish this mode of production but their will to defend the economic interests of their class ally, the faubourgeoisie, against others. At a more abstract level, the Islamists' objections to capitalism are not about the market economy or capitalist exploitation as such, but about the hierarchical relationship between monopoly capital and smaller capital.

In this regard, Turgut Özal's perspective was similar to Erbakan's. In a report for Süleyman Demirel in 1973, Özal criticized existing lending practices. Producers could obtain loans with terms of up to a decade if they did business with foreign suppliers, but domestic suppliers did not have this option and the Turkish banking system's credit terms were much shorter.[31] After he was not nominated by Demirel to the national assembly in the late 1970s, Özal presented a personal political manifesto, "The New Outlook of Development" (*Kalkınmada Yeni Görüşün Esasları*), in 1979. The longest section of that text deals with industrial policy. Unlike the RPP's industrialization policy, which focused on capital and intermediate products, his plan focused on the production of finished goods with a strategy of gradually creating backward linkages in domestic production chains.[32] More importantly, Özal advocated restructuring the financial markets to favor small producers. Similar to the NSP's promises in the 1970s, Özal advised transforming banks into profit-sharing financial institutions that would share both the profits and the risks of new investments because banks favored larger companies that could use their capital as collateral.[33] Both the focus on finished goods and this plan point directly to small manufacturers. With the approval of the junta, he established Turkey's first Islamic financial institutions in 1983 as the first step in transforming financial markets.[34] In the wake of multiple reforms to lift restrictions on imports and support manufacturing exporters with tax subsidies, he liberalized capital accounts in 1989.[35] Just as the title of Özal's 1979 manifesto, "New Outlook," was reminiscent of "National Outlook," the ideology of Erbakan's NSP, Özal's reforms in the 1980s turned small industrialists into a major economic interest and fleshed out the alliance Erbakan had strived to establish since the 1970s.

The 1990s. The protection of small producers with subsidized credit continued to be a policy priority for the Islamists in the 1980s and became the core of the only political economic doctrine Islamist parties produced in Turkey: the short-lived "Just Order." Written by notable intellectuals of the movement such as Süleyman Karagülle, Arif Ersoy, and Süleyman Akdemir, the text introducing this doctrine referenced a variety of historical figures, including the utopian socialist (and middle-class industrialist of his time) Robert Owen and Yugoslavia's Josip Broz Tito, whose socialist doctrine of self-management aimed to promote small industrial units directly controlled by workers.[36]

The text tells a civilizational history since the Mesopotamian empires, treating the Turkish Republic, the Ottoman Empire, and even the rise of Islam as indistinct moments in the long story of humankind. The outstanding feature of the age, the rise of a merchant class and the factory system, replaced commodity exchange with the sale of the accumulation of human labor power: "When a Mercedes car is sold, it is valued on the basis of the calculation of all the labor power used to produce its parts, not on the value of these parts. In this way, humanity entered 'the period of labor exchange.'"[37]

The text goes straight to a peculiar form of labor theory of value that focuses on industrialization to explain what is yet to come. Despite parallels to basic socialist discourse, the narrative is explicitly nonsocialist in that workers are denied agency in this history of civilization. For instance, the term *trade union* is used only twice and is defined as "a professional association."[38] The text treats the working class as a passive factor of production and as a vulnerable group seeking a guardian.

The seemingly contradictory structure of the argument begins to make sense if the text's authors are treated as theorists determined to justify the spiritually emancipatory role of the faubourgeoisie in the teleology of human history. The following is a refined version of the ideas in the 1970s Islamist party materials, illustrating the kind of capitalism that serves the interests of the faubourgeoisie:

> The capitalist system has given room to "interest," which is an unjust instrument of exploitation and oppression, along with "profit," which is a regulating and motivating factor [in the economy]. The same capitalist system promotes "free market competition," which regulates the economy favorably, but is also unable to stop trusts and monopolies in actual economic relations. In contrast, the communist regime fundamentally rejects the concept of interest, but it also contradicts human nature by rejecting "the right to private property" and "profit." Since it abolishes "free market competition" and directs the economy through "armchair price-fixing" [central planning], it actually harms the economy. . . . The Just Order . . . allows profit, but not interest. Moreover, [the Just Order] recognizes the advantages of free market competition and private property, while protecting the economy and the people from monopolization and profiteering.[39]

The envisioned political economic order is a paradise for small producers, a utopia of competitive capitalism. The enemy is monopolies, and the solution lies in the formulation of alternatives that could take the place of interest. Fortunately, Islam provides bases for this task, such as the promissory bill on future production (*selem senedi*) promoted by Prophet Mohammad.[40] In addition to *selem senedi*, the text lists six types of interest-free forms of credit: partnerships, measurement loans, employment loans, pledge loans, tax loans, and project loans.[41] These financial instruments are various forms of forward contracts:

> The entire history of civilization and political economic analysis served as a justification for these forms of forward contract, which would turn monopoly capitalism back into a competitive state and allow small producers to survive or even thrive. As the fierce opposition of the Zionists and their collaborators undeniably demonstrates, the salvation of humanity lies in the widespread use of these forms of forward contract, which represent a great leap. It is not possible to fight the capitalist system, imperialism and Zionism, which exploit humanity, with atomic bombs, but it is possible with promissory bills. . . . If it's so beneficial, why doesn't everyone use IOUs? That's a naive question, because imperialism and Zionism protect the interest-driven

capitalist order. They will not allow us to move away from this order. They can even wage a war, because we should never forget that the interest we pay ultimately goes into the hands of imperialism, Zionism and their collaborators, who together hold global capital in their hands.[42]

The Action

Subsidies and Social Policy. The Islamists have not turned the Turkish economy into a collection of multi-shareholder manufacturing enterprises, as Erbakan envisioned well into the mid-1990s, but they have supported competitive nonmonopoly manufacturers with a neoliberal mindset since coming to power. One important component of their policymaking has been a myriad of direct and indirect subsidy programs.

Under the active workforce programs, the Islamist government regularly compensates small business owners' worker benefits and, in some cases, wages. These programs cost about $3.3 billion in 2022 (about 0.4 percent of GDP) and benefited the employers of an average of 596,000 workers (2.5 percent of the nonagricultural workforce and 6 percent of the industrial workforce) annually between 2018 and 2022.[43] The direct support for the SMEs under the various "SME development and support" programs of Turkey's Small and Medium Enterprises Development Organization (KOSGEB) increased from around $320 million to $617 million between 2012 and 2022,[44] and the share of the KOSGEB budget in the central government budget grew by 220 percent over the same period.[45] In 2022, the Ministry of Industry and Technology spent $692 million on various support programs for industrial SMEs and direct transfers to the KOSGEB budget. These employment, development, and support subsidies together accounted for 2 percent of the general state budget. This calculation does not include many of the investment support programs implemented by several ministries to aid domestic manufacturing SMEs. The amount of investment supported in 2022 under such programs was $24.7 billion. The total value of domestic manufacturing SMEs' investments supported by such government subsidies between 2002 and 2022 was $316 billion.[46] If these difficult-to-measure investment supports—including tax breaks, subsidized interest, fringe benefit subsidies, and subsidized land provision—were included in the calculation, the total volume of subsidies could be quite close to the budgets on national security, public education, and health care, which respectively spent 5.8 percent, 4.6 percent, and 4 percent of the general state budget in 2022.[47] In addition to these direct subsidies, the entire social policy structure was redesigned to benefit small producers. In 2022, 2.7 percent of the central government budget was spent on poverty reduction programs and social solidarity measures; 4.42 million households, 17 percent of all households in Turkey, received some form of assistance from various government agencies, including the Ministry of Family and Social Security (MoFSS), the second largest spender of this budget.[48] MoFSS alone implemented forty-eight different cash or in-kind transfer programs.

On the surface, this looks like a remarkable redistributive initiative that presents the Islamists as the guardians of the poor. However, the goal of these programs is not to reduce poverty but to supplement the wages of workers at small enterprises. For instance, general health insurance was introduced in 2006, which made the Ministry of Labor the largest spender of the social policy budget.[49] The basic idea of the program is to insure those who are not enrolled in the three other public insurance schemes for workers, entrepreneurs, and public-sector employees, using a separate plan based on a small flat-rate contribution. Employers now can offer their applicants salaries slightly higher than the minimum wage if they are willing to work without legally mandated benefits. Younger workers who have no hope of a pension tend to accept that offer. This may explain why there has not been a meaningful decline in informal employment in Turkey during the AKP governments.[50] More importantly, these programs do not reduce poverty despite their considerable budget. On average during 2006–22, the income level of only seven of every hundred poor people rose to the European Union's relative poverty line after social transfers. The corresponding rate for the EU-27 was 34 percent in the same period. Turkey performed far worse than all members of the EU-27 during this period.[51]

Unions and Education. A second political priority is the containment of organized labor. The annual average ratio of Turkey's trade union density to that of Organisation for Economic Co-operation and Development (OECD) member countries was 87 percent between 1984 and 1994, 64 percent between 1995 and 2004, and 47 percent between 2005 and 2019. More importantly for the purposes of this book, union density in manufacturing SMEs is virtually zero. The complete de-unionization of manufacturing SMEs is the main reason for the weakness of independent trade unions in large industrial plants. Unions now represent only a small proportion of employees. The dual labor markets impair their ability to negotiate with the owners of large companies, who threaten to use their subsidiaries on a larger scale if unions demand better conditions and higher wages.

De-unionization is coupled with the Islamists' strategy to dismantle the already inferior public education institutions to further undermine the bargaining power of the white- and blue-collar proletariat. Elementary school enrollment rates were at their lowest since the 1970s under AKP governments. In the 2010s, Turkey fell behind the global average on this indicator for the first time in the past half century. Turkey has consistently achieved the lowest results among OECD members during this period on the Programme for International Student Assessment, which compares the performance of fifteen-year-olds in mathematics, science, and reading in member countries.[52] In higher education, unemployment among graduates grew as fast as the number of graduates. In fact, college graduates were the second largest category of unemployed in 2022, after high school dropouts.[53] Probably for this reason, the number of unfilled positions increased fifty-six-fold for public universities between 2002 and 2017.[54] In the absence of well-educated younger generations, sweatshop owners claim to be the essential source of economic growth.

Credit. The Islamist narrative changed significantly, within the last half century, on topics such as the position of women in social life, government structure, and perspectives about Western countries and the European Union. The Islamists gave up their developmentalist and semi-corporatist perspective about economic policymaking. One component that has survived is their promise to provide subsidized credit for the faubourgeoisie. Hiding within a theological and historical discourse about the evils of usury, this promise made itself visible in plans about forward contracts and banking regulations, not only in party documents under Erbakan's leadership, but also in documents drafted and legislative changes engineered by Özal. Since they came to power in 2002, the Islamists under Erdoğan's leadership have delivered on this promise. Subsidized credit for the faubourgeoisie is the main pillar and defining element of the political economic perspective of Turkish Islamism.

Within the first quarter of the twenty-first century, the Islamists have diligently and successfully worked to bring SMEs into the financial system. Ironically, the faubourgeoisie's dependence on the global financial structure grew in these years despite the anti-interest/usury rhetoric of the Islamist movement. For example, only 29 percent of SMEs had access to bank loans in 1995.[55] To help SMEs overcome this problem, KOSGEB initiated the SME

Finance Support Program when the AKP came to power in 2003 to cover the loan interest of selected SMEs.[56] The AKP government expanded the scope of the previously tiny Credit Guarantee Fund (KGF), established in 1991, so that it could provide collateral for the loans SMEs applied.[57]

When Erdoğan sought the unconditional support of the faubourgeoisie for a constitutional referendum in 2017 to gain unprecedented executive powers and dominate the judiciary, the KGF's budget for collateralizing SME loans was increased from $550 million to $6.8 billion. New KGF funds for SMEs were also made available before the 2018 elections.[58] New KGF-supported loans accounted for 13 percent of all SME loans between 2016 and 2022, with a peak in 2017 at 47 percent.[59] In 2022, the KGF-supported loan volume amounted to $38 billion (702 billion TL) or 31 percent of the total bank loan portfolio of SMEs.[60] As a result of the KGF and other measures, the total amount of loans taken out by SMEs rose from $42 billion in December 2006 (7.5 percent of GDP) to $131 billion in April 2023 (12.7 percent of GDP).[61]

This policy made the government the largest guarantor of SME loans and tied the interests of the bourgeoisie more closely to growth in the volume of loans taken out by the faubourgeoisie. When the AKP came to power in 2003, the banks' total interest income amounted to around $8 billion, or 2.6 percent of GDP. In 2019, this reached $54 billion, or 7.2 percent of GDP. If the ratio of the banking system's interest income to GDP had remained at the 2003 level, the banks' income would have been around $30 billion lower in 2019.[62] In a sense, Erdoğan has realized Erbakan's utopia for small producers by paying the country's long-established bourgeois families and international capital what they were due.

In return, part of the $30 billion was transferred back to the government with a tax policy that favored the faubourgeoisie over the bourgeoisie. In 2001, small, medium, and large manufacturing companies paid an average of $66,000, $221,000, and $2.4 million in taxes, respectively. In 2016, they paid $143,000, $375,000, and $8.1 million. Between 2002 and 2016, taxes per large manufacturing company increased 54 percent and 97 percent faster than those of small and medium manufacturing companies respectively.[63] This is an interesting cycle: Islamists are providing the collateral for the loans of SMEs, which are gradually expanding their borrowing volume. This is a transfer of income to the bourgeoisie to let the faubourgeoisie have access to credit. In return, the Islamists tax the bourgeoisie at higher rates to finance the process and keep it sustainable.[64]

The direct and indirect subsidies promised by the Islamist parties since 1970 and delivered since 2002, essential to the proletarianization of younger generations, strengthened the faubourgeoisie over other social classes even if they drove the country into what some call "the middle-income trap." This clientelist connection is only one component of their relationship. Another major factor that lets the Islamists claim to represent the faubourgeoisie is the evolution of their ideology into a narrative that defines the faubourgeoisie's class identity. The concept of Islamist businessman played an important role not only in the promotion of a new political cadre in strong support of this new ideology, but also in the dissemination of the message to small producers:

> Not all of these petty entrepreneurs, whether the small-scale industrialists in provincial towns or the intermediaries in poor neighborhoods of Istanbul, are necessarily Islamist, but the Islamist segment of the business class comes primarily from among this sector. . . . The findings of a survey conducted in 1993[65] indicated that small entrepreneurs, including those who were self-employed in the informal sector, combined Islamist tendencies in social and cultural matters with "liberal" attitudes in matters of government economic policy. The populist rhetoric of political Islam appealed to these small businessmen who were recent immigrants to the cities and seeking upward mobility from their humble backgrounds.[66]

Not all members of the faubourgeoisie have internalized this new business narrative as an extension of Islamism, but it has defined the norms and values of the faubourgeoisie in general. Members of the faubourgeoisie see Islamists as the agent that implements these values and enforces these norms, even though they have different political views as individuals. In this context, activities by the members of Müsiad (Independent Industrialists and Businessmen Association) illustrate the efforts of Islamist businessmen to present the Islamists as the representatives of the faubourgeoisie in politics and form a narrative that tied Turkish Islamism to how members of the faubourgeoisie conceptualized their class interests.

The official history of Müsiad includes multiple accounts of founding members traveling to distant cities in Anatolia to mobilize local industrialists and open new branches of the club in Kayseri, Ankara, Adana, Kahramanmaraş, and Konya. During these early trips to Anatolia, Müsiad's founding members were warmly received, and they quickly developed interesting contacts. Through these new relationships, the founders of

Müsiad, most of whom were not typical Anatolians, gained a broader view of the country. With the help of these new allies, they succeeded in spreading the word.

When they first arrived in Anatolia, Müsiad's strategy was reminiscent of the civilizing mission of the early Kemalist bureaucrats and intellectuals of the 1920s. Abdurrahman Esmerer, one of its founders, described the motive behind Müsiad's mobilization efforts as changing the world's impression of Anatolia from a land of scarcity to one of opportunity: "We wanted to show the world the power of business in Anatolia."[67] In other words, it was not the Anatolian Tigers but the Istanbul entrepreneurs who built a pan-Anatolian network of small businesses.[68]

A New Business Mindset

The Müsiad leadership's narrative presents profit making and national economic development as two compatible goals prescribed by Islam. The richer an entrepreneur becomes, the better he serves the development of the nation as a whole. Following Friedrich Hayek's doctrine, government should intervene only minimally in markets. Apart from charity and *zakat* (alms, usually 2.5 percent of savings, religiously prescribed for rich people), redistributive measures are against Islam, as people are not created equal and the transfer of resources from the rich to the poor is unjust. Therefore, taxes are legitimate only under certain circumstances. For example, because taxes are levied to pay interest to foreigners, it is religiously acceptable not to pay taxes, especially for those who give charity to the poor. Because workers and their employers are like "different organs of the same body," unions are superfluous, if not outright illegitimate: strikes are forbidden in Islam.[69]

The success of an entrepreneur depends on his ability to build social networks with other Muslim entrepreneurs.[70] However, discussion of social networks among Muslim entrepreneurs is limited to the religiously accepted forms of credit.[71] As of December 2023, there were 188 research reports, books, brochures, and other publications on Müsiad's website, as well as twenty-six issues of its peer-reviewed journal, *Afro-Eurasian Studies*. These publications offer advice on foreign markets, monetary and financial policies, and business practices.

Within this extensive corpus, only four documents focus on the conditions of competition and partnerships. Published in 2007, *The Partnership Culture* (*Ortaklık Kültürü*) provides advice on overcoming the cultural and psychological difficulties of establishing effective partnerships, especially between relatives.[72] *Management and Institutionalization in Family Businesses* (*Aile Şirketlerinde Yönetim ve Kurumsallaşma*), published in 2003, encourages the transfer of power to professional managers, as the second or third generations of family members tend to "finish off" the family businesses.[73] According to a third book published in 2023, *Being a Public Company* (*Halka Açık Şirket Olmak*), the biggest concern of entrepreneurs is the disclosure of business secrets required of public companies.[74] *Competition and Growth Strategies for the SMEs* (*KOBİ'ler İçin Rekabet ve Büyüme Stratejileri*), published in 2005, does not mention cooperative strategies for the growth of SMEs. The small companies are expected to grow by reducing their costs, creating customer loyalty, or increasing their export volume. Only one paragraph is dedicated to "growth through mergers," with the following remark: "Mergers and partnerships are the most difficult methods for business growth in our country. Since SMEs are established with the small capital of entrepreneurs, they have psychological difficulties in merging with other companies."[75]

Müsiad does not encourage companies to have multiple partners. In a booklet published right after the 2001 financial crisis, *Suggestions for Businessmen during the Crisis* (*İşadamlarına Kriz Dönemi Önerileri*), none of the thirty suggestions is about the merits of collaboration with other SME owners in the industry. The only call for a form of cooperation is the twenty-seventh bullet point: "Avoid illogical competition."[76] In terms of business practices, the typical Muslim entrepreneur is portrayed as very competitive, transactional, and individualistic. Ethical norms are limited to compliance with the law, honoring contracts, and the ban on specific forms of interest by Islam. He does not trust his managers, partners, or even family members.

Given this individualistic narrative, it is not surprising that its members, including the founders, saw Müsiad primarily as an opportunity to expand their business relationships.[77] In the meantime, whether based in Istanbul or in smaller provinces, they presented themselves to the public as Anatolian Calvinists[78] or vanguards of the Anatolian people.[79] Müsiad flattered its members as "decent and hard-working entrepreneurs who have humble backgrounds" with a public narrative that established a link "between Islamic values and post-Fordism" and gave them a voice against rent-seeking big business.[80] The term used to summarize Müsiad's aspirations was *the Bazaar of Medina*, the ideal example of competitive markets in the golden age of religion.[81] This, a reference to the commercial regulations set by Prophet

Mohammad in the local market of Medina, was the faubourgeoisie's answer to something the mayor of Çorum, a medium-sized conservative Anatolian city, mockingly said in those years to Ayşe Buğra, the eminent scholar of the business community in Turkey: "Nowadays, everyone is busy looking for Qur'anic verses that are compatible with capitalism."[82]

Anatolian Tigers

One key empirical question is how this narrative found significant appeal among the owners of small and medium manufacturing enterprises. I took part in or independently conducted a number of research projects in 2002, 2007, and 2008 that directly or indirectly focused on aspects of the relationship between the faubourgeoisie and the proletariat, such as the Islamists' social assistance networks;[83] industrial home-based work networks employing probably hundreds of thousands of women and consolidating the Islamist patriarchal order in major cities;[84] and the factory and sweatshop labor practices in the garment industry, which is the biggest in terms of its workforce.[85] I concluded that I needed a more nuanced approach to address this question, in order to have a better understanding of the relations among those small manufacturers. Accordingly, I conducted a four-year research project about business relations among these industrial entrepreneurs in the three cities in Anatolia (Kayseri, Gaziantep, and Denizli) with the fastest industrial growth rates since the 1980s.

These cities provided ideal settings for this more nuanced case study. By 2008, Kayseri, Gaziantep, and Denizli were the largest manufacturers in terms of value added, after the five traditional manufacturing centers (Istanbul, Bursa, Izmir, Kocaeli, and Ankara) and two cities in the hinterland of Istanbul and Izmir (Tekirdağ and Manisa). These three Anatolian cities were well suited for this project in that they were not close to older industrial centers. As a result, they had no logistical or resource-related advantages like Manisa had thanks to its proximity to Izmir and Tekirdağ to Istanbul. If I wanted to see whether cooperative labor relations existed anywhere in Turkey, these small cities in Anatolia were excellent candidates.

Each of these cities has several major industries. In Denizli, the cable, textile, and marble processing industries are particularly strong; in Kayseri, furniture and metal processing; in Gaziantep, carpet, pasta, and petrochemical manufacturers. Despite these differences, the composition of the industries in each city broadly represented the growth of labor-intensive activities such as furniture and readymade garments that had their roots in the 1980s and resource-intensive activities such as wire and petrochemicals that had their roots in the first decade of the 2000s. These industries were the results of the two-step outsourcing movement, mostly from European countries, where larger corporations first gave up on labor-intensive industries and then on resource-intensive ones. The first wave of outsourcing was a result of the search for cheaper labor, and the second wave reflected corporations based in the North Atlantic externalizing the risks associated with the global price volatility of basic resources, from ores to oil, and the costs related to environmental protection.

Over the course of my research between 2012 and 2015, I spoke to representatives of 101 large manufacturing companies from various sectors, including textiles, ready-to-wear garments, furniture and woodworking, metalworking, machinery, wire and cable, marble processing, pasta, and carpets. Many of them worked with smaller subsidiaries in their cities.[86] In addition to these interviews, I conducted another forty-six in Ankara and the three cities with representatives of business associations, municipalities, various government agencies, journalists, and a few other people recommended to me by the main people I interviewed.

Verifying the work of other researchers,[87] unlike in Istanbul, where entrepreneurs did not seem very religious, the opposite was true in these cities. Most of the employers and sweatshop owners I interviewed were pious and conservative. If, as I suspected, piety was an independent factor in supply chain politics, then these cities would be the ideal setting for this project and offer the chance to observe a less competitive environment among entrepreneurs. Even here, few of them were die-hard Islamists. The Islamist businessmen's narrative found appeal among these entrepreneurs because it represented, justified, and to some extent reproduced their highly individualist and competitive business mindset. No common theological motif guided their business practices.

Relations among the entrepreneurs in these cities were toxic. The carpet industry in Gaziantep was a vivid example of how ingrained and destructive the competition had become. At trade fairs, carpet producers routinely took unauthorized photos of their competitors' designs and reproduced them in their own factories. They spied on their competitors as they tried to develop relationships with new customers. Competitors often bribed customs officials to steal the portfolios of international customers and bribed the staff at local hotels to learn the names of the guests staying there. In one case, the competition got so bad that two major carpet producers opened warehouses in the same city in Germany, right across the river from each other.

The businesspeople I talked to were convinced that this business milieu had no alternative. The toxic competition was a consequence of a myriad of factors that had a close connection to the complex web of social relations in each city, which fall into three broad categories: the internal logic of the local supply chains, the historical conditions of industrialization opening a schism between old and new money, and the older generations' determination to keep the younger generations and professionals under control. Each of these broad factors motivates or urges these businesspeople to tacitly or openly support the Islamists.

Hostile Supply Chains. Like in Istanbul, whose business environment I studied in 2007–8, the large companies in these cities worked under enormous pressure imposed by their international customers, and they passed this pressure on to their local subsidiaries. Over 85 percent of them told me entrepreneurs in the same sector did not cooperate among themselves. What is more, again contradicting my assumptions, shared religious beliefs and affiliations did not establish harmony among local businessmen; rather, they produced different forms of tensions.

In the labor-intensive industries in these three cities, medium and large enterprises tended to use many sweatshops to reduce their labor costs. These included the marble processing factories in Denizli and the furniture industry in Kayseri, both of which looked very much like the larger factories I observed in Istanbul in 2007 and 2008. To remain competitive in Anatolia, the larger producers intervened directly in the management of their subsidiaries, as they did in Istanbul. In Kayseri, for example, large companies in the furniture sector parted ways with their subsidiaries after receiving defective items in shipments more than once. In Denizli, textile companies required their subsidiaries to submit documents from their banks to prove they had no outstanding bills. In the carpet industry in Gaziantep, manufacturers closely monitored the output of their subsidiaries to prevent these smaller companies from stealing their designs.

In resource-intensive industries, the larger manufacturers used local supply chains to reduce their risks and investment costs. For example, Erbakır in Denizli, the second largest wire manufacturer in the country, encouraged the development of a huge cable industry in the same city, making sure it became completely dependent on Erbakır's wire production. Thanks to this strategy, Erbakır was able to outsource the costs and risks associated with marketing the final product by using these companies as marketing intermediaries and mitigating some of the seasonal risks in foreign markets. When demand peaked, Gaziantep's Oba Makarna, the third largest pasta company in the world, and Deniz Tekstil and Kocaer Tekstil, two large textile companies in Denizli, sporadically made higher demands on their local subsidiaries. This placed the burden of increasing capital investment on the subsidiaries, forcing small sweatshop owners to hold more fixed capital stock than they needed for their daily operations.

Old Money vs. New Money. Beginning in the 1980s, conflicts between the establishment and young entrepreneurs who were beginning to break into the market contributed significantly to the hostile business environment in these three cities. Competition between old and new families played an important role in defining business dynamics. I heard many stories about the marginalization of the families of younger entrepreneurs by the old guard. In Kayseri, for example, families who had established themselves years before in the city center called themselves "the locals" (*yerli*). They referred to every-one else as "the peasants" (*köylü*) and ridiculed them. According to one run-ning joke, a peasant brought yogurt to the city center to sell. A local put his finger in the container to check its firmness, then rejected it. But since he put his finger in the container, he contaminated the yogurt, forcing the farmer to go home empty-handed.

Other disparaging stories described the opportunistic behavior of immigrant entrepreneurs from Babadağ, a rural district of Denizli, who had built the city's massive towel industry. According to the old-timers, people from Babadağ did not have manners the way townspeople did. When they complained about fellow townspeople being aggressively opportunistic in the garment industry, they accused them of acting like the peasants of Babadağ.

Gaziantep has flourished in recent decades thanks to the connections between Turkish-citizen Kurdish entrepreneurs and Kurds living in Iraqi Kurdistan. Bitter about their success, jealous townspeople never let their competitors forget they were Kurds. They never missed an opportunity to complain about the negative impact Kurdish entrepreneurs were having on business dynamics in the city.

Even when they tried to sound sympathetic and protective, members of the older families adopted a condescending attitude toward the smaller, newer business owners. Small producers were well aware of the true message behind this patronizing talk. Older families who had amassed considerable wealth had little interest in helping the newcomers. They only wanted to buy out smaller and financially struggling companies under the guise of helping those younger entrepreneur families. These same old families also bought land in industrial parks, known in Turkey as organized industrial districts (OIDs), to rent to the new entrepreneurs at inflated prices. While OIDs provided subsidized electricity to young businesses operating on their grounds, they lost much of the money they saved from these subsidies by paying exceptionally high rents to the older families.

The new families looked for ways to show solidarity with one another by establishing symbolic boundaries between themselves and the older ones, using a combination of Islamist and racist narratives to claim moral superiority over the older families. For example, in Gaziantep and Kayseri, they spread gossip about the ethnic roots of older families, suggesting many of them came from Armenian Christian families and had converted to Islam. With stories like these they accused members of the city's old families of being of "infidels."

Islamism coupled with racism, in this context, was an instrument of social cohesion among the younger business families, and the ensuing conservative pressure urged all of them to pretend to have an almost ascetic lifestyle. It was a common practice among Kayseri industrialists to drive forty miles to have wine or liquor in touristy Cappadocia. Some of my interlocutors, who were among the richest in Gaziantep, felt obliged to spend Ramadan in Europe, in particular in Paris, to avoid the monthlong fast. Many businesspeople in Denizli had a second house in Izmir's vacation resorts to avoid the pressure of the local business community.

This tension was reminiscent, and maybe constitutive, of the broader Islamist party narrative that monopoly capital is a foreign element in the Turkish economy. Regardless of their lifestyle, political views, or stance on religion, the older families faced the constant risk of being labeled infidels in one way or another. The old money–new money binary, I realized during the final stages of my project, was more about the size of their capital than the actual age of the business families. Especially in 2013 and 2014, during the height of the rift between Islamist cliques led by Erdoğan and Fethullah Gülen, a Muslim cleric—which eventually triggered a coup attempt by allegedly Gülenist military officers in 2016—I gradually became aware that many Gülenist industrialists were young and pious business families, but they were treated the same as the older industrialist families who owed their success to the early republican regime. In the eyes of their subsidiaries, these Gülenist families were toys of Christian-Masonic-Zionist puppet masters just like the older secularist business families.

Fathers and Sons. Greed worked against these entrepreneurs in multiple ways. Instead of making strategic decisions, they tried to keep everything under their personal control. Few would willingly invest their money in business opportunities with multiple partners. This recurrent theme in Istanbul and these cities puzzled me because their reluctance to pool capital with their local competitors was a major obstacle to the growth of their businesses.

However, in one interview after another, I saw a pattern that had a lot to do with their self-perception. First-generation entrepreneurs believed that their acumen and skills made them successful, rather than favorable global market conditions or the country's political and economic changes. As the patriarchs of their families, they felt entitled to do what they wanted with the wealth they had accumulated. In their calculus, anything that relied on factors beyond their immediate control was a threat to their status in the family.

As a result, they avoided delegating authority to professionals, and they distrusted managers and engineers in particular. Although I never asked about the role of professional managers in their companies in my interviews, about a quarter of the respondents raised the issue themselves. In doing so, these patriarchs revealed the magnitude of their problematic relationship with their sons. In the eyes of the patriarchs, their sons used professional managers as Trojan horses to wrest control of the company from them. As a small furniture manufacturer in Kayseri complained about other first-generation entrepreneurs like himself, "They do not have open minds. As for their sons, they have wasteful habits. So, I am pessimistic about the future of Kayseri. What worries me the most is that when father and son have a disagreement, it often leads them to make mistakes. For example, I once witnessed an argument between a father and his son about the manager they had just hired: the son wanted his father to step aside and let the new manager oversee the shop floor while he, the son, took care of the customers. The manager was summarily fired."

The degree to which first-generation self-made men tried to keep control of their companies out of the hands of their sons was impressive. According to a representative of one of the biggest textile companies in Gaziantep, the first generation's distrust of financial institutions had everything to do with their obsession with preventing their sons from obtaining information about the company's finances. They obscured this obsession by reciting popular wisdom: "The best fortune is the one under the pillow." Sons often got "fed up," observed a representative of what is now one of the biggest textile companies in Denizli. Frustrated by living under their fathers' supervision and control, many members of the second generation left home and moved to Istanbul or Izmir, preferring to take jobs that paid little money over continuing to serve their domineering fathers. Freedom meant more to them than a life of luxury—at least until their fathers died, at which point they would take over the family business.

This problematic relationship between fathers and sons provides a lens for examining two long-term organizational strategies that large manufacturing companies in Denizli, Gaziantep, and Kayseri used to strengthen their businesses. The first and most common strategy could be called mitosis: expanding capital investments horizontally in unrelated industries. For example, as the managing director of one of the largest textile manufacturers in Kayseri explained to me, they opened a yarn factory in 2002 so that one of the sons could have a business of his own, preferably in a different sector. According to a representative of a major pasta manufacturer in Gaziantep, fathers also used this strategy because these first-generation entrepreneurs did not trust their sons' business skills: "The way [entrepreneurs] think about the future of their companies is simple. They say, 'I have three sons. I will ask the eldest to run this factory. Then I'll open two more factories for younger children in other industries like fruit juice or cookies. In this way, I can both spread the risk across different industries and prevent them from selling this factory to divide the money among themselves.'"

The second strategy involved opening new companies that produced the same product within the same sector to create a local cluster of enterprises owned by members of the same family. The Kaplan family was a successful example of this in Gaziantep's carpet industry. The family started its business in 1983 with mechanical looms. In following generations, the youngest boys were sent to college while the older ones did manual work on the looms in one of the factories. The college-educated brothers helped the family convert the first factory from mechanical to electronic looms after the 1990s. By 2015, the family had eighteen independent businesses owned by various members of the extended family. Although competing with each other, the owners of these individual businesses helped their brothers and cousins who were struggling financially.

This strategy made some sense from a marketing point of view. When foreign customers came to Gaziantep to buy a carpet, they saw more than a dozen companies with different variations on the same family name, such as Kaplan, Öz Kaplan, and Yasin Kaplan, suggesting that the brand was important. On the whole, however, this was a very poor use of resources. Nevertheless, the family apparently considered it a good way to keep the overall pool of resources relatively safe. It seemed far less risky than having a single company with multiple shareholders in which internal family feuds would likely erupt. The family opted for a strategy of survival of the fittest, knowing full well that brothers and cousins do not normally get on well. Each of them would vie to become the next patriarch.

Toxic Competition and Collaboration

My observations did not support the narrative that Muslim entrepreneurs created a flourishing industrial oasis in provincial regions of the country thanks to a sense of collective religious spirit. The competitive structure of supply chains promoted by foreign and domestic big business instead produced a toxic relationship among individual entrepreneurs. The highly individualistic and patriarchal narrative of the Islamists only emphasized the business values I had seen in Istanbul, inspiring cutthroat competition and unreliable supply chain relationships.

Although the people I interviewed were largely hopeless about the problem, they were still looking for ways to keep toxic competition under control. One way they tried to tackle it was to introduce a citywide pricing policy. In the early 2010s, for example, representatives from Yasin Kaplan Halı tried to convince their competitors to raise their prices by 5 percent in exchange for a 3 percent increase in input prices. The others agreed but kept their promises for only a year.

As I mentioned earlier, joint-stock companies were rare and fragile. Even older and successful cases did not survive the new business climate introduced by Özal's reforms in the 1980s. For these older companies, the problem was not only that the basic political economic conditions changed, but also that the emerging new individualistic mindset eclipsed even the provincial cynicism of the Cold War–era merchants. For example, in 1953, nearly one hundred small clothing manufacturers and retailers in Kayseri founded the company Birlik Mensucat so they could pool their resources to buy fabrics in bulk with a 10 percent discount from the city's state-owned fabric factory, Sümerbank. Even though it started with this minimalist goal, the company quickly became a pioneer in the private fabric industry. Orta Anadolu, the largest textile factory in Kayseri during the period in which I was doing research, was founded by the same investors who had been involved in Birlik. Both companies experienced serious management crises during the 1980s due to conflicting investment demands from their shareholders. With the hope of double dipping, some investors wanted Birlik and Orta to become the customers or suppliers of their other privately owned manufacturing companies. Other investors objected. In the end, the two companies were sold to larger private investors. In sum, the same political and economic environment that led to the proliferation of small manufacturing companies also created the conditions for toxic competition that destroyed solidarity among local entrepreneurs. That solidarity had sustained successful joint-stock companies for decades before the 1980 coup, which marked the end of the import-substituting industrialization strategy.

After the 1980s, attempts to revive older forms of cooperation in the new business environment were similarly doomed to failure. One outstanding example is the effort to create the EGS Bank in Denizli. Local textile and garment manufacturers founded the bank in 1995 to gain access to cheap capital. The project was a great success at first, and it played an important role in the efforts of local entrepreneurs to establish a cooperative supply chain in the city. In just a few years, the bank became the center of a holding company that expanded its activities from insurance, leasing, and factoring to logistics, machine production, tourism, foreign trade, and even grocery stores.[88] This success story did not last long: in 2001, the company lost its solvency and was seized by the Deposit Insurance Fund of Turkey, a supervisory authority founded in 1993 that was given far-reaching powers to monitor banking operations after the 2001 financial crisis.

Everyone I asked about EGS Bank agreed that the main problem undermining the company's financial strength was the decision to expand its operations to too many sectors in too short a time, especially to sectors that were unrelated to one another. This expansion was partly due to the company's poor management strategy, fueled by the optimism many felt in the 1990s, when the continued depreciation of Turkish lira gave industrialists and managers the illusion that growth had no limits.

But the bank's faulty strategy was not the only reason it collapsed, observed Kudret, head of the Denizli branch of a major bank in those years. When I interviewed him, Kudret was the financial and administrative coordinator of a large textile manufacturer in Denizli. In Kudret's opinion, an important but less visible factor in EGS Bank's downfall was its practice of granting risky loans to shareholders and business partners whose companies were in crisis. As in the case of Birlik Mensucat, the shareholders, he continued, plundered the bank's savings, using the funds to cut corners as they tried to shore up failing enterprises and get ahead of their local competitors.

The result of these failures was the same in each city: continued dependence on different sorts of monopoly capital. Small industrialists depended on major banks for credit, foreign producers for equipment, and global retail chains for marketing. In some cases, entire industries depended on importing equipment exclusively from a particular company or country. For example, carpet manufacturers in Gaziantep almost always imported carpet weaving machines from a single company based in Belgium, Vandewiele.

This dependency had a long history: I was repeatedly told of a major machinery manufacturer, Hemaks Makine, that initially competed with Vandewiele with great success, but eventually lost the battle for mysterious reasons. When I contacted him, Mr. Helvacıkara, the owner of Hemaks Makine, assured me the true story was less enigmatic. Until the mid-1990s, carpet looms had hardly used any electronic devices; then, small but meaningful innovations turned Turkish looms into globally competitive products. In 1995, both Vandewiele and Hemaks debuted their new electronic Jacquard looms in the globally renowned Itma fair. Both companies bought the electronic parts of their new looms from a Japanese company, which later signed an exclusive contract with Vandewiele and stopped selling these items to Hemaks. Mr. Helvacıkara went bankrupt after a few years, only to later start a new business with new product lines for fiber manufacturers in Gaziantep. The Japanese company's decision changed the fate of Gaziantep's carpet industry.

As one of the people I interviewed said, the dependence on the Belgian company was so great that the carpet manufacturers of Gaziantep felt compelled to buy new machines every five years to prevent Vandewiele from selling to competitors in other countries. This was an incredibly distorted view. As much as Vandewiele was the monopolist, the carpet manufacturers in Gaziantep were collectively the monopsonist. However, competition among these manufacturers was so intense that none of my interviewees in this industry even thought of proposing a joint purchase agreement with the Belgian company.

In this respect, the narrative of Müsiad reflected the mindset of its members, whether an entrepreneur in Kayseri or a sweatshop owner in Istanbul. This narrative portrayed the members of Müsiad as role models for these entrepreneurs and thus taught them how to be a proper businessman, even if not an Islamist. These proper businessmen created a business ecology characterized by adversarial supply chains, the gap between old and new money, and generational tension between patriarchs and sons. Each structural, historical, and generational factor confirmed the relevance of the individualist narrative of the Islamist businesspeople and their associations, including Müsiad. The Islamists successfully presented themselves as the actors facilitating social cohesion within hostile supply chains, protecting new money from the pressure of the old, and giving them a moral compass to regulate their relationship with the young. This patronage reinforced these entrepreneurs' aspirations and concerns.

THE CLERIC

Religious Orders as Intellectual Centers

The Islamist political cadre offered the faubourgeoisie a new vision of policymaking to calibrate their relationship with monopoly capital. The Islamist business community defines its individualist mindset as a core element of its class identity. Without that element, it would be difficult to identify these nonmonopoly manufacturers as a major economic interest. What turns this economic interest into the core of a social class, the faubourgeoisie, is the idiosyncratic relationship of these entrepreneurs with their workers. The Islamic religious orders produce the narrative that frames this relationship.

The religious orders have a significant presence in the government bureaucracy, make a substantial impact on policymaking, and control significant economic resources.[89] However, more important than these in terms of the political consequences of their activities for the Islamist movement at large is their role in producing this narrative. The Islamist cadres would possibly continue to control the government bureaucracy and nurture crony capital groups even if the religious orders were not active in the bureaucracy and economy. The religious orders are indispensable for the Islamist movement, however, due to their success in turning Islamism from a mere political ideology into a cosmology governing the everyday lives of the workers, their relationship with their employers, and their emic perspectives about politics. They are the primary intellectual centers of the Islamist movement.

During my fieldwork as an unskilled worker at different garment sweatshops in 2008 in Turkey's largest working-class district, Bağcılar, I observed that very few of my coworkers regularly attended meetings of the religious orders or acted as their followers, even though most of them were devout Muslims. Moreover, my interviews with and observations of small manufacturers between 2008 and 2014 gave me a strong impression that just as with the Islamist party, the primary target of the religious orders was local business owners, not the workers.[90]

Thanks to an interlocutor, introduced to me by the owners of one of the sweatshops I worked at, I attended one such session held by a religious order in 2008 on the second floor of the 2,500-square-foot building of a neighborhood beautification association. The gathering began with an hour-long sermon by the sheikh on the moral threats, such as lust, that Muslim men faced in their daily lives. Some attendees wore religious robes with turbans (*sarık*), while those standing in the back next to me looked like working-class men with conventional, poor clothing. After the sermon, two young men in religious costumes started collecting money. Men in the front rows closer to the sheikh, also in religious costumes, put in hundred-lira bills—about a fifth of a worker's monthly salary. When the box came to our row, the bills dropped to five and ten lira. I could see the disappointment on the faces of the poor participants. As the members of the order prepared for the *dhikr* ceremony, we were kindly invited out. This was the moment when outsiders like us were given a clear signal as to who really belonged to the order and who did not.

I asked my interlocutor, who claimed to be a descendant of the seventeenth-century Kurdish Sufi poet Ehmedê Xanî, about the background of the insiders. I was not surprised to learn that most of them were local businessmen, including shopkeepers and sweatshop owners. Unlike my interlocutor, however, most were of Turkish descent. He told me the outsiders "are looking for salvation, a form of atonement for their sins and a form of protection from future sins."

I found these observations counterintuitive, so I checked their validity with a content analysis of videos posted on the internet by representatives of different religious orders. A strong pro-labor or pro-poor rhetoric in the narrative of the religious orders would cast severe doubt on my observations, while the absence of such rhetoric would support them.[91] My research assistants and I focused on ten Naqshbandi and seven Salafi groups or leaders generally regarded as the most important religious orders in Turkey (see appendix A) and on ten local groups in Bağcılar (including the local mufti's office). I used the Outline of Cultural Materials (OCM) classification system to develop our codebook. Our findings were exciting for two reasons. First, although the material was mostly silent about the working class, and the bits and pieces about the poor were highly negative and almost insulting, it glorified the shopkeepers. Second, the religious orders' narrative was the basis of a moral order justified and framed by the phobic themes that defined the corporeality of the believers. The religious orders did not glorify the class position of the working poor but rather used the element of fear to diminish their capacity to think and act like a social class.

The Social Class

The Poor Muslim. At first, the material we studied did not tell us much about the religious orders' position on the notion of social class. Work-related OCM categories such as occupational specialization, wages and salaries, industrial relations, and work organizations each applied to less than 1 percent of the codes (see appendix B for details). For example, we did not find a single excerpt referring to labor organizations. Among 1,434 extracts, the code for labor relations (OCM 460) was used in only two cases. What individuals do for a living (*rızk*) was mostly irrelevant in the material we dealt with. In other words, the concept of labor was overlooked in the narrative, yet this is still significant: workers are denied an identity based on their occupational status.

The few excerpts we caught gave us a good sense of why the Sunni preachers were not enthusiastic about the topic. Workers' labor was denigrated because productive activity poses an opportunity cost against the time a believer could otherwise spend in worship. As Mahmut Ahmet Ünlü, one of the most famous preachers representing one of the strongest religious orders, İskenderpaşa Cemaati, argued in a sermon watched over 140,000 times on YouTube, the poor male believer cannot fulfill two conflicting expectations: his duty to provide for his family and his duty to serve Allah. Work is legitimate only if it facilitates worship.[92]

In the hierarchy of professions, craftsmen have lower status than religious warriors (jihadists) or farmers. A warrior wins or loses by the will of Allah.

Farmers' yields depend on meteorological events, so their earnings also reflect the will of Allah. The only ones in this taxonomy who have power over their labor are craftsmen, and this power is defined not as a capacity in the service of the deity or the religion but as a corrupting result of their efforts to conceal their shortcomings in their relationships in the marketplace.[93]

Furthermore, different rules apply to the rich and the poor. For instance, according to Ömer Öngüt, the spiritual leader of the Hakikatçılar Grubu, smoking is a sin for the poor, because the poor spend their "children's necessities on pleasure," but "for the rich it is [only] abominable [because] he can take care of his children and his family."[94]

Rewards are also distributed according to the class position of the believer in what Osman Nuri Topbaş, the leader of the Erenköy Cemaati, called "the marketplace of salvation": "It is not enough for us to be pious [*takva*]. We will receive *sadaqah jariah* [the charity of offspring that promotes the status of their parents in the hereafter]. . . . In this place [this world], heaven is marketed [*pazarlamak*]."[95] The rich man can collect *sadaqah jariah* after his death and improve his status in the afterlife. He is also subject to less stringent criteria of pollution than a poor person.

Representatives of these religious orders argue that this idea is supported by sources from the early years of Islam. According to Mahmud Esad Çoşan, Zahid Kotku's successor and technically the shaikh of Erbakan, "Our Prophet told ten people that they would go to heaven [and one of them was Abu Bakr]. . . . He gave up all his gold for the way of the Prophet. . . . He was a nobleman. . . . His Holiness, Uthman, showed [similar] generosity. He donated his herd of one hundred camels. . . . Our Prophet said that after this generosity, 'No matter what [Uthman] does, he will not make any loss. He will surely go to heaven'. . . . He was rich as well."

For Çoşan, the Prophet's favorites were the rich, because they sacrificed more than the poor. Their sacrifice is described as a commercial investment defined in terms of the gain-loss binary ("making a loss"). Abu Bakr and Uthman (the first and third caliphs of Islam) made a considerable investment by giving up part of their wealth and joining the ten people who were promised a place in heaven before they died. They are the role models of religion. Those who follow their path are promised paradise. Their sacrifice of their possessions trumps the suffering of the poor.

Being aware of this cosmic asymmetry, the religious leaders are under no illusion that the rich and the poor are in a harmonious relationship: "[The employer] does not trust his worker. The worker betrays his property. This is not how it should be. . . . The boss is supposed to pay the wages while his workers are sweating. He cheats them. . . . What does the worker do in return? He damages his boss's property, he does everything he can to harm him, he betrays his boss."[96]

The solution to creating harmony is for the poor to accept poverty as a defining part of their social identity and then expect some material benefits. One of these benefits is zakat, a religiously enforced alms, usually equivalent to 2.5 percent of the savings of the rich: "If the rich person gives his zakat to the poor person, the poor person would be happy about it. He would think: 'Allah Almighty, this man has given me zakat this year. Give him more wealth so that he can give me more.' In other words, he would want the rich to have more property."[97] The language about the poor is condescending. The poor person is portrayed as an unintelligent human being who cannot realize that zakat is used to manipulate him into loving the rich person and that the source of zakat is his work anyway.

The Salafi preacher Feyzullah Birışık answered the next logical question, which is also the title of his video, "Is Poverty Our Destiny?":

> If no one is poor, how can the institution of zakat continue to exist? [The poor] cannot participate in jihad. He cannot give *sadaqah jariah*. . . . Does Allah punish this [poor] person? In the name of Allah, no. . . . The poor person should say, "If only I had half the wealth of the rich, I would help the poor and the lazy . . . I would equip the jihadists." . . . Then your reward [*ecir*] will be accounted for as if you had already done all these things you promised. In reality, you would have to spend ten, fifteen years of your life to have all that money so that you can give it back [to the poor, the jihadists, etc.]. The poor person can earn all these rewards without doing all the extra work to become rich. . . . You should not misunderstand this. You should not say, "I am content to be poor. I will remain poor." Allah . . . says: "The hand that gives is superior to the hand that receives." Allah promotes wealth. Yet poverty is destiny.[98]

Birışık made three interrelated points. First, poverty is a religiously necessary and desirable component of the moral order because zakat is one of the five main pillars of Islam. Zakat must exist, so poverty must exist. Second, all the good deeds a rich person can do are beyond the financial means of the poor—and those good financial deeds secure a path to heaven. Yet a poor person could be rewarded in the same way if they dream of being a rich person. Third, the poor person is spared all the hard work the rich person does to become rich. Wealth is justified as the result of hard work, and the poor are portrayed as lazy. Thus, the rich are superior to the poor.

Poor people's labor is devalued, their religious duty is harder, they are not granted priority in heaven, and they depend on the alms of the rich. The poor are left with few choices other than embracing asceticism, yet that path is also closed according to Alparslan Kuytul, one of the most popular Salafist leaders in Turkey. In one of his videos from 2017, which was viewed over 190,000 times, Kuytul commented on the class position of the ideal Muslims:

> Muslims should live like middle-class people [*orta halli*]. They should be the middle class of their time. Our Lord lived his life like a middle-class person. Even with a slightly lower standard, namely asceticism [*zühd*]. . . . If [the Prophet] had wanted to, he could have lived in a palace. . . . In other words, you live a modest life even though you have the means. [He raises his voice in anger] If you do not have the means, you are poor, you live a life of the poor. You are already poor. You must live a life of the poor. What other option do you have? This is not asceticism. Asceticism is living like a poor person even though you are rich.[99]

The Shopkeeper. Who is this middle-class person whom Kuytul represents as the ideal Muslim? Another section in Birışık's material provides further details about this persona:

> We now have one of these periodic crises in Turkey. The shopkeepers . . . have goods in their warehouses, but there is no money, no cash. . . . [Why?] It is Allah who dictates all these factors. . . . Poverty and wealth have nothing to do with intelligence. What did a child [born in a wealthy family] do to become a trillionaire? . . . Was he smart? No. It is because Allah willed it so. Does . . . economic wisdom play a role in this? Of course it does. But it is Allah who gives his slave this commercial wisdom. . . . A person may see [a commercial trend] and say, "If I buy this property at this price and wait for five years, the price will go up fifty times." But it is Allah who has put this idea in his mind. . . . [Then] pray, "My Allah, let the customers remember my business and the brand I sell so that they will come to my store and buy my shoes."[100]

The persona Birışık speaks of here is a shopkeeper, not a worker earning middle-class wages. Unlike the trillionaire prodigal child, they earn their wealth with their commercial wisdom. Nonetheless, this shopkeeper's livelihood (*rızk*) is still a result of their Allah-given good fortune and not their labor. Their biggest asset is the will of Allah that their customers are reminded of their merchandise in a chaotic global marketplace.

In contrast to the middle-class shopkeeper, that "trillionaire prodigal child" or monopoly capitalist is portrayed as a persona in potential defiance against Allah. For instance, Halis Bayancuk, another major Salafi leader, commented on Croesus, "When the ignorant poor saw the wealth of Croesus, they said, 'I wish Allah would give me some of it. I wish I had benefited from this wealth.' The scholar told them, 'The reward of Allah is much more auspicious [than the wealth of Croesus]'. . . . Then Allah destroyed all the wealth of Croesus. The ignorant did not see the turmoil, but the learned did."[101]

As in the narrative of the Islamist political party, monopoly capitalists are treated with tacit hostility because they control the source of the shopkeeper's wealth: credit. Because this urgent problem truly bothers their shopkeeper audience, the religious orders promote *murabaha* (sales contract) over *riba* (interest) to offer a solution compatible with the Islamic principles. İsmail Hünerlice, another preacher of the influential İsmailağa Cemaati, offered such a solution answered in one of his 2020 hadith interpretation sessions, which was viewed ninety-eight thousand times:

> Why is interest a sin? Let me put it this way: . . . Ninety-five kuruş of every lira is deposited [in savings accounts] for interest today. We say, "Down with America." Very well, but you take your money to [the Americans] anyway. . . .
>
> What does our religion demand? Our religion asks . . . the intelligent person . . . to [use] . . . murabaha. . . . America did this. They called it "risk economy." It allows the owners of capital to lend money to those who do business. . . . The Americans did this in the land of the infidels. . . . But the Muslims do not understand. [The Americans] turned the sin into a good deed. What Islam wants is this: I give you 100,000 liras . . . we now have 120,000 liras. You get ten and I get ten. . . . What if we do not make a profit? . . . [In this scenario] there is a loss of 3,000 liras. Islam tells us that the entrepreneur's entire year was ruined while the capital owner lost 3,000 liras. However, the interest dictates . . . that the capital owner should still receive his 5,000 liras. The man has lost his entire year, he has failed. There is no malicious intent here. The other says: "I do not care. . . . Do what is necessary and pay the 5,000 lira." This is where interest becomes a sin.[102]

In this description of *murabaha*, the anti-interest sentiment has more to do with small business owners' conflict of interest with monopoly capital than with an all-encompassing rejection of interest as a practice. The speaker acknowledges the inevitability of the credit mechanism, although he also shares the resentment of small business owners about the interest they pay.

Small businessmen are portrayed as the main victims of the infidels' financial system. Finance capital should bear the risk, not them. Unlike craftsmen or workers, their labor is precious. If their efforts do not pay off, that is Allah's will, so finance capital should not punish them for their failure.

They feel exploited and are looking for a spiritually viable solution to their problems. Their religious order defines their status vis-à-vis their workers: they are the benefactor of the poor. Their religious order defines their relationship with other shopkeepers: they will compete with an opportunistic mindset, begging Allah to favor them over their competitors. Their religious order defines the tension with the prodigal child: as a victim of an economic system based on the religiously prohibited *riba*, they will use the religiously accepted *murabaha* to circumvent the prohibition.

Toxiphobia

The religious orders do not make a substantial effort to expand their follower base among the working class or to appeal to them with a proletariat-friendly narrative, but rather target the shopkeepers as their ideal clientele or followers. Nonetheless, they still frame the actions and beliefs of the working class effectively because their narrative provides norms and guidance about the moral order of their urban community.

When my assistants and I first checked the frequency distribution of the codes applied to the excerpts, our first observation was the considerable effort the religious orders make to explain the world. As shown in table 3 and further elaborated in appendix B, the OCM themes I have grouped under the theme *Social Theory* rank after the religious themes in terms of the number of excerpts used. In addition, two-thirds of these codes belong to the natural sciences and humanities (OCM 810): 204 excerpts (14.5 percent) in these videos refer to science (OCM 815) to explain natural and social phenomena.

The preachers generally accept the epistemological legitimacy of science, but they also discuss potential paradoxes in scientific reasoning to show the epistemological superiority of their narrative. Their cosmological narrative contains possible answers to the believers' problems in their lives. The preacher derives his authority from the scope of his narrative.

For instance, in a recording dated 1971 and viewed 156,000 times, Kotku, the sheikh of Erbakan, related the inability to fight desire (*nefs*) to the domination of a materialistic or technical, and thus inadequate, understanding

TABLE 3 Topics by OCM subjects

OCM topic	Frequency	Share of total
Religion[a]	923	64%
Social Theory[b]	433	30%
Norms[c]	315	22%
Toxicity[d]	303	21%
Relations[e]	272	19%
Sex & Reproduction[f]	193	13%
Politics[g]	166	12%
Public & Everyday Activities[h]	141	10%
Stratification[i]	107	7%
Economy[j]	55	4%
Production[k]	44	3%
Space[l]	13	1%

SOURCE: Courtesy of the author.

[a] 770 Religious Beliefs, 780 Religious Practices, 790 Ecclesiastical Organizations.

[b] 530 Art, 140 Human Biology, 150 Behavior Processes and Personality, 160 Demography, 170 History and Culture Change, 180 Total Culture, 800 Numbers and Measures, 810 Sciences and Humanities.

[c] 670 Law, 680 Offenses and Sanctions, 690 Justice.

[d] 250 Food Processing, 260 Food Consumption, 270 Drink and Drugs, 290 Clothing, 300 Adornment, 730 Social Problems, 750 Sickness, 760 Death.

[e] 200 Communication, 570 Interpersonal Relations, 580 Marriage, 590 Family, 600 Kinship, 620 Community.

[f] 830 Sex, 840 Reproduction, 860 Socialization, 870 Education, 880 Adolescence, Adulthood, and Old Age, 890 Gender Roles and Issues.

[g] 630 Territorial Organization, 640 Government Institutions, 650 Government Activities, 660 Political Behavior, 720 War, 740 Health and Welfare.

[h] 520 Recreation, 540 Commercialized Entertainment.

[i] 550 Naming, Prestige and Status Mobility, 560 Social Stratification.

[j] 420 Property, 430 Exchange and Transfers, 440 Marketing, 450 Finance.

[k] 460 Labor, 470 Business and Industrial Organization.

[l] 340 Structures, 350 Equipment and Maintenance of Buildings, 360 Settlements, 370 Energy and Power.

of the cosmos. Kotku had a particular form of knowledge that let him make better use of scientific data than the scientist to explain the cosmos. This knowledge shows the believer the way to fight *nefs*:

> Man does not sin suddenly. . . . First they make you not pray. They say, "Do not pray. Later you can repent your sins. Allah will forgive you." . . . They can slowly, step by step, tempt you to sin. . . . Then you become the enemy of religion, of preachers, of elders. . . . Swords [against our desires—*nefs*] are the keys to heaven. . . . You must have the knowledge to wage [this] war. What you call "technique" cannot be useful without the knowledge. If you have good knowledge, you can master the technique. To defeat the seduction of

your soul, you must know the methods by which your soul can be seduced, like the tricks of the enemy.[103]

The distinction Kotku made between technique and knowledge assigns the religious leader spiritual hegemony over proper life practices. Technically, it is possible for any Muslim to repent their sins at any time, provided they promise not to commit the same sin again. Kotku acknowledged this but pointed out the inevitable consequence of this behavior: the gradual but certain exit from the religion. A religious leader acts like a sword, transforming his knowledge of the cosmos into a guide that can help believers in their struggle against their desires in the daily practice of life.

The task of the religious leader is thus never finished. The narrative is never complete. What religious leaders produce is not epistemic but phronetic knowledge. Thus, the videos we analyzed covered a wide range of topics, such as cryptocurrencies,[104] online gaming,[105] and menstrual pads.[106] The speakers claimed the authority to regulate every aspect of social life, as it is their task to curb desire, which, according to them and in line with Lacan's perspective, is an insatiable motive.

The object of desire is other humans. Desire is associated with sin. Thus, the relationship among community members may be toxic. In fact, the connection in the narrative between purity and spiritual salvation is much weaker or less direct than one may expect. Rather, what brings these community members together is their shared toxiphobia, instigated by themselves and by aliens. The narrative defines the relevant objects, activities, and cure of the toxiphobia.

Objects. Among the excerpts, 21 percent touched upon spiritually toxic substances and practices that could harm the spiritual purity of the Muslims, including food processing and consumption, drinks and drugs, clothing and adornment, social problems, and sickness and death. These substances and practices were treated not as metaphorical or figurative but as literal objects. For instance, Ahmet Mahmut Ünlü dedicated an entire twenty-seven-minute video to the question of how quickly a man should perform ablution between two prayers:

> You do not have to perform the full ablution [*gusül*] between two prayers. . . . The man is already so tired after sexual intercourse [*muamele*] that he would not even have the strength to perform the regular ablution. . . . [However,] Angel Gabriel comes to the funeral of those who have not died dirty. . . . Then

why do we cleanse the deceased? . . . To eliminate the risk that the deceased did not perform a full ablution before his death. And when someone dies, the body ejaculates. It is very difficult for the soul to leave the body. Therefore, the body releases itself.[107]

This video was viewed over 1.8 million times between 2020 and 2023. For the sake of clarity of the references here, Muslim men are expected to shower after sexual intercourse, which is called *gusül*. All Muslims are expected to perform the regular ablution (*abdest*) before their daily prayers. The scenario discussed here is that a man has sexual intercourse before he goes to bed but fails to perform *gusül*, then wakes up and performs it before the morning prayer.

Mahmut Ünlü draws a fine line, as Kotku underlined many decades ago, between the path to the denial of religion and the path to the true creed. The line touches upon the most private activities with an astonishing level of detail. It is not just to perform the ablution. It is about its time, its actual practice, the events preceding and succeeding it. It is about the possibility of death in the middle of the night and then the risk of denial by Angel Gabriel at the funeral.

Probably because its corporeal nature opens various possibilities of toxicity, sexuality was explicitly addressed in 13 percent of the excerpts we analyzed. Men want to know more about the religious prescriptions on sexuality, probably to extend their sexual hegemony over women, and women see their husbands as a potential threat to their spiritual purity. These tensions between devout partners can be the subject of intense negotiation over religious norms. In a 2011 video viewed by 280,000 people, Salafist leader Abdullah Yolcu addressed an email from a woman whose husband urged her to have anal sex. The woman asked Yolcu for his religious opinion.[108] Her husband was a religious-order follower with a good record of religious practices. In a thirty-minute video, Yolcu called anal sex a sin:

If you observe the three restrictions [*nifas, hayz,* and *dubur*: sex after childbirth, sex during menstruation, and anal sex], you can have sex with your wife in any position you want. . . . In the meantime, I would like to make a comment here. Sometimes we get questions: some women do not let their husbands touch them from behind. This is also wrong. The man can move his organ on the woman's body, let it touch the buttocks, use the buttocks for [vaginal] sex. There is no restriction between married couples. . . . Let us now answer another question that we are often . . . asked. . . . Is the woman allowed to put the man's sexual organ in her mouth? . . . Yes. However, there is one condition. The man should not ejaculate into the woman's mouth. Also, the pre-ejaculatory fluid comes from the penis. . . . Both [fluids] are dirty.[109]

Yolcu's classification of dirtiness as a pathogenic taxonomy of bodily fluids allows one to see Ünlü's comment on postmortem ejaculation in its proper context: menstrual blood is the dirtiest, pre-ejaculatory fluid is less dirty, and ejaculation is again slightly less dirty than the first two. Saliva is a fluid that can be cleaned with ablution. Thus, sexual activity is primarily an actual or potential exchange of bodily fluids rather than a reciprocal interaction between individuals. The properties of these fluids and the conditions of their transfer between partners determine the risk of spiritual corruption.

Contagion. The object of toxification has a contagious character. A salvation seeker's efforts can be easily ruined by improper contact with the contaminant or the contaminator. For instance, according to Mahmud Esad Çoşan, the successor and son-in-law of Kotku of the Naqshbandi İskenderpaşa order, in a 1990 video that has been viewed sixty-two thousand times, perfume as a contaminating or pathogenic liquid in the air is the equivalent of the visual cue ("showing the flesh") as an object of the gaze: "Our Prophet says that he saw that most of those in Hell were women. Why? Women [tend to] deny [and not appreciate] the benefits of their husbands. . . . If a woman walks on the street wearing perfume, she will be cursed until she returns home. . . . The woman should not show her flesh in public [*açılmak*]. She should not leave the house without her husband's permission. She should protect her honor."[110]

The danger of contamination is not limited to women's sartorial, sonic, and aromatic practices: women drivers pose a threat to religion.[111] The cause of economic crises is women's unchastity.[112] Within this broad spectrum, sin is not just a personal matter. It is a threat to the entire community. In an interview that was viewed 136,000 times, Rukiye Genç, a representative of the Menzil order, another important Naqshbandi current, clearly related religious mandates for individuals to the moral standing of the community. For her, the well-being of the whole community is exposed to a spiritual threat as soon as the privacy of the individual's body is compromised. The issue at stake is as much political as private: "As you know, Satan deceived our father and mother [Adam and Eve] by making them show their *adytum* [*mahrem yer*]. . . . [Satan] first attacks their genitals [*edep yeri*]. In other words, he invades their privacy [*mahremiyet*]. . . . In a community that has lost its decency [*edep*], there is no more peace and well-being [*afiyet*], because that community becomes a plaything of Satan. So protect your private parts, like your heart."[113]

The internal elements of contagion risk are closely connected to the external risk factors that similarly pose a threat to the spiritual well-being of the community. Abdullah Yolcu, whom I quoted above, explains the interest of men in anal sex with these external factors:

> When we were young . . . there were rarely [pornographic] pictures. Then the magazines started popping up like mushrooms. The scum of European civilization. . . . Then the internet. . . . Now every woman, every young man . . . watch all sorts of things. . . . It's the reflection of their filthy culture. . . .
>
> The relationship of man to man was the act of the primal tribes. . . . Where does AIDS come from? From anal intercourse. They had sexual intercourse with a species of monkey in Africa. . . . Eighty percent of the spread of AIDS in Europe is due to anal sex. . . . Women who do that in movies are prostitutes [*fahişe*]. . . . [Now responding to the woman who emailed him] If he . . . insists on [his demand], you have the right to divorce him.[114]

The forbidden forms of sexual intercourse directly challenge the core of Yolcu's classification of impurity, which ensures sexual homogeneity and solidarity within his heterosexual male group. Therefore, he must present these threats as alien to the dominant culture. The threat is successfully used to draw a line between European infidels and Muslims.

As his advice to his female follower to divorce her husband indicates, concern for the spiritual purity of an individual takes precedence over the sacred status of the family. Enforcing the principles of moral order to reaffirm the hierarchy between bodily fluids, aromatic substances, and sartorial practices is a political priority for the peace and well-being of the entire community.

Because the protection of the woman's body from pollution is essential to overcome any danger of a spiritual pandemic, a religious leader may even affirm divorce. Separation has the same function as isolation amid a pandemic. Affirming Mary Douglas's insightful dictum that dirt is "matter out of place,"[115] an object could be a toxicant in one place and a safe material in another. This need to arrange space to avoid toxicities assigns religious leaders the authority to call for broader political intervention. What makes the issue political is that toxicity has a contagious form. These substances and practices can be seen, heard, touched, or even ingested. The role of politics is to establish and enforce certain visual, aromatic, and acoustic boundaries between people to reduce the risk of contagion.

Salvation. With its emphasis on toxiphobia, the narrative of the religious orders justifies an individualist notion of salvation as the spiritual goal of the Muslims. In the words of Osman Nuri Topbaş, "heaven is marketed" to those who have the resources. Rukiye Genç confirmed this point in the interview I quoted above. According to her interpretation, this world is a "game" with losers and winners: "When we bid for paradise (*cennete talip isek*), when we bid for the blessings of God, the book in our hand is clear. The rules in the book are clear. If the world is a game, the rules are in front of us. Those who play the game by its rules will go to the promised Heaven."[116] A collective effort to isolate individuals from each other is a must in order to reduce the risk of contagion, yet everyone is on his own in this game. Collaborative interaction between Muslim individuals is justified only if it contributes to the individual salvation.

Indeed, the individuality of salvation is so crucial that not only strangers but also family members must negotiate the terms of their relationships carefully, lest they jeopardize their personal salvation. Men can and do pose a toxic threat to their wives. Women, in return, can spread toxicity in the community with their sartorial, sonic, and aromatic practices. The alien evil forces are waiting just outside the gates of the community.

To give order to this chaos, the narrative of the religious orders creates two boundaries and three actors to define the social. The actors are the individual, the community, and the outside world. The individual is susceptible to contamination and can contaminate others. He or she (there is no "they" as a community member in this narrative) must be protected, but he or she is also a risk factor. Redemption is the result of individual effort and riches, not collective effort.

In the narrative, individuals atomize the community. The outside world has the opposite effect, so the community should take political measures to minimize potential harm from it. Formation of the community reflects a balance between the centrifugal effects that isolate individuals from each other for the sake of spiritual hygiene and the centripetal effects that establish the basis of policies in the public sphere to protect members of the community from the external risk of pollution. The result is a phobic community. Its members are afraid of the toxic properties of other members and they are also collectively afraid of the toxic effects of the outside world. These two types of fears are difficult to reconcile. Therefore, although the moral order promises protection from the phobias, it also generates them.

The Islamists have sought the support of the faubourgeoisie since the 1970s. Promotion of nonmonopoly industrialists has been a policy priority for the past half century. What has been kept, modified, and quit in their discourse and policymaking during this period illustrates the significance of this goal for the Islamists. The faubourgeoisie's interest in and later support for the Islamists has been conditional. Three factors turned the Islamists into a close ally of this social class.

First, the political cadres used every resource at their disposal to subsidize small producers. If one political economic component identifies Turkish Islamism, it is the provision of cheap credit for small manufacturers. The ideological adaptation of the movement in the 1990s was a consequence of the new conditions to fulfill this promise, not a metamorphosis of the Islamists from an antimodernist or even anticapitalist current to a neoliberal one.

The second factor is the historical role of the pious business community in the dissemination of this promise along with a new business mindset to a growing population of small manufacturers since the 1990s. The pioneers of this community were mostly entrepreneurs in metropolitan regions, not provincial cities. The core identity they shared was not their religious or even political perspectives but the size of their businesses: small and medium manufacturers in Istanbul spread a new business narrative to the rest of the country in pursuit of a civilizing mission. This narrative framed and affirmed the toxic competition among these manufacturers, so the Islamist political cadres benefited from this campaign.

The third factor is the historical role religious orders played in the Islamist movement. The central function of religious orders within the movement is to generate a narrative the Islamist-faubourgeois alliance can use to reach out to the proletariat. The core of this narrative is not the promotion of an ascetic worldview to credit the working people's toil and poverty but the formation of a dynamic set of norms as the basis of a moral community. Although these norms are tailored for individual classes, they apply to everyone, so the narrative cuts across class lines or makes the class element invisible. The narrative is not a misrepresentation of the interests of the faubourgeoisie but the universalization of those interests as the hegemonic values of entire working-class communities.

The next and maybe the most critical question is how the alliance between the Islamists and the faubourgeoisie helped both parties frame the perspective of the proletariat about their everyday life practices, work experiences, and communities in a way that helped the alliance come to power in 2002 and stay in power since then.

The Alliance in Action

FOUR

The Faubourgeoisie and the Proletariat

TRUST AND PHOBIA

I WOULD OCCASIONALLY STOP by my cousin Fazıl's jewelry store to talk to him about his business and about daily living conditions in my 2007–8 research setting, Bağcılar, a district of Istanbul in the middle of the largest working-class region of the country. At one of these meetings, we sat as usual on short stools on the narrow sidewalk in front of his store in the middle of the district's central neighborhood as the day drew to a close. After the fourth tea, we had run out of things to talk about. In our silent cognitive fatigue, we stared at the cars on the busy street. Then Fazıl pointed his *misbaha* at a woman crossing the street and sucked his teeth to express displeasure at her clothes: her T-shirt and jeans revealed too much of her body.

Then, as if she had heard us (and maybe she had), the woman turned around and walked in our direction. As she approached the store's entrance, Fazıl jumped from his stool and held the door open for her. After rummaging through some gold jewelry with the help of the now very polite Fazıl, she gave him a sincere, warm smile and said, "Maybe later [*Belki sonra*]." As the woman left, Fazıl looked embarrassed for a brief moment, perhaps because I had witnessed this scene. He overcame the discomfort, as indicated by a change in his posture, and whispered, "You can't trust these people."

As discussed in the previous chapter, trust is almost an alien sentiment for entrepreneurs like Fazıl. He did not trust other jewelry store owners. He had a couple of tenement projects in the neighboring district; he did not trust other small contractors. As the picture of a slightly younger version of him in a karate uniform (*gi*) with a black belt and clenched fists that hung on the front window of the jewelry display in his shop indicated, he was not an easy man to tackle. He did not trust his customers.

Committed Justice and Development Party (AKP) voters shared Fazıl's trust issues. In a 2020 street interview posted on a YouTube channel based in Antalya, a relatively liberal metropolitan city, a reporter asked random people on the street for their opinion of a statement about foreign policy, saying it had been made by the secularist main opposition leader. In the middle of the interview, she corrected herself per the script, told the interviewee it was actually President Tayyip Erdoğan of the AKP who made the statement, and asked the interviewee again for his opinion. Here is an excerpt from one of these interviews:

REPORTER: Are you happy with the AKP?

INTERVIEWEE (a man in his fifties): Yes, of course.

REPORTER: The opposition leader Kemal Kılıçdaroğlu said yesterday that we should change our course toward America and Europe. How would you comment on that?

INTERVIEWEE: Kılıçdaroğlu makes no sense. He says one thing today and something else the next day. He does not know what he's talking about.

REPORTER: Do you think we should change our course toward America and Europe?

INTERVIEWEE: No, no, no ... Europe is hostile toward us. We can take care of ourselves. We do not need them. They are the ones who depend on us.

CAMERAMAN: [He corrects the reporter as part of the script] It was Erdoğan who said that, not Kılıçdaroğlu.

REPORTER: Sir, I am sorry. I am absentminded today. Yes, it was Erdoğan who said that we should change our course toward the West.

INTERVIEWEE: If it was Erdoğan who said that, then that's right.

REPORTER: Should we change our course toward America and Europe?

INTERVIEWEE: [Now reluctantly] I do not want to talk about politics, but they [the Erdoğan clique] know better. We [the people] should not discuss these things. If Erdoğan said that, then that's right.[1]

The relationship of people like Fazıl with his female customer can help make sense of this interview. Fazıl and others with a similar status in the local community shape the social identity of working people in favor of the Islamists. In Cedric Johnson's words, the working people eventually "equate [their] social identity with [their] political interests."[2] This equation turns the neighborhood into an echo chamber of the alliance between the Islamists and the social class Fazıl personifies, the faubourgeoisie. The narrative of the alliance absolves this local elite and its favorite political cadre of responsibility for hardships the working people experience in these echo chambers. Persistent intergenerational poverty, thirteen-hour workdays, and unemployment are the fault of foreign powers or the secularists. Because those theories split opinions from the facts, the working people, like those under a totalitarian regime, are expected to give up their political opinions and adopt new and starkly contradictory ones whenever the Islamist political cadre changes its mind. The relationship between the proletariat and the faubourgeois-Islamist alliance is rooted in the domination of the proletariat by the alliance, not in a common past or clientelist transactions.

THE SWEATSHOPS

The first time I suspected that domination could be the right concept for describing the relationship between the proletariat and the faubourgeois-Islamist alliance was during my 2007 pilot project for the yearlong participant observation I planned to conduct in 2008 at manufacturing sweatshops owned by the local elite. At that point, my main goal was to observe differences in labor practices between smaller and larger manufacturing facilities operating in the same supply chain. In theory, finding such enterprises should not have been difficult. There were literally thousands of them in Istanbul. However, it was not easy to get access to these sweatshops. In the pilot study, I conducted 107 interviews with owners of such establishments, and none of them accepted my request to work and conduct research, with one exception: what I call Center Factory, a relatively large garment plant employing roughly 250 workers.

The invitation looked to me like a golden ticket to a large pool of sweatshops. Center Factory sat atop a complex local supply chain composed of over four dozen smaller sweatshops employing over three thousand workers. I assumed it would be easy to work in a sweatshop affiliated with this larger facility. This proved not to be the case. The owner of Center Factory decided to invest in Ethiopia to cut costs and reduce his footprint in Turkey. Furious with this decision, its subsidiaries turned down my request, one after another, even though management had warmly recommended me.

After this failure, I began working undercover at a medium-sized garment facility that had no long-term relationship with the Center Factory or other major garment factories in the district and revealed my identity a few weeks later. It was not until the final stages of my observations at this facility, which I refer to as Independent Sweatshop, that I received permission to work at one of Center Factory's subsidiaries, which I call Follower Sweatshop, thanks to a referral from a coworker at Center Factory. I later worked in a fourth and much smaller facility employing fewer than ten workers, which I call Family Sweatshop, thanks to another recommendation from a coworker friend, a socialist activist, at Independent Sweatshop.

This struggle to gain access to these workplaces both before and during my research told me that small industrialists were trying to keep the eyes of outsiders like me out of their neighborhoods and workplaces, even though their facilities could use my unpaid labor. They would not have had this concern if they had shared a religious-fraternal relationship with their workers or provided them satisfactory material conditions and wages.

My yearlong experience as an unskilled worker at four garment plants employing between ten and 250 workers only verified my initial suspicion during the pilot project. From the smallest, the Family Sweatshop, to the largest, Center Factory, each workplace enabled the local elite, who allied with the Islamist movement, to dominate their workers in a complex ensemble of social relations that framed not only workplace dynamics but also the norms of the neighborhood and their workers' perspective about their neighborhood and community. My observations at one plant after another let me see that three dynamics lie at the center of the relationship of workers to the faubourgeois-Islamist alliance. These dynamics constitute three interrelated regimes of domination: *the labor regime* about work and employment conditions, *the gaze regime* about community relations, and *the hygiene regime* about the ontological perspectives of the proletariat.

Family Sweatshop

My observations at Family Sweatshop, a small facility employing eight family members, were the most useful in enabling me to see the impact of the labor regime, which is about the relationship of the workers to the Islamist-faubourgeois alliance on the shop floor and in the local labor market. This sweatshop's struggle to survive in a chaotic market environment and its later success illustrated how the class position of small industrialists often trumped other aspects of their identity when it came to their relationship with their workers. When I met the owner, whom I am calling Mr. Survivor, he was planning to open a sweatshop with a partner. I was introduced to him by Cahit, one of my coworkers at Independent Sweatshop. He expressed interest in my project, especially when I told him that although I would be doing research, I wanted to work as a simple laborer. He could use an extra hand, he told me, at least for a few weeks.

Mr. Survivor was Kurdish. In 1996, he and his family moved from Diyarbakır, the unofficial capital of Turkish Kurdistan, to Istanbul after the Turkish military forcibly evacuated his village in order to prevent, they claimed, logistical support of fighters in the Kurdistan Workers' Party (PKK), a common practice in the 1990s. Like his partner, who came from Diyarbakır in 1998 under similar conditions, he was an internally displaced person. At the age of seventeen, Mr. Survivor began working in sweatshops in Istanbul and soon became a foreman. He gained enough confidence to open one of his own in 2003. It was a failure, as was another in 2006, and he returned to work in the last sweatshop that had employed him. Now, in 2008, I was witnessing Mr. Survivor's third attempt.

Two partners rented a five-hundred-square-foot store front on the first floor of an apartment building for about $300 per month. They purchased used sewing machines and convinced their sisters and wives to work for them for a pittance. For an office, the partners curtained off thirty square feet on the shop floor of their modest operation and set up the sewing machines in the remaining space. There was no kitchen.

All eight family members, including the partners, operated sewing machines. One of them also acted as foreman, a job that entailed organizing and training family members as workers, four of whom had no experience at all. The partners had neither applied for a permit nor registered their business, having decided they would do the tedious paperwork only after they completed their first order—if they had a first order. Which they did.

Initially, the partners worried the pace was too slow. After they failed numerous times to set up a functioning assembly line, they realized there were too few of them to assign each worker a specific task, as they had been doing. As they debated the problem during a tea break, one of the partners suggested they try what he had seen at another sweatshop. Instead of assigning different tasks to each of the eight of them, they should assign everyone the same task and then move to the next one. This was precisely the strategy that Stephen Marglin described as an ingenious alternative to what Adam Smith had famously recommended in his imaginary pin factory.[3] To Marglin, the Smithian assembly line was more an instrument of domination than a technological innovation that boosts the dexterity of the workers. Confirming his prediction, the plan proved a great success and the partners delivered their first order on time.

The new system worked better than the traditional assembly line because it saved time and lowered transaction costs by not having the workers move parts from one to the other. In a sweatshop consisting exclusively of family members, who had an incentive to work as fast as they could—they were all in this together—the partners of Family Sweatshop did not have to use a traditional assembly line to pressure laborers to keep things moving. Family solidarity gave this microscopic enterprise a chance in a business environment where only the cruelest employer won the game.

The mastermind of the strategy, Mr. Survivor, had a complex personality. He was an ardent supporter of the PKK—which is on the terror list of many countries, including Turkey and the United States—and a staunch supporter of its leader, Abdullah Öcalan: "If Apo [Öcalan] said this white wall is black, I would see it as black." Deeply engaged politically, he was curious about my views on Kurdish and national politics, which I shared with him. Although the PKK was widely considered leftist, Mr. Survivor's beliefs were deeply imbued with Sunni Islamic values.

One Friday, the men in the sweatshop, including myself, attended an illegal mosque for prayers. Located on the first floor of a residential building, the mosque, which occupied about three thousand square feet, had all the necessary ceremonial accoutrements: rugs on the floor, a *mihrab* indicating the direction of Mecca, and a pulpit. It also had public toilets. But it was not registered with the Directorate of Religious Affairs, to prevent the authorities from choosing the imam, who would probably be Turkish. The imam of this underground mosque preached in Kurdish, which, in the eyes of the authorities, was an even more serious offense than the fact that the mosque was not registered. The mosque offered a safe haven from the racism of everyday life, a sacred space where Sunni Kurdish men felt part of their ethnoreligious community. In their mosque, they could pray with people like themselves and ignore the political or class differences among them.

However, this sense of peace, serenity, and ethnic solidarity did not extend beyond the walls of the mosque. Mr. Survivor had launched his business with the assumption that one of his acquaintances would provide them enough orders to keep their sweatshop running. The two men had met a few years earlier, when Mr. Survivor was working as the foreman at another sweatshop. Not only was this middleman not Kurdish, their relationship was purely transactional. This acquaintance expected to earn a hefty commission for the orders he provided for Family Sweatshop. These expectations were not being met on either side—both the orders and the commissions were too small.

During summer 2009, about a year after I worked for Mr. Survivor, I visited him to see how things were going. Over the course of that year, Mr. Survivor had moved his sweatshop to a larger site in the same area. He now employed about twenty workers and his company was working for clients selling to foreign markets. The contracts he received paid better than those from the previous year. Given the growing volume of business, he could no longer rely on his relatives because, as he explained, "We have grown so much that we can no longer manage alone. We need to employ strangers whom we can scold when they are not performing well enough. You can't shout at members of your own family."

As Harry Braverman has discussed, the "deskilling process" assigns the conception part of the capitalist labor process to management and the execution part to workers. This separation weakens the position of workers, who lose their ability to see their productive role in the overall labor process.[4] A Smithian assembly line had to replace Marglinian teamwork if Mr. Survivor was to survive the market conditions. He saw himself as a victim of Michael Burawoy's market despotism[5] and blamed mystical global forces for low wages and tough work conditions. He felt he did not need to work with the family anymore, because he knew that Kurdish workers tired of discrimination in the labor force[6] would keep knocking on his door for a job.

Soon, like thousands of others in his and other, similar neighborhoods, he joined the faubourgeois-Islamist alliance. The bait that trapped him was his aspiration to grow rich enough to overcome the hardships he had experienced after his family was forced to leave Diyarbakır and move to Istanbul. He pushed himself to work harder and harder in hopes of turning a haunting nightmare into a dream come true. In the meantime, he would become a cog of local labor relations, perpetuating the suboptimal working and living conditions of his workers and many others.

Follower Sweatshop

If an entrepreneur like Mr. Survivor does well for a decade, his business might become a medium-sized enterprise, employing dozens or even a few hundred people. If that happens, perks like a fancy car, a summer house, and perhaps even a mistress would be within his reach. More importantly, the entrepreneur would enjoy high respect from his neighbors and relatives. Now a member of the local elite, he would feel a duty to enforce the social norms of the community.

Mr. Follower was one of those successful businesspeople. Until recently, his main customer had been Center Factory, yet he let me work at his sweatshop (unlike the other subsidiaries of Center Factory) because I was introduced to him by Deniz, one of my coworkers at Center. Like the owner of Center Factory, Mr. Follower had immigrated to Istanbul from Iğdır, a small, impoverished town on the Armenian border. After working in various sweatshops for a few years, he, like Mr. Survivor, borrowed a few thousand dollars from relatives and opened a sweatshop in a seven-hundred-square-foot store in 1988 in Halkalı, one of the neighborhoods where I had spent two months for my 2008 research project. Together with other members of his family, he bought nine sewing machines to launch the new enterprise. By 1993, Mr. Follower and his partner had moved to a new, larger space measuring 2,200 square feet, which had room for twenty sewing machines. By 1995, they had moved again and were renting five thousand square feet in the nearby neighborhood of İkitelli, where they had room for forty sewing machines. His growth was closely tied to the growth of Center Factory, and the growth of Center in turn depended on his capacity to make his employees work for longer hours and lower wages than Center.

My observations at Follower Sweatshop convinced me that relations between these sweatshop owners and their workers are framed not only on the shop floor and in the local labor market but also in the neighborhood through social pressure, what I call the gaze regime. Mr. Follower had vast knowledge about the local community: who was who and who did what. Given the suboptimal wages and work conditions, labor force volatility was high in these sweatshops. Thus, he had to be an active member of his community and engage with workers like Deniz if he wanted to have access to a pool of workers large enough to let him have the upper hand over his current and prospective workers. This practical concern put him at the center of a gaze regime that fostered three interconnected practices.

First, as in Michel Foucault's treatment of Jeremy Bentham's panopticon,[7] the disciplinary function of the gaze is embedded in the physicality of urban spaces[8] and is reproduced by actors to produce the often violently sexualized other in their social landscape.[9] His involvement in the social life of his workers was an asset.

Second, rather than being a unidirectional exercise of power, gaze has a reciprocal character.[10] The panopticon metaphor obscures the dialectical nature of the gaze as a relationship.[11] Observations visualized with the panopticon metaphor are accurate but incomplete. Despite being in a weak position, workers, women, and members of ethnic and religious minorities contribute to the making of the gaze regime as well.

Third, the actions and reactions of actors in different layers of local power hierarchies make the gaze regime a formative process that shapes the identities of these actors. In Maurice Merleau-Ponty's lexicon, this is referred to as "intercorporeal"[12] or "carnal intersubjectivity."[13] Merleau-Ponty rejected Cartesian body-mind dualism, which regards behavior "as an external representation of an internal state." This process cannot be based on the assumption that the other can be reduced to the actor's thought of the other. Thus, Merleau-Ponty's intercorporeal subjectivity makes the gaze a formative experience for those gazed upon.[14] Agency does not depend on the contingencies of context for social interactions. Agency has an agenda that is shaped by this carnal intersubjectivity. Reaction to the gaze cannot be reduced to a pragmatic response to the scopophobic effect of an independent mind that resists domination with stable subjectivity. In simpler terms, the gaze regime entails a distinct socialization process that demarcates deviance and conformity for community members.

Independent Sweatshop

The growth prospects of individual entrepreneurs are closely related to their success in presenting the gaze practices and the labor process as pillars of the moral values of the community and identifying themselves as the moral guardians of the community. The owner of Independent Sweatshop, Mr. Independent, was not an exemplary entrepreneur in this regard. He had owned his business since the flourishing 1990s. In the 1980s, at the age of only twenty-two, he was a foreman in a small sweatshop. In 1991, he opened his own sweatshop, initially with ten sewing machines. By the mid-1990s, he owned a factory employing 180 workers with an annual turnover of $1.5 million.

His business grew faster than Mr. Follower's during those years, so he was about to move up to a higher business league. He had an aggressive growth mindset. All he needed was a little bit of luck and good decisions about his loan portfolio. However, by 2008, when I worked on the assembly line in his company, Mr. Independent employed only about seventy people and had annual turnover of $700,000.

Unlike Mr. Follower, Mr. Independent enjoyed talking about politics, maybe because of his business's decline. He blamed the downturn of his business on the AKP's monetary policy in the first decade of the 2000s: "The monetary policy has ruined us. . . . This new system has led to the exploitation of my workers by foreign powers [*dış güçler*]." The policy he referred to was the International Monetary Fund–backed strong Turkish lira strategy, which the Islamists inherited from the secularist coalition government after the 2001 crisis and continued to implement well until the 2010s because growing global demand allowed currency appreciation without significantly compromising phenomenal export growth.

It surprised me that Mr. Independent did not seem to care that I had started to work at his sweatshop as an undercover agent. Later, I realized that our conversations about monetary policy and many other political subjects were not just talk, but were his way to make me part of his parallel struggle in the Istanbul Textile and Apparel Exporters Association (ITKIB). His candidate in ITKIB elections, Abdi Köse, wanted to turn the association into a political platform representing the interests of small industrialists against bigger ones.

At his request, I took part in Köse's propaganda meetings as Mr. Independent's aide. While carrying mocktails to the friends of Mr. Independent in large hotel halls, I eavesdropped on their conversations about the administration's Turquality project, which provided subsidies for bigger exporting companies but left theirs no support. Köse's supporters frequently interrupted his speeches with slogans, gave their own intense short speeches, and even read poems they wrote for him. Having a PhD in textile engineering and owning a medium-sized textile and garment facility in Istanbul, Köse was the perfect candidate to represent thousands of entrepreneurs against the bigger players in Istanbul's chaotic textile and garment industries. The result was less than satisfactory. Köse received no more votes than the number of participants at his meetings. Another candidate, who was not an Islamist but was on good terms with the government at that time, won the election. The small industrialists I talked to on election day had a reason not to support Köse: to them, entrepreneurs who complained about the Islamist government were avoiding responsibility for the business decisions they made. They needed to find a leader to negotiate with the government, not to fight it.

Center Factory

Mr. Independent tried to substitute his business association politics for the connection Mr. Self-Made Man had with his workers. Mr. Self-Made Man was one of the rare success stories in Bağcılar. Working in his favor was the fact that he came to Istanbul a decade earlier than the other three entrepreneurs discussed in this chapter. Still, he started his business, which I call Center Factory, in 1986 with only five sewing machines in a sweatshop in Zeytinburnu, a district that had been in the center of the Istanbul garment sector well into the 1980s. He established a good reputation as a hardworking entrepreneur. In 1988, Mr. Self-Made Man met his future partner, who spoke German fluently and developed business connections in Germany. When they agreed to collaborate, Mr. Self-Made Man took full responsibility for the business side of things in Istanbul, and his partner established contacts in Germany.

In 1991, Mr. Self-Made Man and his partner moved the business five miles from Zeytinburnu to Bağcılar, the preferred district of rural migrants from his hometown, Iğdır. About a quarter of the workers were immigrants from Mr. Self-Made Man's hometown, and 12 percent of them lived in the nearby neighborhood where Mr. Self-Made Man's father and brother lived. Mr. Self-Made Man encouraged his fellow countrymen [hemşehris] to open their own sweatshops and become part of his local supply chain. This strategy gave Mr. Self-Made Man access to reliable labor, a privilege many sweatshop owners did not have, and helped his German-speaking partner find long-term customers in Germany.

As Center Factory became the hub of a large network of supplier sweatshops—like the one Mr. Follower owned—the volume of orders from Germany grew. By 2005, Center employed four hundred workers, and its subsidiaries in and around Bağcılar employed over three thousand. Those working in subsidiary sweatshops earned wages 10–20 percent below what laborers were paid at Center, and they rarely received benefits.

Given the depressed salaries paid by Center Factory's satellite sweatshops, the model of expanding the number of satellites proved highly cost effective. Soon, the company became one of the largest clothing manufacturers in the country. With an annual export volume of $50 million, the factory was one of the five hundred largest industrial companies in Turkey for four consecutive years between 2001 and 2004, according to the Istanbul Chamber of Industry.

What distinguished Mr. Self-Made Man from Mr. Independent was the former's capacity to find himself a position in the local politics of the neighborhood as the guardian of a moral order discursively constructed by the religious orders, which is what I call the hygiene regime. The main motif, which entrepreneurs like him borrowed from those Muslim religious orders, was something I initially overlooked during my 2008 research: my coworkers repeatedly referred to the concept of pollution in different contexts. I gradually became aware of a pattern that points to the old binary of sacred and profane.[15] As mentioned in the previous chapter, the scholar who turned this age-old trope into a useful tool for my observations is Mary Douglas, who came up with the well-known formula of dirt as "matter out of place."[16] According to this, pollution and the fear of it refer to the positions or places of individuals in relation to others. Boosting the toxiphobia emerging from this notion of dirt, local industrialists defined the symbolic boundaries of their community and, therefore, their respectable position in that community. Because they saw it as an instrument to help them endure the drudgery and the gaze, workers would be immersed in the narrative, which ultimately represented the self-image of the faubourgeoisie.

Encouraged by Center Factory's success, Mr. Self-Made Man overlooked the significance of this factor and made a bold move around 2005. He wanted to repeat what he achieved in Bağcılar in a distant part of the world, only at a larger scale. At about the same time that I started working there, management began downsizing the plant in Bağcılar and moving production to Addis Ababa, Ethiopia. The new factory in Addis Ababa (see figure 14) had the capacity to hire ten thousand workers. Center Factory had invested $100 million in this facility, making it the largest textile operation in East Africa and one of the largest industrial plants in Ethiopia. According to the company's predictions, by 2013 the plant was expected to account for more than 60 percent of Ethiopia's textile and clothing exports.[17] Earning about thirty dollars per month, or 10 percent of the minimum wage in Turkey, the laborers wove high-quality Ethiopian cotton into cloth, destined for making garments for the German market.

FIGURE 14. Shop floor in Center Factory's facility in Addis Ababa. Photograph by Utku Balaban, May 31, 2010.

During a two-week pilot study in Addis Ababa in 2010, I realized that Center Factory's Addis Ababa campus was not the only Turkish investment in that city. Turkey was at the time the largest investor in terms of the number of foreign companies in Ethiopia and the second largest, after China, in terms of volume of capital investment. As I learned my way around the city, I found the main expat hangout at the Sheraton Hotel. With an unmistakable colonial feel, its large, lavish lobby was filled with entrepreneurs from all over the world: representatives of European agribusiness companies looking for land to acquire, Chinese entrepreneurs looking for ways to sell their countrymen's products, and of course Turkish entrepreneurs who owned and ran companies of all sizes. In this broader picture, Mr. Self-Made Man looked like an agent of what I call "the second tier of globalization." He was in the process of incorporating relatively untouched regions of global capitalism into the economies of the non–North Atlantic world as an agent of monopoly capital.

My initial impressions in Addis Ababa persuaded me that Mr. Self-Made Man was on his way to becoming a new member of the transnational bourgeoisie, yet that did not happen. In 2018, Mr. Self-Made Man's factory in Addis Ababa filed for bankruptcy.[18] Lack of proper infrastructure was one reason for the failure. For instance, transportation of finished products was routinely delayed because the railway the Chinese were building from Addis Ababa to Djibouti was not yet fully operational in 2010. However, the core issue was the human factor. According to a brief survey I conducted at the facility, only 5 percent of the employees had worked in a textile factory before. The workers I talked to were unexceptionally unhappy with the long work hours, even though they were much shorter than those of their Turkish counterparts. The Turkish administration had a limited understanding of the social dynamics among workers of Oromo, Amhara, and Tigray origin. Mr. Self-Made Man had a workforce that had not been fully proletarianized. Unlike in Bağcılar, he did not have a special connection to his Ethiopian workers to facilitate the proletarianization process.

In fact, this factory was just a bloated subsidiary of European retailers. Mr. Self-Made Man was merely an actor on a much wider stage who was given the role of testing the feasibility of proletarianizing the urban workforce in Addis Ababa on behalf of his European partners. As the role model for much smaller entrepreneurs like Mr. Survivor and an object of envy for others like Mr. Independent, multimillionaires like Mr. Self-Made Man may employ, directly or indirectly, hundreds or even thousands of workers in complex local supply chains. However, the source of the fortune of these nonmonopoly entrepreneurs is not their small capital but their exclusive relationship with the workers of their home country, hometown, ethnicity, or religion. They are only buyers of money and technology, not sellers. They are not "too big to fail."

THE NEIGHBORHOODS

The Iğdır Neighborhood

A factor in Mr. Self-Made Man's success in Turkey was his privileged access to a sizable pocket within the vast labor pool in Bağcılar and its neighboring districts. Roughly half a mile away from Center Factory, this pocket of about half a square mile was called the Iğdır neighborhood because most of its thirty thousand residents were migrants from Iğdır, a city on the Armenian border, who followed the Shia-Jaferi faith and spoke the Azeri dialect of Turkish.

I lived in this neighborhood for about two months during my fieldwork. My observations there informed my experiences at Center Factory and illuminated the role of the local elite. This neighborhood came close to what one might call an ethnoreligious ghetto. Most Iğdır migrants had moved to the neighborhood in the mid-1980s, when much of the building stock was still simple single-story houses. The new community set up informal credit mechanisms that enabled the relatively affluent to build apartment buildings and a mosque for the Shia-Jaferi faithful. Migrants from various Iğdır villages founded associations. The community was organized around a complex network or federation of village associations that marked kinship status at different levels. These associations operated under the spiritual leadership of the mosque community.

The formation of this network was coupled with the ideological transformation of the inchoate community. In the 1980s, the Iğdır community was home to many socialists who had immigrated to the city in earlier decades and moved to the growing neighborhood from older working-class areas of Istanbul. In the early 1990s, the mosque community pushed these activists out of the neighborhood. Young coworkers from the neighborhood told me about the "cleansing" of the neighborhood to eliminate the "terrorist" activities of "some alcoholics" by leaders of the community who had "high moral values" (*maneviyatı yüksek büyüklerimiz*).

On my first visit to the neighborhood, I wanted to meet one of my closest friends from Center Factory, Ahmet, and enjoy a sunny Sunday away from the dust and stress of the shop floor. As I walked from the bus stop, I noticed that the street was closed to traffic and a large group of people had gathered. Before I could figure out what they were doing on the street, the sonic shock of a strong beat in the air reached my ears. The beat was impressive but its source was unclear. Then I saw a black mass in the middle of the crowd, moving slowly on the street. I later discovered that this group of young men dressed in black was commemorating and mourning the Holy Twelve Imams. The source of the rhythmic beat, which I could hear from almost a hundred yards away, was the pounding of these young men's fists on their chests. The entire street was decorated with black flags. Another reason the scene was impressive was that the spectators were in complete silence. Apart from the symbolic power of the ritual, this silence, a rarity in any working-class neighborhood in Istanbul, was extraordinary.

As chairman of his village association, the father of Mr. Self-Made Man was a leading patron of such religious activities. For example, Shiite believers celebrate Newroz, the spring festival. Although Center Factory management did not give its workers the day off for this important event, my Jaferi friends and I decided to attend. During our lunch break, we hurried to the two-acre field in the neighborhood to catch part of the festivities. When we arrived, my friends told me with great pride that the speaker was the father of the factory owner.

As the head of the preparatory committee, he opened the ceremony. The Islamist mayor followed, emphasizing brotherhood between Sunnis and Shiites in his speech. Among the speakers on the podium, another person caught my eye. I remembered seeing him a few weeks earlier in the neighborhood barbershop when I stopped to get a shave and make a few observations around the store. Everyone in the shop paid their respects, and the man and the barber were obviously displeased with my presence.

At that moment, I had been unaware that I had run into the religious leader of the neighborhood community, Selahattin Özgündüz. He lived in the neighborhood. The main entrance gate of his building, located next to the mosque, was decorated with reliefs of flowers and geometric shapes in gold-colored brass to signal its occupant's high status. Many Iğdır migrants saw him as the leader of the Jaferi community in the country. My Jaferi friends at Center Factor rarely went to the mosque, yet they undoubtedly accepted Özgündüz's moral authority. Even though he did not speak, his aura radiated from over fifty yards away.

Despite his considerable wealth, Mr. Self-Made Man's father chose to live in this poor neighborhood. As we passed his building on another Sunday, my coworker friends not only let me know he lived there but also told me he kept all the other units in the building empty. This show of wealth amazed them, though I would not have known this detail had they not shared it with me: unlike Özgündüz's house, the building was so unassuming that it easily blended into the concrete jungle around it.

There was not a single liquor store in this neighborhood, eyes were everywhere, and outsiders were under close scrutiny. This was a very conservative and exceptionally homogeneous community in terms of the ethnic and religious background of its inhabitants. Still, even though I lived there only a short time, I was able to get to know quite a few people, many of whom were very welcoming. This rapid socialization process was the result of my worker friends' introductions to the community in my absence. People were curious about me because my friends knew I was a researcher. Nonetheless, it was a challenge to find an apartment, despite all the positive recommendations from my worker friends, because I was a single man and therefore a potential threat to the honor of the neighborhood. Thus, the extremely damp basement I rented—not only from the owner but also from the cockroaches that enjoyed their daily morning walk on my chest—was a blessing, even if I had to pay twice as much as he would have charged a family desperate to live in this suboptimal place.

The close relationships between the Center Factory owners and the community went beyond religious and regional events. As the largest employer in the neighborhood, the owners were willing to give anyone from the community a chance to work in their facilities. Their eagerness to recruit their compatriots, I believe, was closely related to a one-day wildcat strike in 2003 that resulted in the firing of about sixty workers. The strike was initiated by the owners' compatriots who came to the city before the 1980s; those who had come to Istanbul more recently sided with management. In return, these loyal workers received employment in the factory for themselves and their families.

Despite his concerted effort to maintain close relations with the neighborhood, the owner would not recruit his entire workforce from fellow countrymen because he knew they could use their ethnic, regional, and religious connections to organize against their employers. After all, the 2003 wildcat strike was initiated by their compatriots. However, as a minority in the factory, these workers could serve as a tool for the employer's overall strategy to divide and rule the workers.

In other words, the sociocultural order of the city unequally distributes rewards for small and medium entrepreneurs in labor-intensive industries. Through an alliance with the religious leader, Mr. Self-Made Man was able to turn the Jaferi community into a reliable labor pool for his factory. As he built an elaborate local network of subsidiary sweatshops using that labor pool, he was able to dramatically expand the scale of his production with docile labor and minimal worker turnover and resistance. Mr. Self-Made Man took this for granted when he made a nine-figure investment in Ethiopia.

The 2004 Mukhtar Election in Yenimahalle

Most working-class neighborhoods in Bağcılar and its surrounding districts were more ethnically, regionally, and religiously heterogeneous than the Iğdır neighborhood. There, the footprint of the local elite on local politics was subtler. Thus, the stories I was told by my socialist-activist friends in one of those neighborhoods, Yenimahalle, about the 2004 local election drew my attention as a case that describes that effect.

I moved to Yenimahalle in the third phase of my fieldwork, when I started working at Independent Sweatshop. I had relatively close ties to Yenimahalle. Some of my relatives lived there, and during my student days from the late 1990s to the early years of the 2000s, I was involved in the grassroots of a socialist political movement that had a base in this neighborhood. The place, known as Solidarity House (Dayanışma Evi), functioned as the local branch of the Socialist Solidarity Platform (SODAP).[19] Another socialist branch was allegedly affiliated with the illegal Revolutionary People's Liberation Party/ Front (DHKP-C). As a student, I visited Solidarity House to tutor high school students for their national college entrance exams. Some of these young people came from conservative families and grew up with conservative values. Most of our young female participants wore a hijab except in school.[20] I had good access to a wide variety of interlocutors.

In 2004, the position of neighborhood head (*mukhtar*) had been contested in an election. Mukhtars collect and manage neighborhood residents' basic data and help the authorities with local social welfare actions.[21] This key political position connected urban communities with government authorities. The race was between the incumbent mukhtar and two challengers representing two regional groups that together made up about 9 percent of the neighborhood population. The contest became politicized after the two socialist groups offered support to each challenger. The socialists had certain conditions for their support. For example, mukhtars charged residents roughly two dollars for the official documents they issued. Yenimahalle had a population of about twenty-nine thousand in 2006, so this service brought in considerable revenue. Both socialist-backed candidates promised to put this revenue into a neighborhood fund to finance community-based services and help the poor. They also promised to establish a neighborhood assembly that would make collective decisions about the community. This town meeting would directly intervene in the neighborhood's social problems, such as crime and drug use.

SODAP and alleged DHKP-C supporters ran an active and systematic campaign. They reached almost every household and made contact with most of the residents. Nevertheless, the incumbent mukhtar received fifty-eight hundred votes, and the two candidates supported by the socialist groups together received about forty-nine hundred votes.

Although the split between the socialist factions did not help either of them, another reason for their defeat was the support the mukhtar received from the local elite. The mukhtar was a major donor to the neighborhood mosque and a regular in the community of mostly elderly mosque-goers who often gathered in its courtyard. Most members of the mosque community supported the incumbent mukhtar unconditionally. His two socialist-backed opponents courted support from their compatriots in the neighborhood.

Thanks to the mukhtar's mediation, I was able to attend these courtyard meetings four times. The number of participants varied between one and two dozen people. In addition to exchanges about the history of the neighborhood, their lively conversations about daily happenings provided me interesting insights into their view of politics. Most members of the group were apartment building owners and fathers of sweatshop owners. The topics of the day focused on criminal and morally unacceptable incidents such as burglaries and female debauchery, the business success and failure of their mostly wealthy acquaintances in the neighborhood, and their personal health situations.

Another frequent topic of conversation was the current state of their businesses or those of their sons. Those whose sons owned sweatshops in or near their neighborhoods shared with the others up-to-date information about the availability of workers and the regularity and deadlines of their businesses' orders. Most in this group owned several apartments, so rental income was important. At one meeting, group members had an intense discussion about what percentage of rent increase would be fair for their tenants. I felt I was sitting in a secret trust meeting where the base rent for a neighborhood of twenty-nine thousand residents was being determined.

A third major topic was politics. Tensions between the AKP and the secularist opposition Republican People's Party (RPP) usually headlined the daily conversations, with strong support for the AKP. Bashing of the RPP was followed by praise of AKP policies that had saved them from oppression by the infidel RPP. With a certain wariness of the threats and challenges ahead, the mosque community was generally optimistic about the future.

This optimism was not unfounded. Just before the 2008 crisis began to show its effects on the domestic economy, export volumes had grown phenomenally over the past five years. The AKP government had issued three amnesties for unregistered additions to their residential buildings, effectively increasing the value of their residential buildings by 20–35 percent. As discussed in the previous chapter, the AKP also developed a universal health care program that allowed their sons to avoid paying benefits as their workers gained access to health care through this program.

The mosque frequenters I spoke to in 2008 still had strong opinions about the 2004 race:

UB: What do you think of the candidates running against our mukhtar in the 2004 election?

MEHMET (one of the men in the courtyard, over sixty years old): They were terrorists. If one of them had become mukhtar, we would have lost our neighborhood honor [*mahallenin namusu*], and promiscuity would have prevailed.

UB: Did any of your relatives or acquaintances vote for them?

MEHMET: How should I know? Of course I told everyone to vote for our mukhtar. I made my family members take an oath not to vote for the other two. We let people know what kind of people they are.

Two competing electoral strategies had been at work. The socialists ran a grassroots campaign with great energy and good promises, and the mosque community reached out via word of mouth, propagandizing that the candidates supported by the socialists would bring vice and debauchery to the neighborhood. The mosque community had the moral high ground.

The competition was not fair. The mukhtar had government-funded tools at his disposal. For example, the Islamist government gave him considerable power to guide social workers as they selected some of the families among the poorest 10–15 percent of the neighborhood for welfare. A complex social network of the mukhtar's local allies reminded them of the potential consequences of their political decisions, and some of them must have changed their minds. Furthermore, the socialists had only two branches in a large neighborhood. The mosque community and its allies had numerous businesses, sweatshops, and apartments. As economically prominent members of their communities, the mukhtar's supporters could participate in the social and cultural life of the workers and stage political discussions in public spaces like the district's 477 male-only coffeehouses, roughly one every five streets.[22]

Members of this local elite were also active in the associations founded by migrants from the same hometown or village. As the funders of these associations, they had say over their activities. This was the case in the association of my home village in Bağcılar, which my father had established in 1998 after the 1980 coup failed to kill his interest in civic life. The association became a success in the later decade, and other relatively well-to-do fellow villagers took part in the administration, donated money, and gradually added religious elements to the activities. For example, they insisted that meetings start with prayers. The activities were not visibly political, yet these new religious motifs showed who was welcome in the community and who was not.

The biography of the mukhtar explains how he gained the support of this local political network. He had immigrated to Istanbul in 1958 at the age of sixteen to work in a textile factory near Zeytinburnu, one of the first and most important squatter settlements in Istanbul. This district was the center of Istanbul's garment industry before the 1980s and remains an important location for clothing sweatshops. For several years, he worked in this and other factories in the region, occasionally returning to his hometown, Sivas in central Anatolia, to work in construction. In 1972, he migrated to Germany as a guest worker at a factory in Stuttgart. This was within the framework of the special agreement between Turkey and Germany, which led to a growing number of Turkish migrants in Germany. The Islamist movement was particularly strong among guest workers in Germany, and this was when he first came into contact with the Islamists. He returned to Turkey in 1978 after he had saved a considerable sum of money.

In our long conversations, he emphasized several times that he had returned because he did not want to raise his children in a non-Muslim society. I was convinced he was sincere in this concern, but his decision was also linked to promising economic prospects in Istanbul. Upon his return, he settled in Bağcılar, then just slightly bigger than a village outside the city limits. He used his savings to acquire some cheap plots from local farmers and sold the land at a high profit margin to subsequent immigrants. Together, they turned this village into a new town. By 2008, he had been the mukhtar of the neighborhood for a quarter century.

The story of his first election to this office provides valuable insight into the foundations of local politics. In 1983, migrants from Erzincan and Kars in Yenimahalle had not been satisfied with the mukhtar. Bağcılar was not its own municipality then, and mukhtars had the power to draw legally binding boundaries between individual lots and determine the location of streets and avenues. Often, they served as de facto city planners and designed the street network. Everyone with savings was eager to enclose the land and build multistory homes, and a development-friendly mukhtar could give the rural-to-urban migrants and local speculators a head start over others.

The decision of which street in the grid would become the main artery of a block or neighborhood could significantly increase or decrease the value of properties.

The migrants from Erzincan and Kars were determined to take the lead in this race. It was in their best interest to act together, but each group wanted a compatriot to become the next mukhtar. Although or perhaps because he was from a different region of the country, the incumbent mukhtar earned the respect and trust of the community as a small construction contractor and land developer. He won five consecutive elections.

In 2004, circumstances were very different. The land rush was over. The Islamists had been in charge of the Bağcılar municipality since 1994 and had established a rigid pro-Sunni political milieu. Most of the Erzincan residents in Yenimahalle were Kurdish-Zaza and Alevi. In other words, they were neither Turkish nor Sunni, so they were not satisfied with the pro-Turkish-Sunni sociopolitical transformation of their neighborhood. Kars, my family's hometown, had been a stronghold of leftist politics until the 1980s, and a significant minority of Kars migrants had sympathy for socialist movements.

It was an epic coincidence. A quarter of a century later, the mukhtar again faced a challenge from these two regional groups, now working with two different socialist factions. They had needed someone to bring them together in the past; when they parted ways with the mukhtar, the support of the socialists was not enough for them to act together.

The mukhtar, for his part, built a new coalition based on class rather than the migrants' regional or ethnic origin. His business profile made him the perfect candidate for slumlords, construction contractors, and small industrialists. Because he had succeeded in maintaining an equal distance from the various regional groups, he could act as a neutral actor in local politics. His Sunni conservatism served as a political canopy under which those regional groups of Sunnis could come together. This network was realized in the courtyard of the neighborhood mosque, the all-seeing eye of the neighborhood.

From my own experience, I knew that the local elite had done their best to keep young people away from Solidarity House. My friends were often called "terrorists," and my female students complained that their families put immense pressure on them and warned them the community would label them "prostitutes" if they returned to Solidarity House.

Like the clientelist provision of social welfare, systematic police harassment of patrons of local branches of socialist groups helped the local elite's ongoing smear campaign. The harassment let residents know that contact with socialists posed a significant risk to the poor people in our neighborhood. The residents were aware that the Left was unwelcome in the eyes of the local elite and the government authorities.

In 2008, there were only two police stations in Bağcılar, which had a population of over seven hundred thousand. Despite the high population-to-police ratio, the police officers I interviewed at these stations had no major complaints about their workload. Brawls were common, but they were not a police concern unless someone died or was stabbed. Apart from the occasional car theft and some trafficking in illegal narcotics, not much was happening.

In addition to the police stations, Bağcılar had an antiterrorism unit located in its central neighborhood. This had a much larger area than the two police stations, and it was surrounded by twenty-foot-tall barbed-wired walls and protected by a thick steel gate. Half a dozen armored combat and antiriot vehicles were in the parking lot, ready to intervene as needed. Anyone's first impression would be that Bağcılar was ready to explode with riots, looting, and political demonstrations, but the members of the antiterrorist unit I spoke to had a relaxed attitude.

In fact, most working-class districts, including Bağcılar and its neighbors Bahçelievler and Esenler, had lower crime rates than the rest of Istanbul. Nevertheless, according to a 2012 research project, Bağcılar was among the three neighborhoods where residents felt the least safe at home.[23] This discrepancy between facts and the general perception indicated the effectiveness of the gaze regime in working-class communities. The narrative that these communities were a hotbed of crime was factually contestable, but it deterred outsider activists and heightened the residents' fear of crime, or scelerophobia. In fact, the scopophobic urban milieu turned these neighborhoods into sites of mass scelerophobia.

During my conversation with the representative of the antiterrorism unit, I noticed that my interlocutor was standing in front of a map of Bağcılar and its neighbors showing reported incidents and "the most important places" for potential criminal or "terrorist" activities. One of these places was, unsurprisingly, Solidarity House. Law enforcement did not seem as concerned about local criminal activity as they were about our grassroots organization.

What was special about the 2004 election in Yenimahalle was that the mukhtar's challengers, the socialist groups, had a firm place in the social context of their neighborhood. Most other neighborhoods had no trace of socialist activism. In this rare case, however, the efforts of socialist activists over the years had earned them partial recognition from the community, and almost all of them were residents of the neighborhood. Therefore, it was difficult for the local elite to simply discredit the socialists' political campaign as a "colonial intervention" by secularist outsiders. So they played the terrorism card, implicitly threatening workers with possible consequences if they supported the socialists, ranging from blacklisting in sweatshops to persecution by police antiterrorism teams.

TRUST AND PHOBIA

The control wielded over the proletariat by the alliance between local urban elites and Islamists is multifaceted and pervasive in Turkey's working-class neighborhoods. The motives of the elite and the Islamists have been structured in the complex history of business and politics since the 1960s. The Islamist political cadre, the pious businesspeople, and the religious orders led non-Islamist businesspeople to define their class interests with an individualist mindset. Urban development and new industrial connections to the global economy since the 1980s also played a role in how the local elite connected to the working class. Between the workers and their employers, among the businesspeople, and between the elite and the Islamists, the missing element was trust. In the end, the streets, shop floors, and narratives turned out to be sites and media of domination by the elite, the faubourgeoisie, over the workers.

Notwithstanding its unity at the phenomenological level, I fragment this domination in the next chapter into a matrix of three interrelated regimes that help me discuss how working people conceptualize and respond to various manifestations of the domination. Michel Foucault's discussion of technologies of domination was useful for this fragmentation process. His technologies of power, production, and sign systems respectively correspond to the regimes of the gaze, labor, and hygiene in these neighborhoods. In my framework, the element that turns this triad into operational concepts is phobia. In the absence of trust, each regime produces and perpetuates a distinct phobia. The first is *scopophobia*, fear due to being under constant surveillance in public spaces and work environments. The second is *ergophobia*, fear derived from work-related cognitive and physiological depletion, identity-related tensions among workers, and the omnipresent risk of unemployment. The third is *toxiphobia*, fear of symbolic impurity. Composed of identifiable contributions by the political cadre, the business community, and the religious orders—as the tripartite structure of the Islamist movement discussed in chapter 3—to the discursive making of each respective phobia, the Islamist narrative defines measures for individuals coping with these phobias and responding to each of the three regimes of domination.

Foucault also mentioned "the technology of the self" as a fourth and broader epistemological canopy that individuals use to "transform themselves in order to achieve a certain state of happiness, purity, wisdom, perfection, or morality."[24] Within the context of my research, this last component refers to a moral order that emerges as a result of the interactions among the first three technologies. The three regimes of domination construct a moral order that determines the strategies the workers use to define their self in their neighborhood community.

Thus, internalization of the measures prescribed by the Islamist narrative frames the community's self-image. Each regime draws different boundaries between the gazer and the gazed, the employer and the worker, the contaminated and the pure. However, each boundary is permeable because the community is located in a city, in a country, and in a global market. In this respect, the work of Fredrik Barth is useful for linking that self-image of the community to the processes of boundary making.[25] Barth's discussion of ethnicity fleshes out Foucault's "technology of the self."

The proletariat seek symbolic protection from constant surveillance by the local elite of small industrialists, small construction contractors, shopkeepers, and slumlords. Precarious employment, tensions among workers, and the cognitively and physiologically painful experience of work lead to dissonance between the vagaries of the labor market and the routine of the work process. The urban poor embrace the Islamist narrative as an instrument to cope with surveillance and dissonance because the narrative helps them make sense of both and grants them symbolic agency in their community, which they envision as a part of what Barth called "stratified poly-ethnic systems."[26] They are members of a phobic community, which is a part of a broader cosmological polyethnic system. The agency of the worker is defined as a constructive element of that system. Thanks to that agency, they are granted an identity in this system.

Barth's focus on the relation between boundary making and identity formation helps one avoid defining the ethos of the community as an essence, a permanent categorical object such as religious scripture or a mystified cultural code. Any attempt to define such a categorical essence fails to convincingly explain why workers adopt the Islamist narrative, describe the complexity of the changing social interactions at the local level, or document the historical background leading to the hegemony of the local elite and its narrative. Instead of an essence, one should look for a relationship as the ethos. That relationship is between the proletariat and the faubourgeois-Islamist alliance.

Barth's ethnic communities are embedded in a stratified relationship. What makes this relationship sustainable is the conviction of the members of communities at the bottom of the hierarchy that the conditions that determine their position in the hierarchy are the same conditions that define their community. The stratification among communities justifies the domination within individual communities. This model provides a useful vantage point for seeing the relationship between the processes of boundary making between and within communities.

The Islamist narrative as the core of the moral order motivates or urges workers to view their relationship with the faubourgeois-Islamist alliance as the ethos of their communities. The phobic individuals form a community in reference to the nonphobic individuals, who are a threat to the community as pollutants. Then the stratification among communities is no longer defined as a vertical hierarchy, but rather as a horizontal platform of concentric rings from the purest (the pious individual) to the potential pollutant (the community) to the pollutant (outsiders). Stratification, the foundational feature of the ethos of their phobic moral community, must not be dismantled with a revolution but be carefully preserved as the context preserving the purity of the individual.

The three regimes of domination, as the interactional, material, and ontological components of this moral community, are mutually productive. If the social and physical topography of the city had taken a different shape in the 1970s, the current labor and hygiene regimes could not have prevailed for the past four decades in the same way. If Turkey's incorporation of market despotism had not been as dramatic as it was in the 1980s, the political effect of the gaze and hygiene regimes would have been much less dramatic. If the Islamists had failed to recalibrate their narrative in the 1990s, the gaze and labor regimes would have faced stronger collective resistance by workers. Under the actual circumstances, however, voting for the strongest Islamist party becomes an act of promoting moral order, even when it undermines their social and material conditions. Returning to Johnson's formulation, the workers' social identity is equated with their political interests as a result of this association. The next chapter will look into the factors that framed the emic perspectives of my 2008 coworkers in regard to these regimes of domination and, ultimately, the equation between their social identity and political interests.

FIVE

The Proletariat

ONE OF MUSA'S FAVORITE ACTIVITIES during his thirteen-hour shifts in Center Factory was watching his male coworkers go to the toilet. This practice not only let him cope with boredom at his sewing machine, but also allowed him to spot freeloaders who were spending an inordinate amount of time in the restroom. He believed he could pass that information to management to save his job if further layoffs occurred. His ability to predict the timing of his coworkers with great precision was extraordinary. While I was working with him, he would interrupt our conversations to point out a male employee who was about to go to the restroom. He was invariably right: that employee would indeed leave his machine to go to the restroom in the next few minutes.

Musa's cognitive exercise gives insight into each of the three regimes of domination introduced in the previous chapter. He was the eyes of the employer on the shop floor as part of the gaze regime. While his excuse was a need to save his job—and precariousness was an integral component of the labor regime—his other strong motivation was, I believe, to cope with the excruciating boredom that posed a challenge to his mental health. Another objective of the activity was to make observations about his male workers' bathroom routines, to distinguish legitimate acts of self-purification from illegitimate ones. He judged whether the discharge of excrement was an act of purification or a source of moral pollution. Right and wrong were defined on the basis of the purity of the act in the eyes of Musa. The hygiene regime framed his perspective about the gaze and labor regimes.

In this chapter, I discuss the emic perspectives of my coworkers about these regimes I observed during my 2008 fieldwork. In essence a composite phenomenon, these regimes interact in such a way that my coworkers accepted the Islamist narrative as an instrument to define their agency under those relations of domination. Musa became part of the gaze regime to cope with the labor regime, even though the same gaze regime challenged his own personal autonomy. The labor regime motivated him to look for patterns and meaning in the seemingly erratic behaviors of his coworkers. These patterns framed his notion of morality as a form of symbolic purity, and he internalized the gaze, which he now believed served as a pillar of his moral community. Exposed to and producing this matrix, Musa was unsurprisingly a loyal supporter of the Islamists.

THE GAZE REGIME

The Punk

One day when I was discussing my observations with the owner of Follower Sweatshop, a medium-sized garment plant I worked at as an unskilled worker in 2008, he complained about "obnoxious types" (*garip tipler*) in the neighborhood. At that moment, a female worker's T-shirt really bothered him. Although she was wearing a headscarf, the owner feared that her short sleeves could turn the whole shop floor into chaos as male workers competed for her attention.

A few minutes later, he had a small argument with the foreman. The foreman had talked with two men in their early twenties about working conditions at Follower Sweatshop. They needed workers immediately, to finish a job within two weeks, and the conversation was cordial and encouraging. However, Mr. Follower's partner refused to hire these workers because he knew that a male relative of one of the applicants had long hair and wore earrings. This applicant was related to a punk (*zibidi*). Both applicants lost the tender.

Sweatshop owners' close monitoring of their workers' sartorial practices, habits, relationships, and families surprised me time and again throughout my 2008 fieldwork. Their pickiness could hurt their business because they usually worked on contracts with tight deadlines. Gradually, it became clear that they knew a more tolerant view might isolate them from the community of sweatshop owners in their neighborhood who collectively consolidated the moral order of the community. The sweatshop owners' rigid attitude toward their workers' clothing practices was a show of power, as they were (or pretended to be) ready to fire anyone who did not conform to the norms. It was a political stance, reminding their workers of their role as moral guardians of the shop floor and the neighborhood.

The gaze was not limited to sartorial practices. Ethnic tensions were similarly reflected in the workshop. Kurdish employers were no different from their Turkish counterparts in their relationships with Kurdish workers. As discussed in chapter 4, Mr. Survivor, a Kurdish sweatshop owner expelled from his hometown by the military, was not enthusiastic about hiring his compatriots on more favorable terms than those customary in the industry. Similarly, Turkish sweatshop owners adopted a functionalist nationalism to remind their workers of each other's ethnic identity. The presence of Kurdish workers was tolerated, not cherished or overlooked. The employers' attitude was reflected in or accompanied by subtle rifts among Turkish and Kurdish workers. In Independent and Follower Sweatshops, Kurdish and Turkish workers sat at different tables and rarely spoke to each other. Center Factory was more relaxed, but the Turkish workers never missed an opportunity to remind their Kurdish friends of their ethnic differences. Constant surveillance operated not only as a form of social control in public spaces but also as a form of organizational practice to keep the workforce under the discipline of the small industrialists, both on the shop floor and in the neighborhood.

This surveillance was possible because of the urban, industrial landscape of the neighborhood that emerged in the 1980s as tens of thousands of manufacturing sweatshops mushroomed in distant, growing corners of industrializing cities. This urban-industrial transformation was materialized in new working-class neighborhoods of the metropolitan cities as the spatial-economic setting where the Islamists have thrived politically for the past three decades.

Bağcılar, the setting of my 2008 research, was one of those growth poles of Istanbul where sweatshops changed the structure of the national economy in the 1990s. At least twelve districts around Bağcılar (see map 1) went through a similar urban and industrial transformation after the early 1980s. These districts can be treated as the largest working-class region of the country, with Bağcılar at its center. The region had a population of 6.9 million in 2023[1] and accounted for 8 percent of the total votes the Islamists received in the 2023 presidential election.[2] In 2008, Bağcılar was the largest district in this region (and in Istanbul), and it was the third largest in 2024 after being passed by nearby Küçükçekmece and Esenyurt. Apart from being representative of the

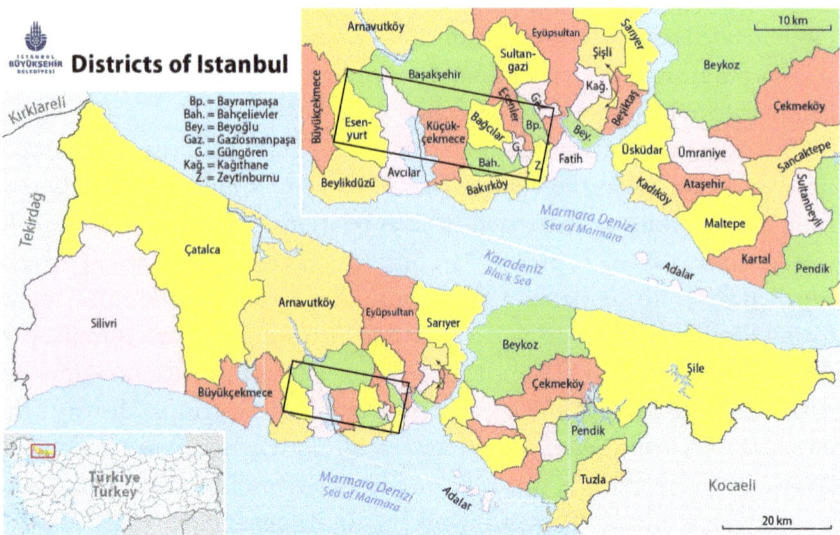

MAP 1. Districts of Istanbul. Rectangles indicate the rough boundaries of the working-class districts in the European part of Istanbul. The research was located in this European part of the city, between several features not shown on the map: the Golden Horn and the Büyükçekmece Lagoon and between the highways E5 (or D100) and TEM (or E80). Source: Maximilian Dörrbecker, *Map of the Districts of Istanbul.*

country's urban political dynamics, this geographically microscopic region is the most important source of electoral support for the Islamists.

Like its neighbors, Bağcılar has been a stronghold for the Islamists. It had phenomenal growth due to rural-to-urban migration between 1980 and 2000. As its population grew from 100,000 in 1980 to 292,000 in 1990 and 557,000 in 2000, the Islamist parties increased their municipal election vote share in Bağcılar from 35 percent in 1992 to 48 percent in 2002, the year the Islamists first won the majority in Parliament. When the Islamists emerged as the first party in Istanbul and Ankara in the 1994 local elections, the strongest support among Istanbul's working-class districts came from Bağcılar (37 percent), a figure 50 percent higher than their vote share in Istanbul at large (25 percent).

The Islamists' support base continued to grow after the 1990s to 58 percent in 2023,[3] as Bağcılar's population rose to 740,000.[4] In other words, the Islamists expanded their votes in this district after the rural-to-urban migration slowed and city-born generations joined the population. This detail draws attention to the physical and industrial landscape of Bağcılar as an endogenous factor behind the success of the Islamists in working-class districts since the 1980s.

The Urban Landscape

Unlike in the two decades preceding the 1980s, when squatter settlements characterized working-class neighborhoods, the construction of over twenty-five thousand multistory buildings every year between 1980 and 2000 led to urban sprawl and created a new urban landscape in the periphery of the city.[5] Instead of building and occupying their own dwellings, rural-to-urban migrants after the 1980s became tenants of the owners of these buildings in districts like Bağcılar. As discussed in chapter 2, this process helped these owners, many of whom were rural-to-urban migrants in previous decades, accumulate capital and emerge as the nucleus of the local elite in the working-class neighborhoods.

This construction frenzy led to a scopophobic physical landscape. The elite used the landscape features of the district to control social life. Their eyes were everywhere: on the street, at work, even in the home. What turned this practice into a regime was the participation of the nonelite in it. Narrow streets and sidewalks make passersby targets of the gaze of residents, shopkeepers, and patrons of all-male coffeehouses. The almost total lack of recreational public spaces also contributed to this scopophobic environment. Green space per person in Bağcılar in 2022 was 7.5 square feet, far less than the 146 square feet in New York City in 2019.[6] Like in other districts in this part of the city, almost none of the apartment buildings in Bağcılar have any backyard or green space. The spaces between the rear facades of the buildings are, almost without exception, unused. The housing units in these buildings were designed to ensure a high degree of specialization of interior spaces in a hierarchy that reflects and constructs the patriarchal order within the family. Privacy is limited,[7] and these dwellings have few if any semiprivate rooms.[8] The constant search for some level of privacy turns curtains into an important part of social life. It is a common practice not only to draw the curtains all the time, but also to use curtains to visually isolate balconies from the neighbors (see figure 15).

The regional, ethnic, and religious composition of the population only boosted the scopophobic effects of this physical landscape. In the first decade of the 2000s, Bağcılar was still a community of first-generation rural-to-urban migrants. According to the 2006 Bağcılar Municipal

Household Survey, less than a quarter of households had lived in Bağcılar for more than two decades, and about 40 percent of the population had moved to Bağcılar less than a decade ago. The origin of migrants in relation to the city and region is an important social marker in Turkey's metropolitan regions, yet Bağcılar was not a collection of regional ghettos. Even the largest regional migrant groups from Eastern Anatolia and the Black Sea regions did not make up more than 15 percent of the total population in Bağcılar's twenty-two neighborhoods. The same pattern applied to the Kurds, the biggest ethnic minority in the country. According to the same survey, 15 percent of respondents stated that Kurmanji or Zazaki, two Kurdish dialects, was spoken at home. However, none of the neighborhoods had a Kurdish-speaking population of more than 22 percent of the district's total, and the neighborhood with the largest Kurdish-speaking population accounted for 13 percent of the total such population in Bağcılar. In other words, Bağcılar and its neighboring districts were predominantly minority-majority settlements in terms of migration and ethnic origin, and they had low dissimilarity and isolation index scores.[9]

One reason for the regional and ethnic heterogeneity was the high residential mobility between and within Istanbul's neighborhoods. About a quarter of households in Bağcılar had lived in their current residence for less than two years, about 70 percent had spent less than a decade in their current residence as of 2006, and 44 percent had moved from elsewhere in Istanbul to their current residence in Bağcılar.

The Industrial Landscape

This last piece of information relates the history of the physical landscape to the transformation of the industrial landscape as the second endogenous factor that empowered the local elite and the Islamists. In the 1960s and 1970s, rural-to-urban migration was coupled with the expansion of large industrial facilities. In the 1980s, small manufacturing enterprises began to absorb rural-to-urban migrants as the new industrial workforce of the country. Over two thousand new ones were established every year between 1992 and 2002 in Istanbul. According to the 1992 and 2002 industrial censuses, Istanbul's industrial workforce grew from 108,030 to 719,716 in that decade. This accounted for roughly one-third of the growth of the entire industrial labor force in the country.[10]

These two censuses, however, provide at best a minimal estimate of the actual size of the growing citywide industrial complex. When I started my research in 2008, I had only a rough idea of the scale of industrial production in Bağcılar. According to the 2002 national industrial census, the 2,888 manufacturing companies employed 32,683 workers. These impressive figures were one reason I chose Bağcılar as a research site, but when the Bağcılar municipality provided me part of their 2006 household survey, I realized the actual numbers were much bigger. According to this local census covering 89 percent of the population and virtually all the buildings, Bağcılar had 9,736 industrial establishments among its fifty thousand residential buildings, and roughly seven thousand of them were garment sweatshops. In other words, on average, there were about 3.6 industrial establishments on every street and an industrial establishment in every fifth building—one for every seventy-two people. The district had around thirty-two thousand commercial businesses, including grocery stores and men-only coffeehouses. That number represented about two-thirds of buildings in the district. Based on the 2002 national industrial census, over 110,000 workers (about one in four adults under the age of sixty-five) were employed in manufacturing establishments, typically located on the first floor of residential buildings in Bağcılar.

Industrial home-based workers are not included in this estimate, however, as they are invisible to official statistics because of the completely informal nature of piecework employment. I studied various piecework distribution

networks with two of my colleagues in 2002–3 and 2006, and observed
Center Factory's own distribution network in 2008, including reviewing
their records and conducting a time-use survey among home-based workers. Like all other networks employing probably hundreds of thousands of
women in Istanbul, each of these networks hired the home-based workers
exclusively for short-term jobs such as cleaning threads or embroidering
almost microscopic beads on the finished garments. The average monthly
earnings of the home-based workers we interviewed in 2006 in three different districts of Istanbul, including Bağcılar, was 22 percent of the minimum
wage, even though our interviewees worked an average of more than seven
hours per day. The samples for the 2006 and 2008 projects, with sizes of
ninety-one and twenty-eight home-based workers, respectively, were remarkably similar in terms of their life course–related choices. In both projects, 91
percent of the women surveyed were married. In 2006 and 2008, the average age of the home-based workers was thirty-seven and thirty-five years,
respectively; 89 percent and 77 percent had started working as home-based
workers because they had childcare responsibilities or because their husbands
did not allow them to work outside the home; 38 percent and 42 percent of
respondents in 2006 and 2008, respectively, were previously employed in
factories or sweatshops; and 39 percent of respondents in 2008 worked
in the garment industry.[11]

Thanks to these observations, I began to realize that Bağcılar's claustro-
phobic apartments served not only to isolate women from their local community in various ways, but also to integrate young women who used to work
outside the home into global industrial supply chains in their new lives in
prison after marriage and children as industrial home-based workers. In fact,
Bağcılar, like many other working-class neighborhoods in Istanbul, was not
just a residential area for workers. It was their factory. The urban landscape
was the industrial landscape.

The goods produced in these sweatshops and houses, often destined for
foreign markets, brought in considerable revenue, which expanded services
and construction. Districts like Bağcılar would look like Loïc Wacquant's
hyperghettoes in the United States[12] if these sweatshops did not play a consequential role in the local economy. Thus, sweatshop owners were key actors
not only as major employers but also as the central actors of the local elite;
13–18 percent of the district population had either a manufacturing business,
a store, or an apartment to rent in 2008. This group had different interests
than the rest of the population, many of whom moved between streets,

neighborhoods, and districts every few years. This minority was the concrete embodiment of the faubourgeoisie. The elite maintains its central position within the gaze regime thanks to its power over workers on the shop floor.

The Ortacı

Mazlum's mother brought him and his siblings to Istanbul in the late 1980s after his father was killed in a feud in their hometown in the central Black Sea region. After elementary school, he began working for many years without receiving any social benefits. He did not have children, yet his wife refused to work and kept telling him she would not have married if she had known he would ask her to work. He had trouble sleeping at night. Sometimes he could not move his shoulders and legs properly while working when he thought about the risk of future layoffs. His anxiety reached a climax whenever the foreman at Center Factory measured the performance of individual sewing machine operators by taking a count of the pieces they completed. As he shared his biography and emotions, I realized why Mazlum did not open his mouth during the first week I worked with him. He was not a talkative person because he did not find much relief in talking to his coworkers.

I listened to stories similar to Mazlum's when I assisted sewing machine operators, who need someone to fold the parts they finish and pass them on to the next operator on the assembly line. These assistants are called *ortacı* or *meydancı* in Turkish, a pejorative that refers to low-status workers who "loaf around" the shop floor. They are an integral part of what I call "the conveyor belt of flesh." They also mediate the relationships between sewing machine operators and their employers. Operators enjoy having someone to yell at when stress becomes unbearable, and employers want operators to believe they have a high social status in the workplace. Because ortacıs are usually young workers who are unhappy with this treatment, they are eager to become the next generation of sewing machine operators.

This was a good position for my research goals because I was able to talk to other ortacıs and machine operators like Mazlum while working. I also worked in other departments at Center Factory, including quality control and packaging, cutting, strip printing, and machine embroidery. I likewise worked in the sewing and cutting departments at Independent Sweatshop. Work in these departments had idiosyncrasies and distinct personalities.

In the cutting departments, for example, the main work consisted of placing hundreds of pieces of fabric on a ten-yard-long table before the actual cutting was carried out, either manually by the master cutter (*makastar*) or by a robot. This allowed or urged workers to talk for hours. In contrast, there was intense competition in the ironing department at Center Factory, as the foremen regularly counted the pieces completed by each ironer. Under the constraint of direct control, the ironers were mostly silent men who minded their own business. With the exception of sewing and final packaging, there was a strict gender division of labor in each department. The capital-intensive strip printing, embroidery, and cutting departments were assigned to men, and the labor-intensive quality control department, which I observed the least, employed only women, as they were believed to have a longer attention span than men—an unsurprising reflection of the patriarchal order. Thousands of hours of work and hundreds of hours of conversation with my coworkers provided me valuable insights into their daily routines, political views, and fantasies.

At Center Factory and Independent Sweatshop, I initially concealed my identity as a researcher, to ensure that these workplaces would serve my research goals and to minimize the impact of this information on my coworkers' behaviors and narratives. However, a completely covert observation would have jeopardized the basic ethical principles of research; therefore, over the coming weeks, I gradually gave my collaborators clues about my objectives and eventually revealed my identity as a researcher and asked for their permission to use my observations while preserving their anonymity. I call this ethnographic strategy "gradual disclosure." In my case, it minimized the potential ethical problems and the distorting effects of full disclosure at the beginning of the project. Because I lived in Bağcılar that year and became friends with some of my coworkers, I could observe their daily lives outside the work environment.

These experiences and observations helped me identify three intertwined components of labor practices that turned the work experience into a foundational element of politics. The first factor is toil, the drudgery and hardship of work. The second factor is market despotism, the taming of the workers with unemployment risk due to market conditions. The third factor is lack of trust among workers of different identity backgrounds, a result of the atomizing effect of the assembly line and a transmuted form of the male gaze on the shop floor. Under these circumstances, collective action is almost impossible and social solidarity among workers is weak.

The Islamist-faubourgeoisie alliance effectively capitalizes on the ensuing vulnerability of workers like Mazlum.

Toil

Toil plays an indirect but foundational role in the formation of workers' political views. The capitalist industrial labor process is an overwhelming experience. By definition, the employer's goal is to use the worker's capacity, or labor power, to its fullest extent. However, a typical sweatshop, especially in labor-intensive industries, is not efficient. Indeed, productivity is of less concern for sweatshop owners than the availability of a large pool of workers, low wages, and long shifts. Sweatshops are disorderly spaces.

I made my most graphic observations of chaos on the assembly line at Independent Sweatshop. One day, we had a major bottleneck in the assembly line because a bucket of blue ribbons used by the sewing machine operators was missing. After a long search, the foremen discovered that the bucket had been sitting under a table for many hours. In another case, a young and healthy male coworker fainted in the middle of the day. It was common for female sewing machine operators to cry at their desks if they failed to keep up with their team members. The foremen were so confused that one of them ran out of the shop in the middle of our shift having a nervous breakdown. The desperation was so palpable that about 10 percent of the workers quit by the end of my first month, some to accept offers from sweatshops paying below minimum wage.

I was not immune to the pressure. Just like Ronald Roy in the 1950s,[13] I thought about quitting the project altogether several times in my first month at the Center Factory. I felt trapped during the workday, which triggered strong feelings of claustrophobia. I was supervising about five machines a day, which meant I had to walk eight to ten miles a day and make about twenty-four hundred pit stops between machine operators. In the meantime, I also counted the changes in the sequence of sewing machines in the assembly lines to get a better overview of the organizational dimensions of the work. As the months went by, I found it increasingly difficult to count fifty, then thirty, and finally even ten machines. As an assistant to the sewing machine operators, I was sometimes tasked with counting the number of parts my coworkers sewed. Without a pen and a piece of paper, it was impossible to add even simple numbers. I cannot emphasize enough how much this work-related cognitive fatigue minimized my coworkers' engagement with community developments or with politics in general. Given the cognitive hardships they experienced on the shop floor, it was simply unrealistic to expect these workers to thoroughly contemplate the factors behind the oppressive and exploitative conditions in their workplaces and communities.

Despite my own transformation, I did not initially recognize the political significance of this effect. I tended to attribute my coworkers' lack of interest in political matters, including work and employment conditions, to their lack of education or the power of the Islamist narrative. In other words, even I was mystifying the effect of the Islamism on their psyche.

Only in my final month at Center Factory did I begin to understand the source of the cognitive distance of my friends from all sorts of social issues. During a lunchbreak, I joined three of my close coworkers to go to a big Home Depot–like hardware store that was a couple hundred yards away from the factory. Our mission was to buy fishing rods. The Sazlıdere Dam was nearby, and they were planning to go fishing on Sundays.

As we entered the store, all of us stopped for a few seconds in utter silence until Cüneyt came to his senses and said, "Let's go, we don't have much time." The soothing music, the calmness, and even the bright white lights, which would disturb many nonworkers, were components of a phantasmagoric experience after all the hours of work under tremendous stress running a sewing machine, ironing thousands of pieces of garments, or overseeing the dull routine of a machine. In the end, we did not buy the fishing rods. The commute to the dam was too long using public transportation, as was the line at the register; the price was too high for a garment worker; and we had to run back to the factory. The fishing rods were only an excuse for my coworkers to have a moment of serenity.

Market Despotism

Needless to say, there were no trade unions. Employers could fire anyone if they offered them severance pay; in many cases, the severance pay was not offered or was offered only after a considerable delay. Thus, workers were constantly concerned about job security. The tension surfaced in different ways. For example, during a week when around a dozen workers were laid off at Center because of the plans to move the facility to Addis Ababa, Cüneyt and I had a quick bite at the cafeteria so that we could arrive in time to find a good spot in the mosque for Friday prayers—part of the courtyard was full of water and the cardboard we prayed on would not protect us from the moisture on the floor. While we discussed this, Cüneyt started mumbling to himself. When I asked him to repeat himself, he raised his voice and said, "I have other options. If they fired me today, I could find a job tomorrow. I'll be fine."

In smaller workplaces, it was not just the jobs of my coworkers that were at stake, but the survival of their workplace. Aware that their sweatshop needed a steady stream of orders to stay in business, many felt they had to work as hard as they could to save both the sweatshop and their jobs. A frequent topic of our lunch-break conversations at Independent Sweatshop was that the foremen were ringing the bell a few minutes early to shorten the breaks. Süphan, who migrated from Bitlis, an eastern Kurdish province, to Istanbul in 2003, was particularly frustrated by this practice:

> If we come to work on time, the foremen warn us and insult us, as if we do not know that they will ring the bell before our break is over. The other day I was on the verge of talking back to the foreman because I thought "enough is enough." I said to myself, "Fuck it. I can look for a job somewhere else." [He then stopped talking for a few seconds.] But if I quit, we'll just drop dead. Even if I do not find a job for a few weeks, the landlord will kick us out of our apartment. [Another short silence.] If we don't deliver this job, the boss will close the place down. In that case, I don't know what to do.

By and large, Burawoy's market despotism describes the nature of the relationship between the workers and the owners of the sweatshops very well.[14] My coworkers were under the constant and debilitating stress of precarity, while at the same time being aware that their employers' position was not much different from their own.

As discussed in chapter 3, these companies had a short life span. According to membership data for the first decade of the 2000s, provided by the Istanbul Garment Exporters' Assembly, about a quarter of the exporting members were replaced by new ones every year. My brief interviews with 107 sweatshop owners during my 2007 pilot study showed that the average age of a sweatshop was about five years. In other words, workers knew that their employers were only one level above them in the global market. As Burawoy pointed out, this gave employers strong leverage over their workers. In the sweatshops where I worked in 2008, the way the foremen ensured discipline was primitive but sufficient. Their constant shouting and running around reminded them that they were in the same boat.

Even though foreign clients and the global market were mostly abstractions for my coworkers, some of them had the rare opportunity to see who these outsiders were and what they looked like: unlike my other workplaces in 2008, Center Factory received inspectors from its long-term German client. During my three months at Center Factory, a one-hour inspection took place on the shop floor, a cursory check of working conditions. These inspectors returned to their headquarters to report that work practices met basic standards while pretending not to know that Center Factory produced only a fraction of the orders it received. Its subsidiaries, such as Follower Sweatshop, did most of the production and paid much less attention to the already problematic labor laws in Turkey. Nor did they seem to care that Center Factory workers worked at least eleven hours a day, from 8:30 a.m. to 7:00 p.m., most days of the year and until 11:00 p.m. if overtime was worked.

The inspector was a blonde, somewhat heavyset woman with colored eyes, wearing sparkly sneakers and jeans. She held a cell phone in a glittery case and spoke to the head of the sewing department, Kemalettin Bey, through her translator, whose German was not very good. She picked out a few pieces at random and did not bother to speak to the workers. She strolled carelessly through the three assembly lines, which at the time had over 120 workers. My female coworkers were envious of this woman's high status and commented on her physical appearance with negative remarks about her weight. One of my male coworkers agreed with his female coworkers, saying that the previous inspector, also a woman, had been much more attractive. As I moved from a team of female operators to a team of male operators, I could hear their gendered comments. Unsurprisingly, conversations among the men centered on their sexual fantasies, and the female employees scrutinized her outfit with snide remarks about her old jeans.

The child of a Kurdish father and an Azeri-Jaferi mother, Kemalettin Bey was from Ağrı, a small town in eastern Anatolia bordering Iğdır, the owner's city. A confident man in his fifties, his body language gave the workers the impression that he did not bow to the authority of the inspector. Regardless of the minimum courtesy he was obliged to show, he adopted his usual upright posture to demonstrate that this was his territory and the inspector was welcomed as a guest: "Kemalettin Bey knows how to deal with these guys," Selvi, an eighteen-year-old female sewing machine operator, told me with great pride. "I'm sick of these people ordering us around as if they own us."

This was one of those moments when the volatile nature of global market forces served as an element of solidarity between employers and employees and between men and women: Selvi's fate depended, at least in part, on this foreign woman's report. Their employer could lose an important partner, and Selvi and her coworkers could lose their jobs. Indeed, the precariousness of the workers' employment conditions indirectly contributed to the formation of a boundary between the local community, consisting of both the workers and their employers, and their foreign clients from an unknown world who were the true contingency in their lives. They were in this battle together, on this side of the line, in a perpetual war against the alien polluters for whom they worked.

Collective Action

In addition to ethnic and gender tensions, shop floor dynamics made collective action difficult for workers. Unsurprisingly, the assembly line pitted my coworkers against each other. Different versions of what Burawoy called "making out"[15] were common. Sewing machine operators would hide a few pieces on their lap for a while and later put the stack next to their desk as a reserve supply to stress and slow down the next operator on the line. In the quality control, ironing, and packing department at Center Factory, the ironers took finished pieces from the cart to the ironing board so that the same piece would be counted twice for that worker. Because the pieces that came from different workers were placed in the same cart, once the foreman unknowingly counted the pieces a second time and placed them back in the cart, there was no practical way to prove which worker was responsible for the shortage. Despite the complete lack of trust, coworkers did not report these incidents to the foremen because they would do the same given the opportunity. What brought them together was their complicity in the mischief. The practice therefore did not create a basis for solidarity among these workers.

In the absence of solidarity, individual and passive-aggressive acts of defiance were a way for my coworkers to escape the pressure. In the words of Ahmet, one of my closest friends at Center Factory,

Sometimes I think to myself, "I'm not going to work today," which is exactly what I did the other day. Of course, it went quite wrong. [He laughs.] [The foreman] yelled at me and Kemalettin Bey [the manager] called me into his office. It was a bad idea and he was right. I feel bad now because I skipped a day of work for no reason. I feel like I let them down, but I don't know why I did it. When I skip a day, I feel free, like I am not dependent on anyone. I feel independent. I feel like I can do whatever I want. It's not just about having a good life. Money is not the real issue here. Okay, we live under tough economic conditions, but what counts here is what I think, what I feel. What can I do? If I don't feel like working this week, I go out. If I don't have any money, I stay at home.

He had good reasons to feel defiant. Ahmet started working as a shoe-shine boy on the streets of his neighborhood when he was seven years old. He collected waste paper and sometimes stole coal from people's basements to sell to a garbage collector: "When you are a kid, you do not know fear. You are not afraid of humiliation. . . . You can turn the world upside down." After I realized he was actively thinking about his class position thanks to such stories, I defined the concept of surplus value to him and asked him to think about it:

UB: There is a concept I would like to ask you about. For example, think of how an employer pays for the electricity, other costs, materials, etc. And the machines.

AHMET: Yes, he only pays once for the machines.

UB: Yes. And then when you add everything up, including your salary, there is still a gap between these costs and the price of the final product. Where does the rest come from?

AHMET: Well, I've thought about that before. Okay, we make the garments, right? We do the sewing. He [the employer] sells a pair of jeans for a hundred dollars, so I make a hundred dollars for him. He pays me twenty dollars. Twenty dollars is mine. All he gives me is twenty dollars. Look at the money he's making here! [He laughs.]

UB: Don't you think that's unfair?

AHMET: Yes, it is.

UB: How do you deal with it then?

AHMET: Because you have to. What else can you do? Either you accept it or you do not.

UB: Yes, if you're lucky, sometimes it turns out well. But why don't people get together?

AHMET: You mean people fight for their rights?

UB: Yes, indeed.

AHMET: Do you know why? Because nobody trusts anyone anymore. Nowadays, people just mind their own business. All this pointless stuff. Everyone over the age of fourteen is cyber-crazy now.

Ahmet was aware he was being exploited, but he also felt helpless and isolated. He started working in sweatshops when he was eleven years old. Before Center Factory, he had worked in more than ten sweatshops and garment factories. Although he was not sure exactly how many jobs he had, he remembered his first one vividly. The shift was just too long for an eleven-year-old. He also remembered that one of his friends had stopped coming to the sweatshop after his father asked the foreman not to push his son to work overtime and received a negative answer from the foreman. Ahmet's father did not do the same for him:

> You know I told you about the boy in the jeans sweatshop [Ahmet's first sweatshop]. His father had this four-, five-story building. He didn't have to put his kid to work. But if he was suffering from [economic] hardship, his kid would have had to work there. I have told you before, if I had money, I would defy everyone. Seriously . . . everyone needs a father like that, one who has money. You know what I mean? His dad came in and told the sweatshop boss that his kid was not going to work overtime. I said to myself, "Look, this man has money and his kid doesn't have to work overtime." The man just took his child and left. Do you see the difference between a rich man and a poor man?

Ahmet's search for a stronger father figure in his life pointed to a gap he had repeatedly addressed in different ways in our conversations. Like Mr. Self-Made Man, his father had immigrated to Istanbul in 1974 and began working in sweatshops in Zeytinburnu, an older working-class neighborhood and one of the city's first major squatter districts. He later found a job in a textile factory with over 150 workers. He was one of the strikebreakers in this factory in 1979, but he was fired soon after the strike ended. Many of his compatriots locked up a piece of land in Bağcılar and Küçükçekmece. Others opened their own sweatshops, just like Mr. Self-Made Man. Ahmet's father was not one of them, and this failure was a source of resentment for Ahmet. While it was true that he was exploited, he knew this was not everyone's fate. He blamed his father for their family-size desperation.

Despite his anger, his father and he shared a passion that bound them together: treasure hunting. Before Armenians rushed to leave Iğdır with the retreat of the Soviet Union in the early 1920s, some hid their gold in their homes or around their villages in hopes they would get their valuables back when they returned to their hometown. It then became common practice for the Muslims who occupied these villages to search for what the Armenians had left behind. Few of them found these treasures, and their stories created myths for those who hoped to change their fate in the same way.

Ahmet believed he had found a unique place that could hide a huge treasure. It was not easy for him to talk to me about this subject, because secrecy was a must, but he showed me pictures of this place, a massive stone that seemed to have very ancient manmade symbols engraved on it. After his repeated requests, I spoke to an archaeologist friend of mine, for whom these prehistoric symbols did not mean a location of any specific find. Although he was very disappointed, he did not completely give up on the project, which represented a connection to his father and possible redemption from poverty.

The isolation, precariousness, lack of trust, and exploitation made it difficult for Ahmet and my other coworkers to develop the will to take collective action against their employers. One of the rare moments when the workers overcame this difficulty was the work stoppage at Center Factory in 2003 that I mentioned in chapter 4. The workers walked off the job to demand higher wages. It was a poorly coordinated wildcat strike. For instance, at that time, the current Center Factory administration building, about thirty yards from the main building, was still being used for production. The workers there were not informed about the work stoppage. In the end, the management refused to negotiate with the workers. About a fifth of the workers were dismissed the next day. The rest resumed work. The action lasted only one day.

Despite the complete failure, the workers kept the memory of this incident alive. The same story was told to me by many workers, some of whom were not even working at Center Factory in 2003. The two most common tropes in different versions of the story were the workers' lack of coordination and the employers' financial power to overcome the work stoppage. The workers agreed their employer had enormous resources and would not hesitate to fire dissenting workers even if it cost the employer their severance pay. They also believed they were easily replaceable, as wages were slightly higher and payments were made without delay.

A similar incident occurred during my 2008 fieldwork at Independent Sweatshop. When they learned payroll would be delayed, the workers started discussing what to do during the tea break. One of my close friends, Cahit, a socialist Alevi Zaza worker I met at Solidarity House, advised them to work slower in the coming days to increase pressure on the employer.

Most of the workers doubted the feasibility of this idea, as they had never experienced or heard of the concept of slowdown. Nevertheless, the situation was grim. Despite all the ethnic, religious, regional, and gender differences, many of them agreed. After the tea break, the workers established an almost poetic harmony among themselves with perfect coordination. In the absence of a real conveyor belt, the only factor that could speed up the output of the assembly line was competition among the workers. So, it took a while for the foreman to realize he was dealing with collective resistance. He gave the workers an ultimatum, which did not work. He tried to convince them their reaction would not put the owner of the sweatshop in a better position to be able to pay them, which was a very strong motivation to be obedient despite all the hardship they were experiencing. This time, however, the threat was met with uncomfortable silence. Celal, a respected worker over fifty, asked the foreman how they could be expected to work if they were not paid. They had their own debts to pay and their own mouths to feed.

That was the crux of the tension. The foreman verbally attacked Celal and dominated him. The last sentence of the conversation was the foreman's "official statement" that he "did not give a shit [*sikimde değil*]." Celal was in no position to respond to this harsh attack. His coworkers decided they did not stand a chance. They silently resumed their work. The whole incident lasted no longer than an hour.

With a Che Guevara tattoo on his left bicep, a reputation among his comrades as a good fighter, and a criminal record that included stabbing his former father-in-law in the leg, my socialist friend Cahit was not someone the foremen could have easily cowed if he had intervened at this critical moment. However, he chose not to intervene. When I later asked Cahit why he had not sided with Celal, I realized I was still unable to recognize the power dynamics among my coworkers. Cahit believed that Celal's case could be just another instance of a common tactic, that of older and respected male workers posing as mediators between workers and management in such tense moments and then pretending to represent the workers in the employer's room to get small favors for themselves, such as an advance payment or a promise of tolerance for future absences. Having witnessed such underhanded dealings before, Cahit waited to see the reaction of the other workers before taking the initiative. The workers immediately submitted to the foreman's authority, so there was no reason for him to risk his own job just to support Celal's possible scheme during this brief chaos.

THE HYGIENE REGIME

The Lover

Gülizar, an ortacı at Center Factory like me, was an excellent storyteller. The second half of lunch breaks was her time to take the stage and tell religious stories to her half-dozen-strong all-female audience on the empty shop floor. Although the stories were made for women, I was allowed to listen to her while pretending to work on the sewing machines, thanks to my low status as an ortacı in the hierarchy among the workers. Sometimes I had trouble figuring out whether she was telling these stories to call the young female workers to true religion or using these religious motifs to give her audience a legitimate reason to listen to these elegant tales.

Once, she told her audience about the assassination of the fourth caliph of Islam, Ali. The murderer's lover threatened to end her relationship with him if he did not commit the crime. The explicitly misogynistic message of Gülizar's story was that women were essentially sinners and morally corrupt. On the one hand, she seemed to be simply conveying a story of and about men. On the other hand, it was also a reminder to her female coworkers, especially the sewing machine operators who were above her in the shop floor hierarchy, that they had a lower position in the gender hierarchy.

However, the reinterpretation of Selvi, the young female coworker I mentioned earlier, took a completely different and surprising turn. She was mesmerized by the power his lover wielded over Ali's murderer. With great awe in her voice, she blurted out, "You mean the murderer killed His Holiness Ali because of his love for his girlfriend?" While Gülizar looked perplexed at Selvi's reaction, others began to laugh and one of them commented, "Selvi, you didn't get it." After Selvi had unintentionally decontextualized Gülizar's story, the storytelling session was over and everyone started to chat in smaller groups.

Another self-proclaimed proselytizer was İhsan Abi at Center Factory. He was not a follower of any religious order, yet he would not miss the opportunity when a guest preacher came to the mosque in his Altınşehir neighborhood, one of the newest working-class communities. While I assisted him, he would tell me semi-philosophical religious stories about the meaning of life for a worker spending most of his active life under the duress of the capitalist labor process. As discussed in chapter 3, the religious orders denigrate laborers' work as a waste of time that could be spent on worshipping if the worker did not have to work. One of his stories had the exact same message: "Do you know the story of the shopkeeper who never stopped complaining? Let me tell you his story. He complained about his loss at the end of every day. The other shopkeepers could not understand why he was so grumpy, because they knew his business was doing well. One day they asked him what was really going on. And he said, 'I made money, but I lost the day.'"

The main character of the story was not a toiling worker but a shopkeeper waiting for his customers. İhsan Abi identified with this shopkeeper in terms of their supposedly shared dilemma. What should worry him was not that he was poor and could lose his job at any time but that he had a higher purpose and work stood in the way of his quest for salvation, just like that busy shopkeeper.

As the themes of the next three subsections, three interconnected processes helped Gülizar and İhsan Abi have a good audience for their stories. First, as a direct consequence of the labor regime, my coworkers were looking for any kind of material, religious or not, to beat the cognitive and emotional effects of the drudgery. What Gülizar and İhsan Abi offered emotionally empowered them in different ways and helped them cope with the never-ending cycle of the assembly line. Second, they looked for useful elements in this material to understand the meaning of the dual pressure of precarious work and community surveillance. The notion of purity, a key theme in their narratives, helped them cope with their dual vulnerabilities under the labor and gaze regimes. Third, my coworkers used these purity-driven narratives to define and redefine the symbolic boundaries of their community. Depending on the context, anyone could be an outsider, so my coworkers treated the Islamists (and their stories) as a moral compass whenever they felt uncertain about those symbolic boundaries.

The Drudgery

The capitalist labor process had two related effects on my coworkers' perspectives on the political and the social. First, capitalist toil distanced my coworkers from politics for the simple reason that they did not have the energy to engage with it. Second, my coworkers needed something to entertain themselves with during the long working day to withstand the attrition. During work, various forms of daydreaming and cognitive exercises helped them cope with the monotony and stress of work. The cognitive effort behind these fantasies was the first step to formulating their political opinions.

My first proper conversation with Şeyhmuz was my cue to identify this relationship between fantasies and political opinions. My taciturn ironing coworker in Center Factory was a stocky man in his late forties. While he was working, he avoided talking to his coworkers, including me. All my efforts in my early days in the interim ironing department to encourage him to join conversations with the other ironers failed completely. This was understandable, as the other crew members were teenagers living in a different world. Furthermore, the job was tough. Each us had to use the iron's heat to glue thousands of small polyester sheets on the fabric to protect it from the sewing machine's needle.

Şeyhmuz's silence was also, I thought, an indication of the cognitive effort he was putting into ironing the myriad pieces of fabric. Then, one day, our young coworkers talked briefly about a popular telenovela, *Valley of the Wolves* (*Kurtlar Vadisi*). The show was about a conservative, pious secret agent who infiltrated the world of crime by assuming a covert criminal identity. Islamists extensively used the conspiracy theories in this series about the evil plans of foreign powers against Turkey to serve current politics.[16]

I said a few things about the show's characters—I was a fan in my own way—and he finally got involved in the conversation: "I love the show. I love it so much that I even enjoy watching the commercials." I was surprised by his reaction. This was the first time he had opened his mouth in a week, and he was very excited. Despite this pleasant surprise, I wanted to provoke him a little:

UB: The actor does not even act like a real actor, though. I don't understand why you enjoy the show so much.

ŞEYHMUZ: No, you don't know anything about acting. He acts like a real hero saving the State from the scum. . . .

UB: Well, I think you're right. I mean, a guy like him would probably act like that in a real situation.

ŞEYHMUZ: It's so good that I think about it all day when I am working here. I replay the cool lines in my head and imagine myself in the scenes of the show.

Şeyhmuz obviously enjoyed thinking about this TV show much more than talking to his teenage coworkers. The reflection of himself in a world full of danger and sin as the savior of the victims apparently entertained him during eleven-hour shifts facing piles of fabric waiting at his ironing board.

The Islamist narrative provided rich material for making sense of and coping with drudgery. Gülizar's story about the murderer of Ali gave Selvi material to think about—later in the afternoon while I was assisting her, she shared that she was fascinated by the story. While İhsan Abi was inviting me to his ontological cosmos as a self-proclaimed proselytizer, the stories he was telling helped him present all the past decisions that brought him to the shop floor as a part of a bigger cosmic plan. The plot Şeyhmuz was attracted to demarcated the world between the good and the evil. In none of these stories was Islam the core content. The murder of Ali was a story of betrayal. İhsan Abi was looking for an emotional redemption of his past mistakes. Şeyhmuz was looking for a cognitive escape from his ironing board. In other words, even though the Islamists were on the good side of these stories, my coworkers' interest in them was not a consequence of their interest in Islamism. Even though the connection between their interest in these stories and the drudgery they experienced gradually looked obvious to me, I still could not understand why stories prioritizing other political actors were not their favorite. The appeal of the narrative was still a mystery to me.

The Purity

A Risk Society. While I struggled with this difficulty, I found myself in another puzzle. Almost every day after my shift, I came to my room with a little story, comment, or complaint from my coworkers about their bad habits or lack thereof. For example, Hasan at Center Factory emphasized more than a dozen times during the three days we worked together that he had no bad habits: "I have been working at Center Factory for seven years. I do not have any bad habits: I don't drink, I don't smoke. I don't go to a coffeeshop. I buy two kilograms of tea and drink it for a month."

Ahmet, the close friend I mentioned earlier, used to drink one or two beers a month, but he gave up this habit after his friends and he made too much noise when they got drunk in the neighborhood late at night and were beaten up by the community. He also stopped his internet service because it kept him up late at night, a luxury a garment worker cannot afford. He used to buy a lottery ticket now and then, but he said he had given up this "addiction" too. In his words, he had "repented all his bad habits." I overlooked these comments until I figured out the centrality of spiritual purity as the main motif in the stories my coworkers chose to listen to and used as objects for contemplation during long work hours.

What helped me establish this connection was that the fear of moral pollution expressed in my coworkers' comments about their daily habits was often coupled with the constant fear of a future catastrophic event. Slightly more often than my other coworkers, Celadet in Center Factory's packaging department kept our coworkers and me on our toes with all sorts of disaster scenarios that would be triggered by spectacular events such as the death of an immediate family member, an economic crisis, or an earthquake. Even if his scenarios did not lighten our mood, his creativity was admirable. The moral of his narrative, which I agreed with, was clear. We lived in a high-risk world, so we should find grace in our lives: "No one knows what will happen to us tomorrow," and "it's not even clear if we can go home without an accident," so "you should have grace that you are granted a life."

With a similar attitude, and as an indirect consequence of the hegemonic despotism, my coworkers went to great lengths to express their grace and appreciate the state of security they were enjoying at that moment: they had a job, and no one in their family had a serious health problem. My coworkers usually expressed their grace with a sigh and religious expressions such as *yarabbi şükür* (Thank Allah), repeated once or twice an hour. This *dhikr*-like practice was an attempt to harmonize the routine of the work process with an informal prayer practice. In this way, Mutlu, another good friend at Center Factory, found contentment in his life: "I find grace for my life. I do all this for my children. The majority of Turkish people are selfless people like me. Everyone thinks about their children. There are people who are much poorer than us. We should be grateful." The irony was that Mutlu had recently sent one of his two children to live with his parents in his hometown because his wife had to work and they could not afford the cost of childcare or other expenses for their children. Mutlu was going to send his second child to his parents soon.

I realized gradually that many of my coworkers viewed their bodies as fragile objects, susceptible to various corrupting influences from the outside world. In fact, they perceived the precariousness of their employment conditions as one of the two major corrupting influences. As a structural component of the labor regime, unemployment was not only a material but also a spiritual risk. Bad habits were a sign of lack of determination to combat spiritual contamination.

A second corrupting influence I identified was directly related to the gaze regime. A worker with the right spiritual profile (not *zibidi*), they believed, had a better chance to avoid unemployment and cope with various types of community surveillance and pressure.

Given the significance of the gaze regime to the organization of social interactions in their community, this spiritual profile had to be coupled with visual, sonic, and aromatic cues such as sartorial practices. For this reason, another and even more obvious reflection of the search of my coworkers for spiritual purity was their effort to make sense of the hijab mandate.

Gendered Perspectives. My coworkers' perspective on this mandate was particularly useful for me in connecting their search for spiritual purity with their standing in the community. Their perspectives differed in accordance with their gender and their perspective on social class. There was a visible difference between my male and female coworkers in their readings of the hijab mandate because the social role of the mandate was different for the sexes.

My male coworkers actively sought advice about religiously proper practices. One person my male coworkers at Center Factory consulted with was the imam of the mosque at the end of the street. He would occasionally come to the tea room across the street, where we usually spent our lunch break, and answer my coworkers' questions in half-hour conversations.

My coworkers could not get enough of the conversations about the proper form of hijab. The imam taught the workers a complex taxonomy that categorized types of hijab from the most desirable to the less desirable minimalist forms consisting of headscarf and cloak. The imam's tone was diplomatic. Although burqa-like practices occupied a higher position in his taxonomy, he ensured that the minimalist practice did not violate core doctrine.

He chose his words carefully because the minimalist option was the common practice in Bağcılar and in my workplaces. The imam knew it would be a challenge for these men to convince their wives, sisters, and daughters to switch from the cloak-and-headscarf combination to a burqa-like style. In the eyes of my male coworkers, piety was in the service of purity as defined by the moral order, an ontological instrument that helped them fulfill the moral expectations of their community. It was not the end but the means of purity.

My female coworkers in hijab shared a major motivation of my male coworkers regarding the practice. Wearing a hijab attributed meaning to the scopophobic pressure under the male gaze regime and gave them a means to deal with this pressure. The gaze, like their potentially pollutant bodies, was the inevitable consequence of men's God-created nature (*fitrat*). In this context, the hijab served as a protective suit that shielded them from the potentially defiling effect of the male gaze. Probably for this reason, roughly two-thirds of the female workers I worked with in 2008 wore a hijab.

Where my male and female coworkers differed was about their own role in the male gaze as a relationship. Adopting the hijab as a religious dress practice required accepting the principle that women were a potential source of moral pollution. This principle was not easy for my female coworkers to internalize because it meant recognizing a permanent character trait that affected all women. The principle limited the ways they could define their agency. One of my exchanges with Selvi and her sister Sema, who unlike Selvi did not wear a hijab, is illustrative in this respect:

SELVI: Utku Abi, does your mother wear a headscarf?

UB: No, she doesn't. What about yours?

SELVI: My mother wears a headscarf. Actually, I never wore a headscarf until recently. . . . I was planning to wear a headscarf only after I got married, but then I read this book, *The Long Path After Death* [*Ölümden Sonraki Uzun Yol*], which is about people's suffering after death. Even if you are a believer, you will have to suffer because of your sins in this life. I was really worried. Women have more important tasks than men.

SEMA (Selvi's sister, who worked next to her in the same work unit, laughed and cheerfully joined the conversation): Yes, Utku Abi, I also started reading the same book, but [with a sarcastic tone] I got so depressed that I couldn't finish it.

UB (to Selvi): How did your parents react?

SELVI: My father wanted us [Selvi and Sema] to wear a headscarf when I was thirteen, but we didn't want to. Then when I decided to wear a headscarf . . .

UB: When?

SELVI: Three years ago. . . . He then changed his mind and asked us to wait until we were married. I don't know why he changed his mind. I also started praying when I decided to wear a headscarf. But right now I'm depressed [and no longer praying] because I broke up with my lover [*sevgili*].

UB: Excuse me, who?

SELVI: I mean, my boyfriend [*erkek arkadaş*]. . . . He never prayed. Then I convinced him that praying is the right thing to do. Now we've broken up, but he still prays.

I cannot speculate why Selvi's father changed his mind about the timing of the hijab for his daughters, but her defiance was her way to reclaim agency, just like her romantic relations with men despite the strict religious ban before marriage. Her reference point to justify her strategy was a book, which was, I assume, *On the Remembrance of Death and the Hereafter* (*Ölüm ve Sonrası*), Book 40 of the most important work by Ghazali, a prominent conservative Muslim cleric from the thirteenth century: *The Revival of Religious Sciences*.[17] In other words, unlike for men (or at least some men), the hijab mandate for my female coworkers was not merely an instrument to deal with community pressure. Given the specifications superimposed by the mandate on the way they defined their agency, my female coworkers were in an active ontological effort to reconcile the mandate with their strategy to define their agency.

Class Perspectives. This effort, unsurprisingly, motivated my female coworkers to think about their relationship to other women wearing hijabs. As a spatial arrangement that demarcates the pure and the toxic, the hijab practice asked my female coworkers not only to relate their agency to their corporeality, but also to internalize the idea that women in hijab formed an imagined community of solidarity that was supposed to cut across class lines.

My female coworkers had to find their own way of dealing with this factually weak idea. The perspectives of Zeliha and Sakine, two female workers at Center Factory, show the differences in this regard. The first time I noticed the depth of these differences was in a conversation initiated by Zeliha:

ZELIHA (with a slightly patronizing tone): Tell me your name.

UB: Utku.

ZELIHA: What does that mean? I've never heard it before.

UB: It means "victory."

ZELIHA: Hmm, okay. So you are a revolutionary?

Since Zeliha was a worker wearing a hijab and I had just started helping her, this question caught me by surprise:

UB: Well, I don't know. It depends on what you mean by "revolutionary." If you mean that you are calling for progressive social change, yes, then maybe I am a revolutionary. But I don't know.

ZELIHA: My boyfriend is a revolutionary. That's what I meant.

UB (still trying to understand the semantics): Alright, so. . . . Does he belong to a political party or something?

ZELIHA: He's a student at Akdeniz University. [With a tone of pride] He's a revolutionary, an Atatürkist!

This last remark made it clear that what Zeliha had in mind was Turkey's official state ideology, Atatürkism or Kemalism, not some form of socialism or anarchism. The followers of this ideology were proud to call themselves "revolutionaries" because Atatürk's reforms in the 1920s were instrumental in bringing down the ancien régime of the Ottoman Empire:

UB: I think it's good that your friend is interested in politics.

ZELIHA: I think everyone should be a revolutionary at some level.

Our conversation was interrupted for the next fifteen minutes because the foreman began to look past the sewing machines to monitor the pace of work. In response to the foreman's presence, the workers from the previous unit sped up their work and we were in a hurry to keep up with them. Eventually we caught up and Zeliha continued our conversation in a relaxed manner:

ZELIHA: Does your mother wear a headscarf?

UB: No, she doesn't, but I am not so happy about the prejudice against women who wear a hijab.

ZELIHA: That's true, but I also support Atatürk's revolutions and secularism. I don't believe that women wearing a hijab should be allowed to enter college campuses. People should abide by the rules. [She referred to the ban on female university students wearing the hijab that was actively enforced between 1997 and 2002. The ban was formally lifted in 2013.]

As I continued to work with Zeliha in the following days, new clues about her past helped me realize the main reason for her seemingly contradictory position about the ban on female students wearing hijabs. Zeliha's father was a civil servant in Ağrı, an eastern province inhabited mainly by Kurds. She was of Turkish descent, and when I asked her whether Kurds made up the majority of the population of Ağrı, her answer was: "Unfortunately." Zeliha came from a relatively privileged position in terms of her father's profession and her ethnic background. Therefore, she was dissatisfied with her social status as a worker in the garment industry. She could have been one of the students who were not admitted to the college because of their political views (and sartorial practices).

This led to a particular form of tacit resentment against these students. Zeliha was aware that the problems these students and she experienced in everyday life had different origins. The Islamists' active political campaign in those years against the banning of the hijab in certain public spaces, such as college campuses, and the publicity this campaign received bothered her because she knew she did not have much in common with these students. They would fight for the civil rights of women wearing hijabs, and perhaps tell Zeliha's story too, but in their version and in their own words. Zeliha believed she was deprived of her agency, not by the secularists, but by the daughters of the local elite who monitored her on the streets and in the sweatshops of Bağcılar. In fact, the female students who protested the headscarf ban were just as much outsiders as the secular women, at least from Zeliha's point of view. Her Atatürkism was a telling way of using the secularist-Islamist binary to express a visibly class-based grievance about the appropriation of one of the few practices or symbols that could give her some space, some status in the neighborhood community.

Based on my experience, I am certain Zeliha was in the minority. For most of my coworkers, like Sakine, the protective function of the hijab as an enabler was more important. It gave them, albeit with severe restrictions, the logistical advantage of leaving home and joining the urban community without being symbolically defiled by it or defiling the community.

Sakine's solidarity with the educated and privileged women wearing hijabs was thus not necessarily an expression of her political views on a just world in which women wearing hijabs would no longer be discriminated against, but rather an extension of her strategy to form an alliance with those privileged (faubourgeois and petty bourgeois) women. Like Zeliha, she was aware that many hijab-wearing female graduates and students protesting the headscarf ban on campus were demanding privileged permanent positions in the public sector and that they would get these jobs if the ban were lifted. In this respect, Sakine knew, these protesters had almost nothing in common with her.

Unlike Zeliha, however, Sakine felt no visible resentment about the difference in status between herself and these privileged women in hijab. She accepted that these students and she did not belong to the same social cosmos or class. As in Zeliha's case, they were distant figures for Sakine. Nevertheless, or precisely because of this, these privileged women could be her strategic allies (but not members of her imagined community) who could expand her social and physical mobility. Sakine's pragmatism reflected her complex identity as a pious woman and a go-getter:

SAKINE: I wrote this poem for my manager, "Müdürüm" [My Manager].

UB: [I quickly read the poem, which was an encomium for Kemalettin Bey, the manager of the sewing section] It looks good. Why don't you send it to a competition?

SAKINE: Women wearing a hijab cannot take part in such competitions.

UB: That's a shame. Which poems do you like best?

SAKINE: I don't really read poetry. It sounds pointless. The last book I read
was something my former boyfriend asked me to read. The author was
a revolutionary. I did not understand anything. It was nonsensical, too
abstract. Are you a left-wing or right-wing?

UB: I'm not interested in politics.

SAKINE: I think everyone should dress how they want. Because of
the headscarf ban, families do not let their girls go to school. Pressure
is being exerted. Whenever I go to my friend's family, who by the
way is from Artvin [a relatively liberal city in the eastern Black Sea
region], they tell me to give up the headscarf. They do not respect
my beliefs.

Even though it sounded like a digression, the seemingly sudden shift from
her poetry to politics was her way to express her effort to identify with
college students wearing hijabs, like herself. Sakine was a poet, so she and
those college students had common intellectual interests. Sakine believed
her encomium for Kemalettin Bey would not be accepted for a poetry competition because she wore a hijab, just as those college students were denied
access to university campuses. Just like those students, who were interrogated at the campus gates by hardcore secularist (often female) professors
about why they were wearing hijabs, Sakine was put under pressure by the
parents of her friend.

The happy irony is that the complex amalgamation of Sakine's religious-
political ideals and pragmatism, two forces in tension, helped her break
her cocoon. I discovered this to my pleasant surprise when I visited the
new Center Factory facility in Addis Ababa two years after my research
in Istanbul. She was the only woman in the team of foremen who had
been transferred from Istanbul and was head of the factory's first sewing
department. At full capacity, the department would employ over a thousand workers. Sakine was offered this position because management had
decided to employ only women in the sewing department after realizing
Ethiopian workers were aware of their brief socialist past and many of them
were not as proletarianized in their minds as workers in Turkey. Drawing
on their experiences in Istanbul, they believed female workers would be
more docile. As she quickly learned Amharic, Sakine began to commu-
nicate with the rapidly growing group of female workers. When I asked

her how it felt to be a manager herself now, reminding her of her poem for Kemalettin Bey, she replied in her usual cheerful voice, "Maybe one day one of these girls will write a poem for me too!"

The Demarcation

External Threats. My coworkers' social constructions regarding their religious duties, including the hijab mandate, helped them symbolically demarcate their community and look for a place in it. This search had an apparent class element. Their emotional state regarding their class position often swung between anger and insecurity because the immediate object of their anger was not the faubourgeois-Islamist local elite but outsiders, whom they did not know much about. The secularists were the ideal typical form of such outsiders. They believed that secularists were categorically rich. Hence their anger. They rarely interacted with them. Hence their insecurity. To cope with these mixed feelings, my male coworkers often turned their encounters with those rich secularists into epic stories.

In one of these stories that Cüneyt, one of my closest coworkers at Center Factory, told us during a lunch break, he and a few friends visited Kadıköy, a district in the Asian part of the city. The district was a stronghold of the secularist petty bourgeoisie, many of whom had a strong negative opinion of the residents of Bağcılar, much like the opinions New England or Bay Area liberals have of southern Republicans in the United States. As part of their adventure, they entered an upscale restaurant and ordered rotisserie chicken, even though they were not sure they had enough money. As the waiter with the bow tie was about to serve the chicken, one of his friends stopped the waiter and broke the chicken into smaller pieces with his hands. The other customers stared at them with astonishment and disgust. The waiter asked them to leave.

For Cüneyt, this was a symbolic demonstration of power: breaking the chicken with his bare hands was the gesture his friend used to show his dislike of other privileged customers. Cüneyt and his friends believed these other customers saw them as dirty. So, they wanted to show them that they had different standards of purity. Because of their working-class background and Bağcılar identity, they did not mind getting their hands dirty with the greasy chicken—they did not define their purity by this simple gesture. As the protagonists, their role in this story was to show their counterparts their impermeable purity.

As I watched my other coworkers affirm Cüneyt's courage, I realized the story served as collective reassurance that we did not belong to Kadıköy. Their fear of being soiled by the alluring milieu of this and other petty bourgeois neighborhoods was symbolically expressed as an act that disrupted life in this restaurant for a moment. The grease in the hands of Cüneyt's friend was a dirty substance for other customers. This was a skirmish in a long war of mutual destruction between the pure and the toxic.

My closer coworkers' mystification of the class status and lifestyles of the secularists was not unique. An anonymous survey I conducted at each workplace (except Family Sweatshop) documents the degree of mutual isolation between these petty bourgeois neighborhoods and working-class neighborhoods. About 30 percent of my coworkers had not visited any of the non-working-class neighborhoods on the list, including nearby ones like Bakırköy, another petty bourgeois stronghold of the secularist parties around six miles away. The figure rises to a whopping 69 percent if we limit the list to Bosporus neighborhoods. Only 9.5 percent had visited Bebek, a wealthy neighborhood on the Bosporus.

Thus, anger was coupled with a deep insecurity. Even though Cüneyt's fictional or real story was epic, not every encounter with secularist outsiders had a happy ending. Çağlar and Deniz were young, handsome men who dreamed of becoming fashion models. One day Çağlar came with the news that a modeling agency was holding an audition in Bakırköy. We talked about their plans all week, but later they changed their minds. Deniz explained succinctly why they had abandoned the plan: "We don't belong there. What would the guy who picks the applicants say? 'Two guys from Varosh[18] are coming here and I'm going to make them famous'? I don't think so. And even if we were successful, what would happen then? Fame corrupts people. Look at the artists and singers who came out of the Varosh? They all lost their honor, without exception!" Then, the indisputable reality sank in: "Outside of this workplace, we are nobody. Here we can hang out with people and kill time. But outside of this place, we are like pears sitting on a table."

Shortly afterward, Deniz had a new idea. He read in a newspaper that Norway would take in a hundred thousand foreign workers. This could be his way out of poverty, insecurity, and toil. To my surprise, everyone in our close circle attacked the idea. Cüneyt commented that he would never apply because he would not "go to another country to clean their shit and wipe [the foreigners'] asses." Ahmet did not miss the opportunity to irritate Deniz with several sentences in a row: "I would rather pick up the garbage from the streets here, steal the electricity cables and sell them, . . . , survive here on bare bread than go to the land of infidels." If a little sadistic, Ahmet's parrot-like hyperbolic assertions were really funny. Deniz laughed at his friends' treatment, saying, "Hey, it was just an idea, okay? I didn't say I was going for sure."

In both cases, advancement through fame or migration was discredited as a source of pollution. Leaving the community would amount to "cleaning the shit" of the corrupt, like the petty bourgeois residents of Kadıköy and the Norwegians. The activity of cleaning (the feces of) the corrupt could transfer the pollution to the cleaner.

The Enemies Within. My coworkers made constant efforts to define an external common enemy to demarcate their community. The enemy was defined and redefined circumstantially: it could be the secularists of Kadıköy; the German inspector woman; the Norwegians; or the residents of their own neighborhood such as the Kurds, the Alevis, the leftists, the men with tattoos, women wearing no hijab, and so on. The demarcation process was permanent and context dependent. None of these efforts on the part of my coworkers, however, eliminated the fact that they were heavily exploited by their employers. Formulating the narrative for the hygiene regime, the Islamists played a dual role to help my coworkers come to terms with this fact.

First, the Islamists played a mediating role for my coworkers in this active demarcation process whenever they felt betrayed by their employers. Islamism served as a reference point for defining purity amid all the dirt produced not only by the external enemies, but also by these employers who claimed to be the guardians of their moral community.

The political opinions of Murat Abi, one of my regular lunchmates at Center Factory, were the critical input I needed to establish this connection. Regardless of topic, he showed unconditional support for the AKP in almost any conversation, which I later realized was closely linked to the weakness he felt in relation to Mr. Self-Made Man. During a lunchtime conversation about party politics, he said, unmistakable pride in his tone, that "the country has been ruled by the Left until now. Now it should be ruled by the Right for a while." This remark surprised me because Turkey had not had a strong left-wing government since the 1970s. What he meant by "Left" was all secularist parties, including liberals or non-Islamist conservatives.

He was from Çorum, a central Anatolian city with a very conservative Sunni majority, so it was not surprising that he had sharp opinions even when the topic did not sit visibly on the right-hand side of the ideological spectrum. But it was also true that he was a worker in his mid-fifties. He had spent enough time in various factories to understand the nature of his relationship with his many employers:

MURAT ABI: I also worked in Çorum. . . . [Out of a hundred workers] they only paid fringe benefits to twenty workers. . . . The [government] inspectors saw all the unused machines, of course, but they never fined the employer.

UB: So the government did not do what it was supposed to do.

MURAT ABI: Listen, Utku. I don't know about your political views, but this government has done a very good job. It has given tax breaks to newly hired workers. But companies are abusing all these good measures. They fire people in March [income tax is paid in March in Turkey] and hire them back the next time. Our people are faggots [*ibne*]. They always abuse everything.

Cornered from all directions and abandoned by his employers for many decades, he shared with great and genuine effort at that lunch table all the facts about the employers' little schemes to deceive the Islamists, who, he believed, were the only trustable force in his life. In this context, the contaminated, "the faggots," were the employers.

Second, the Islamist narrative defined the terms of their resistance against their employers as an essential component of the hygiene regime. My coworkers used religious symbols and rituals as a shield against their foremen, employers, neighbors, and government officials. Friday prayers were practically mandatory for the male workers at all my workplaces. Many of them took this opportunity to take an extended lunch break. Only a few skipped the prayer, but only a few spent more than the minimum duration at the ritual in the mosque. In addition, daily prayer was allowed at Center Factory. Sunni Muslims are required to pray five times a day, and at least three of these times coincide with working hours. This was an unusual practice in the industry at the time, but Center Factory could afford it and its owners were not Sunni, so they may have seen this policy as a way to increase motivation among Sunni workers.

The policy was a success, but in a different way than management envisioned: the Sunni workers did not see it as an act of kindness but as a concession. A longtime worker at Center Factory, Ebuzer contrasted the brief work stoppage in 2003 with the company's prayer policy as a factor that helped him feel strong and as a cue that let me see the connection:

> I don't want to go into details, but I have experienced a similar incident [he is referring to the work stoppage at Center Factory] one other time in my fifteen years in this business. Like these [recalcitrant Center Factory workers], they got their benefits paid and were immediately . . . fired. . . . They put a list of their names on the front gate so they could not come in. They could only go to the accountant's office to do the paperwork. Bosses talk to each other and these lists sometimes become a blacklist. That would be your execution order, at least for a year. In fact, you cannot expect to be spoon-fed by your employer. [Center Factory] is a pleasant working environment. We are allowed to perform ablution and pray here.

Ebuzer felt that, by invoking the higher authority of religion, the workers were getting something the employer would not give them in other circumstances. In addition to the materiality of this reward, the time also helped them deal with the problem of the shopkeeper in İhsan Abi's story: labor was not a redeeming activity. It was a sacrifice they had to make to live at the expense of their future conditions in the hereafter. Praying during work partially ameliorated the damage done by their own labor. My coworkers were listening to İhsan Abi and Gülizar because those stories helped them relate their dissent to their search for purity.

The Neighborhood and the Nation

The neighborhood dynamics are important for two reasons. First, the working-class votes in big cities are crucial for the Islamists in elections. The answer to the question of how the Islamist AKP and its leader Erdoğan can still receive 35–50 percent of the votes after a decade-long decline in wages, rampant corruption, and political oppression lies in the domination of the working people at the neighborhood level. Second, the same working-class votes are crucial for the Islamists to be able to claim the ideological representation of the working class and, indirectly, the leadership of the nation as a whole.

If it had not been for the local dynamics discussed in this chapter, Islamists could not have stayed in power in Turkey for multiple decades and their support would have declined in the 2010s as dramatically as support for right-wing parties had declined in the 1990s. A number of historical factors turned these dynamics into instruments favoring the political hegemony of the Islamists in the working-class neighborhoods of cities that had significant manufacturing activity.

The political cadres have persistently sought the support of small producers since the 1970s and have calibrated their policymaking to deliver various subsidies, including cheap credit, to them since they came to power in 2002. The pious business community boosted the already individualist mindset of the small manufacturers and made them politically dependent on the Islamists. The religious orders framed the normative terms of their relationship with their workers and granted them moral superiority in their community. The almost chaotic nature of the relations between individual entrepreneurs and their customers played an independent role in the transformation of the urban and industrial landscape and created the social context where workers would see them as respectable members of their community.

The combined effect of all these factors is the political hegemony of the Islamists in urban working-class neighborhoods. In other words, the key historical message of this material is that the city, not the provinces, was the birthplace of Turkish Islamism. Its hegemony in the city was not produced in a distant past but in the current generation. Unless the conditions for this hegemony disappear or change, the Islamists will continue to be strong actors in these neighborhoods and in the nation as a whole, even if they lose power in coming years.

The growing hegemony of Islamists over the industrial working class has certainly been susceptible to numerous contingencies since the 1970s. Islamist clerics, including Zahid Kotku and Said Nurs-i in the early years of their careers, were well aware that those who controlled industrial production would control politics. However, their strategic decision to train a technocratic cadre for the government bureaucracy could easily have failed if pro-small industrialist charismatic figures such as Necmettin Erbakan and Turgut Özal had not taken the lead. As in Egypt, the secularist leadership of the 1970s could have opted for a much slower export-led growth strategy. As in Tunisia, the socialists could have developed successful practices of political mobilization among manufacturing workers in the 1980s. As in Indonesia, the electoral base of the movement could have split into two or more electorally relevant Islamist parties in the 1990s.

One structural advantage minimized the effect of all these contingencies for the Islamists in Turkey: the competing political actors cannot or do not penetrate Islamists' hegemony at the neighborhood level. The socialists' political capacities in the working-class neighborhoods were irreversibly damaged by state oppression after the 1980 coup and by their reluctance to discuss the core of their theory in the post–Cold War context. Other actors similarly failed to or chose not to challenge the Islamist hegemony. As shown in the next chapter, this was the main reason the Islamists not only survived the 2010s as the leading political movement of the country but also expanded the scope of the regimes of domination from neighborhood settings like Bağcılar to the nation as a whole.

SIX

Rifts and Authoritarianism

THE CONCERTED LETHARGY

IT WAS PAST 3 A.M. The cigarette smoke, the leftover food, and the empty tea glasses on the large coffee table told of a long night of debates over the economic promises of the opposition Republican People's Party (RPP) for the 2018 elections, just a few months away.

We were on the top floor of party headquarters in the office of our patron, the vice chairman for economic policy. Our entire team, including myself, had been purged from academia a year earlier after protesting the 2015 killings of civilians by government forces in the Kurdish region. We took our unconstitutional firings as signs of the further dismantlement of weak democratic institutions. RPP was the only challenger to the Islamist Justice and Development Party (AKP) that had a sufficient electoral base to reverse that process.

Members of Parliament and deputy party leaders came by, sometimes for ten minutes, sometimes for over an hour, to listen to the conversation. They were curious because a sincere strategic and political debate was rare in the party at that point. The scene probably looked extraordinary to them because most people in the party were careerists.

Our team wanted to send a clear message to the working class. The party had failed to expand its voter base over the past two decades, and it was time to say something new. Along with a universal income support program, we argued for promising workers not populist measures such as a raise in minimum wage but a voice in economic matters, an institutional framework to expand a nationwide network of workers' cooperatives and social enterprises. The plan was not radical or even new. The RPP had a long history of similar initiatives, such as the State Industrial and Labor Investment Bank, established in 1972 in coalition with the Islamists. The context was different, so the model should be different, yet the basic message could be the same: give initiative to workers in nonmonopoly industrial (and, later, commercial) enterprises. This would be a direct attack on the hegemony of the faubourgeoisie at the local level. This structural intervention in the faubourgeois-Islamist alliance could destabilize the bond between the alliance and the proletariat.

Others in the room held that the recent decline in wages should sweep the Islamists from government, so there was no need to propose specific programs. The erosion in living standards would take care of political change. Unlike our team members, these people had little to lose if defeated at the ballot box. Some of them had successful small businesses that mainly worked for wealthy secularist clients or for local governments. The RPP governed the wealthiest cities and regions in the country and roughly a fourth of the municipalities. The sizable budgets gave the party leadership considerable control over the party apparatus and attracted small businesspeople. A leftist ideological and programmatic change would have jeopardized the positions of leadership and these entrepreneurs. Our patron's political career depended on the approval of those within this complex matrix of relationships. At one point, he lost his temper during one of my tedious monologues: "Utku, I understand what you are getting at, but forget about the AKP voters. Just tell me, how am I supposed to explain these ideas to my own constituents?"

There was silence in response. He was right.

I had been working for about two years as an advisor to the party's highest officials after being fired from Ankara University for protesting military operations in Kurdish cities. My interactions with party members in 2017–18 had convinced me that many rank-and-file members disapproved of the lethargy of the party. Yet they would not sacrifice their resources and privileges, give up their Sundays, or skip their long summer vacations to incite a revolt in the party. Many of them were convinced it was impossible to break the almost mystical bond between the working class and the Islamists. To them, the legacy of the Islamic imperial order remained: workers were uneducated, and they prioritized their interests over the nation's. Even though they would call themselves "leftists" or even "revolutionaries," the first reaction of many party members to a rights-based universal income program like ours was "Wouldn't this policy reward free riders?"

In the RPP's broader narrative, redistribution was treated as a detail. The mission of the century-old party, most of its members believed, was to advance the country into the league of modern nations after defeating the antimodernist Islamists. Ironically, the very presence of the RPP as a modernist rather than leftist party allowed the Islamists to claim the legacy of the entire pre-republican history; obscure the fact that they were as new or old a political current as the socialists, Kurdish separatists, and ultranationalists; and claim outsider legitimacy despite having ruled since 2002.

Our patron was aware that a hidden dimension in the narrative of Turkey's supposedly social democratic main opposition party was the main obstacle to an ideological transformation that could challenge the Islamists' legitimacy. With a Rawlsian mindset, the leadership and members would be happy if the living conditions of the working class improved, but only if their own living conditions improved faster. Growth, not redistribution, was the priority. Many party cadres were small businessmen, just like those in the AKP. As a group of small manufacturers, contractors, shopkeepers, and slumlords, the faubourgeoisie was therefore a potential ally of the party, or at least a social class to negotiate with. Our team had been asked to develop a plan to win the support of the faubourgeoisie, not to attack them as a class actor. From an organizational and ideological point of view, the RPP was a scaled-down version of the AKP. Its leaders shared an economic policy vision that was very similar to that of the Islamists, only less convincing.

We drafted a good part of the economic section of the election manifesto and managed to sneak some of our ideas into the text. Social entrepreneurship became part of the official party line. During the election campaign, however, the political cadre chose to overlook these ideas. They instead told a fairy tale about Industry 4.0, advanced cybernetics, and high value-added production, as if not knowing that these ideas would sound, to many unskilled workers, like threats to their jobs.

The RPP lost the 2018 presidential elections, like so many previous ones. This proved the subtext of the party's message a failure, yet no one within the RPP seemed to care. In 2023, the RPP used the same narrative in another presidential election. It lost again.

In the early 2010s, however, there had been good reasons to believe the Islamists would not succeed in circumventing democratic practices and institutions. As a result of a series of politico-judicial operations and a controversial referendum in 2010, the secularist leadership of the military, whose 1980 coup had empowered the Islamists in the first place, was largely pacified. With the military out of the way, the usual electoral process could have sent the Islamists back into opposition.

Not only did this dialectical redemption not happen, but the Islamists also managed to oust or pacify their three main challengers from the political stage:

the secularists; the Kurdish movement; and the Gülenists, an Islamist faction rivaling the Erdoğan clique. The victory of the Islamists, now led exclusively by the Erdoğan clique, enabled them to assume an increasingly authoritarian position and present the faubourgeoisie as the vanguard of the Turkish nation.

In chapters 4 and 5, I defined the basic terms of the faubourgeois-Islamist alliance at the local level. In this chapter, I use the lessons drawn from those chapters to discuss the unfolding of these three rifts at the national level in the 2010s. Each rift debunks a different myth about Islamism in Turkey. The way the rift with the secularists ended illustrates that it was not existential. These camps could reconcile their interests under the right circumstances. The Islamists' attacks on the Kurdish movement and civilians show that Islamism in Turkey is antidemocratic. The internal rift between Islamist factions led by Tayyip Erdoğan and Fethullah Gülen showed that the Islamists did not have an integrated and long-term agenda to move the country to a theocratic regime.

This chapter presents an alternative regarding national politics. The growing hegemony of the Islamists in the 2010s demands a comprehensive assessment of those three rifts, and the Islamist-faubourgeois alliance needs to be at the center of this discussion. The secularist-Islamist rift ended with reconciliation between the faubourgeoisie and the petty bourgeoisie—the social class composed of professionals, bureaucrats, and scholars—because the petty bourgeois secularists, as a beneficiary, were reluctant to interfere in relations between the faubourgeoisie and the proletariat in the working-class neighborhoods. The growing visibility of the Kurdish faubourgeoisie disturbed both the Islamist and Kurdish movements for different reasons and facilitated the end of the peace process in the mid-2010s. Resentment among small industrialists against the major Gülenist business families helped the Erdoğan clique muster the local support of the faubourgeoisie and present itself as the leader of the Islamist movement.

THE SECULARISTS: FROM TENSION TO RECONCILIATION

A Tacit Coalition

When Necmettin Erbakan began his journey as the first leader of the young Islamist movement in the late 1960s, he had a modest goal. He wanted to represent small businessmen, then a politically and economically weak interest group. In those years, the vanguards of the nation were the soldiers and the bureaucrats, as symbolized in the mausoleum of Kemal Atatürk, the

FIGURE 16. Vanguards of the nation. (Left) *Turkish Men* statue group, Atatürk Museum-Mausoleum (1953). Courtesy of İlker Yavuz. (Right) Statue of Ahi Evran (1171–1261) holding a piece of fabric, Kırşehir (1991). Source: Süleyman Alkan / Alamy Stock Photo.

founder of the republican regime. The *Turkish Men* statue group in front of the mausoleum's Freedom Tower consists of three men (see figure 16). The two standing in front are a soldier in uniform and a bureaucrat holding a book—the pioneers of the petty bourgeoisie. The third figure is a shepherd standing behind them in traditional dress, symbolizing the rural working class whose political support made it possible for the petty bourgeoisie to rule the country for most of the twentieth century. None of these figures exist politically today: the soldier and bureaucrat now work on the Islamists' payroll, and the shepherd moved to the city.

Erdoğan offered an alternative symbolization of the nation, one embodied by Ahi Evran, who established the Ahi Brotherhood of Muslim craftsman guilds in the thirteenth century. After appeasing the bureaucrats and the generals, Erdoğan declared 2021 the "Year of Ahi Evran" and defined the shopkeeper as "the safeguard of the nation":

Our ancestors are renowned of their skill to establish new states in the world.... These states were established not only with the sword. Ahi Evran's... guild organization [*ahilik*] established the basis of commerce and solidarity in this land. ... This organization with its judges, scholars, masters, journeymen, and apprentices established the cadres of the state [*devlet erkanı*] and supported the sultans.... The shopkeeper is not just a person who buys, sells, trades. The shopkeeper is also the eyes, ears, voice, conscience, guardian [*hami*], guide [*yol gösterici*] of his neighborhood [*muhit*]. The ancient culture inherited from Ahi Evran lets the shopkeeper make predictions that are superior to those made by research companies, sociologists, and political scientists.[1]

To Erdoğan, "shopkeepers and artisans are the backbone of this country and nation."[2] The most notable success of the Islamists in the 2010s was that they identified the faubourgeoisie as the vanguard of the nation. As representatives of the faubourgeoisie, the Islamists represent the entire nation. Today, this ideology is unchallenged, hegemonic, and supreme.

The key factor that helped the Islamists redefine Turkish nationalism was, ironically, the tacit support they received from the secularists. Their seeming conflict gave both the Islamist AKP and the secularist RPP a secure place at the center of party politics. This political constellation resulted from a tacit agreement between the faubourgeoisie and the petty bourgeoisie about the redistributive terms of national politics. As a collection of professionals, government officials, and scholars, the petty bourgeoisie was a beneficiary of the Islamists' economic policies. Professionals and managers were the two major occupational groups with the highest annual average gross earnings between 2006 and 2022. During that time, there was no substantial change in the ratio of their earnings to those of other major occupational groups.[3]

The petty bourgeoisie was also a major beneficiary of the construction frenzy under AKP governments. The number of building permits increased from 162,000 in 2002 to 518,000 in 2009 to 995,000 in 2016. The registered value of these units increased from $6 billion in 2002 to $62 billion in 2016,[4] and construction as a share of Turkey's total value added grew by 79 percent, from 5.3 percent in 2002 to 9.5 percent in 2017, a period during which the global average decreased from 6.2 percent to 5.6 percent.[5] However, between 2006 and 2022, the home ownership rate in Turkey fell from 61 percent to 57 percent for the national population and from 59 percent to 49 percent for those living below the EU-defined poverty line.[6] According to the OECD, rental price index values in Turkey increased by 369 percent between 2003 and 2016, while the average country value in the same dataset increased by 149 percent.[7] The share of households that owned a second house grew by 55 percent, from 5.8 percent in 2003 to 9 percent in 2016.[8] More importantly, the share of those between the eightieth and the ninety-ninth percentiles of the wealth distribution (i.e., the nonbourgeois households who had above-average wealth) grew by a whopping 8 percent between 2002 and 2021, without any interruption except for 2009–10.[9]

In short, the Islamist governments treated the 19 percent of the population who were petty bourgeoisie or faubourgeoisie well. Notwithstanding his constant laments and apocalyptic predictions about the country's future under Islamist rule, the typical petty bourgeois secularist has been satisfied with the progress of his finances over the past two decades. As an RPP politician in a key party position told me privately, "Our voters want the AKP to rule the country and RPP to protect their interests." This golden formula has shaped the basic lines of politics since 2002.

Nonetheless, the petty bourgeois secularists had some real concerns about the future. The current generation is doing well, but they worry their resources might not be enough to save their children from proletarianization, especially after the Islamists diminished the prestige of education as a means of class mobility or stability. The discrepancy between the immediate economic benefits of Islamists' policies for them and their fears for the future triggered two somewhat contradictory reactions in the 2010s. These reactions illustrate how the petty bourgeoisie defines its class interests and why the rift between the secularists and the Islamists did not pose a major challenge to the latter and may have even helped the Islamists consolidate their position in government.

The first reaction was the consolidation of a de facto coalition between the Islamists and the secularists, which assigned the Islamists the national government and the secularists the municipal governments of the richest cities. The second reaction was the co-optation of the mass demonstrations in 2013, known as the Gezi protests, by cosmopolitan secularist protesters as a bargaining chip against the faubourgeois-Islamist alliance.

Negotiating the Slice of the Pie

The first reaction of the petty bourgeoisie to Islamist rule was to contribute to the formation of a de facto two-party system in the 2010s. This process began with the 2002 elections that brought the Islamists to power. Deniz Baykal, the leader of the RPP between 1995 and 2010, changed his party's ideology from social democracy to right-wing secularism and turned the RPP into an anachronistic version of the Republican Trust Party of the 1960s and 1970s.[10] This shift spared the Islamists political pressure from the left. Baykal's RPP would represent the petty bourgeois secularists and Erdoğan's AKP the pious workers under the leadership of the faubourgeoisie.

After Kemal Kılıçdaroğlu replaced Baykal in 2010, he vowed to distance the RPP from Baykal's hardline secularist position. The new leadership initially looked eager to end the Baykal–Erdoğan charade and mobilize the working class with a left-oriented political agenda. It soon became clear that Kılıçdaroğlu's strategy was to move the party further to the right in order to appeal to pious and ultranationalist voters.

The first step in this direction was the RPP's alliance with the ultranationalist Nationalist Movement Party (NMP) for the 2014 presidential elections. Although neither party was Islamist, their candidate was a devout Muslim with antirepublican family roots: Ekmeleddin İhsanoğlu, the former chairman of the Organization of Islamic Cooperation. İhsanoğlu's candidacy was an unofficial declaration by the RPP that the secularist-Islamist cleavage was over. The experiment only helped Erdoğan become president.

This election result should have sent a strong signal to the secularists that the reason the working class supported the Islamists was not Islam as such. But the message fell on deaf ears. The 2017 constitutional referendum, which replaced the parliamentary system with a presidential system, further solidified a de facto two-party system that was no longer characterized by the secularist-Islamist binary. For this referendum, the NMP sided with the AKP and the RPP found new allies in the new ultranationalist Good Party and some smaller Islamist parties founded by former AKP members. In 2018, this alliance called itself the Nation Alliance. In turn, the AKP founded the People Alliance with the NMP and smaller secularist parties. Both alliances contained Islamist and secularist elements. In the last years of the 2010s, not only was the secularist-Islamist divide that had troubled the public since the 1990s over, but it was also becoming increasingly difficult to distinguish between the RPP and AKP in terms of their policymaking priorities.[11]

Fighting for a Bigger Slice

The petty bourgeois secularists' second response to the Islamists was to get involved in street politics. They joined and later dominated the wave of protests in the early 2010s. The peak demonstrations were in summer 2013, when more than three million people rallied against the government in all but one of the country's provinces.[12]

According to the standard narrative, the driving force behind these demonstrations, which became known as the Gezi protests, was "the concern of the country's secular population over the shrinking ground of their lifestyle as a result of government pressure."[13] As a liberating moment for the country, the protests represented "a new threshold for democracy, where old dividing lines between authoritarian secularism and Islam are overcome and new forms of citizenship are rehearsed."[14] The epic echoes of this narrative are tantalizing, but two small problems disrupt the core of the argument.

First, the Gezi demonstrations were a peak in a broader and longer wave of protests. According to David Clark and Patrick Regan's database of mass mobilization protests, there were more political protests between 2011 and 2013 than in the first nine years of the AKP government, between 2002 and 2010.[15] In other words, the Gezi protests were merely one moment in a longer process. The secularist–Islamist tension was only one of many motives that drove people onto the streets. Second, the focus of these "worried secular people" was on "connective actions" rather than collective actions,[16] and the Gezi protests "faded away without leaving a trace on the national political map of Turkey."[17] After the 2013 protests, the liberal cosmopolitan protesters vanished from the political scene.

In this regard, the literature's emphasis on and tacit glorification of the reluctance of protesters to engage in long-term mobilization efforts and collective action is revealing. Young professionals, artists, and students from elite schools dominated the representation of the protests with iconic images and performative actions that symbolized their "dashed liberal hopes."[18] The resulting milieu has been called "the Gezi spirit" that helped these petty bourgeois protesters "become subjects of their own lives."[19] The embedded individualism in their artistic and political performances was a form of resistance against the oppressive Islamist collectivity.

One notable moment during the protests was the performance of Erdem Gündüz, known as the Standing Man. He stood motionless for hours in the public square next to Gezi Park where the protests began.[20] The public attention his performance attracted illustrates the kind of political action the cosmopolitan protester was prepared to take: passive, distanced, and self-centered. The literature helps identify the hidden power dynamics between the protesters, who portrayed the Gezi protests as a "middle-class revolt,"[21] and socialist workers like Ethem Sarısülük, shot in the head by police on the second day of the protests in Ankara, just two hundred yards away from where my friends and I were standing in the crowd.[22]

My firsthand experience as a participant in protests in Ankara, Diyarbakır, and Istanbul convinced me they were as much a struggle against the government as a contest between cosmopolitan protesters and socialists. The socialists vehemently tried to convince demonstrators to take the protests from the squares or parks they were occupying to working-class neighborhoods, but the petty bourgeois demonstrators were satisfied with what they had achieved. They would not beg workers and the poor to join their struggle. If they wanted to emancipate themselves, they would have to join the petty bourgeois protesters on their terms. They did not need or want to compromise between their class agenda and that of the socialists.

Everything I saw at these protest sites was reminiscent of what I had seen at the Occupy Wall Street protests in Philadelphia in 2011. As a nonnative Philadelphian, I attended protests and led a teach-in in Dilworth Park. Almost exactly as in Ankara and Istanbul, the protesters were split into two camps. A small minority of socialist protesters invited everyone to go to the predominantly African American working-class neighborhoods, while most protesters invented a perfect tactic to justify their reticence: they were in no position to impose their political will on the African Americans. This would have amounted to taking away their agency—it would have been cultural imperialism. I recall that one of those who defended this position even used the term *white man's burden* against these mostly young and inexperienced socialists. In Philadelphia and Istanbul, everyone knew that a decision to go to those neighborhoods would have serious consequences, including exposing oneself to unfiltered violence not only from law enforcement but also from local elites of various stripes. Two years later, in Istanbul and Ankara, the Turkish version of the same petty bourgeois mentality dominated the protests, albeit with slightly different terminology. The universality of the petty bourgeois ideology surprised me once again.

Ultimately, the petty bourgeois protesters ousted the socialists from the collective memory of the event, both during the protests and after.[23] These same petty bourgeois protesters, having appropriated the collective memory, lost interest in politics almost immediately after they ended. The people who had pretended to be revolutionaries on the streets quickly returned to their normal lives. Those who paid the price with their lives or years in prison, including nonsocialist human rights activists like Osman Kavala, found no sustained, substantial support from these so-called revolutionaries.[24]

In fact, like the individualism expressed by the artistic and political performances during the protests, the subsequent lethargy of the secularists was telling. The protest wave was not over in 2013. According to Clark and Regan, democratic political momentum increased after the Gezi protests: protests between 2014 and 2016 outnumbered those between 2011 and 2013. However, the petty bourgeois Gezi protesters acted as if they had lost not only the battle, but also the war they claimed to be fighting. They did their best to turn the protests into a moment of nostalgia, a relic of the past.

This sudden change of collective mood among the secularists points to the petty bourgeoisie's collective motivation for participating in the 2013 protests. Taking advantage of the antisystemic nature of these demonstrations, the petty bourgeoisie used this moment as a bargaining chip to advance its class interests against the Islamists, rather than joining a coalition with the working class to end Islamist rule. As the divide between Islamists and secularists became less central to Turkish politics, this negotiation process, expressed in both electoral alliances and street protests, reflected the reconciliation of class interests between the faubourgeoisie and the petty bourgeoisie after the latter had accepted the hegemony of the former.

From the Islamists' perspective, both their resilience to the waves of protest between 2011 and 2016 and the willingness of the secularist petty bourgeoisie to play the two-party game were crucial opportunities to claim the new political establishment for themselves. The waves of protest during this period presented the Islamists with a unique challenge. They had no repertoire for a meaningful conversation with labor unions, chambers of professionals, feminists, LGBTQ people, and many other dissenting groups. Moreover, up until this point, they were the ones protesting the establishment. Now, they were obliged to respond to these various demands. Perhaps most importantly, they had been playing the role of "the democratic and democratizing Islamist" for over a decade and it was now time to test their sincerity.

The Islamists failed this test because the protesters' demands were in direct opposition to the moral order they wanted to establish in working-class neighborhoods. Had they given in, the resulting political milieu could have sparked resistance like never before. A single image of many garment workers wearing hijabs protesting their employers on the streets of Bağcılar would have put a major dent in the political hegemony of the Islamists in these neighborhoods as well as on petty bourgeois secularists' claim to represent the opposition.

The Islamists' success against the protesters strengthened them considerably. They won against the seemingly all-powerful Turkish military. They continued to win at the ballot box. The only serious threat remained popular action triggered by nationwide democratic demonstrations such as the Gezi protests. The concerted lethargy of the petty bourgeois secularists after these protests helped the Islamists overcome this last barrier of fear. From that moment on, they felt so empowered that they believed they could do anything without any serious backlash from the public. In this respect, the Gezi protests helped the Islamists take a big leap in an authoritarian direction.

THE KURDS: FROM NEGOTIATION TO CONFLICT

A Long History

A rupture with the Kurdish movement in the 2010s helped the Islamists further consolidate their power. Most Kurds are devout Sunnis, and Kurds and Islamists have a long history. Some Kurdish uprisings against the early republican regime had a religious character. The Islamists exploited this background in the 1970s to gain the support of local landowners and religious leaders in the Kurdish region as an alternative to Süleyman Demirel's center-right Justice Party. Devout Kurds' continued support of the Islamists was a key factor in the survival of the Islamist movement in the 1970s.[25]

In the 1980s, the separatist Kurdistan Workers' Party (PKK) initiated an armed resistance movement and expanded its support base. The PKK was a secular movement with a socialist background. In turn, the Islamist movement continued to gain significant support among the devout Kurdish electorate. The antisocialist and racist regime had denied the existence of the Kurds for decades and was eager to harshly punish supporters of an ethnic leftist movement. Religious conservatism offered Kurds limited recognition as members of the wider Islamic community, albeit in an underprivileged position, and a haven from the state's wrath. Turkish Kurdistan was electorally shared between the Islamists and the pro-socialist Kurdish movement.

The military conflict in the 1990s triggered massive outmigration of up to 10 percent of the country's entire Kurdish population, from the Kurdish provinces to the Turkish metropolitan regions, as part of the military's expulsion policy.[26] This exodus continued under AKP governments after 2002, as the Kurdish region continued to be the poorest part of the country due to

TABLE 4 Rate of change in AKP's vote shares (2007–2015)

Vote share (rate of change from previous election)	2007	2011	2015 (1)	2015 (2)
Kurdish-prominent provinces	45%	41% (−10%)	25% (−39%)	35% (+41%)
Non-Kurdish provinces	49%	54% (+10%)	46% (−14%)	55% (+20%)

SOURCE: Supreme Election Council (YSK, "Açık Veri Portalı").

NOTE: According to the 1965 census, Kurdish-prominent provinces are Adıyaman, Ağrı, Batman, Bingöl, Bitlis, Diyarbakır, Hakkari, Kars, Mardin, Muş, Siirt, Şanlıurfa, Şırnak, Tunceli, Van (Devlet İstatistik Enstitüsü, *Genel Nüfus Sayımı 24.10.1965. [Census of population, social and economic characteristics of population]*).

the AKP's decision to invest a third less per person in that region than it did in other regions.[27]

The Kurdish movement tacitly endorsed the transfer of power from the secularist establishment to the Islamists, and the Islamists began secret negotiations with the PKK around 2009. These negotiations, known as the "peace process," helped the Islamists pass constitutional amendments in 2010 that curtailed some of the military's administrative powers and expanded the AKP's control over the judiciary. The Kurdish movement boycotted that 2010 constitutional referendum, allowing the Islamists to pass these amendments.

The peace process benefited both parties electorally. The AKP won 49.8 percent of the vote in the 2011 parliamentary elections, its biggest electoral victory to date, while the Kurdish movement expanded its voter base among Kurds at the expense of the Islamist movement (see table 4). This observation contradicts the common perception that Turkish voters were not satisfied with the negotiations. In other words, the Turkish electorate kept the Islamists in power despite its strong nationalist sentiments and suspicions of the peace process, and the Kurdish electorate split from the Islamists despite the success of the peace process. Thus, negotiations with the Kurdish movement were a give-and-take process for the Islamists. Between 2011 and 2015, the Islamists lost a larger share of the vote among Kurdish voters than among Turkish voters. The decline of support for the Islamists among the Kurds was a major factor in the Islamists' loss of their majority in Parliament in the June 2015 elections.

Erdoğan unofficially ended the peace process shortly before the June 2015 elections because he knew the peace negotiations would no longer help him at the ballot box. The AKP sabotaged the coalition negotiations and abused a loophole in the constitution to rerun the election. Mysterious episodes of violence before the second election, including a suicide attack killing 101 peaceful demonstrators at a "Peace and Democracy" rally on October 10, 2015, helped the AKP increase its vote share from 40.9 percent in June to 49.5 percent in November.[28]

During this period between the June 2015 and October 2015 elections, the Islamists initiated a military operation in densely populated Kurdish cities. According to the Turkish Human Rights Foundation, at least 310 civilians died in clashes between August 2015 and March 2016.[29] Thousands of Kurdish activists were arrested and imprisoned, including many high-ranking left-oriented leaders of the pro-Kurdish Peoples' Democratic Party (PDP) such as Selahattin Demirtaş and Gültan Kışanak. Almost all PDP municipalities were appointed government trustees in place of elected mayors. Harassment and violence by government forces are now part of Kurds' daily lives.

Albeit factually correct, this political and military history of the relationship between the Islamists and the Kurdish movements is silent about an actor whose changing political stance framed the positions of both parties in the negotiation process: the Kurdish faubourgeoisie. Based on their locations and business practices, there are three distinct groups within the Kurdish faubourgeoisie.

The Kurdish sweatshop owners in Turkey's metropolitan regions constitute the first and numerically largest of these categories. Like many others in Istanbul and other major cities in the country, Mr. Survivor, one of the central figures in chapter 4, was a victim of internal displacement and a staunch supporter of the Kurdish movement. However, he was also an instrument of the proletarianization of the Kurdish rural refugees who came to the major cities under similar circumstances. Thus, as long as the Kurdish movement lacked political legitimacy, he posed no substantial threat to the Islamist-faubourgeois alliance in the working-class neighborhoods of these cities, regardless of his political beliefs and ethnic identity. The rest of this subsection describes two others who affect the evolving relations between the Kurdish and Islamist movements: Kurdish exporters and entrepreneurs in Turkish Kurdistan.

The Kurdish Exporter. Like the smaller Kurdish entrepreneurs in major Turkish cities, such as Mr. Survivor, the larger Kurdish exporters, the second prominent group within the Kurdish faubourgeoisie, play a crucial role in the economy by connecting manufacturers in Turkey with the Iraqi and Syrian markets. My observations between 2012 and 2015 as a researcher, during my project on the industrializing cities of Anatolia and as a project expert for the Ministry of Family and Social Policies, provided me with insights about these entrepreneurs.

Gaziantep was one of the three cities I studied for that 2012–15 project. Near Syria, it increased its share of the country's GDP more than any other city between 2004 and 2021.[30] During my research in Gaziantep in 2014 and 2015, twelve of my fifty-five interviewees mentioned the Kurdish entrepreneurs in their city, even though I did not ask a direct question about that topic. My interviewees agreed that Kurdish entrepreneurs make up a significant part of Gaziantep's business community and that the expanding trade volume with the Kurdish regions in Iraq and Syria contributed to the economic growth of the city. The net turnover of the companies belonging to my interviewees who identified themselves as Kurdish and were included in the Istanbul Chamber of Industry's First and Second Top 500 Industrial Enterprises Lists (ISO1000) in the early 2010s accounted for roughly 10 percent of the total net turnover of ISO1000 companies in Gaziantep, or approximately $760 million. Some of the interviewees did not want to reveal their ethnic identity, so I suspect the actual number is higher. These entrepreneurs had privileged access to markets in Kurdish areas in Turkey, Syria, and Iraq. Those with connections to the Barzani family in Iraqi Kurdistan not only boosted the volume of their business but also helped other businesses in Gaziantep succeed.

An outstanding example is Kadooğlu Holding. When I interviewed Celal Kadooğlu, a member of the owning family, the company's annual net sales were around $152 million. Between 2003 and 2006, after the US invasion decimated Iraq's infrastructure, the company refined and exported $700 million of oil to Iraq. After starting their business just to distribute major Turkish brands in Iraqi Kurdistan, the family opened multiple facilities in Gaziantep. For instance, their cooking oil plant, the fourth largest in Turkey, began its operations in 2007.

Thanks to this success, Ömer Sabancı, a member of the country's second richest family and chairman of Tüsiad, the business association of the country's largest industrialists, invited Tarkan Kadooğlu, the chairman of Kadooğlu Holding, to join Tüsiad in 2008. He first served on the board of Türkonfed, Tüsiad's SME organization, from 2005 to 2009. He joined the Tüsiad board in 2013–14. He also served as Türkonfed's deputy chairman from 2009 to 2015 and as chairman in 2015.[31]

The Kadooğlu family was not happy with being portrayed in the media as "the Kurdish figurehead of Tüsiad." In a 2013 interview, Tarkan Kadooğlu emphasized that the commonality of Tüsiad was not the ethnic identity of its members. Although he supported the peace process as a proud Kurd, he believed that 95 percent of Kurds would remain within Turkey if there were a referendum: "The Kurds are the only people who have remained loyal to the Turks since the Ottoman Empire. . . . If I secede from Turkey, will I be able to enjoy the view of . . . the Bosporus from my office?"[32]

Nonetheless, in his opinion, poverty was not the only reason Kurds joined the PKK, because "both the rich and the poor joined the armed resistance [*dağa çıkmak*]." Thus, he supported the peace process, but not just for the Kurdish cause. The negotiations, he knew, could also bring new investment opportunities: "We cannot expect people to invest in a region ravaged by violence. The capitalists are nervous and timid [*korkak, ürkek*]. Unless he dominates [*hükmetmek*], he does not feel safe, he will not invest. As soon as the violence in the [Kurdish] region and in the country comes to an end, it will be our task to make investments in the region. Not only the members of Tüsiad, but all of us must invest in the region."[33]

Kadooğlu Holding's Tüsiad membership embodied the bourgeoisie's alternative to the Islamist and separatist answers to "the Kurdish question" and was an attempt to establish and utilize Türkonfed as a Trojan horse within the faubourgeoisie.[34] In return, Kadooğlu had his own agenda: to dominate the Kurdish region as a member of the Kurdish bourgeoisie. However, just as Türkonfed, a secularist SME business association, was no alternative to Müsiad's narrative and actions, neither could Tarkan Kadooğlu achieve his goal. He was charged as the instigator of the murder of one of his business partners in 2018 and sentenced to life imprisonment in 2022.[35]

The Businessman of Kurdistan. The third outstanding personality of the Kurdish faubourgeoisie, the Kurdish businessman in Kurdistan, was the strongest candidate for changing the political dynamics of the Kurdish polity if negotiations between PKK and the Islamists came to fruition. According to Ayşe Seda Yüksel's research in the early 2010s in the industrial park of Diyarbakır, the largest Kurdish city within Turkey, most owners of these businesses had moved there from rural areas in the 1970s or later. Some of them had been activists in the Kurdish movement in their youth.[36] Nevertheless, these businessmen had a bad reputation among the city's inhabitants as greedy and unreliable rentiers. For instance, when some Kurdish businessmen, including Raif Türk, the president of the Diyarbakır Chamber of Industry (DISIAD) and a former activist in the movement, declared their support for the constitutional amendments in the 2010 referendum, Kurdish militants burned their construction equipment and vehicles.

This negative perception of these businessmen slowly changed when this group established a close relationship with the Kurdish movement in the early 2010s. This reconfiguration posed a new risk to the Kurdish movement: "We know DISIAD is actively working to support the municipality [in the project to renovate the old city walls of Diyarbakır]. Such developments are changing the negative perception of Kurds toward capitalists, who are now seen as a class that is necessary [for the city's growth. . . . However], if you create jobs within the framework of wild capitalism, you contribute to exploitation. This class division is one of the most important points in the Kurdish question. A very radical neoliberal transformation is taking place. The [resulting] class conflict could prove to be a major problem in the future."[37] The peace process was not only about the high-level negotiations to end the military conflict, but also about everyday life practices and economic relations that could change the fabric of urban Kurdish society.

I made similar observations during this time. For example, in 2014, after I provided training to the Diyarbakır municipality staff as an expert for the Ministry of Family and Social Policies project, my host asked whether I would like to go to a DISIAD meeting with the municipality— I had told him about my ongoing research project. I gratefully accepted this offer. Because the tables were reserved for DISIAD members and PDP representatives, we sat in a corner of the large hall. First, Mayor Gültan Kışanak, who would be imprisoned in 2016 and sentenced to fourteen years in prison for her alleged participation in the 2014 protests against the Turkish invasion of the Kurdish region of Syria, spoke to the all-male audience, the industrialists of Diyarbakır. She emphasized that their business success was closely linked to the success of the PDP, as no other party would ever seriously intend to develop the city economically. Her tone was warm but guarded: she implied her listeners were not the movement's main interest in Diyarbakır. The body language of the businessmen was generally tense. No one touched their plate during the speech; many had their hands on their laps, not on the tables. Kışanak's message was that PDP politicians did not consider these businessmen to be pioneers of the Kurdish people. Rather, the Kurdish movement tolerated them. After all, Kışanak was a socialist politician.

After Kışanak, Altan Tan spoke to the audience. An Islamist Kurd, he had been a member of the central executive committee of the (Islamist) Welfare Party in 1990. During the peace process, the PDP included non-leftist figures like him in order to reach out to conservative Kurds, and he was elected as a PDP member of Parliament in 2011 at the height of the negotiations. Tan's tone was highly critical of Kışanak. Although he did not address her directly in most parts of his speech, he touched on similar themes to highlight his differences. He emphasized that it was necessary to support the industrialists if the Kurdish movement wanted the peace process to succeed. The Diyarbakır municipality should have taken additional steps beyond its normal municipal duties to boost the local economy.

His most notable point concerned a new tram project in the city center, which Kışanak briefly mentioned in her speech as good news. Tan attacked the project: "Dear mayor presents this as a success story, but Bursa [one of the most industrialized cities in the country] is now producing the cars of these trams, while we present the laying of the tracks as a major step forward. I would call it a success only when we start building our tram cars." Tan offered a different vision that would encourage the small manufacturers in Diyarbakır. His defiant position ran counter to the political line of the movement, because he saw Kışanak's position as unrealistic.

This exchange surprised me: by 2014, it was obvious that the peace process was about to end. Although the people of Diyarbakır, including my host, were optimistic about the future because of the social and cultural renaissance in the city, there was every indication that the Islamists were not acting in good faith. Therefore, I did not expect Kurdish politicians to be embroiled in an internal dispute over the politics of the day, because the storm was coming.

Upon reflection, I should not have been surprised. A striking observation I had made the year before, during the Gezi protests, gave me every indication that the peace process intersected with a growing rift within the Kurdish movement. After participating in the protests in Ankara and Istanbul and being disillusioned by what I saw, I decided to attend a conference on Kurdish studies in Diyarbakır.

The presentations on the historiography and methodology of Kurdish studies were excellent, yet I was surprised that the participants paid no attention to the ongoing Gezi protests. For most if not all of them, this was a nonissue, a detail. When I attended a pro–Gezi Park demonstration the next day, I was almost shocked to see no more than fifty protesters in this highly political city of more than 1.7 million. Nevertheless, a huge riot police vehicle was waiting in the narrow street where a few of us had gathered, pointing its water cannon at us. As far as I could tell from their style of dress, most demonstrators were teachers, professionals, and intellectuals. Almost no one in this small group was speaking Kurdish, and few were residents of the city. The Gezi protests did not take place in Diyarbakır.

In the evening, we were invited to a nice (but not fancy) restaurant, a meeting place for the city's intellectuals. It was a wonderful night, and almost everyone was a bit tipsy within the first hour or two. The conversations were intellectually intense and satisfying. I sat near a PhD student from Istanbul and a young man who had an interesting conversation about the city's changing cultural scene. I introduced myself and asked them about their professions. The young man (YM) replied,

YM: We [he and his family] have a local business here.

UB: What kind of business is that?

YM: We are building contractors.

UB: How nice! Is there a tender you are working on at the moment?

YM: Yes, we are working on the extension of the prison in Diyarbakır.

I was puzzled: I knew the AKP had been investing heavily to expand prisons and build new ones for some time, probably an indication of the Islamists' intention to turn the peace process into a hell for Kurdish activists. The $49 million Diyarbakır Prison Project, initiated in 2012, was the biggest of these projects, 9 percent of the total budget.[38] I had many questions about various issues, but the most important was how he could find a place in this highly politicized group that was critical of the Turkish state, the hegemonic and colonialist Turkish culture, and so on. But first, this question crossed my lips almost reflexively:

UB: How do you transport the building materials to the construction site? Don't the local people protest or attack your vehicles?

YM (with a smile): We hang the flag on the windshield.

UB: What flag?

Y M: Well, it does not matter which flag it is, as long as the colors green, red, and yellow are on it [the colors of the Kurdish flag].

U B: How can the government staff allow you to do that? Aren't they making your life difficult?

Y M: Not at all. . . . As long as the construction keeps going, they are happy.

This was a clear indication that the Islamists were determined to end the peace process as early as 2013. They were in a hurry to finish these prison projects in order to lock up the Kurdish activists after negotiations ended. They did not care what flag flew over the walls of these prisons as long as these activists were pacified by force.

After this conversation, I wanted to ask all the questions that were buzzing around in my head, but the guests suddenly fell silent. All eyes were now on a small television in the opposite corner of the crowded restaurant: the police had attacked the protesters to drive them out of Gezi Park in Istanbul.

The loud reactions varied. Some berated the police and the Turkish state. Others expressed satisfaction with laughter and relaxed comments. I heard heated discussions between people at almost every table. One camp expressed frustration at the incident. The other celebrated it as a moment when the Turks—the nationalist/racist Turks—finally got a taste of their own medicine: those Turkish protesters had found a safe haven in something like "White ignorance"[39] for years and their protests had been tolerated for weeks, a privilege that had never been granted the Kurds. Those in this second camp had a good point: despite the supposedly transformative experience of the Gezi protests, we knew that most of the petty bourgeois Turkish protesters would return home with the same racist ideas they held about the Kurds and their struggle for self-determination. It was all about them. It was always about them.

Because most of the evening's participants were Kurds, the division did not have much to do with ethnic backgrounds. The Turkish participants looked just as divided as the Kurdish ones. This was an almost purely ideological dispute. Perhaps that is why the division shocked the whole group. They were used to showing similar reflexes at such historical political events.

Then I sobered up a little and looked at the young man sitting across the narrow table, the builder of the prison that was to take many Kurdish activists hostage just a few years later. With a smile, he turned to me and said: "Don't [the Turkish protesters] deserve it? Am I not right, professor [*hocam*]?"

The Class Question of the Kurdish Movement, the Kurdish Question of the Islamist Movement

The changing profile of Kurdish entrepreneurs has both potentials and risks for the Islamist movement. Unlike in the 1990s, the new Kurdish businessman was more like Kadooğlu than Türk. Like the members of Müsiad who often boarded Turgut Özal's plane for profitable business trips to Turkic Central Asian countries, Kadooğlu developed a dual connection with the Kurdish working class and the Iraqi Kurdish elite. Kadooğlu made Turkish businessmen in Gaziantep richer, and he was not the only one to challenge the underprivileged position of Kurds in business and politics.

My Kurdish interlocutors in Gaziantep openly complained—perhaps due to the tolerant political milieu during the peace process—about the discrimination they faced despite their contribution to economic growth. One of them, a mill owner and one of Gaziantep's tax champions, said during a meeting with his business friends: "Erdoğan gives something with a spoon but takes it back with a shovel. I love Gaziantep, I made my money here, but [the Kurdish businessmen] cannot contribute as much as they could to the economy and politics here because they are uprooted, separated from their land, their people."

At that meeting, all Kurdish businessmen openly spoke in favor of the pro-Kurdish PDP, even though the group also included ultranationalist NMP supporters. At that time (2014), the NMP was critical of the AKP. They had a common enemy despite targeting the AKP for opposing reasons, namely its ultranationalism and its tolerance of the Kurdish movement. Regardless of the reason, however, this interesting collection of middle-aged men was a sign that the Islamists might lose their decades-long role as mediators between them.

That same Kurdish businessman made clear his concern that they had not gotten their due share of the pie: "I have twenty-five thousand tons of flour stored right there [pointing his finger at the large storage area on the other side of the plant's yard]. If we sell that, it will make money for the country [and] save [Erdoğan]. Will anyone applaud us? No … however, they have a lot of [racist] jokes about the Kurds in their pockets." The Kurdish businessmen were the ones who boosted Turkish exports when the AKP was struggling with competition from China and other East Asian countries. They were the ones who established new trade networks in Iraq and Syria. As in the case of Mr. Survivor, they were also the ones who kept the Kurdish working class under control in Turkish cities like İstanbul, İzmir, and Gaziantep.

During the peace process, the AKP was confronted with the prospects of a new Kurdish movement under the leadership of the Kurdish faubourgeoisie. Such a transformation of the Kurdish movement could have posed an existential threat to the Islamists, as the Kurdish faubourgeoisie could have dissolved the ideological unity of this social class, which was originally based on the pro-business Islamism of Müsiad. It was not only the results at the ballot box but also this challenge that motivated the Islamists to end the peace process.

The return to war against the Kurds helped the Islamists in two ways. First, it silenced the Kurdish faubourgeoisie and forced them to cooperate with the Turkish faubourgeoisie, even though the latter still had "a lot of jokes about the Kurds in their pockets." The class unity of the faubourgeoisie was consolidated. Second, the 2015–16 war displaced five hundred thousand people from the Kurdish region, according to estimates by the Migration Monitoring Association, many of whom left their hometowns to work in cities like Gaziantep and Istanbul.[40] As the resistance was broken in Kurdistan, more young hands were provided for sweatshops in Turkish cities.

The new Kurdish businessmen also posed a challenge to the Kurdish movement. In the 1980s and even in the early 1990s, mostly landless peasants formed the backbone of a movement that had relatively uniform class composition. In the 1990s, however, the expulsion of many Kurdish villagers by the Turkish military brought the Kurds and their identity to Turkish cities in large waves. The Kurdish movement became a nationwide political force at this point, and the Kurdish industrial proletariat, together with the landless Kurdish peasantry, became an important class actor in the movement. Later, the Kurdish faubourgeoisie emerged as a smaller but still significant player. Many of them, like Mr. Survivor, were now employers of these Kurdish migrant workers. Others, like the Kadooğlu family, made their fortunes outside Turkish Kurdistan. For these entrepreneurs, being Kurdish was an advantage despite the discrimination they faced from their Turkish counterparts. At least some of them wanted Kurdish politics to succeed, but in their own way and with their participation in it.

The success of the peace process may not have empowered the Kurdish worker, but it would have given a bigger voice to the Kurdish faubourgeoisie.

In the meantime, although the doctrine of the Kurdish movement had evolved since the 1990s, the left wing of the Kurdish movement was and is failing to develop a narrative and strategy to politically mobilize displaced Kurdish workers in Turkish metropolitan regions and to reverse or at least slow down their assimilation.

This gap in the narrative and strategy legitimized the position of the Kurdish faubourgeoisie in the movement during the peace process. With the end of the negotiations, the Kurdish faubourgeoisie distanced itself from the movement, as the "domination" of the proletariat in Turkey's Kurdistan, in the words of Tarkan Kadooğlu, was no longer a viable plan. The representative of the Kurdish faubourgeoisie, Altan Tan, left the PDP in 2018, and the collapse of the peace process indirectly contributed to the current leftist leadership regaining its supremacy. However, this consolidation of power came at a high price for the same leftist leadership: Gültan Kışanak was not released until May 2024, having spent more than seven years in prison, and many other, similar cases are pending against her.

THE GÜLENISTS: FROM COMPETITION TO PURGE

Two Rival Cliques

The Erdoğan–Gülen conflict was an internal division between the two leading cliques of the Islamist movement. The Gülenist clique has had a tense relationship with the dominant faction of the Islamists since the 1970s, and the rift culminated in the failed 2016 coup attempt. The conflict put an end to the narrative that Islamism is an antisystemic movement. The secularist version of the narrative had long portrayed Islamism as an unbreakable entity acting out of a single motivation: to establish a theocratic regime in the country. However, the Erdoğan and Gülen cliques started fighting each other right after they pacified the secularist cadres of the Turkish military, so it became clear that the Islamists' supposed antisystemic unity to change the secular regime was an illusion.

Born in 1938 in Erzurum, a very conservative city in northeastern Turkey, Gülen was an imam on the government payroll until the 1980s.[41] He was a follower of the Nurcu Yeni Asya (New Asia) group, a Sunni religious circle inspired by the Kurdish cleric Said Nurs-i.[42] In the 1970s, Gülen distanced himself from this group and built a support base in Izmir, the country's third largest city and the metropolitan stronghold of secularism in western

Anatolia. In 1974, his followers opened the first college exam preparation center for high school students as a strategic move to raise a new generation of highly educated Gülenists.[43]

Gülen kept his distance from the Islamist party in the 1970s. The strategic value of this became clear when the Nurcu groups failed to dethrone Erbakan at the National Salvation Party congresses in 1974 and 1977.[44] Erbakan was extending his influence at the expense of the religious orders within the party. Rather than the clerics, the political cadres would play the leading role in Erbakan's party, and Gülen did not want to be part of that.

Gülen's strategy was a bloated version of the tactics of other religious orders: like Zahid Kotku, Erbakan's spiritual leader, Gülen's goal was to get his young and educated followers into key positions in the government bureaucracy. Erbakan offered Kotku the amalgamation of this strategy within the bureaucracy with a mass movement that would be strong at the ballot box.

The difference between Gülen and other clerics like Kotku was his effort to create an ideology tailored for those bureaucrats without an appeal to the proletariat or the faubourgeoisie. He called these bureaucrats members of "the golden generation" (*altın nesil*) who were destined to bring Turkey back to the glorified position of the imperial era.[45]

The extraordinary success of Gülen's strategy has led to curiosity and accusations for many decades. He was and is commonly accused of working for the United States.[46] In a 1999 interview, Mehmet Kutlular, a leader of the Nurcu Yeni Asya group, claimed that state authorities had selected Gülen to establish links with pious groups at the expense of the Welfare Party, and Gülen admitted to Kutlular that the state had helped him build an international private school network in over 170 countries. These allegations may have some merit. Gülen publicly called on Erbakan to resign after the military memorandum of February 28, 1997, against the Islamist Welfare Party. He had good relations with most important political figures, such as Demirel, Çiller, Alparslan Türkeş, and Bülent Ecevit, but not with Erbakan.[47]

Nonetheless, the Gülen movement has been and remains highly secretive about its relations with domestic bureaucratic cliques and political movements and foreign governments, so there is little beyond individual testimonies and indirect evidence of these connections. But a discussion that puts exclusive emphasis on these connections would be misleading about how Gülen's Islamism differed from Erbakan's (and, later, Erdoğan's)

Islamism. The goal of Erbakan's Islamism was to promote and ally with the small industrialists. The spoils system in government bureaucracy was an instrument for this purpose. Gülen had a diametrically opposed goal: the Gülen supporters in the economic sphere would extend the position of his supporters in the government bureaucracy at the expense of their secularist (and Islamist) rivals.

On one level, the confrontation between Erdoğan and Gülen was a struggle between class and cadre movements in Turkish politics. Erdoğan's (and Erbakan's) was a class movement representing the interests of the faubourgeoisie within the state apparatus. Gülen's was a cadre movement aiming to control the state apparatus on behalf of the cadre.

On another level, the Gülenist cadre resembled the secularist bureaucrats, whom they had helped the Erdoğan clique oust from power in the early 2010s, more than the Erdoğan clique itself, in terms of its relationship with and vision for smaller and larger industrial capital. Even though the Gülenist cadre wanted Gülenist capital to replace the older (secularist) big capital, it did not want or offer any structural change in the relationship between big and small industrial capital in favor of the latter. In this respect, the Gülenist cadre looked like an Islamist current within the petty bourgeoisie that had already established a political economic regime in favor of big capital in the 1960s. From this perspective, the confrontation between Erdoğan and Gülen was another round of the redistribution struggle between the faubourgeoisie and the petty bourgeoisie, only in a purer form because the Islamism-secularism tension was largely irrelevant to the relationship between the Erdoğan and Gülen cliques.

Given their different goals and raisons d'être, it is not surprising that Erdoğan's and Gülen's cliques began plotting against each other immediately after the resignation of the entire high command (except for the head of the gendarme) in July 2011, which marked the end of secularist leadership of the Turkish military. Initial skirmishes as the cliques appointed their supporters to key positions in the security bureaucracy were quickly followed by police raids on the homes of high-ranking bureaucrats and the sons of ministers. These were part of a large-scale embezzlement operation allegedly initiated by Gülenist prosecutors and police chiefs immediately after the 2013 Gezi protests, possibly to exploit protesters' discontent with the government. In the same year, numerous wiretapped telephone conversations and videos of important political figures, including Erdoğan, were leaked, allegedly from the Gülenist police. In one of these, Erdoğan asked his son Bilal during a raid to move a sum of money from their house to a safe place. Bilal had difficulty finding a truck large enough to stack the money.

However, none of these actions fundamentally affected Erdoğan's popular support. He lost the June 2015 elections but regained those votes just a few months later. The Gülenists' handicap was similar to that of the Kurdish movement in two respects. First, perhaps because the complex and corrupt spoils system they had established over the years gave them considerable power in the government bureaucracy, they tended to see the Erdoğan clique as a mere cadre sitting on a critical structural hole in the vast network of Ankara's politics. They overlooked the potential impact of growing tensions within the faubourgeoisie in various parts of the country, including Denizli, Gaziantep, and Kayseri, where I studied in those years. In the meantime, Erdoğan had won the support of the lower echelons of the faubourgeoisie against the richer Gülenists by turning tensions in their supply chain relations into a political conflict long before the coup attempt. Second, the Gülenists expected the petty bourgeois secularists to support them in their fight against the Erdoğan clique as their "common enemy." They overlooked the fact that the petty bourgeois secularists had already accepted their fate as representatives of a politically weakening social class; ironically, the Gülenists had been involved in this process until they came into conflict with the Erdoğan clique. The petty bourgeois secularists wanted (and still want) to negotiate the interests of their social class with the Erdoğan clique, not to overthrow the clique.

In a way, the Gülenists' theoretical blindness to the role of class relations in politics brought about their political downfall. When the 2016 coup attempt took place, the Gülenists had few allies among the petty bourgeois secularists, much less in faubourgeois business circles or, by proxy, in the working-class neighborhoods. On the night of the coup, the streets were filled with Erdoğan supporters, not Gülenists.

The Gülenist Businesspeople

Along with the unconstitutional dismissal of over 125,000 public employees from mostly tenured positions because of their alleged connections to the Gülenists,[48] the most important consequence of the failed coup in the economic sphere was the seizures of the businesses of suspected Gülenists. Over the years, these businesspeople had expanded their influence within their industries and began to act as an independent force in the Turkish economy.

The Gülen-affiliated business association Tuskon had forty-three thousand members, and the corresponding figures for Türkonfed, Müsiad, and Tüsiad were eleven thousand, sixty-five hundred, and six hundred, respectively. In 2009, Tuskon was represented by forty-five companies in the Istanbul Chamber of Industry's list of the five hundred largest industrial companies (ISO500), while Islamist Müsiad was represented by thirty-one. Of the thirty-nine companies on the 2019 ISO500 list that are commonly considered Islamist, twenty-one (54 percent) either were Tuskon members or were confiscated by the government after the 2016 coup attempt for alleged links to the Gülenists.[49] Although enterprises affiliated with these Islamist organizations were a minority within the league of big industrialists, Gülenist capital was the majority within this minority.

It is impossible to determine the exact size of the Gülenist-linked business community because it is very secretive, but the figures on the seizures of businesses allegedly linked to Gülen after the failed coup attempt in 2016 give an idea of its economic and regional composition. First, the scale of the seizures was massive: 985 companies allegedly affiliated with Gülen were seized in 2016 following the coup attempt. The total net revenue and total assets of these companies amounted to $8.14 billion and $16.4 billion, respectively, in 2017. This was probably the largest confiscation in the country since 1915, when the property of hundreds of thousands of Armenians was confiscated or looted in various violent ways.

Second, thirteen of these 985 companies made it onto the ISO1000 list. The net sales and total assets of these thirteen companies amounted to $2.6 billion and $2.1 billion, respectively, representing about one-third of the total net sales and 13 percent of the total assets of the seized companies.

Third, for the remaining 972 companies, average net sales and assets were $5.9 million and $15 million, respectively. Some of the businesses seized were small cafés and local restaurants. It is clear that the main target was the largest Gülenist businesses, but some small Gülenist businesses were also targeted, possibly to spread fear among those businessmen. If Tuskon's membership figures are a minimum for the size of the Gülenist business community, most small Gülenist entrepreneurs were spared this wave of confiscation.

Fourth, all the confiscated businesses that made it to the ISO1000 list were in five cities: Istanbul, Izmir, Denizli, Gaziantep, and Kayseri. Kayseri and Istanbul shared first place, with four companies. As luck would have it, I had completed my research in Denizli, Gaziantep, and Kayseri about a year before the 2016 coup attempt. When I started this project around 2012,

I did not realize that my research topic, the politics of local supply chains, was closely linked to one of the most critical political tensions in the country. In fact, what I saw before my eyes was a struggle between the businessmen at the top and those at the bottom, a tension that would tip the political balance in one direction or the other.[50]

Two Stages of the Conflict

The Prelude. Relations between Gülen and Erdoğan did not take up much space in my 2012 and 2013 interviews. Neither my interviewees nor I raised this issue in our conversations. As with the Kurdish issue, I avoided asking about the relationship between Gülen and Erdoğan in order to focus on relationships in local supply chains, as discussed in chapter 3. Moreover, I assumed that my interviewees would be reluctant to talk about this topic because small business owners, whether Gülenists or not, are rarely transparent about their politics. Furthermore, like many others, I could not see any close connection between my interviewees' business practices and the growing Gülen-Erdoğan tensions. At the time, those tensions seemed more like a struggle between political cliques for the spoils of cushy political offices in Ankara than one of the defining issues of local business relations in Denizli, Gaziantep, and Kayseri.

However, the situation changed over the next two years. At the end of my research project, thirty-four of my 147 interviewees brought up their relations with the Gülenists or the impact of the Gülen-Erdoğan conflict on their businesses and local economies. The comments on Gülen in these interviews were characterized by opposing positions and emotions. Some interviewees expressed gratitude for the economic benefits of their association with the Gülenists, even though they were not followers or members of this clandestine network. A manufacturer of marble products in Denizli, for example, was very grateful to the Gülenists for their support:

> [The Gülenists] have helped my business a lot. They have helped me find contacts in overseas markets. We have to work together as local businessmen, but we do not have that culture here. The Cemaat [Gülenists] have helped us learn how to work together. I have attended many of their meetings. I traveled with them to Macedonia. I don't want you to get the wrong impression: I am not a Gülenist. I once told them that I drank *rakı* [a Turkish liquor] and that I didn't want anyone to interfere in my lifestyle. They told me, "It does not matter to us. Just do not come to the meetings after drinking rakı."

Supporting the Gülenists was not just about business contacts in foreign markets. That businessman believed close ties with the Gülenists also helped him in his dealings with the government bureaucracy and business chambers: "Once, the president of the Chamber of Commerce asked us about our expectations of the chamber. I said: 'Just don't ask for money.' He made sure our previous contributions to the chamber were returned. If he was not close to the Gülenists, he would not do us this favor." When he applied for a regional investment grant, a representative who helped applicants with their documents emphasized that his connections to the Gülenists would ensure the success of his application. He received the grant and felt even more grateful toward them.[51]

One reason this entrepreneur had such a high opinion of the Gülenists, at least until pressure from the Erdoğan clique led him to cut his relations with them, was the simple structure of his local supply chain. His main input was marble, and his output was various marble products. His biggest tensions were with the owners of marble quarries, and his dream was to find a new quarry one day and purchase that land for himself. He had a relationship with Gülenist bureaucrats, not Gülenist businesspeople.

In many other industries, however, supply chain relationships were more complex, and the prominent pro-Gülen families had much more control over their local suppliers. Two, the Nakıboğlu family in Gaziantep and the Boydak family in Kayseri were particularly close to the Gülenists. The Boydak family was more aggressive than the Nakıboğlu family in its expansion strategy. They were constantly trying to buy up their biggest competitors in the Kayseri furniture industry. Many local suppliers I spoke to in those years did not seem to object to this hierarchical relationship. Some of them saw it as something they could not change. Others believed they were treated better than other suppliers to these families because of their explicit support for the Gülenists. However, others felt the large Gülenist companies in their city exploited their local suppliers and saw their aggressive growth strategy as an effort to increase their influence over small manufacturers.

The representatives of other large companies in the city were also not happy with this strategy. One of them was one of the largest denim producers in the world, working for global brands such as Levi's and Wrangler. The Boydaks posed no threat to their business because they operated a highly integrated facility that reduced their dependence on the local supply chain. Nevertheless, they were concerned about the Boydaks' strategy. As my interlocutor put it: "Kayseri is in a dangerous position. If Boydaks collapse, the whole city will collapse. We need to diversify the customer profile of Boydak's local subsidiaries."

The Boydaks would take this criticism as a compliment, as the representative of Merkez Metal, the flagship of the Boydak Group, commented when I asked about their predictions for the economic future of Kayseri: "I don't think Boydak and Kayseri will grow at different rates. They will probably have similar growth patterns in the future." Behind these modest sentences was a lot of pride and joy at the power the family held. Boydak's destiny was Kayseri's.

This connection seemed intuitive to my interlocutor, given the size difference between the Boydak Group and its subsidiaries. In addition to the manufacturing industry, like the Ülker Group, whose owner Murat Ülker is the third richest person in the country, the Boydak Group had a significant stake in Anadolu Finans, the Gülen-backed Islamic bank. The five companies owned by the Boydak family in the ISO500 had net turnover of $1.23 billion in 2016 and an export volume of $281 million. These companies directly employed 7,143 people.[52]

The Boydaks' strategy, I was told several times, was to achieve economic hegemony over Kayseri through methods ranging from buying up key local competitors to building an exceptionally large local supply chain. They also helped marginalize the professionals in the management of their subsidiaries. As many of my interviewees argued (and sometimes defended), professionals were not valued in Kayseri, and the Boydak family fostered this culture. As the small machine parts manufacturer put it: "All who work for the Boydaks are robots. They work for the minimum wage. For example, we cannot convince the interns to come here because they all want to work at Boydak, even though they cannot use their skills there: they just package the products." An indirect but perhaps intended consequence of the Boydak family's efforts to promote anti-intellectualism and anti-technocratism was to limit their subsidiaries' independent access to global markets and maintain their dependence on the Boydaks. The professionals employed by those smaller manufacturing companies could have disrupted this relationship.

At least some small subsidiaries were aware of this strategy or outcome and were critical of it. For example, a small manufacturer of industrial chemicals, who was born and raised in Germany and came to Turkey in his thirties as a chemical engineer to open a business, said, "If [Boydak's main furniture company] İstikbal coughs, its subsidiaries will get sick." He produced a special compound used in PVC window frames and cable coating. Boydak's

HES Kablo offered to buy his entire capacity, but he declined the offer in order to keep his independence. Nonetheless, he was content to have a business relationship with HES Kablo, which helped him find other customers. Furthermore, he was still selling specialized, high-value-added, low-volume inputs like flame retardants to HES Kablo.

However, this relationship was exceptional. Eight of the ten members of the local branch of the Plastic Producers Association in Kayseri worked almost exclusively for Boydak. According to this interviewee, the Boydak family kept competition among its subsidiaries alive with a long-term strategy: it gradually increased its demand to enable the subsidiary to invest in new equipment and thus expand its debt stock. This deepened the subsidiary's dependence on the Boydaks because it lacked the connections to find other customers, especially in foreign markets.

Another factor that perpetuated this dependency was the pressure the Boydaks exerted on their subsidiaries to tailor their product range to their specific requirements, as expressed by a machine parts manufacturer:

> Yes, the Boydaks are really big. Seventy, maybe eighty percent of all small producers in Kayseri work for them in one way or another. But don't let that fool you. The biggest obstacle to the growth of Kayseri is the Boydaks themselves. . . . The Boydaks prevented a major investment in a car factory by [South Korean] Hyundai because they feared they would have lost their workers to this new plant. . . . They helped some [of their subsidiaries] and ruined all the others. First, they push their subsidiaries to invest in a machine, then they change their product line and push them again to invest in the machine. The old machines that are still fully functional are then thrown away. Most of the time they are bought with leasing, so the money spent on them is usually completely lost. They want to enslave everyone here. But good things happen too: they have lost half of their old capacity. I stopped buying Koç products [the epitome of secularist capital] after the Gezi protests. Now, I no longer work for the Boydaks.

Despite his angry stance, this manufacturer of machine parts gave small scholarships to two students who were supported by the Gülenists until 2014.[53] It was interesting how he linked the Boydaks, who were considered devout Gülenists, to the Koç family, who he believed headed the Masonic Lodge in Turkey. Politics and business did indeed go hand in hand.

The experience of a small furniture producer, Cemal, is another good example of how these business conditions have created hostility among small producers toward the Boydaks. Cemal worked almost exclusively for the Boydaks between 2001 and 2013, having received his first contract in 1997 thanks to his nephew, who worked as head of the planning department in one of the Boydak companies. He appreciated the Boydaks' success in changing the image of Kayseri's furniture industry outside the city. The auxiliary industry (*yan sanayii*) had developed over the previous two decades after the Boydaks pushed their subsidiaries to adopt new technologies, which improved the city's production capacity.

However, the same process concentrated wealth in the hands of the Boydaks. Like the small manufacturer of industrial chemicals that sold calcid products to the Boydaks, Cemal believed the lack of connections to customers beyond the city limits was the main reason local producers were dependent on the Boydaks. His solution to this problem was to establish a large, year-round fair in Kayseri like the one in İnegöl, a city near Istanbul with a large furniture industry:

> The money and power have become concentrated in the hands of a few. Growth has not been distributed fairly. We can now go to other cities, but the big companies are doing everything they can to prevent us from doing so. If I were allocated a space at the trade fair, customers could find me at any time. However, the big companies would not like this idea because I would not serve them if I learned about the birds and bees. In turn, they would not find new subsidiaries. Besides, Kayseri would grow faster than İnegöl if the Organized Industrial District issued letters of credit for small producers like me. . . . The small producers are grumbling now, and I don't know how much longer the big companies can hold us back.

When I conducted this interview, I thought the idea of a year-round trade fair just reflected Cemal's personal opinion, but I later realized that small producers were actively working to convince the Kayseri business community to take a step in this direction. As Cemal said, one opponent of the idea was the Boydak family.

This issue was raised at a meeting of the Kayseri Chamber of Industry (Kayso) in 2015, which I attended by invitation to make observations about relations between local industrialists. Kayso had met with the chairman of the Union of Chambers and Commodity Exchanges of Turkey (TOBB), Rifat Hisarcıklıoğlu, about the fair idea in recent months, though the head of Kayso, Mustafa Boydak, had not attended due to his busy schedule. Many details were discussed at this meeting, including the size of the rooms and the allocation method for the space. Mustafa Boydak was a gentle person who was careful to use the finest words and expressions, but his tone became a little more aggressive when this issue came up on the chamber's agenda: "Some here in Kayseri, who have nothing to do with trade, keep pushing the idea of setting up a fair. Do not worry: we will take care of it. . . . There used to be an abundance of money in the world. That is no longer the case. That's why we have to calculate carefully before we take an irreversible step. Please be aware that we, the businesspeople, are the ones footing the bill. I am taking care of this project."

The Clash. The plan to establish this year-round fair did not come to fruition, even after Mustafa Boydak was sentenced to seven and a half years in prison for his involvement in what the government now called the Gülenist Terrorist Organization. After being on the run for many months after the verdict, he was caught in a safe house in Istanbul in June 2023.[54] At the height of the conflict between Gülen and Erdoğan, the outcome was difficult to predict for my non-Gülenist interlocutors. They were happy to have Erdoğan on their side, as one of the major big bag makers in Gaziantep pointed out: "I was very worried about the clash because the Gülenist members were so self-confident that they restricted their business relations with the non-Gülenist businessmen. I began to believe that we would not be given room to survive economically. However, after December 17 [the police raids on the safehouses of Erdoğan supporters], the situation has changed fundamentally. Nobody wants to be associated with the Cemaat [Gülenists] anymore. Even though I am not voting for Erdoğan, I am relieved." He had every reason to be worried, because many of their suppliers were on the side of the big Gülenist business families and the Gülen movement until 2013, such as the two thousand small manufacturers working for the Boydaks in Kayseri. In contrast to the political milieu surrounding the 2008 ITKIB elections in Istanbul discussed in chapter 4, the growing tensions between Gülen and Erdoğan helped those at the bottom turn their dispute with their Gülenist clients into a political rift and improve their position in this unequal relationship.

The story of Mehmed, a small furniture manufacturer, is instructive in this regard. He ran against the Boydak representative for the chair of the Kayseri Chamber of Industry's Furniture Commission in the early 2010s. The Boydak representative was confident because 70 percent of the member companies in this commission were their subsidiaries. Mehmed told him that unlike them, he had nothing to lose, and the Boydak representative said he "should get the votes if he puts his money on the line" (*resti çekiyorsan sandıktan çıkacaksın*).

The election ended in a draw. The next step was a decision by lot, which Mehmed won. Boydak's representative went to court: the judge decided to draw a second lot, which Mehmed won again. Mehmed succeeded in mobilizing an ideologically diverse coalition of ultranationalist NMP, Islamist AKP, and secularist RPP small furniture manufacturers against the Boydaks. To Mehmed:

> The Boydaks know how much their subsidiary earns. They control him. The subsidiary buys his car and his house, has a decent life, but he also lives in despair because everything he enjoys depends on the Boydaks' will. He does not like the Boydaks. The result of this election was the result of this disenchantment with the Boydaks, a reflection of this dissatisfaction. . . . They are aggressive when their subsidiaries no longer want to work with them, but they become even more aggressive when new competitors emerge that produce the same inputs for their subsidiaries. For example, they took down Big Mattress [a pseudonym for one of the local competitors of the Boydaks] because Big Mattress had a large synthetic sponge plant. Big Mattress is now an ordinary company.

When I asked him about the politics of Big Mattress's owners, he said: "They are leftists. Last year, they served alcoholic drinks at a cocktail party in Gaziantep. They even served champagne at this party." This was an interesting observation because Cemal was one of Mehmed's supporters in that election and he had his own observations about Boydak and Big Mattress: "Big Mattress was in decline until last year, when the Boydaks lost favorite status in the eyes of the government. Now Big Mattress is growing rapidly in Kayseri thanks to the public tenders they were granted recently."

The openly Gülenist businessmen in Kayseri were closer to this second approach. The pro-Gülenist owners of a large steel door manufacturer commented that the local businessmen were acting hypocritically. First, as I was warned several times by other Gülenist businessmen, they argued that it would be wrong to associate the Boydaks closely with the Gülenists. They supported, probably for strategic reasons, several religious orders in the city. Moreover, I was told more than once, some family members, such as Mustafa Boydak, were not spiritually connected to the Gülenists. Second and more importantly, they believed that the Gülenists' efforts had contributed greatly to local growth, but the businessmen who benefited from this growth remained silent while tension was boiling up in the city. They saw this as a redistributive struggle among the big industrialist families, not a political feud in Ankara. The steel door producers saw the Boydaks not as instigators of tensions but merely as their victims, heroes with unadulterated values: "We call ourselves democrats. Despite our differences, we can talk to each other today, can't we? But now we are being called by name, and we cannot accept this injustice."

Because of these tangled connections and relationships, the political milieu in Kayseri was very tense in 2014. I was told on several occasions that family members were having heated arguments about which side they should have taken in the dispute between Gülen and Erdoğan. At a dinner I attended in 2014 as an expert for a Ministry of Family and Social Policy project, the participants at my table, top-level local bureaucrats and medium-sized industrialists, spontaneously opened the subject, which I believe was a sign of the intensity of the tensions. After a brief conversation, they agreed that Gülenists and Erdoğan supporters were as close as bark to a tree, and they quickly changed the subject with a visible sense of unease.

Just a few months later, in late August, two of my interlocutors independently told me about rumors that Erdoğan was planning a major police operation against Gülenist businessmen in Kayseri. This operation apparently waited until the failed 2016 coup attempt, but more and more people began to tell me stories of people forced by Gülenist bureaucrats at the Ministry of Finance to donate to Gülenist NGOs.

The tense situation also affected the city's political milieu. Before the clash, the Gülen-supporting business association GESIAD had around two hundred members, compared to thirty Erdoğan-supporting Müsiad members. GESIAD lost most of its members between 2013 and 2016. Another indication of declining Gülenist support was the sale of the Gülenist newspaper *Zaman*. An interviewee told me that the number of newspapers delivered to his gated community, where mainly local industrialists lived, was forty before 2013; the number dropped to two in 2014.

The Erdoğan clique also took steps to defame Gülen-supporting business circles, including the Boydak family. The family had been given a building on Erciyes Mountain, next to which was a large "Boydak" sign that was visible to the entire city. This sign, a symbol of the family's power, was removed in 2014, and the building was taken away from the family.

Nevertheless, the Boydak Family was still hopeful about the future of their political and economic position. At that Kayso meeting in August 2015, Mustafa Boydak took about ten minutes to explain his views on the June 2015 elections:

<blockquote>
Our president [Erdoğan] has done a very important service for our country. . . . The economy is being managed very successfully. . . . [However], it would not be the end of the world if we had a coalition government. . . . We would also like to thank Prime Minister Davutoğlu for his efforts. He has a huge burden on his shoulders. He is working both to lead the government under difficult circumstances and to form a new coalition. Also, the hope that the AKP might win the next round of elections just excites me. . . . The candidates will be visiting us next month, and we wish them the best of luck.
</blockquote>

Notwithstanding his compliments about Erdoğan, Boydak's emphasis on the merits of coalition governments indicated how much the Boydak family hoped Erdoğan would lose at least some of his power in the coming months, giving the family some relief from the pressures since 2013. However, the developments that followed did not meet their expectations. In addition to the confiscation of their business empire, family members were imprisoned after the failed 2016 coup attempt, as mentioned above, and seven of them were still in prison as of July 2024.[55]

The Gülen-Erdoğan conflict was not just about the loyalists occupying important positions in the government bureaucracy. It was not just about state power as such. It was also about a score that the upper and lower echelons of the faubourgeoisie wanted to settle. Similarly, it was about the aspirations of the upper echelons of the faubourgeoisie to replace or join the biggest business families, who had made their fortunes as comprador industrialists, particularly in the 1960s and 1970s, with the help of a new state under the rule of the Gülenist bureaucrats.

The Boydaks were big industrialists, but not monopoly capitalists. Ultimately, the country's largest industrialist families were mostly a product of the 1960 coup. In an alternate universe, if the vision of Kemal Kurdaş, the finance minister of the junta's first cabinet in 1960, or even that of Erbakan had prevailed among junta members, these families would have had a different economic history.

In fact, the 1960 coup and the 2016 coup attempt are morphologically similar from the perspective of class relations. The 1960 coup enabled the rise of the comprador industrialists to the center of the Turkish economy, and the failed 2016 coup had the potential to bring the richest Gülenist faubourgeoisie into a new class position. The final leap from the upper echelons of the faubourgeoisie to the lower echelons of the bourgeoisie requires political action in the world of monopoly capitalism. Ironically, a key factor that prevented this group from achieving its goals and led to the downfall of the Gülenists was resistance from the lower ranks of the faubourgeoisie, the Gülenist businessmen's own suppliers.

As already mentioned, with the exception of Istanbul and Izmir, all of the allegedly Gülenist large-scale enterprises the Erdoğan clique confiscated after the failed 2016 coup attempt are in Denizli, Gaziantep, and Kayseri, my research setting between 2012 and 2015. Not all, but many suppliers in these cities resented the power of Gülenist businesses and argued that their cities and individual businesses would be better off if the Gülenists went out of business. This happened after the coup attempt. The Gülenist small business owners I talked to, however, argued the Gülenist industrial conglomerates had turned their cities into growth poles.

The GDP growth of Denizli and Kayseri between 2016 and 2022 was slower than that of the country as a whole. The manufacturing and industrial sectors of these cities grew at about the same pace as the Turkish economy. Gaziantep's GDP has grown much faster than Turkey's. However, the influence of the Nakıboğlu family, who allegedly owned the biggest Gülenist industrial enterprise in Gaziantep, on the city's economy was more limited than that of the Boydak family in Kayseri. The Nakıboğlu family, the new owners of the decades-old petrochemical company Pil-Sa, or with its new name, Nak-Sa, focused on industrial chemicals.[56] Unlike the furniture industry, in which the Boydak family thrived in Kayseri, the Nakıboğlu family did not need to establish an extensive local supply chain for this raw-materials-based industry. Rather, Nak-Sa developed a highly vertical structure, taking on even the most labor-intensive processes, such as big bag weaving, at its gigantic campus in the city. The city ranked third in GDP growth between 2016 and 2022, but so did Kilis and Mardin, two neighbors of Gaziantep, both of which share a border with Syria. It seems Gaziantep has grown faster than the country (as it did before 2016), not because of (or despite) the Gülenists but because the city borders a war-torn country in need of the most basic industrial products.[57]

In other words, data since 2016 do not support the claims of either the Gülenists or the Erdoğanists that they have been the reason for the growth of their cities. Seizure of the allegedly Gülenist big businesses did not collapse the local economies of Denizli and Kayseri, and the post-Gülenist new business environment has not allowed these cities to flourish, at least so far. The struggle has not benefited local business circles in these cities, but it has helped the Erdoğan clique consolidate its power in national politics.

In the Islamists' struggle with the secularists, the faubourgeoisie acted as gatekeepers and cut the non-Islamists' links to the working class. In the struggle between the Kurds and the Islamists, the faubourgeoisie's position led to a crack in the ideological unity of both movements. The struggle between the factions of the Islamist movement led by Gülen and Erdoğan was an extrapolation of the split within the higher and lower ranks of the faubourgeoisie at the level of national politics. The struggle also contrasted the political aspirations of the Islamist petty bourgeois Gülenist bureaucrats and the Islamist pro-faubourgeois Erdoğan clique.

What appears to an outside observer today as a strongman regime in Turkey under the leadership of Erdoğan is the result of the changing conditions of the alliance between the Islamists and the faubourgeoisie since the 1970s. Any discussion that reduces the particularities of these political struggles to a history of the Erdoğan clique or Erdoğan himself overlooks the historical significance of the transformation of the state along the class interests of the faubourgeoisie.

The surprise that many experienced after the 2023 elections in Turkey clearly shows, in my opinion, the limitations of perspectives that avoid a class analysis of politics or use a simplified version of it. Many expected Erdoğan to lose in the 2023 elections because they believed that the depreciating Turkish currency would lead to discontent among voters. Indeed, life became more difficult for many before the elections, mainly as a result of Erdoğan's persistent policy of lowering interest rates. Some commentators called this policy irrational[58] and said the markets would teach Erdoğan a valuable lesson.[59] The opposition in Turkey quickly bought the story: Erdoğan was an uneducated man. He could not understand the political implications of his economic policies. He pushed down interest rates in the country because Islam banned interest.

However, the situation looked different to me even a year before this election.[60] No one bothered to check the data, which told me that Turkey was going through the impoverishment of the working class, not an economic crisis. Employment was booming in the new sweatshops. The Erdoğan clique had an effective and straightforward plan. At the center of its strategy was something the Islamists had been trying to deliver to the faubourgeoisie since Erbakan's time in the 1970s: low interest rates. In other words, the unorthodox policy decision that the opposition believed would end Erdoğan's political career was at the very core of his 2023 electoral strategy.

The equation was simple. Erdoğan's seemingly irrational interest rate policy contributed to the erosion of wages. The monthly minimum wage fell by 31 percent from $430 in 2016 to $295 in 2022.[61] The reduction in wages enabled a boom in the number of new sweatshops and medium-sized factories. As the last stage of a trend uninterrupted since 2012, the annual net growth in the number of new manufacturing companies reached 17,967 in 2022, the highest since 1999. Between the 2019 municipal election, when the Islamists lost Istanbul and Ankara, and the 2023 presidential election, the population of manufacturing SMEs grew by 16 percent, from 403,000 to 466,000.[62] This boom was associated with the largest expansion in job creation in the AKP period and probably in modern Turkish history: 1.35 million, 1.04 million, and 1.41 million jobs were created in 2020, 2021, and 2022, respectively. The total corresponded to 14.4 percent of the people covered by the social security system in 2022.[63]

With this strategy, Erdoğan economically satisfied the faubourgeoisie and politically cornered the working class. The faubourgeoisie had cheap credit and a devalued currency, and the working class had jobs, even if their wages fell by a third. Families who were able to find new jobs for their unemployed members were able to offset some of the fall in wages. While they knew they were being collectively exploited, in the absence of political alternatives they forced themselves to see this situation as a result of the vagaries of global markets rather than the Islamists' decades-long strategy to impoverish the working class. As long as impoverishment was not accompanied by any direct political action by the opposition to reach the working class, it would not have much impact on the voting behavior of workers enclosed by the thick walls of the echo chambers in their neighborhoods.

My story, however, fell on deaf ears. The same people who explained the rise of Islamism by way of a mystical centuries-old bond between the Islamists and the subaltern masses—a textbook example of cultural essentialism deeply rooted in Orientalism—now hoped the "falling wages = falling support" formula, the most vulgar form of economic reductionism, would bring democracy back to the country. The 2023 elections dealt a severe blow to both cultural essentialism, which idealizes the Islamist movement as representing the underprivileged, and economic reductionism, which portrays the political success of the Islamist movement as the result of economic growth.

Both views deny the possibility that the Islamist movement is pursuing a class agenda that has its own utopia and nostalgia. The 2023 election was an important step for the Islamists' goal of transforming the whole country into a "great Bağcılar," their utopia, which was nostalgically frozen in its political heyday in the 1990s when the Islamists were widely recognized as the voice of the subaltern. Indeed, Islamism has been the most class-conscious movement in the country's recent political history. The hard-to-see detail here is that the class interests the Islamists seek to protect and advance are not those of the proletariat, the bourgeoisie, or the petty bourgeoisie, but those of the social class I call the faubourgeoisie.

The faubourgeoisie's growing role in the Turkish economy since the 1990s has framed politics in a variety of ways. The turbulent 2010s was the stage for this class to settle its score with the bourgeoisie and the petty bourgeoisie, recalibrate power dynamics among its members, and consolidate its domination over the proletariat. Each of the three rifts discussed in this chapter corresponds to these changes in class relations. Taking the form of reconciliation, conflict, and purge, the relations of the Islamists to the secularists, the Kurds, and rival Islamist cliques resulted in a new political establishment and complex power network under the leadership of the Erdoğan clique. A thirteenth-century guildsman weaving fabric is now the personification of the nation, rather than an early-twentieth-century bureaucrat preparing a five-year development plan.

As discussed in chapter 3, this political and economic transformation did not help the country prosper. The Islamists' economic policies have failed to deliver growth, and this failure has continued for so long that this simply cannot be the result of a strategic miscalculation, incompetence, or cronyism. Figure 17 compares Turkey's per capita income with four units: the world, the countries of the Middle East and North Africa (MENA), upper-middle-income countries, and Muslim-majority countries. Turkey's per capita income slowly grew by 76 percent with respect to the upper-middle-income countries between 1960 and 2005. Per capita income caught up with the world about when the Islamists came to power. Except for the 1970s, when petrodollars began to flow to the oil-rich Muslim-majority countries and the figures for the MENA region and those countries shifted, Turkey's per capita income grew faster than them until the first decade of the 2000s.

There was no sustained relative decline in per capita income in Turkey in the postwar period until the end of the 1990s. Ironically, the Islamists came to power under extremely favorable conditions. Global growth rates were high in the first decade of their rule. The European Union did its best to support the Islamists and initiated EU accession negotiations with Turkey in 2004. This geopolitical move boosted foreign direct investment to a pace the

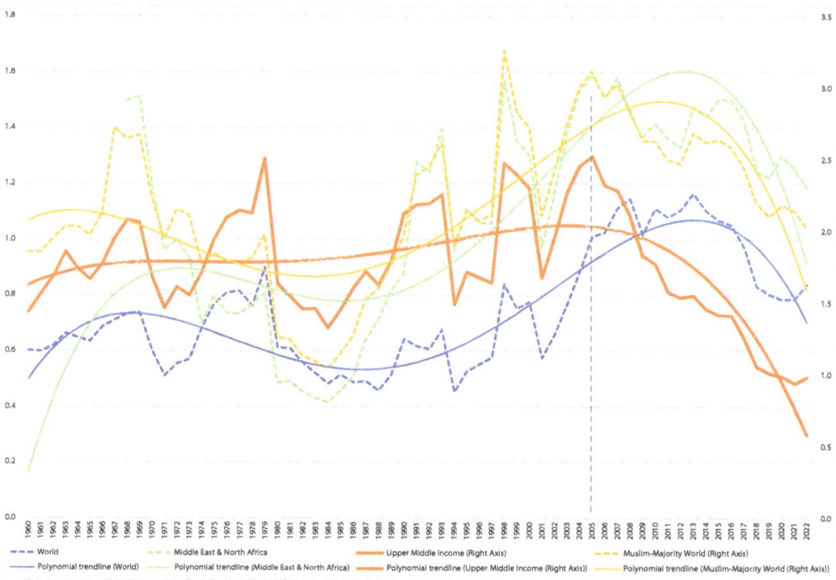

FIGURE 17. Relative GDP per capita of Turkey (1960–2022). Calculated by the author using World Bank country indicators.

country had never experienced. In addition, the Middle East was destabilized by various military conflicts, including the US invasion of Iraq. This opened new business opportunities for Turkish entrepreneurs.

However, the decline in Turkey's relative per capita income has been uninterrupted since the Islamists came to power. The most dramatic and important trend concerns Turkey's income group: the upper-middle-income countries. When the AKP came to power in November 2002, the ratio between Turkey's per capita income and this group of countries was at its highest level since 1979. The difference was a factor of 2.5, and the trend had been positive since the 1960s. The decline began in 2005, just three years after the Islamists came to power, and it has not stopped. Turkey's GDP per capita fell below that of upper-middle-income countries in 2020 for the first time since 1960.

This last piece of information also shows that one cannot attribute this utter failure of the Islamists to their neoliberal policies. Turkey adopted and implemented a neoliberal agenda after the 1980 military coup. Even though per capita income dropped by 40 percent in just four years after the coup and several financial crises destabilized the economy, the two decades between

1980 and 2000 were not a period of relative decline in per capita income. Under Islamist rule, there is only a straight downward trend. The unilinear nature of this trend supports the argument that the Islamists have not been unhappy with this consequence of their economic policies.

This is why I call the Islamists' economic strategy "sustainable decline." The strategy pursues two overarching goals. The first is to subsidize the faubourgeoisie with public resources as a shield against domestic and foreign big business in finance, trade, and manufacturing. This ensures that the number of these entrepreneurs grows, as does their collective dependence on these funds provided by the Islamists. The second is to use public policy to raise new generations of sweatshop workers with poor public education. Coupled with intolerance of labor unions and clientelist welfare measures, this strategy makes the younger generations dependent on the faubourgeoisie in different ways, necessary because the Islamists cannot maintain their political hegemony in a country where these younger generations have other options and can develop a collective will against the faubourgeoisie. So, the working class should be impoverished, even if this policy means the impoverishment of the entire country.

The Erdoğan clique's victory over the secularists, the Kurdish movement, and the Gülenists turned sustainable decline into Turkey's unofficial economic doctrine. Just like my coworkers in Bağcılar, the country has been systematically impoverished with this policy mindset. The class dimension of the history of Turkish Islamism invites reconsideration of the relationship between economic growth and political support for parties in government. Under certain conditions of class relations, such as those in Turkey, political movements could opt for employment over growth if economic decline at a certain pace could help them muster the support of the proletariat. That calculation of the Islamists helped them corner or appease their rivals in the 2010s with a remarkable outcome: continued support of the proletariat despite the slow but sure impoverishment of the country.

SEVEN

The Theory

A GROUNDED THEORY ABOUT THE MIDDLE CLASS

MY RESEARCH SINCE THE LATE 1990S has falsified more than once my initial propositions about the rise of the Islamist movement in Turkey. I was surprised to see that the industrialization-Islamization connection pertained not only to Turkey but to the Muslim-majority world (MMW) at large. Islamists' persistent efforts to connect to small producers since the 1970s were astonishing. During my fieldwork, I expected to see pious businessmen with a collaborative spirit in the industrializing towns of the country, and religious orders delivering appealing and positive messages to the proletariat. I expected the workers to be much more pious and religiously dedicated.

I was proven wrong many times, and each failure provided input to the three arguments I have advanced in this book. First, the more industrialized a Muslim-majority country is, the more visibly it goes through the Islamization process, by which I mean the growing use of religious motifs in politics. Second, instead of tension between Islamists and secularists, the alliance between Islamists and nonmonopoly industrialists, who are the core of a social class I call the faubourgeoisie, is at the center of the Islamization of politics in Turkey. Third, the raison d'être of the alliance of the faubourgeoisie with the Islamists is not to wage a war against modernism, establish a theological political order, or advance the interests of the subaltern masses, but to intensify the exploitation of the proletariat in capitalist labor process.

I suspect this social class plays a similar role in other countries. The Islamization-industrialization connection pertains to the MMW at large, and two-thirds of this meta-region's population[1] lives in countries similar to Turkey in the ways discussed in chapter 1. Relatively recent globalization studies document the rise of a new global middle class as a new component of the global class structure.[2] Furthermore, a smaller number of studies point to the significance of the middle class in the politics of the MMW,[3] yet these contributions fall short of defining this actor within a general theory of class formation. In this chapter, I discuss how my observations about Turkey can serve such a theory and lay the groundwork for a research framework for other country contexts.

The Marxist framework has good potential for developing this theory, given that the research material points to domination in the local dynamics of the capitalist labor process as the key factor behind the continued political success of the Turkish Islamists. I use Marx's *Capital* to formulate a three-layered typology of major class actors in terms of their position, function, and motives in capital accumulation.

Marx's model offers an integrated theory of capital accumulation and class formation. Each volume of *Capital* defines the proletariat, the landowners, and the bourgeoisie—the three main social classes of a bourgeois society—in relation to the production, circulation, and appropriation of surplus value as the constitutive processes of capital accumulation. The connection between capital accumulation and class formation in his model turns the major conceptual innovation of this book, the faubourgeoisie, into an operational category for further research in Turkey and elsewhere.

This chapter advances and presents the book's fourth argument: There is a middle stratum in wealth distribution that is categorically different from the proletariat and the bourgeoisie. One can empirically identify this stratum with a simple quantitative metric. There are different social classes in this middle stratum of wealth distribution. These social classes differ from each other, not in terms of the metric but in the function they serve in what Marx calls "the circulation of surplus value." In other words, the factor that identifies the middle stratum is their position in the wealth distribution, and the factor that identifies the social classes within that middle stratum is their function in the circulation process. Based on Marx's analysis, the circulation process is composed of three interconnected metamorphoses of capital. Each social class in the middle stratum—the faubourgeoisie, the petty bourgeoisie, and the technocracy—plays a function in one of these. This book focuses on the faubourgeoisie and its relationship to the petty bourgeoisie, the bourgeoisie, and the proletariat. By serving their functions in one of the metamorphoses of capital, those social classes help the bourgeoisie recuperate what Marxists call "the surplus profit," an essential component of capital accumulation, or simply economic growth. The middle classes are, in fact, "circulation classes."

The monopolization of capacities by members of the circulation classes is the process that yields them above-average wealth. Thus, the revenue of the circulation classes is rent, not wages or interest. The circulation classes are rentier classes. For the members of these social classes to remain in this wealth stratum, they must preserve the capacity that lets them serve their function in the circulation process from what Marxists call "the deskilling process," the destruction of a capacity, usually via the routinization of that capacity.

The key component of the deskilling process is the separation of conception from execution. The process is inherently epistemic, like the capacities the circulation classes strive to monopolize. Each of the three circulation classes produces, promotes, and uses a different form of knowledge: *episteme, techne*, and *phronesis*. They work to prevent others from the legitimate and practical use of these forms of knowledge and to epistemologically demote the other two forms of knowledge. The circulation classes are epistemic classes.

The circulation classes work to muster the political support of the proletariat for use as a bargaining chip against the bourgeoisie and to advance their epistemic turf vis-à-vis the other two circulation classes. Most politics in bourgeois society today is an outcome of this dual struggle among these social classes. Thus, there is a structural relationship between the redistributive and epistemic aspects of class relations. For instance, the rift between secularists and Islamists in Turkey has never been just about lifestyle, nor has it been only about the redistributive elements of the relationship between the faubourgeoisie and the petty bourgeoisie. Secularism and Islamism refer to different capacities that favor these two social classes in the circulation process. The victory of one over the other in the epistemic field points to the potential proletarianization of one class actor in favor of the other.

Each component of this fourth argument is informed by the research material I presented in previous chapters to substantiate the book's other three arguments. I flesh out this last argument in the following sections in relation to the first three arguments. For an analysis that substantiates the discussion about rent in this chapter, see appendix C.

The first argument of this book, the connection between Islamization and industrialization, is related to the two major redistributive consequences of post–Cold War globalization. First, the wealth of billionaires expanded immensely. In a sense, the world is in an advanced stage of monopoly capitalism ruled by a microscopic transnational elite, the bourgeoisie. Second, growing economic interconnectivity boosted a new global middle class, particularly outside the North Atlantic region. The relationships of this new global middle class to other social classes have framed major political shifts in this period, such as the rise of Islamism in the MMW and the emergence of authoritarian movements in various parts of the world.

This new global middle class is part of the middle stratum in the wealth distribution. Unlike the poorest stratum, the proletariat, which comprises approximately 85 percent of the world population and has a smaller share of global wealth than if it were distributed equally, members of the middle stratum can save enough wealth to pass their privileges on to their children. Nonetheless, even the wealthiest members of this stratum, approximately 15 percent of the world population (and 12–31 percent of the population in individual countries for 2021), are much poorer than those on the other tail of the spectrum. Five to eight thousand individuals in a few thousand families owned roughly 6 percent ($26 trillion) of total global wealth in 2021.[4] To put the wealth of this small population in perspective, the average wealth of the top 1 percent of the global population was six ten-thousandths of the average wealth of the superelite that year.[5] Unlike nonmonopoly entrepreneurs, the magnitude of their wealth lets this global elite move their capital freely across corporations, industries, and countries. Competition is not a threat to their status in the wealth distribution. It is an instrument they use to dominate everyone else, including nonmonopoly entrepreneurs.

Marx's critical contribution is about the kind of revenue the middle stratum earns. The proletariat in the bottom 85 percent produces most of the value and receives a share so small that their offspring find themselves under the same duress of wage labor. The bourgeoisie, the microscopically small global elite, and the middle stratum just below them appropriate the rest.

Marx dedicated at least half of the third volume of *Capital*, parts 5–7, to identifying the revenue sources of the nonproletarian social classes. This provides a simple metric for distinguishing these three wealth strata. According to his trinity formula (in chapter 48), the proletariat receives a portion of the value it produces in the form of wages. The bourgeoisie appropriates the rest of this value in the form of interest as the revenue of capital. Any arrears left to those in the middle stratum above the prevailing wage are a third form of revenue, rent.[6] The rent the members of this middle stratum receive enables them to accumulate above-average wealth.

In other words, the revenue of the middle stratum could be, in theory, as small as the average wage of the proletariat. In practice, it is much bigger because of the gap between the value the members of the middle stratum produce and the revenue they receive. Examples materialize the idea: a slumlord is of course a rentier. So is a physician if their occupational organization can put an effective limit on the number of new graduates in their country. The ensuing monopoly of physicians in their occupational field delinks the value of the service provided from its price and helps the bourgeoisie recuperate a substantial and growing portion of the wages of the proletariat. The physicians receive some portion of this recuperated value as their share in the form of rent. A tenured scholar has job security and saves above-average wealth over their life span because they produce knowledge that increases what Marx called the intensity of labor or reduces wages by justifying the existing class structure. A corporate executive receives bonuses much larger than their typical predecessor in the 1950s if they find new suppliers of manufactured goods in countries with a small GDP per capita. A sweatshop owner could receive much more revenue than a factory foreman's wages if they can keep unions and socialists out of the neighborhood. In all cases, these personas expand the surplus value.[7]

In these examples, a technical, cultural, or legal boundary facilitates the progressive exploitation of the proletariat. Those who draw or maintain those boundaries help the bourgeoisie accumulate capital at a growing rate in the form of surplus profits, and they receive much more revenue than they would if there were no such boundaries. The difference between their revenue and the value of what they produce (if they produce anything at all) is rent, which is a portion of the surplus profit. Those in the middle stratum are members of rentier classes.

Because the total revenue of the middle stratum can theoretically range from the average wage to the total amount of surplus profits, the social classes in the middle stratum seek alliances with political movements as they wage two simultaneous fights. First, they work to suppress the proletariat to generate surplus profits for the bourgeoisie. Second, they fight the bourgeoisie to expand their share of the surplus profits produced by the proletariat.

This proposition shows why Islamism in Turkey has neither become a working-class movement nor exclusively represented the interests of the bourgeoisie since the 1970s. As I argued in chapter 2 on the history of the Islamist movement and in chapter 3 on the relationship between the Islamists and the faubourgeoisie, the movement emerged as a third option after the Islamists had won the support of nonmonopoly entrepreneurs, a segment of the middle stratum of the wealth distribution. Islamism is a class movement that both defines and represents the interests of nonmonopoly entrepreneurs. On the one hand, the Islamists negotiate their interests vis-à-vis monopoly capital and shape state and security policies to suppress and reproduce the proletariat. On the other hand, the Islamists reinforce the competitive tendencies of the individual nonmonopoly entrpreneurs and make themselves an indispensable mediator for the faubourgeoisie in its relations with other social classes.

The link between Islamization and industrialization is the result of the relative strength of nonmonopoly entrepreneurs in the production relations of their countries and the idiosyncratic historical conditions of the alliances they have formed with the political actors leading the process of Islamization. As I argued in chapter 1, the success of Turkish Islamism is no exception. That chapter not only demonstrates the similarities between Turkey and the overwhelming majority of Muslim-majority countries but also shows what to look for in the relationship between Islamization and industrialization in the Turkish context. On a broader level, the link between Islamization and industrialization illustrates the political consequences of an alliance between Islamists and nonmonopoly entrepreneurs, who are playing an increasingly important role in production relations in the post–Cold war era.

THE SECOND ARGUMENT AND THE CIRCULATION PROCESS

Marx's analysis of the circulation process in the second volume of *Capital* helps distinguish these nonmonopoly entrepreneurs, the faubourgeoisie, from the two other social classes in the middle stratum of wealth distribution. In this volume, Marx described three metamorphoses of capital as moments in the circulation of capital. Money capital transforms into productive capital, which transforms into commodity capital, which—at the end of this metamorphic cycle—transforms back into money capital, together with the surplus value attached to it. This underlines the role of the circulation process in class formation. Every metamorphosis is a social relation

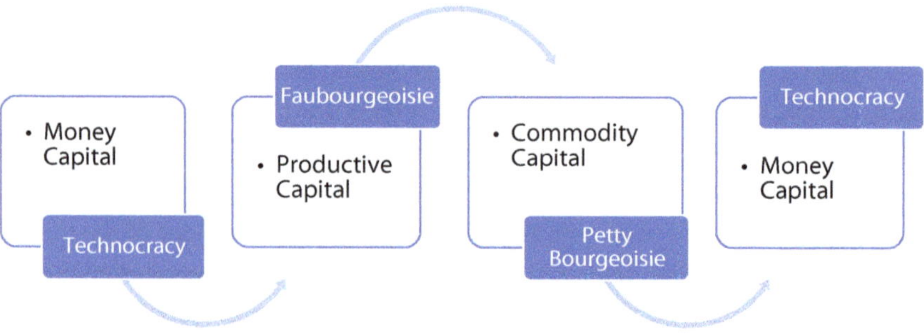

FIGURE 18. Social classes originating from the circulation process. Courtesy of the author.

rather than a purely technical connection between different forms of capital. Different social classes play distinct roles in these three metamorphoses. In other words, the middle stratum of the wealth distribution hosts three distinct circulation classes that serve functions in particular metamorphoses. This is illustrated in figure 18.

The raison d'être of the petty bourgeoisie is the metamorphosis of commodity capital into money capital. A second circulation class takes part in the metamorphosis of money capital into productive capital by overseeing and expanding the investment of the bourgeoisie. I call this managerial class technocracy, following Nicos Poulantzas, who used the same term for professional managers,[8] and Alvin Gouldner, who carefully distinguished between technical intelligentsia and intellectuals.[9] The last and, for the purposes of this book, most important social class, the faubourgeoisie, takes part in the metamorphosis of productive capital into commodity capital by overseeing the capitalist labor process on behalf of the bourgeoisie and, in non–North Atlantic countries, on behalf of global corporations. Each class played crucial roles in the expansion of wage labor and market relations.

The petty bourgeoisie creates and maintains the commodity markets. Members of this class spread new consumer trends through what Jacques Lacan called "the purification of desire."[10] They define what desire should mean with various intellectual products that appeal to different segments of the working class. Similarly, bureaucrats and state officials create and direct the political institutions that structure national and supranational markets. The petty bourgeoisie has historically been the actor behind the formation of nation-states in both high- and low-income regions of the world.

Members of the technocracy design social and sometimes material technologies to build horizontal supply chains and vertical corporate structures.

Of the three social classes, they work most closely with members of the bourgeoisie. As the predecessors of the technocracy, previous generations of corporate managers had been highly paid administrative workers, hired to develop and administer the deskilling process at the corporate level. However, the successors of these managers became the core of the emergent technocracy as they began to play a critical role in the formation and expansion of the transnational operations of corporate capital.

High-income countries now host the battleground of these two classes. The petty bourgeoisie has lost most of its status in recent decades as the technocracy has invented creative methods to isolate the skills of the petty bourgeoisie within contractual arrangements so that they cannot lay claim to the outcome of their own work. The strategies pursued by the technocracy to undermine the status of the petty bourgeoisie include the commercial pressure on the mom-and-pop shops; the proliferation of contract work among petty bourgeois content creators; the gradual expansion of the influence of business schools and other career-oriented disciplines, such as criminology or social work, within academia at the expense of the humanities and social sciences; the gradual transformation of the sciences into STEM fields and subfields of medicine; the resurgence of nonacademic research centers that indirectly exploit the resources of academia; and the replacement of tenured government bureaucrats with freelancer professional experts.

The last and, for the purposes of this book, most important circulation class is what I have called the faubourgeoisie. The term comes from the French historian Henri Pirenne, one of the most influential exponents of the Annales school. He discussed the impact of the rejuvenation of Roman roads around the eleventh century on socioeconomic relations in Europe, after the Islamic Empire had cut the northern Mediterranean off from the rest of the known world. This process, Pirenne argued, was the main reason for the dissolution of the Roman order. During this period, the expansion of cities gave rise to new groups of merchants and artisans on the outskirts of flourishing cities, in places he called *faubourgs* or *forisburgus*. Unlike their counterparts within the city walls, they were rootless, but they played an important role in a "real industrial revolution" that transformed rural industries into urban ones. According to Pirenne, these merchants and artisans gradually merged with their counterparts within the city as the guild system slowly lost its importance in the new era.[11] Their emergence was linked to growing economic interdependence in the northern Mediterranean, which is now called Europe. This historical moment serves as a good analogy for naming this social class.

Small industrial producers played a significant role in other periods as well. In the sixteenth century, they triggered what some historians call "protoindustrialization" in northwestern Europe.[12] Similarly, such producers played an important role at the height of the Industrial Revolution. In the first volume of *Capital*, Marx distinguished the formal subsumption of labor, a relationship between small producers in the countryside and urban merchants (like the Verlagsystem), from the real subsumption of labor, which took its ideal typical form in the factory system. Historians have underpinned Marx's emphasis.[13] According to Bythell,[14] the putting-out system competed effectively with the emerging factory system well into the second half of the nineteenth century. This lasted until the share of consumer goods, such as readymade clothing, in British exports dropped in favor of intermediate products such as fabrics, followed by the mushrooming of similar small-scale manufacturing practices in the colonies of the British Empire.

Unlike the technocracy, a significant portion of today's faubourgeoisie operates in global faubourgs as it conducts business outside the metaphoric or sometimes actual walls that surround the cities or the richer nation-states. The members of this social class not only made post–Cold War globalization possible but also facilitated new cross-country redistributive dynamics that favored regions other than the North Atlantic. In the North Atlantic, franchisees have a similar class character. Like their counterparts in poorer countries, they are on the periphery of the vertical corporate structures yet play an essential role as a buffer against unionization.

As discussed in chapters 2 and 6, this interpretation shows the historical significance of the tension between Islamists and secularists in recent Turkish history. As discussed in chapter 2, the founding cadres of the Republican regime produced what Erdem Damar[15] called an "Orientalist fantasy" about the Islamists to justify regime change in the first decades of their rule and to differentiate their project, which they defined as a "civilizing mission," from the socialist agenda of the Left between the coups of 1960 and 1980. The secularist cadres have allied themselves with the Islamists against the socialists at every critical juncture throughout the entire history of the republic.

This tacit alliance has been at the heart of the Islamist–secularist divide since the 1980s, as discussed in chapter 6. By squeezing the socialists and the entire spectrum of non-Islamist liberals and conservatives out of party politics, the Islamists and the secularists established a new hegemonic bloc that not only denies all other political actors any space but is also the scene of repeated skirmishes between these camps over the redistributive terms of the relationship between the two classes they represent, the faubourgeoisie and the petty bourgeoisie.

In this complex relationship between classes, represented by the Islamist-secularist divide, the petty bourgeoisie had the upper hand after the Second World War, but the faubourgeoisie has expanded its influence on policymaking at the expense of the petty bourgeoisie since the 1980s. This decisive change in politics is closely related to the political economic role of secularism in Turkey.

As in the nineteenth century, postcolonial state formation under the guidance of the petty bourgeoisie continued to incorporate Turkey into the capitalist world economy during the twentieth century. Secularism in different forms and to different degrees has been on the political economic agenda of the petty bourgeoisie because proletarianization of the rural-to-urban migrant population and the expansion of market relations required a state ideology broader than regional and identity-related particularities.

As this dual process of proletarianization and market making was completed, the petty bourgeoisie's function became less central to the global accumulation process, unlike the faubourgeoisie's key position in global supply chains, as discussed in chapters 3–5. In Turkey, this transformation corresponded to the demotion of secularism to a secondary principle and the secularist petty bourgeoisie to a secondary class actor. Meanwhile, the faubourgeoisie expanded its influence over politics and the economy thanks to its successful alliance with the Islamists.

THE THIRD ARGUMENT AND THE PRODUCTION PROCESS

The notion of multiple middle classes is not alien to Marxist theory. Two eminent Marxist theorists, Poulantzas and Erik O. Wright, identified three middle-class actors in parallel with this discussion. In Poulantzas's framework, these actors are a new petty bourgeoisie, nonmonopoly capital and the managerial technocracy.[16] In Wright's, they are semiautonomous workers, small employers, and managers and supervisors.[17] In other words, albeit with a slightly different lexicon, both thinkers refer to the same class actors to flesh out the notion of middle class with a Marxist perspective.

However, neither they nor others have related these actors to the circulation process, which made it difficult to relate the role of these social classes in the labor process to their political motives. Even the wealthiest members of the circulation classes are not completely immune to the processes the first volume of *Capital* relays about the proletariat, what Harry Braverman has simply called "the deskilling process."[18] The core component of the deskilling process is the separation of conception and execution. In other words, the deskilling process is epistemic in nature. If they are to save themselves from proletarianization, the circulation classes need to produce a specific kind of knowledge that is difficult to alienate from them and minimally accessible to others. This knowledge assigns them a privileged position in the labor process, which they typically use to intensify the exploitation of the proletariat.

The monopolization of a certain form of knowledge as an instrument against monopoly capital is the main motive of the circulation classes. It frames their relationship to the labor process. The knowledge they produce, use, and promote leads to the desired result to the degree it frames the historical conditions of the circulation process. The petty bourgeoisie draws boundaries across countries and professions. The technocracy structures organizations that pierce those boundaries. The faubourgeoisie turns these boundary-making processes into corporeal contingencies in the everyday life practices of the proletariat. This conceptual clarification reveals the nature of the rift among different circulation classes in general and the tension between the Islamists and the secularists in the Turkish case in two respects.

First, my research material repeatedly illustrates the contrast between the Islamist and secularist narratives. Well before concepts such as posttruth politics gained currency in the North Atlantic, observers of Turkey found themselves amid an epistemic war in the 1990s. For the secularists, the republican regime had saved the country. For the Islamists, the reforms of the twentieth century had ruined it. For the former, women should reject religious dogma. For the latter, dogma was salvation. For the former, what would save workers from their drudgery was some form of developmentalism. For the latter, those policies had excluded a large mass from core economic activities in the 1970s. As discussed in chapters 2 and 6, these differences demarcate the epistemic turfs of the faubourgeoisie and the petty bourgeoisie. The themes that justify the rift are about "civilizational" differences, so the public is told that the rift is more important and older than banal problems such as unemployment, low wages, and long working hours.

Second, my research material on the religious orders and my coworkers in the industrial workplaces in Bağcılar in chapters 3–5 shows that the Islamist-faubourgeoisie alliance produces and promotes a particular form of knowledge that cannot be categorically separated from the knower. In chapter 3, I argued that the leader of a religious order has exclusive spiritual access to knowledge that matters for them and their followers. Secularists reject the legitimacy that this form of knowledge confers on religious leaders. In chapter 4, I observed how the faubourgeois members of working-class communities use their knowledge of local urban dynamics to shape the politics of poorer residents. In chapter 5, I discussed the specific practices or technologies that enable this urban elite to utilize this knowledge.

Undergirding its cosmological undertones, the goal of this knowledge is not to present universal principles that can, in theory, be communicated, for instance by an academic, to anyone with proper training, but to explain the individual's relationship to the cosmos, starting with their immediate environs including their body and their community. Within this framework, the knowledge that grants privileges to the sweatshop owner is similar to the knowledge of the religious leader. Instead of a credential documented with a diploma, their knowledge of the local social context, inalienable due to its local character, is the source of their wealth and prestige.

In other words, the circulation classes produce distinct forms of knowledge and challenge the legitimacy of others. The typical petty bourgeois is a firm supporter of credentialism, which lets occupational groups such as teachers, scholars, physicians, lawyers, and engineers have their specific territories.[19] In the case of corporate executives, the ideal typical representative of the technocracy, it could be a cultural milieu that favors highly exclusive social networks and helps the members of these networks keep certain forms of business practices to themselves.[20] In the case of the faubourgeoisie, the knowledge it produces and promotes is by definition local and nonprogrammatic. For instance, the answer to a mystery I left unresolved in chapters 3 and 4—why the Just Order manifesto of the Islamists was discarded only a few years after its dissemination in the 1990s—lies in this local and nonprogrammatic nature: the Just Order was too doctrinal for the faubourgeoisie. Thus, the petty bourgeois scholar typically fails to consider the knowledge this social class produces as a legitimate object of study.

In reference to Bent Flyvbjerg's reading of the related concepts,[21] I believe that Aristotle's distinction between the three forms of knowledge in his Nicomachean Ethics matches the conceptual triad surprisingly well:

Aristotle distinguishes between episteme, techne, and phronesis. Episteme is about establishing universal principles that claim to explain the universe and tend to overlook unfitting phenomena as exceptions. Techne is a form of knowledge that can be obtained by uncovering the layers of a spatially and temporally limited phenomenon such as a machine or an organization. Phronesis is a form of knowledge that is tied to the knower and justified in reference to a specific trait or capacity of the knower, such as virtue. These forms of knowledge respectively refer to the petty bourgeoisie, the technocracy, and the faubourgeoisie. The circulation classes strive to dominate the production of and access to these salient forms of knowledge, to degrade the status of other forms relative to their own, and to make their role in the labor process unavoidable.

BROADER IMPLICATIONS

The discussion of redistributive dynamics provided a metric for distinguishing the middle stratum of the wealth distribution from the proletariat and the bourgeoisie: they are rentiers. The discussion of the function they serve in the circulation process identified three groups within that middle stratum: they are circulation classes. The discussion of their capacities indicates what they do in the labor process: the circulation classes are knowledge-producers, and their raison d'être is knowledge production, so they are epistemic classes. This three-layered discussion of the class identity of those in the middle of the contemporary stratification structure links the theoretical construct of this book, which I have presented in this final chapter, to its three objectives.

The first objective was to offer a historical and ethnographic answer to the question of how the Islamists have been so powerful in Turkey since the 1990s but not before. My answer offers an alternative to two narratives that dominate political discussion in Turkey. The first and intellectually more influential one is the grand narrative, according to which the modernist republican elites of the twentieth century have been in a century-long tension with pious antimodernist masses due to the split of values between these two camps. The Islamists are here represented as the guardians of the masses. This is a form of cultural essentialism that equates the motives of the elites and the masses with their stance on religion. This narrative faces two problems. First, popular support for the Islamists is relatively new, which challenges the idea that the pious masses have an intrinsic political lean toward the Islamists.

Second, the local conditions of support for the Islamists have not been closely studied by the proponents of this narrative. The narrative presupposes some form of social solidarity among local community members without providing empirical and historical evidence other than factually problematic and sometimes even irrelevant bits and pieces such as election results and the narratives of various tropes of elites. I dealt with some of these problematic assertions in previous chapters.

The other prevailing narrative focuses on redistributive dynamics and portrays the Islamists as clientelist providers of resources like means-tested social assistance for the poor and as facilitators of the neoliberal reforms that coincided with a brief period of economic growth in the first few years of their one-party government. This economic reductionism faces two problems. First, the Islamists mustered the support of a growing section of the urban working class before they controlled central government in 2002, so this account, like the first narrative, suffers from a chronological error. Second, after coming to power, the Islamists have received considerable support from the proletariat, despite the economic ups and downs, the corruption scandals, and their complete disinterest in the actual welfare of workers and their families. Per capita income in Turkey declined 32 percent between 2013 and 2020. Moreover, this trend was opposite to the averages of lower, middle, and upper middle-income countries. Only nineteen of the 217 countries in the World Bank database shrank economically more than Turkey between 2014 and 2022, including Yemen, Afghanistan, Libya, Syria, and South Sudan, each the site of an armed conflict. Turkey had not had such a long and steep decline in this metric since 1960. Nonetheless, the Islamists passed constitutional amendments that eliminated the last vestiges of democratic institutions in 2017 and won the presidential elections in 2018 and 2023.

What makes these narratives examples of cultural essentialism and economic reductionism is their failure to provide a holistic perspective on the conditions of popular support for the Islamist movement. The economic reductionist narrative fails to explain why a significant portion of the proletariat continues to support the Islamists despite the economic ups and downs. The cultural essentialist narrative does not explain why the election results are receptive to these ups and downs. This failure is related to the assumption that tension takes place between the pious and the secularists, not between social classes. The failure thus is misrecognizing the actor behind this receptivity. The class reaction is not from the proletariat but from another actor, the faubourgeoisie. This social class emerged from within the circulation of surplus value. Its relationship with the proletariat and the petty bourgeoisie has determined the broad contours of politics since the 1980s.

The second objective of this book was to provide a basis for further research about contemporary authoritarianism in other countries. The Turkish case is not exceptional but rather an example of global trends that may apply to other countries. For instance, the parallels between China and Turkey are remarkable. China and Turkey passed new constitutions in 1982 and 1983, under Deng Xiaoping and Turgut Özal respectively, that brought about a neoliberal transformation. Both countries went through a massive rural-to-urban migration in the following decade. Small producers expanded their share of manufacturing outputs in both countries in roughly the same period. Turkey and China respectively became a negotiating EU candidate in 2004 and a WTO member in 2001. The proportions in metrics on the growth of the industrial labor force and small and medium-sized manufacturing enterprises are very close.[22]

More importantly, as Yue Gong's *Manufacturing Towns in China* vividly illustrates,[23] relations at the local level in Turkey and China are astonishingly similar. As the equivalent of the neighborhood sweatshops in the outskirts of the major metropolitan cities of Turkey such as Bağcılar, town and village enterprises served as the nuclei of similar establishments in semi-urban regions of China. Like his Islamist counterparts, the entrepreneurial bureaucrat replaced the cadres of the revolutionary period and emerged as a new actor promoting this local urban and industrial growth.[24] One of these entrepreneurial bureaucrats, Xi Jinping, is now the paramount leader of the country.[25]

There are interesting parallels between Turkey and the United States as well. Empirically rich studies such as Thomas Frank's *What's the Matter with Kansas?*[26] and Arlie R. Hochschild's *Strangers in Their Own Land*[27] point to the shift of the European American proletariat to the right in response to the outsourcing of manufacturing activities. Even though industrial relations in the United States have been, in many respects, diametrically opposed to those in Turkey, the same global transformation may have brought about new local elites (or empowered older local elites) in the United States with a similarly racist, xenophobic, homophobic, and nationalist agenda: business owners accounted for one-fourth of the prosecuted January 6 insurrectionists. The second largest occupational category, 17 percent, of prosecuted insurrectionists was blue-collar workers.[28]

Common to the spectacular changes in the politics of these countries is the change in the conditions of the appropriation of surplus value across the globe. Redistributive dynamics favored some of those in the middle stratum in some regions of the world and penalized others in other regions. The nature and extent of the favor or penalty framed the modalities of political participation by members of these classes in individual countries.

The processes are identified, yet the key actors behind those processes are sporadically documented without a significant effort to identify their class position. This failure means that observations about similar phenomena in different countries are compiled, but without the tools needed to establish connections among them. If growing authoritarianism is a legitimate political concern, these observations do not offer a vantage point to formulate an effective way to cope with it.

However, earlier Marxist and anarchist thinkers such as Theodor Geiger, Luigi Salvatorelli, Daniel Guerin, and Erich Fromm, who were baffled by mass support for European fascist movements in the 1930s, expressly pointed to the role of the middle classes in this political phenomenon.[29] Antonio Gramsci called the urban middle classes an ally of the bureaucratic military class.[30] Franz Neumann, whose work was widely celebrated in the United States, attributed the rise of Nazism in Germany to the growth of a middle stratum that developed grievances due to the growing income of organized labor and, thus, began to support the fascist movement.[31]

In other words, this is not the first time there has been a connection between authoritarianism and the antidemocratic aspirations of the middle classes, reflecting their desire to maintain hegemony over knowledge production and thereby appropriate privileges in the labor process. However, the growing body of historical experience now allows for a new perspective on the relationship between capital accumulation and class formation that could broaden our understanding not only of fascism or Islamism, but also of other ideological positions of the circulation classes such as developmentalism or secularism.

The material in this book suggests that the dual and correlated slowdown of the Pacific economy and rural-to-urban migration in East Asia will alter the key parameters of the post–Cold War era. On the one hand, this slowdown could encourage a new wave of industrialization outside the North Atlantic, this time not by North Atlantic–based capital but by Turkish or Chinese capital, as in the Ethiopian case, in this second tier of globalization. On the other hand, the faubourgeoisie in the North Atlantic now has more to offer the bourgeoisie and wants to recalibrate its relationship with this ruling class, as East Asia slowly loses its former appeal as a large container for cheap labor. The ongoing protectionism debate in the United States, for instance, is a sign of this growing influence of the faubourgeoisie on US politics. The encroachment of authoritarianism from countries like Turkey to countries like the United States is a result of this political shift.

This new global environment will present challenges and opportunities for Islamists and other pro-faubourgeois movements in countries like Turkey. By allying with a promising political actor, the faubourgeoisie in the North Atlantic could turn protectionist ideas into a (selective) policy package and indirectly undermine the critical role of the faubourgeoisie in countries like Turkey and China. This would cause the Islamists in Turkey to reconsider their class alliances, possibly take an even more authoritarian direction, and perhaps even agree to a transfer of power with the secularists, who, they trust, would in turn do their best to keep the Islamist-secularist tension as the central theme of Turkish politics for the sake of their tacit alliance with the Islamists. The geopolitical vacuum amid and due to the reconfiguration of the global economy, which we can trace back to the 2008 recession, has benefited and continues to benefit the faubourgeoisie in different ways. In the case of Turkey, the European Union's waning interest in Turkey and the victory of the Islamists in Syria give the faubourgeoisie-Islamist alliance every reason to be optimistic about the next decade.

This is a grim picture, for it underscores that the political representatives and allies of the circulation classes will not do much in the coming decades to salvage what is left of twentieth-century bourgeois democracy. As a journey to deeper authoritarianism, the last half century has shown that the circulation classes are competing with each other to be the bourgeoisie's preferred agent of global plunder, rather than offering a "New Deal" that prevents the conflicts and rifts between social classes from taking us back to the 1930s.

The burden of stopping this apocalyptic scenario therefore once again lies on the shoulders of the socialists. There is great potential to turn this authoritarian backlash into an opportunity to build a global movement fighting for a democratic postcapitalist world order. As the material in this book has illustrated more than once, the proletariat resists capitalist exploitation in different ways, even in circumstances like those in Bağcılar. Moreover, the socialists have an invisible but remarkable support base in many nation-states. For instance, a presidential candidate who called himself a socialist received the support of 28 percent of Democratic delegates in the 2020 primaries in the United States. The 2023 elections in Turkey also showed that around 10 percent of voters see themselves as socialists or communists.[32]

This potential has so far remained untapped in many countries. In others, where movements calling themselves socialist have achieved electoral success in the past quarter of a century, those in power have not developed and implemented a comprehensive anticapitalist strategy. Instead, they have offered a flimsy anti-imperialist narrative combined with limited redistributive efforts similar to those of the Islamists in Turkey. Leaders like Lula da Silva and Nicolás Maduro use this narrative and these policies not only to legitimize themselves among the socialists, but also to justify their collaboration with explicitly antisocialist leaders like Erdoğan. This is a failure, which warrants a debate on the key class actors, the dynamics of capital accumulation, and the socialist narrative in the post–Cold War era. This book has addressed these three issues.

Methodology for Analysis of the Religious Orders' Online Content

This project focused on ten Naqshbandi and seven Salafi groups or leaders and on ten local groups in Bağcılar, including the local mufti's office. I selected these groups and leaders with the assistance of three resources: *Verse and Slogan (Ayet ve Slogan)*, by Ruşen Çakır; *Sects in Turkey: History and Culture (Türkiye'de Tarikatlar: Tarih ve Kültür)*, edited by Semih Ceyhan and published by the Directorate for Religious Affairs; and another report by the Directorate for Religious Affairs that was drafted and leaked in 2019.[1] From these three sources and others,[2] we identified forty-six active and prominent Sunni sects or sect representatives. Furthermore, we identified fifty-eight outlets on YouTube and Facebook. I focused on the outlets of seventeen groups and leaders. Ten of these groups and leaders are theologically closer to the Naqshbandis, and seven of them are regarded as Salafi.

After we filtered the initial pool of 1,318 videos on YouTube and Facebook according to their length, number of views, titles, and broad content, we coded sixty-three videos. Their total duration was 2,909 minutes. The average year of release of the videos was 2016, but most of the videos were produced more recently. We coded 1,434 paragraphs or excerpts from the transcripts.

For the codebook, I used the Outline of Cultural Materials (OCM) classification system. The OCM system was developed in the 1940s to aid ethnographic classification of human behavior, social life and customs, material culture, and human-ecological environments.[3] I started with a limited list of preestablished OCM codes.[4] We used 271 of 743 codes from sixty-seven themes of the OCM classification system, grouped these codes into twelve themes, and narrowed down the code list.[5] My assistants worked on fifty-four OCM codes in those twelve categories: religion, social theory, toxicity, norms, relations, sex and reproduction, public and everyday activities, politics, stratification, economy, production, and space. We exclusively used the definitions in the OCM in order to minimize the multiple coding of individual excerpts. One of the most appealing features of this classification system is its global character. For coding purposes, we used Dedoose, a computer-assisted qualitative data analysis software.[6]

My assistants coded the selected videos in a multistep reading process that began with mutual agreement on paragraphs that served as excerpts, blind reading of the excerpts, and consensus building on the excerpts to which they assigned different tags.

We conducted the content analysis in five steps. First, we gave priority to video recordings of the content in the sample available online. We used audio transcription services provided by Trint.[7] Each team member was assigned to be the first reader for individual texts in the initial excerpting process. The first readers shared the excerpts (i.e., the units of content analysis) with the second readers for their approval or objections. I intervened as the tiebreaker on less than 10 percent of the cases, when readers could not resolve their disagreements.

The second step was the blind coding process, in which each reader read the texts independently of the other. In the third step, the first reader read the blind-coded text, marked their disagreements with the second reader, and attached memos to describe the nature of the disagreement as necessary. In the fourth step, the second reader went over the first reader's disagreements and memos to reevaluate their original assessment. In the last step, I acted as the tiebreaker in less than 5 percent of the analyzed excerpts. Each copy of codes for each turn was saved to perform tests for interrater reliability.[8]

Because I prioritized content that had dialogues between sect representatives and followers, the reading process followed the basic methodological guidelines of conversation analysis, a method for assessing the content in dialogues. The research team went beyond the presence (or absence) of a particular code in its list to assess and document the linguistic and discursive choices and strategies in these conversations, such as observable regularities in the talk of participants (i.e., preferences); the sequence of the conversation pairs; repairs of problems with speaking, hearing, or understanding; and turn construction among the participants.[9]

Qualitative content analysis requires the simultaneous occurrence of observation and analysis.[10] As my team compiled the coded transcripts, I worked on the manifest content by examining the frequency and location of the codes.[11] Simultaneously, I wrote memos on the coded transcripts to discuss further with my team members. We used this secondary material to assess the latent content and connect the subjects of this project to a broader theoretical framework.

Thematic Distribution of the Codes

TABLE 5 Thematic distribution of the OCM codes

			Number of codes applied				Percentage of total codes applied			
Theme	*Topic*	*OCM subject*	*Total*	*Bağcılar*	*Naqshi*	*Salafi*	*Total*	*Bağcılar*	*Naqshi*	*Salafi*
Gaze	Norms	670 Law	72	6	24	42	1.3	1	0.8	2.4
		680 Offenses and Sanctions	356	31	202	123	6.6	5.2	6.6	7
		690 Justice	10	2	1	7	0.2	0.3	0	0.4
		Norms—Misc. Applied	5	0	5	0	0.1	0	0.2	0
	Total		**443**	**39**	**232**	**172**	**8.2**	**6.5**	**7.6**	**9.7**
	Public & Everyday Activities	520 Recreation	55	17	23	15	1	2.8	0.7	0.8
		540 Commercialized Entertainment	7	0	3	4	0.1	0	0.1	0.2
		Public & Everyday Activities—Misc. Applied	3	0	0	3	0.1	0	0	0.2
	Total		**246**	**30**	**142**	**74**	**4.5**	**5**	**4.6**	**4.2**
	Relations	200 Communication	0	0	0	0	0	0	0	0
		570 Interpersonal Relations	142	11	74	57	2.6	1.8	2.4	3.2
		580 Marriage	23	1	22	0	0.4	0.2	0.7	0
		590 Family	104	10	72	22	1.9	1.7	2.3	1.2
		600 Kinship	0	0	0	0	0	0	0	0
		620 Community	60	5	32	23	1.1	0.8	1	1.3
		Relations—Misc. Applied	1	0	1	0	0	0	0	0
	Total		**330**	**27**	**201**	**102**	**6.1**	**4.5**	**6.5**	**5.8**

(continued)

TABLE 5 (continued)

Theme	Topic	OCM subject	Number of codes applied				Percentage of total codes applied			
			Total	Bağcılar	Naqshi	Salafi	Total	Bağcılar	Naqshi	Salafi
	Sex & Reproduction	830 Sex	77	5	25	47	1.4	0.8	0.8	2.7
		840 Reproduction	9	3	1	5	0.2	0.5	0	0.3
		860 Socialization	84	10	35	39	1.5	1.7	1.1	2.2
		870 Education	67	7	39	21	1.2	1.2	1.3	1.2
		880 Adolescence, Adulthood, and Old Age	5	0	2	3	0.1	0	0.1	0.2
		890 Gender Roles and Issues	62	0	47	15	1.1	0	1.5	0.8
		Sex & Reproduction—Misc. Applied	0	0	0	0	0	0	0	0
	Total		**304**	**25**	**149**	**130**	**5.6**	**4.2**	**4.9**	**7.4**
	Space	340 Structures	1	0	1	0	0	0	0	0
		350 Equipment and Maintenance of Buildings	0	0	0	0	0	0	0	0
		360 Settlements	5	0	4	1	0.1	0	0.1	0.1
		370 Energy and Power	2	0	0	2	0	0	0	0.1
		Space—Misc. Applied	2	0	2	0	0	0	0.1	0
	Total		**10**	**0**	**7**	**3**	**0.2**	**0**	**0.2**	**0.2**
	Stratification	550 Naming, Prestige and Status Mobility	30	3	16	11	0.6	0.5	0.5	0.6
		560 Social Stratification	71	0	68	3	1.3	0	2.2	0.2
		Stratification—Misc. Applied	2	0	1	1	0	0	0	0.1
	Total		**103**	**3**	**85**	**15**	**1.9**	**0.5**	**2.8**	**0.8**
Gaze total			**1,436**	**124**	**816**	**496**	**26.4**	**20.8**	**26.6**	**28.1**
Hygiene	Religion	770 Religious Beliefs	1,210	142	693	375	22.3	23.8	22.6	21.2
		780 Religious Practices	852	87	623	142	15.7	14.6	20.3	8
		790 Ecclesiastical Organization	590	57	290	243	10.9	9.5	9.4	13.8
		Religion—Misc. Applied	2	0	2	0	0	0	0.1	0
	Total		**2,654**	**286**	**1,608**	**760**	**48.9**	**47.9**	**52.4**	**43.1**

TABLE 5 (continued)

Theme	Topic	OCM subject	Number of codes applied				Percentage of total codes applied			
			Total	Bağcılar	Naqshi	Salafi	Total	Bağcılar	Naqshi	Salafi
	Social Theory	530 Art	6	3	2	1	0.1	0.5	0.1	0.1
		140 Human Biology	3	1	1	1	0.1	0.2	0	0.1
		150 Behavior Processes and Personality	58	15	16	27	1.1	2.5	0.5	1.5
		160 Demography	1	0	1	0	0	0	0	0
		170 History and Culture Change	58	6	38	14	1.1	1	1.2	0.8
		180 Total Culture	162	22	96	44	3	3.7	3.1	2.5
		800 Numbers and Measures	17	1	13	3	0.3	0.2	0.4	0.2
		810 Sciences and Humanities	279	30	95	154	5.1	5	3.1	8.7
		Social Theory— Misc. Applied	1	0	0	1	0	0	0	0.1
	Total		**585**	**78**	**262**	**245**	**10.8**	**13.1**	**8.5**	**13.9**
	Toxicity	250 Food Processing	0	0	0	0	0	0	0	0
		260 Food Consumption	26	1	23	2	0.5	0.2	0.7	0.1
		270 Drink and Drugs	34	3	21	10	0.6	0.5	0.7	0.6
		290 Clothing	38	8	14	16	0.7	1.3	0.5	0.9
		300 Adornment	9	0	8	1	0.2	0	0.3	0.1
		730 Social Problems	60	12	32	16	1.1	2	1	0.9
		750 Sickness	115	13	75	27	2.1	2.2	2.4	1.5
		760 Death	125	16	86	23	2.3	2.7	2.8	1.3
		Toxicity—Misc. Applied	7	0	6	1	0.1	0	0.2	0.1
	Total		**414**	**53**	**265**	**96**	**7.6**	**8.9**	**8.6**	**5.4**
Hygiene total			**3,653**	**417**	**2,135**	**1,101**	**67.2**	**69.8**	**69.5**	**62.4**
Labor	Economy	420 Property	20	1	15	4	0.4	0.2	0.5	0.2
		430 Exchange and Transfers	38	20	8	10	0.7	3.4	0.3	0.6
		440 Marketing	1	1	0	0	0	0.2	0	0
		450 Finance	23	0	17	6	0.4	0	0.6	0.3
		Economy—Misc. Applied	10	0	8	2	0.2	0	0.3	0.1
	Total		**92**	**22**	**48**	**22**	**1.7**	**3.7**	**1.6**	**1.2**

(continued)

TABLE 5 (continued)

Theme	Topic	OCM subject	Number of codes applied				Percentage of total codes applied			
			Total	Bağcılar	Naqshi	Salafi	Total	Bağcılar	Naqshi	Salafi
	Politics	630 Territorial Organization	2	0	0	2	0	0	0	0.1
		640 Government Institutions	59	10	4	45	1.1	1.7	0.1	2.5
		650 Government Activities	8	0	2	6	0.1	0	0.1	0.3
		660 Political Behavior	68	9	1	58	1.3	1.5	0	3.3
		720 War	11	1	6	4	0.2	0.2	0.2	0.2
		740 Health and Welfare	28	4	24	0	0.5	0.7	0.8	0
		Politics—Misc. Applied	27	0	7	20	0.5	0	0.2	1.1
	Total		**203**	**24**	**44**	**135**	**3.7**	**4**	**1.4**	**7.6**
	Production	460 Labor	44	9	27	8	0.8	1.5	0.9	0.5
		470 Business and Industrial Organization	4	1	0	3	0.1	0.2	0	0.2
		Production—Misc. Applied	0	0	0	0	0	0	0	0
	Total		**48**	**10**	**27**	**11**	**0.9**	**1.7**	**0.9**	**0.6**
Labor total			**343**	**56**	**119**	**168**	**6.3**	**9.4**	**3.9**	**9.5**
Grand total			**5,432**	**597**	**3,070**	**1,765**	**100**	**100**	**100**	**100**

The Expanded Reproduction and Rent

INTRODUCTION

Marx's presentation of the conditions of equilibrium between departments of production helps identify the source of revenue for middle classes. In the final chapter of the second volume of *Capital*, Marx identified two departments of production: Department I produces constant capital, which does not produce value, and Department II produces the means of consumption for variable capital, which produces value.[1] However, the dead labor embodied in capital is treated the same as the labor power in market exchanges. Thus, these two departments have divergent growth patterns, and there is an incompatibility between simple reproduction and expanded reproduction.

Below, I argue that these two departments can exchange a portion of their output, which they cannot exchange with each other, with the output of a third department of production. The output of this third department raises the rate of surplus value in the first two departments and allows expanded reproduction. This exchange is unequal: the exchanged output of the first two departments is undervalued and the exchanged output of the third is overvalued. The value transferred to the third department as a result of this unequal exchange is equal to the total rent.

THE MODEL

Marx defines two subdivisions within Department II.[2] These subdivisions produce and exchange necessary means of subsistence for the proletariat and luxury items for the bourgeoisie. I treat the second subdivision as a third department of production and, following Bukharin's presentation of the equilibrium condition,[3] define β as the coefficient of the share of the investment of the surplus value.

$$c: \textit{Constant capital}$$
$$v: \textit{Variable capital}$$
$$s: \textit{Surplus value}$$
$$\beta: \textit{The investment coefficient}$$
$$\beta_{1c} + \beta_{1v} + \beta_{1s} = \beta_{2c} + \beta_{2v} + \beta_{2s} = \beta_{3c} + \beta_{3v} + \beta_{3s} = 1$$

Under the condition of simple reproduction, surplus value is dedicated to the consumption of the bourgeoisie. This is closer to Marx's discussion of the two subdivisions of Department II.

$$DI = c_1 + v_1 + s_1 = c_1 + c_2 + c_3$$
$$DII = c_2 + v_2 + s_2 = v_1 + v_2 + v_3$$
$$DIII = c_3 + v_3 + s_3 = s_1 + s_2 + s_3$$
$$E_1 \rightarrow c_2 + c_3 = v_1 + s_1$$

Under the condition of expanded reproduction, Department III produces a specific portion of the surplus value with a specific function, as I elaborate below:

$$DI = c_1 + v_1 + s_1 = c_1 + c_2 + c_3 + \beta_{1c}s_1 + \beta_{2c}s_2 + \beta_{3c}s_3$$
$$DII = c_2 + v_2 + s_2 = v_1 + v_2 + v_3 + \beta_{1v}s_1 + \beta_{2v}s_2 + \beta_{3v}s_3$$
$$DIII = c_3 + v_3 + s_3 = \beta_{1s}s_1 + \beta_{2s}s_2 + \beta_{3s}s_3$$

I simplify the condition of the growth of the surplus value in Department I as follows:

$$DI => c_2 + c_3 + (\beta_{1c}s_1 + \beta_{2c}s_2 + \beta_{3c}s_3) = v_1 + s_1$$

However, if E_1 holds,

$$E_2 \rightarrow c_2 + c_3 + \beta_{2c}s_2 + \beta_{3c}s_3 > c_2 + c_3 = v_1 + s_1 > v_1 + \beta_{1v}s_1 + \beta_{1s}s_1$$

Then, the following two conditions may satisfy the equilibrium.

First, Department II may have a decline in its organic composition of capital. In other words,

$$\lim_{n \to \infty} (\beta_{2vn} + \beta_{2sn}) = 1$$

Accordingly, Department I can continue to grow its organic composition of capital. This condition looked both intuitive and possible to Marx, because its repercussions for Department II apparently did not bother him very much:

> Nothing is altered in the relation between I_{vs} and II_c if a section of the constant capital in department II is reproduced there—as in agriculture for example, with the employment of homegrown seed.[4]

Second, Department I may exchange its surplus value, which corresponds to the total new demand for constant capital, for a portion of the surplus value produced in Department III for Department I. In other words,

$$\beta_{1c}s_1 + \beta_{2c}s_2 + \beta_{3c}s_3 \rightarrow \beta_{1s}s_1$$

The first assumption is that this (unequal) exchange violates the principle of value identity in exchanges. The second and third assumptions are that the value of the total output of constant capital has a bigger magnitude and grows faster than the surplus value produced in Department III for Department I. Then,

$$f\,(n) = \beta_{1cn}s_{1n} + \beta_{2cn}s_{2n} + \beta_{3cn}s_{3n} \wedge g\,(n)$$
$$g\,(n) = \beta_{1sn}s_{1n} \wedge f(n) > g(n) \wedge f'(n) > g'(n)$$
$$=> \lim_{n \to \infty} \frac{g(n)}{f(n)} = 0 => \lim_{n \to \infty} (c_{2n} + c_{3n}) = \lim_{n \to \infty} (v_{1n} + s_{1n})$$

The price of production of the surplus value produced in Department III for Department I approaches zero in relation to the surplus value produced in Department I and the expanded reproduction approaches the equilibrium condition for Department I in subsequent turnover periods.

Rate of Surplus Value

Department I took part in this unequal exchange because the surplus value produced in Department III for Department I increases the value of the output of Department I. The fourth assumption is that the surplus value produced in Department III has a special quality, which is to increase the rate of surplus value in Departments I and II and, therefore, to compensate this loss of value in the consecutive turnover period. For the sake of simplicity, assume that Department I does not expand its labor force. In other words,

$$\beta_{1v}s_1 = 0 \wedge v_{11} \in \mathbb{R} \wedge v_{11} > 0$$

Then,

$$DI_{Input_{t_1}} = c_{11} + v_{11} + s_{11}$$

$$Rate\ of\ surplus\ value_{DI_{t_1}} = s_{11} / v_{11}$$

$$DI_{Output_{t_1}} = c_{11} + c_{21} + c_{31} + \beta_{1c1}s_{11} + \beta_{2c1}s_{21} + \beta_{3c1}s_{31}$$

$$\beta_{1c}s_1 + \beta_{2c}s_2 + \beta_{3c}s_3 \rightarrow \beta_{1s}s_1 = > DI_{Input_{t_2}} = c_{11} + v_{11} + s_{11} + \beta_{1s1}s_{11}$$

$$Rate\ of\ surplus\ value_{DI_{t_2}} = (1 + \beta_{1s1})s_{11} / v_{11}$$

$$DI_{Output_{t_2}} = c_{11} + c_{21} + c_{31} + \beta_{1c1}s_{11} + \beta_{2c1}s_{21} + \beta_{3c1}s_{31} + \beta_{1c2}s_{12} + \beta_{2c2}s_{22} + \beta_{3c2}s_{32}$$

Both the rate of surplus value and the output have grown in two consecutive turnover periods.

$$(1 + \beta_{1s1})s_{11} / v_{11} > s_{11} / v_{11}$$

$$DI_{Output_{t_2}} > DI_{Output_{t_1}}$$

The Growth Function

Now, I denote the rate of surplus value of Department I and its growth coefficient to formulate a general expression of the growth of Department I:

$$k_1 : Rate\ of\ surplus\ value\ of\ Department\ I$$

$$s'_1 : Growth\ coefficient\ of\ the\ rate\ of\ surplus\ value\ of\ Department\ I$$

The surplus value produced in Department III is used as an (overvalued) input in Department I. Unlike the new constant capital, which typically increases the productivity of labor, the surplus value produced in Department III increases the intensity of labor or extends the duration of the working day.

Except for the first turnover period, when Department I does not exchange its surplus value with Department III, the rate of surplus value of Department I is measured by the ratio of the surplus value in its output to the variable capital in its input:

$$\beta_{1c1}s_{11} + \beta_{2c1}s_{21} + \beta_{3c1}s_{31} + \beta_{1c2}s_{12} + \beta_{2c2}s_{22} + \beta_{3c2}s_{32} = s'_{12}s_{11}$$

$$= > DI_{Output_{t_2}} = c_{11} + c_{21} + c_{31} + s'_{12}s_{11}$$

Both the magnitude of the surplus value and the rate of surplus value are byproducts of the growth coefficient. Thus, I define the change in the rate of surplus value as follows:

$$k_{11} = s_{11} / v_{11}$$

$$k_{12} = \frac{s_{11} + s'_{12}s_{11}}{v_{11} + v_{12}} = \frac{s_{11} + s'_{12}s_{11}}{v_{11} + \beta_{1v2}s_{11}}$$

$$k_{14} = \frac{1 + s'_{12} + s'_{13}(1 + s'_{12}) + s'_{14}[1 + s'_{12} + s'_{13}(1 + s'_{12})]}{\dfrac{\beta_{1v1}}{s'_{11}} + \beta_{1v2} + \beta_{1v3}(1 + s'_{12}) + \beta_{1v4}[1 + s'_{12} + s'_{13}(1 + s'_{12})]}$$

Now, I assign infinitesimal values to the figures for the first turnover period for the sake of the simplification of the general expression:

$$s'_{11} \wedge \beta_{1v1} \wedge \frac{\beta_{1v1}}{s'_{11}} \cong 0 \;=> k_{14} \cong \frac{\prod_{i=1}^{4}(1 + s'_{1i})}{\sum_{i=1}^{3}[\beta_{1vi+1}\prod_{i=1}^{3}(1 + s'_{1i})]}$$

Now, I can define the rate of surplus value as follows:

$$k_{1n} \cong \frac{\prod_{i=1}^{n}(1 + s'_{1i})}{\sum_{i=1}^{n-1}[\beta_{1vi+1}\prod_{i=1}^{n-1}(1 + s'_{1i})]}$$

The first condition for expanded reproduction is now redundant, because the mutual demand of Department I and Department II is tied to the growth coefficient. Then, this growth function of Department I represents the change in the rate of surplus value:

$$d_1(n) = c(n) + v(n) + s_{1n} = \left(c_{11} + \sum_{i=1}^{n}\beta_{1ci}s_{1i-1}\right) + \left(v_{11} + \sum_{i=1}^{n}\beta_{1vi}s_{1i-1}\right) + s_{1n}$$

$$s_{10} = 0 \wedge s_{1n} = k_{1n}v(n) => d_1(n) = c(n) + (1 + k_{1n})\,v(n)$$

$$d_1(n) = c_{11} + \sum_{i=1}^{n}\beta_{1ci}s_{1i-1} + (1 + k_{1n})\left(v_{11} + \sum_{i=1}^{n}\beta_{1vi}s_{1i-1}\right)$$

$$d_1(n) \cong c_{11} + \sum_{i=1}^{n}\beta_{1ci}s_{1i-1} + \left(1 + \frac{\prod_{i=1}^{n}(1 + s'_{1i})}{\sum_{i=1}^{n-1}[\beta_{1vi+1}\prod_{i=1}^{n-1}(1 + s'_{1i})]}\right)\left(v_{11} + \sum_{i=1}^{n}\beta_{1vi}s_{1i-1}\right)$$

This is not a complete analytical treatment of expanded reproduction, which requires the specification of the effects of the changes in the intensity of labor, the duration of the working day, and the productivity of labor both for individual departments of production and expanded reproduction. Nonetheless, these steps support the following conclusions.

First, the origin of rent is not the control or ownership of a scarce resource. Scarcity is a social construction in bourgeois society. I define the maximum magnitude of rent as the magnitude of the value emerging from within the disequilibrium between Departments I and II: no departmental disequilibrium, no rent. Any object, practice, or symbol that raises the rate of surplus value with the effect of shrinking the disequilibrium can be defined or innovated as a scarce resource and generate rent according to this magnitude. Just as value entails both the necessary means for the proletariat and the surplus value in it, rent can be embedded in those objects, practices, and symbols that appear as constant capital or variable capital and also serve as means of production or means of consumption. The disequilibrium indirectly facilitates the expanded reproduction.

Second, following Marx's trinity formula in the third volume of *Capital*, if interest and wages define the bourgeoisie and the proletariat, rent defines a third social class, or, more properly, three circulation classes.[5] Interest is the revenue due to the monopoly over the dead labor accumulated in the past. Wages are paid for both the reproduction of this dead labor and the production of the surplus value now. Rent is the revenue paid for an increasing rate of surplus value to facilitate the growth of the dead labor in the future.

Instead of an archaic form, rent is the revenue accrued to those who participate in increasing the intensity of labor and extending the duration of the working day. For this purpose, the circulation classes produce and implement technologies that range from the design of new forms of fixed capital such as machinery and communications to the formation of institutions and organizations such as nation-states and transnational corporations and to the invention of traditions, such as those I discuss in this book with regard to Islamism. Essential for the expanded reproduction, these technologies underlie the gaze, labor, and purity regimes. The proletariat produces value. The bourgeoisie funnels that value that cannot be exchanged between Departments I and II to Department III. The circulation classes use this value, which now takes the form of rent, to develop these technologies for the intensification of the exploitation of the proletariat.

NOTES

INTRODUCTION

1. TÜİK, "İl Bazında Gayrisafi Yurt İçi Hasıla, 2021."
2. Kandiyoti, "Bargaining with Patriarchy."
3. Azari, "Islam's Appeal to Women in Iran: Illusion and Reality."
4. Azari.
5. World Bank, "Labor Force Participation Rate, Female (% of Female Population Ages 15+) (Modeled ILO Estimate)."
6. Goldin, "The U-Shaped Female Labor Force Function in Economic Development and Economic History."
7. Konda Araştırma, "Barometre."
8. World Bank, "Labor Force Participation Rate."
9. Mardin, "Center-Periphery Relations."
10. Shils, *Center and Periphery: Essays in Macrosociology.*
11. Aslan, *1 Mayis Mahallesi.*
12. Piore and Sabel, *The Second Industrial Divide.*
13. Harvey, *The Condition of Postmodernity.*
14. International Labour Organization, *Small Matters: Global Evidence on the Contribution to Employment by the Self-Employed, Micro-Enterprises and SMEs.*
15. World Bank, "GDP (Current US$)."
16. Milanovic, *Global Inequality: A New Approach for the Age of Globalization,* 5.
17. Milanovic, 19.
18. WID, "World Inequality Database."
19. TÜİK, "Number of Enterprises by Size Class and Economic Activity"; TÜİK, "Number of Persons Employed by Size Class and Economic Activity."
20. Cruz, Keefer, and Scartascini, "The Database of Political Institutions 2020 (DPI2020)."
21. Foucault, *Technologies of the Self.*
22. V-Dem Institute, "V-Dem Dataset Version 12."

1. Geertz, "Thick Description."
2. UN Stats, "National Accounts—Analysis of Main Aggregates (AMA)."
3. Mitchell, *Carbon Democracy*.
4. Wilson, *Islam and Economic Policy*.
5. Galal, *Industrial Policy in the Middle East and North Africa*, 2.
6. Hartshorn, *Labor Politics in North Africa*, 209.
7. V-Dem Institute, "V-Dem Dataset Version 12."
8. This indicator (the ideological character of the government, v2exl_legitide-olcr) shows the degree of agreement among country experts who are asked "how [they would] characterize the ideology/ideologies [promoted by the current government]" from one or more of these options: nationalist, socialist or communist, restorative or conservative, separatist or autonomist, and religious. For Muslim-majority countries, I use the scores on this last option as a measure of the significance of religiosity in government ideology, which I call "religious government ideology" in the following pages.
9. These indicators show the degree of agreement among country experts. There are the following thirteen options for both questions and I use the values for "a religious group" as a measure of the role of religion in politics: the aristocracy, agrarian elites, party elites, business elites, civil servants, the military, an ethnic or racial group, a religious group, local elites, urban working classes, urban middle classes, rural working classes, rural middle classes, and a foreign government or colonial power. V-Dem Institute, "V-Dem Codebook—V12 March 2022."
10. The share of agricultural employment in total workforce took a negative Spearman's rho value (-0.534; $p < 0.01$). Industry and services took similar positive Spearman's rho values (0.459; $p < 0.01$ and 0.492; $p < 0.01$). The proportion of the industry's share to the shares of agriculture and services took the following positive Spearman's rho values: 0.541 ($p < 0.01$) and 0.226 ($p < 0.01$). In other words, industrial employment is more closely aligned with the political religiosity and religious government ideology scores than are agricultural or service employment.
11. Gross fixed capital formation is a measure that has been widely used since the 1950s to assess the net additions to fixed nonfinancial assets. Its relative size therefore gives us a comprehensive picture of the role that capital plays in the domestic economy of each country. Natural resource rent is the difference between the price and the average cost of a harvested or extracted commodity. The most typical and economically important rent-bearing commodities are hydrocarbon resources. Because governments can either tax a significant portion of the revenues from resource extraction or simply own the resource deposits, policies in hydrocarbon-rich countries tend to be very state-centric. Both the political establishment and their competitors in these countries tend to achieve their goals by controlling the state apparatus.
12. World Bank, "Employment in Industry (% of Total Employment) (Modeled ILO Estimate)."

13. UNIDO, "UNIDO Statistics Data Portal."

14. Beblawi and Luciani, *The Rentier State*; Freer, *Rentier Islamism*; Gray, "A Theory of 'Late Rentierism' in the Arab States of the Gulf"; Luciani, "Allocation vs. Production States: A Theoretical Framework"; Mahdavy, "Patterns and Problems of Economic Development in Rentier States: The Case of Iran"; Ross, "Does Oil Hinder Democracy?"

15. Esposito, Sonn, and Voll, *Islam and Democracy after the Arab Spring*, 149–51.

16. Baldaro and Raineri, "Azawad"; Amao, "A Decade of Terror: Revisiting Nigeria's Interminable Boko Haram Insurgency."

17. Cogan, "Partners in Time."

18. Savina et al., "The KOF Globalisation Index—Revisited."

19. Chibber, *Locked in Place*; Harrison, *Developmentalism*; Wallerstein, "After Developmentalism and Globalization, What?"; Said Aly et al., *Developmentalism and Beyond*; Beinin, *Workers and Thieves*, 16.

20. Fuller, *The Future of Political Islam*; Fogg, *Indonesia's Islamic Revolution*; Riaz, "Islamist Parties, Elections, and Democracy in Bangladesh"; Devji, *Muslim Zion*; Joya, *The Roots of Revolt*; Adaman and Arsel, *Environmentalism in Turkey*; Lord, *Religious Politics in Turkey*, 2018.

21. Ajl, Haddad, and Abul-Magd, "State, Market, and Class: Egypt, Syria, and Tunisia," 46–47.

22. Tanuwidjaja, "Political Islam and Islamic Parties in Indonesia"; Robinson, *The Killing Season*; Melvin, *The Army and the Indonesian Genocide*, 7.

23. Antonio, "Islamic Microfinance Initiatives to Enhance to Small and Medium-Sized Enterprises," 252–53.

24. Tuğal, "Fight or Acquiesce?"

25. Bianchi, "Islam and Democracy in Egypt."

26. Dalacoura, "Islamism and Neoliberalism in the Aftermath of the 2011 Arab Uprisings: The Freedom and Justice Party in Egypt and Nahda in Tunisia."

27. El Alami, "Law No. 100 of 1985 Amending Certain Provisions of Egypt's Personal Status Laws."

28. Pripstein Posusney, "Egyptian Privatization."

29. Joya, *The Roots of Revolt*.

30. "Egypt Outlines a Vast Privatization Plan."

31. Jakes and Shakr, "Capitalism in Egypt, Not Egyptian Capitalism," 140–41.

32. Joya, *The Roots of Revolt*, 144.

33. Al-Arian, *Answering the Call*.

34. Masoud, *Counting Islam*.

35. Joya, *The Roots of Revolt*, 144, 151–52.

36. Acconcia, *The Uprisings in Egypt*.

37. Riaz, "Islamist Parties, Elections, and Democracy in Bangladesh," 168.

38. Riaz, 156.

39. Esposito, Sonn, and Voll, *Islam and Democracy after the Arab Spring*, 122.

40. Menchik, *Islam and Democracy in Indonesia*, 68–73.

41. Tanuwidjaja, "Political Islam and Islamic Parties in Indonesia."

42. Bush, "Regional Sharia Regulations in Indonesia: Anomaly or Symptom?"

43. Schneier, *Muslim Democracy*.

44. BPS-Statistics Indonesia, "Statistical Yearbook of Indonesia 2022."

45. ILO, "Number of Strikes and Lockouts by Economic Activity—Annual." The ILO data set covers these Muslim-majority countries: Algeria, Bahrain, Bangladesh, Burkina Faso, Egypt, Guinea, Indonesia, Jordan, Malaysia, Morocco, Niger, Pakistan, Palestine, Senegal, Tunisia, and Turkey.

46. ILO, "Trade Union Density Rate (%)—Annual." The corresponding figures for the last year in the ILO data set are as follows: Bangladesh (2018), 11.9 percent; Indonesia (2019), 13 percent; Pakistan (2016), 4.7 percent; Turkey (2019), 9.9 percent; and Egypt (2010), 23.8 percent. The figure is high for Egypt, yet there are no independent trade unions in Egypt. The Sisi regime dissolved the independent unions in 2018 and allowed only 12 percent of these approximately one thousand unions to continue their work. ITUC, "2019 ITUC Global Rights Index: The World's Worst Countries for Workers," 13.

47. Allinson, "Class Forces, Transition and the Arab Uprisings."

48. Hartshorn, *Labor Politics in North Africa*, 162.

49. Mandaville, *Islam and Politics*.

50. Bayat, *Workers and Revolution in Iran*, 25.

51. World Bank, "Employment in Industry (% of Total Employment) (Modeled ILO Estimate)."

52. Jafari, "The Showras in the Iranian Revolution: Labour Relations and the State in the Iranian Oil Industry, 1979–82," 256.

53. Gohardani and Tizro, *The Political Economy of Iran*.

54. Wilson, *Islam and Economic Policy*; Harris, "A Martyrs' Welfare State and Its Contradictions: Regime Resilience and Limits through the Lens of Social Policy in Iran."

55. World Bank, "Employment to Population Ratio, 15+, Total (%) (Modeled ILO Estimate)"; World Bank, "Employment in Industry (% of Total Employment) (Modeled ILO Estimate)."

56. ITUC, "2019 ITUC Global Rights Index: The World's Worst Countries for Workers."

57. A similar but weaker pattern between growth in manufacturing output and vote share applies to the ultranationalist parties. Industrialization has overlapped with a general shift to the far right in the form of Islamonationalism since the 1980s. Nonetheless, the ultranationalist parties have not placed first in any election since 1973. The Islamists have emerged as the hegemonic party in Turkish politics.

58. Agriculture and related sectors (ISIC A-B) grew much more slowly than the industrial sectors. I excluded these sectors to see the relationship of the two mainly urban sector groups, industry (ISIC C-F) and services (ISIC G-P).

59. For example, Roccu, "Democratization beyond Capitalist Time"; Roy, *Globalized Islam*; Green, *Global Islam*; Robinson, *Global Jihad*; Mandaville, *Islam and Politics*; Esposito, *The Future of Islam*; Pepinsky and Liddle, *Piety and Public Opinion*.

CHAPTER TWO

1. Tunaya, *Türkiye'de Siyasal Partiler, Cilt 1: İkinci Meşrutiyet Dönemi*, 188.

2. Kobal, "Millî Mücadelede İç Ayaklanmalar."

3. T.C. Kültür ve Turizm Bakanlığı, "Yeşil Ordu Cemiyeti"; Arbaç, "Milli Mücadele Dönemi Rus-Türk İlişkilerinde Yeşil Ordu—Çerkez Ethem—Mustafa Suphi ve Arkadaşları Üçgeni."

4. Atatürk Ansiklopedisi, "Atatürk Döneminde Meydana Gelen Ayaklanmalar (1924–1938)."

5. Lord, *Religious Politics in Turkey*.

6. Lewis, *Islamic Revival in Turkey*, 46–47.

7. Zengin, *Akıncılar Hareketi*, 58.

8. Mardin, *Religion and Social Change in Modern Turkey*.

9. Yaşar, "Dergah'tan Partiye, Vakıf'tan Şirkete Bir Kimliğin Oluşumu ve Dönüşümü: Lskenderpaşa Cemaati," 326.

10. Dal and Dilek, "Comparison of Erbakan's Economic Policy Proposals with Turkey's 2002–2021 Economic Policies"; Öztürk, "Adil Ekonomik Düzen' de Artı(k) Değerin Paylaşımı."

11. Özbür, *Necmettin Erbakan ve Gümüş Motor*, 51–54; Zengin, *Akıncılar Hareketi*, 106–7.

12. Yaşar, "Dergah'tan Partiye, Vakıf'tan Şirkete Bir Kimliğin Oluşumu ve Dönüşümü: Lskenderpaşa Cemaati," 325–27; Yaşar, "Mehmet Zahid Kotku," 326–27.

13. Çalmuk, "Necmettin Erbakan," 555.

14. Gündoğan, *Erbakan*, 24–25.

15. Gündoğan, 24–26.

16. Gündoğan, 34.

17. Çetin, "1960 darbesi sonrası Necmettin Erbakan'a hangi bakanlık teklif edildi?—Saadet Partisi Genel Başkanı Temel Karamollaoğlu ile söyleşi."

18. Koçak, *27 Mayıs Bakanlar Kurulu Tutanakları (2 Haziran 1960—6 Kasım 1961)*, 708.

19. Koçak, 718.

20. Koçak, 713.

21. Koçak, 713.

22. Koçak, 717.

23. Koçak, 744. The savings bonds were issued in the 1960s, but they mostly proved ineffective and eventually were abolished, in 1971. Ekonomi Terimleri Girişimci Ajansı, "Tasarruf Bonoları."

24. Koçak, 716–18.

25. Koçak, 741.

26. Koçak, 708.

27. Çetin, "1960 darbesi sonrası Necmettin Erbakan'a hangi bakanlık teklif edildi?—Saadet Partisi Genel Başkanı Temel Karamollaoğlu ile söyleşi."

28. TİM, "History (The Union of Chambers and Commodity Exchanges of Türkiye)."

29. Ersöz, "Prof. Dr. Necmeddin Erbakan-3."

30. Milli Gazete, "Tarihin ilk ayakkabılı eylemi bize ait çıktı."

31. Gündoğan, *Erbakan*, 37–38.

32. Gündoğan, 37–38.

33. Gündoğan, 37–38.

34. Karaveli, *Why Turkey Is Authoritarian*, 153–54.

35. Yavuz, "Milli Görüş Hareketi: Muhalif ve Modernist Gelenek," 591.

36. Sarıbay, "Milli Nizam Partisi'nin Kuruluşu ve Programının İçeriği," 576.

37. Gündoğan, *Erbakan*, 56, 71–73, 66–67.

38. Çakır, "Milli Görüş Hareketi," 547.

39. In turn, İskenderpaşa Cemaati took a hostile stance toward Erbakan, especially after the rise of Esad Coşan, Kotku's son-in-law, to the top of the order in the late 1980s. Çalmuk, "Necmettin Erbakan," 563.

40. Çalmuk, 562.

41. Zengin, *Akıncılar Hareketi*, 72.

42. Çakır, "Milli Görüş Hareketi," 547; Gündoğan, *Erbakan*, 52–53.

43. Buğra and Savaşkan, *New Capitalism in Turkey*, 80.

44. Sarıbay, "Milli Nizam Partisi'nin Kuruluşu ve Programının İçeriği," 584–87.

45. Şahinkaya, "Devlet Sanayi ve İşçi Yatırım Bankası'ndan Türkiye Kalkınma Bankası'na: 1975–2001 Döneminde Kurumsal Yapıdaki Temel Dönüşümler Üzerine Düşünceler ve Bazı Öneriler," 4–5. The number of worker-enterprises continued to grow in the 1970s and finally rose to 322 in 1983. See Gürbüz, "İşçi ve Halk Şirketleri Örneğinde Küçük ve Orta Büyüklükteki İşletmelerin Finansal Sorunları ve Çözüm Alternatifleri"; Ünal, "Çok Ortaklı Şirketlere Genel Bakış."

46. Sarıbay, "Milli Nizam Partisi'nin Kuruluşu ve Programının İçeriği," 588.

47. Çakır, "Milli Görüş Hareketi," 547.

48. Yavuz, "Milli Görüş Hareketi: Muhalif ve Modernist Gelenek," 592.

49. Çakır, "Milli Görüş Hareketi," 547.

50. "YSK Web Portal."

51. Bianchi, *Interest Groups and Political Development in Turkey*, 256.

52. Barlas, *Turgut Özal'ın Anıları*, 88.

53. Yalçın, *Hangi Erbakan*, 16.

54. Evren, *Kenan Evren'in Anılar (Cilt 2)*, 70.

55. Evren, 29.

56. Evren, 119.

57. Feyzioğlu split from the RPP without hesitation in 1967 after it moved to "left of center" (*ortanın solu*) in 1965.

58. Yalman, "The Neoliberal Transformation of State and Market in Turkey: An Overview of Financial Developments from 1980 to 2000," 54–63; Öniş, "Turgut Özal and His Economic Legacy," 123.

59. Alpagu, "24 Ocak Kararları ve Turgut Özal Döneminin Yansımaları," 131.

60. Karluk, "Türkiye Ekonomisini Dışa Açan 24 Ocak 1980 İstikrar Kararları: Öncesi ve Sonrasında Ekonomik Durum," 221.

61. Doğançay, "Neoliberal Kuram Bağlamında Turgut Özal ve 24 Ocak Kararları," 155.

62. Öztürk, *Agriculture, Peasantry and Poverty in Turkey in the Neo-Liberal Age*; Cenk Özbay, Erol, and Terzioglu, *The Making of Neoliberal Turkey*.

63. World Bank, "Urban Population (% of Total Population) | Data"; World Bank, "Population, Total | Data."

64. Işık, "Turgut Özal'ın İhracat Odaklı Büyüme Politikaları ve Sonuçlarının Değerlendirilmesi: (1983–1993 Dönemi)," 231.

65. Yönder, "Implications of Double Standards in Housing Policy: Development of Informal Settlements in Istanbul." Islamists actively supported anti-squatting campaigns. Tayyip Erdoğan, who served as mayor of Istanbul in the 1990s, even toyed publicly with the idea of imposing additional taxes on squatters. Then, after coming to power in 2003, Islamists have refused to enact amnesty laws for squatters (Tercan, "1948'den Bugüne İmar Afları") but relaxed zoning restrictions, which added value to the existing residential buildings (Batuman, *New Islamist Architecture and Urbanism*).

66. Aslan, *1 Mayis Mahallesi*; Erder, *İstanbul'a Bir Kent Kondu Ümraniye*; Işık and Pınarcıoğlu, *Nöbetlese Yoksulluk*.

67. Turkish Statistical Institute, *Statistical Indicators (1923–2008)*.

68. Balaban, "The Enclosure of Urban Space and Consolidation of the Capitalist Land Regime in Turkish Cities."

69. Devlet İstatistik Enstitüsü (Turkey), "Sanayi ve isyerleri sayimi."

70. Basbakanlık Devlet İstatistik Enstitüsü, *1980 genel sanayi ve işyerleri sayımı = 1980 census of industry and business establishments*.

71. TÜİK, "Number of Enterprises by Size Class and Economic Activity."

72. TÜİK, "2002 Genel Sanayi ve İşyerleri Sayımı—İstatistiki Bölge Birimleri Sınıflaması (İBBS) ve Ekonomik Faaliyet Bölümlerine Göre Yerel Birim Sayısı ve İstihdam."

73. T.C. İçişleri Bakanlığı, "Mülki İdare Birimleri."

74. Işık and Pınarcıoğlu, *Nöbetlese Yoksulluk*.

75. The center-left parties (RPP and SDP), the center-right parties (JP, MP, and TPP), and the Islamist parties (NSP and WP) participated without an electoral alliance with another party in the 1977, 1987, and 1995 elections. The difference between the change in the vote shares of the center-left and center-right parties between the 1977 and 1987 elections is 2 percent. The difference between the change in the vote shares of the center-right parties and the Islamist parties between the 1987 and 1995 elections is also 2 percent. At the city level, if the Kurdish cities are excluded from the calculation, the Pearson correlation values are -0.27 ($p < 0.05$) for the changes in vote shares between the 1977 and 1987 elections for the center-left and center-right parties and -0.69 ($p < 0.01$) between the 1987 and 1995 elections for the center-right and Islamist parties. In Ankara, Istanbul, and Izmir, the three largest cities in the country, the vote shares of the center-left parties decreased by 22 percent,

28 percent, and 17 percent, respectively, between 1977 and 1987, while the center-right parties increased their vote shares by 23 percent, 23 percent, and 12 percent, respectively. In the same cities and in the same order, the vote shares of the center-right parties fell by 19 percent, 14 percent, and 9 percent between 1987 and 1995, and the Islamist parties increased their vote shares by 17 percent, 17 percent, and 6 percent. YSK, "Açık Veri Portalı."

76. TBMM, "TBMM Ülkemizde Demokrasiye Müdahale Eden Tüm Darbe ve Muhtıralar Ile Demokrasiyi İşlevsiz Kılan Diğer Bütün Girişm ve Süreçlerin Tüm Boyutları Ile Araştırılarak Alınması Gereken Önlemlerin Belirlenmesi Amacıyla Kurulan Meclis Araştırması Komisyonu Raporu—Cilt 1," xiv–xiv, 122.

77. Çakır, "Milli Görüş Hareketi," 553.

78. Çelik and İşeri, "Islamically Oriented Humanitarian NGOs in Turkey"; Aksular, "Faith Based Organizations in the Struggle against Poverty"; Zencirci, "Markets of Islam"; Çevik, Sevin, and Baybars-Hawks, "State–Civil Society Partnerships in International Aid and Public Diplomacy"; Grütjen, "The Turkey Welfare Regime: An Example of the Southern European Model?"

79. Eligür, *The Mobilization of Political Islam in Turkey*, 6.

80. Delibaş, *The Rise of Political Islam in Turkey*, 233.

81. Arat, *Political Islam in Turkey and Women's Organizations*; Yavuz, "Political Islam and the Welfare (Refah) Party in Turkey"; Sayari, "Turkey's Islamist Challenge."

82. Yilmaz, "The Rise of Political Islam in Turkey," 371–72.

83. Delibaş, *The Rise of Political Islam in Turkey*, 15; Çakır, *Ne Şeriat Ne Demokrasi*, 59–63.

84. Delibaş, *The Rise of Political Islam in Turkey*, 142, 223, 250.

85. White, *Islamist Mobilization in Turkey*, 181–82.

86. Delibaş, *The Rise of Political Islam in Turkey*, 235.

87. Erder, *İstanbul'a Bir Kent Kondu Ümraniye*; Aslan, *1 Mayis Mahallesi*.

88. Aslan, *1 Mayis Mahallesi*.

89. Erder, *İstanbul'a Bir Kent Kondu Ümraniye*.

90. Işık and Pınarcıoğlu, *Nöbetlese Yoksulluk*.

91. Tuğal, *Passive Revolution*.

92. Öniş, "The Political Economy of Islamic Resurgence in Turkey," 758–59.

93. Yankaya, "28 Şubat, İslami Burjuvazinin İktidar Yolunda Bir Milat," 44–48, 95, 146–47.

94. Dönmez, *25 Yılın Hikayesi*, 27, 29, 30, 53.

95. Yankaya, "28 Şubat, İslami Burjuvazinin İktidar Yolunda Bir Milat," 31–32.

96. Dönmez, *25 Yılın Hikayesi*, 5–6, 60, 135.

97. Dönmez, 25, 51.

98. Köksal, *İstanbul'daki Sosyal Demokrat Belediye Başkanları ve Gecekondu*.

99. Yankaya, "28 Şubat, İslami Burjuvazinin İktidar Yolunda Bir Milat"; Buğra, "Class, Culture, and State."

100. Yankaya, "28 Şubat, İslami Burjuvazinin İktidar Yolunda Bir Milat," 31.

101. Dönmez, *25 Yılın Hikayesi*, 117.

102. Çakır, "Milli Görüş Hareketi"; Cagaptay, *The New Sultan*.

103. Yankaya, *Yeni islâmî burjuvazi*, 120.

104. Dönmez, *25 Yılın Hikayesi*, 31.

105. İnce, "Bazı isimler geldi ve Erbakan'ı tehdit etti—Mehmet Bekaroğlu ile söyleşi."

106. Tuğal, "Fight or Acquiesce?," 33.

107. Çınar, "AKP ve İslami Hareketler: Defansif ve Dağıtıcı İktidar Kardeşliği," 311.

108. Karaveli, *Why Turkey Is Authoritarian*, 155.

109. Hürriyet, "Hoca'nın Derneği Kavgalı Kuruldu."

110. Buğra and Savaşkan, *New Capitalism in Turkey*, 183–85.

111. Yavuz, *Erdoğan*, 60.

112. Presidency of the Republic of Turkey, "Presidency of the Republic of Turkey: Biography of Recep Tayyip Erdoğan."

113. Yavuz, *Erdoğan*, 41, 36, 46, 47–51.

CHAPTER THREE

1. IMF, "World Economic Outlook (October 2023)—Inflation Rate, Average Consumer Prices."

2. In Turkish, the expression was *"Bir şey diyemiyorum artık."* https://twitter.com/Zumrut_Imamoglu/status/1319234840806510595.

3. Cumhuriyet, "AKP'li Cumhurbaşkanı Erdoğan'ın hedefindeki TÜSİAD başkanı Orhan Turan kimdir?"

4. İstanbul Sanayi Odası, "İSO—Türkiye'nin 500 Büyük Sanayi Kuruluşu."

5. Buğra, *State and Business in Modern Turkey*; Boratav, *İstanbul ve Anadolu'dan Sınıf Profilleri*; Gürakar, *Politics of Favoritism in Public Procurement in Turkey*; Esen and Gümüşçü, "Rising Competitive Authoritarianism in Turkey"; Yilmaz, Caman, and Bashirov, "How an Islamist Party Managed to Legitimate Its Authoritarianization in the Eyes of the Secularist Opposition."

6. I thank Bekir Ağırdır and Konda researchers for sharing the data.

7. TÜİK, "Small and Medium Sized Enterprises Statistics, 2023"; KOSGEB, "KOBİ Tanımı Güncellendi!"

8. TÜİK, "Tablo-5 Hayatta Kalma Göstergeleri (2016–2020)."

9. TCMB, "TCMB—Sektör Bilançoları—İmalat."

10. TCMB, "TCMB—Sektör Bilançoları—İmalat.

11. TCMB, "TCMB—Sektör Bilançoları—Metaveri."

12. Milli Nizam Partisi, *Milli Nizam Partisi Program ve Tüzük*, 27; Milli Selamet Partisi, *Milli Selamet Partisi 1973 Seçim Beyannamesi*, 59.

13. Milli Nizam Partisi, *Milli Nizam Partisi Program ve Tüzük*, 9.

14. Milli Nizam Partisi, *Milli Nizam Partisi 1. Büyük Kongresi*, 6; Milli Selamet Partisi, *Milli Selamet Partisi 1973 Seçim Beyannamesi*, 21.

15. Milli Nizam Partisi, *Milli Nizam Partisi 1. Büyük Kongresi*, 6.

16. Milli Selamet Partisi, *Milli Selamet Partisi 1973 Seçim Beyannamesi*, 10.

17. Milli Selamet Partisi, 47.

18. Halk Bankası is a state-owned bank founded in 1933 to provide loans to small producers and shopkeepers.

19. Milli Selamet Partisi, *Milli Selamet Partisi 1973 Seçim Beyannamesi*, 60 (italics added).

20. Milli Selamet Partisi, 42.

21. Milli Nizam Partisi, *Milli Nizam Partisi Program ve Tüzük*, 26.

22. Milli Selamet Partisi, *Milli Selamet Partisi Program ve Tüzük*, 21.

23. Milli Selamet Partisi, *Milli Selamet Partisi 5 Haziran 1977 Seçim Beyannamesi*, 52.

24. Milli Nizam Partisi, *Milli Nizam Partisi Program ve Tüzük*, 22.

25. Milli Nizam Partisi, 26.

26. Milli Selamet Partisi, *Milli Selamet Partisi 1973 Seçim Beyannamesi*, 42.

27. Milli Selamet Partisi, 70.

28. Milli Selamet Partisi, *Milli Selamet Partisi 5 Haziran 1977 Seçim Beyannamesi*, 51.

29. Milli Nizam Partisi, *Milli Nizam Partisi Kuruluş Beyannamesi*, 2; Milli Nizam Partisi, *Milli Nizam Partisi Program ve Tüzük*, 19–20; Milli Selamet Partisi, *Milli Selamet Partisi 1973 Seçim Beyannamesi*, 7; Milli Selamet Partisi, *Milli Selamet Partisi 5 Haziran 1977 Seçim Beyannamesi*, 8–9; Refah Partisi, *Refah Partisi 20 Ekim 1991 Genel Seçimi Beyannamesi*, 9.

30. Milli Nizam Partisi, *Milli Nizam Partisi Program ve Tüzük*, 8; Milli Selamet Partisi, *Milli Selamet Partisi Program ve Tüzük*, 6.

31. Barlas, *Turgut Özal'ın Anıları*, 195.

32. Barlas, 231, 233.

33. Barlas, 223–25.

34. Özdemir and Aslan, *Türkiye'de İslami Finansın Dönüşümünün Ekonomi Politiği*, 21–22.

35. Öniş, "Turgut Özal and His Economic Legacy," 123.

36. Çakır, "Milli Görüş Hareketi," 563.

37. Erbakan, *Adil Ekonomik Düzen*, 68–72.

38. Erbakan, 47.

39. Erbakan, 18.

40. Erbakan, *The Just Economic System*, 18.

41. Erbakan, 6.

42. Erbakan, *Adil Ekonomik Düzen*, 41–42.

43. İŞKUR, "İŞKUR İstatistikler"; Hürriyet, "Asgari Ücret Desteği Ne Kadar?"

44. KOSGEB, *KOSGEB 2022 Yılı Faaliyet Raporu*, 37.

45. Hazine ve Maliye Bakanlığı, "Genel Yönetim Bütçe İstatistikleri—T.C. Hazine ve Maliye Bakanlığı Muhasebat Genel Müdürlüğü."

46. Sanayi ve Teknoloji Bakanlığı, "Sanayi ve Teknoloji Bakanlığı Faaliyet Raporları"; Sanayi ve Teknoloji Bakanlığı, "Sanayi ve Teknoloji Bakanlığı Yatırım Teşvik İstatistikleri."

47. Hazine ve Maliye Bakanlığı, "2022 Merkezi Yönetim Bütçe Giderleri Ay İçi Gerçekleşmeleri (Program Sınıflandırması)."

48. ASHB, *2022 Faaliyet Raporu*, 134; Hazine ve Maliye Bakanlığı, "2022 Merkezi Yönetim Bütçe Giderleri Ay İçi Gerçekleşmeleri Ekod4"; TÜİK, "İstatistiklerle Çocuk, 2022."

49. Yılmaz, "The AK Party and the Politics of Healthcare in Turkey in the Last Decade."

50. Elgin et al., "Understanding Informality."

51. Eurostat, "At-Risk-of-Poverty Rate by Sex [tessio10]," 2024, https://ec.europa.eu/eurostat/databrowser/view/tessio10/default/table?lang=en; Eurostat, "At-Risk-of-Poverty Rate before Social Transfers (Pensions Excluded from Social Transfers) by Poverty Threshold, Age and Sex [ilc_li10__custom_6834383]," 2024, https://ec.europa.eu/eurostat/databrowser/view/ILC_LI10__custom_6834383/default/table?lang=en.

52. OECD, "Data—PISA."

53. TÜİK, "Eğitim Durumuna Göre Temel Işgücü Göstergeleri."

54. ÖSYM, "(2002-ÖSYS) Yükseköğretim Programlarına Ek Yerleştirme Ile İlgili Sayısal Bilgiler"; ÖSYM, "Basın Duyurusu: 2009-ÖSYS Yükseköğretim Programlarına Ek Yerleştirme"; ÖSYM, "2017–ÖSYS Ek Yerleştirme Sonuçlarına İlişkin Sayısal Bilgiler"; YÖK, "2020 Yılı Yükseköğretim Kurumları Sınavı Yerleştirme Sonuçları Raporu."

55. Topal, "The State, Crisis and Transformation of Small and Medium-Sized Enterprise Finance in Turkey," 225–26.

56. KOSGEB, Kosgeb Kobi Finansman Destek Programı Uygulama Esasları, 3.

57. KOBİ Girişim Sermayesi Yatırım Ortaklığı A.Ş., "Ortaklık Yapımız."

58. Topal, "The State, Crisis and Transformation of Small and Medium-Sized Enterprise Finance in Turkey," 239.

59. KOSGEB, *Türkiye'deki KOBİ'lere İlişkin Bazı İstatistiki Göstergeler*, 171; BDDK, *Türk Bankacılık Sektörü Genel Görünümü*, 172.

60. KOSGEB, *Türkiye'deki KOBİ'lere İlişkin Bazı İstatistiki Göstergeler*, 117; Hazine ve Maliye Bakanlığı, "TC Hazine ve Maliye Bakanlığı, Hazine Destekli Kefalet Sistemi Raporları- T.C. Hazine ve Maliye Bakanlığı"; BDDK, *Türk Bankacılık Sektörü Genel Görünümü*, 24; TÜİK, "Küçük ve Orta Büyüklükteki Girişim İstatistikleri, 2021."

61. BDDK, "Aylık Bankacılık Sektörü Verileri (Temel Gösterim)"; IMF, "Datasets: Republic of Türkiye."

62. TBB, "Türkiye'de Bankacılık Sistemi (1958'den İtibaren)—2021."

63. TCMB, "TCMB—Sektör Bilançoları—İmalat."

64. For a more detailed discussion of the consequences of the financialization of the Turkish economy in the last quarter century, see the contributions in Yalman, Marois, and Güngen, *The Political Economy of Financial Transformation in Turkey*. Ali Rıza Güngen's "The Neoliberal Emergence of Market Finance," Demir Demiröz and Nilgün Erdem's "Profitability and M&As," and Aylin Topal's "The State, Crisis

and Transformation of Small and Medium-Sized Enterprise Finance in Turkey"
paint a comprehensive picture of the gradual retreat of the older large capital groups
from competitive industries to monopolistic industries and finance.

65. Cited source: Boratav, *İstanbul ve Anadolu'dan Sınıf Profilleri*.

66. Gülalp, "Globalization and Political Islam," 438, 441.

67. Dönmez, *25 Yılın Hikayesi*, 83, 137–38.

68. Yankaya, *Yeni islâmî burjuvazi*, 37–58.

69. Balcı, "İslam'da Çalışma İlişkileri," 125; Buğra and Savaşkan, *New Capitalism in Turkey*, 193–98.

70. Buğra and Savaşkan, *New Capitalism in Turkey*, 194.

71. Zaim, "Ekonomik Hayatta Müslüman İnsanın Tutum ve Davranışları," 108–11.

72. Genç, *Ortaklık Kültürü*.

73. Alayoğlu, *Aile Şirketlerinde Yönetim ve Kurumsallaşma*, 14.

74. Balcı, *Halka Açık Şirket Olmak*, 31.

75. Müsiad, *Yeni Ekonomi Döneminde KOBİ'ler İçin Rekabet ve Büyüme*, 85.

76. Müsiad, *İşadamlarına Kriz Dönemi Öneriler*, 8.

77. Yankaya, *Yeni islâmî burjuvazi*, 78–82, 94; *Buğra and Savaşkan, New Capitalism in Turkey*, 183.

78. Karaveli, *Why Turkey Is Authoritarian*, 63–64.

79. Yankaya, *Yeni Islâmî Burjuvazi*, 102–4.

80. Gülalp, "Globalization and Political Islam," 440; see also Yankaya, *Yeni Islâmî Burjuvazi*, 101.

81. Soylu and Şencal, "Cemaatçilik ve Bireycilik Arasında Piyasa İlişkileri."

82. Buğra, "Class, Culture, and State," 531.

83. Buğra and Keyder, "Social Assistance in Turkey: For a Policy of Minimum Income Support Conditional on Socially Beneficial Activity."

84. Balaban, "Wages and Bottlenecks: Home-Based Work and Factory System in Istanbul; Information Structures of Employment and Rigidities Embedded in the Organization of Home-Based Work."

85. Balaban, *A Conveyor Belt of Flesh: Urban Space and the Proliferation of Industrial Labor Practices in Istanbul's Garment Industry*.

86. I selected the companies from the Istanbul Chamber of Industry's list of the thousand largest industrial companies in Turkey and the Turkish Exporters Assembly's list of the thousand largest exporters (İstanbul Sanayi Odası, "İSO—Türkiye'nin 500 Büyük Sanayi Kuruluşu"; İstanbul Sanayi Odası, "İSO—Türkiye'nin İkinci 500 Büyük Sanayi Kuruluşu"; TİM, "TİM—Türkiye İhracatçılar Meclisi—Türkiye'nin İlk 1000 İhracatçı Araştırması"). I talked to all the companies in Denizli and Kayseri and 84 percent of the companies in Gaziantep that were on the Istanbul Chamber of Industry list in 2012. I also reached out to the subsidiaries of these companies as well as journalists, former politicians, and bureaucrats both in these three cities and in Ankara. In total, I conducted 147 in-depth interviews between 2012 and 2015.

87. Ayata, "Bir Yerel Sanayi Odağı Olarak Gaziantep'te Girişimcilik"; Mortan and Arolat, *Gaziantep Ekonomisine Bakış*; Varol, "Entrepreneurial Networks in

Local Industrial Development"; Türkün-Erendil, "Mit ve Gerçeklik Olarak Denizli"; Meder and Şahin, *Neo-liberal Politikaların İşçi Sınıfına Yansıması*; Özuğurlu, *Anadolu'da Küresel Fabrikanın Doğuşu: Yeni İşçilik Örüntülerinin Sosyolojisi*; Cengiz, *"Yav İşte Fabrikalaşak": Anadolu Sermayesinin Oluşumu: Kayseri-Hacılar Örneği*; Doğan, *Eğreti Kamusallık*.

88. Pınarcıoğlu, "KOBİ'ler, Kolektif Verimlilik ve Sorunları"; Türkün-Erendil, "Mit ve Gerçeklik Olarak Denizli." Türkün-Erendil argues that medium-sized manufacturing enterprises had an overwhelmingly large share in this initiative. Thus, EGS Bank tended to favor the relatively larger companies over the smaller ones. Pınarcıoğlu argues that EGS Bank weakened solidarity within the local network among businessmen in the 1980s.

89. Atay, *Parti, Cemaat, Tarikat*.

90. Doğan, *Mahalledeki AKP*, 108–12.

91. I thank my research assistants, Neşe Şen and Pelin Tuştaş, for their intellectual contributions and diligence.

92. *Dünya ve Ahiret İçin Çalışmada Ölçü*.

93. *Alışverişin Şartları ve Yasaklanan Alışveriş Bölüm—1. Ders—Fatih Bulut*.

94. *"Sigara Mevzusu," Ömer Öngüt -Kuddise Sırruh-*.

95. *Huzurlu Âile Hayatının Şartları—Osman Nuri Topbaş*.

96. *Norşin Seyda Şeyh Abdulkerim Çevik / Müminlerin Vasıfları*.

97. *Norşin Seyda Şeyh Abdulkerim Çevik / Müminlerin Vasıfları*.

98. *Fakirlik Kader Midir?*

99. *Cumhurbaşkanlığı Sarayının Harcamalarına Gösterilen Tepkiye, "Itibarda Tasarruf Olmaz" Anlayışı*...

100. *Fakirlik Kader Midir?*

101. *Fitne ve Fitnelerden Korunma Yolları | Nasihatler 35 | Halis Bayancuk Hoca*.

102. *Kıyâmet Alâmetleri Ortaya Çıktı Mı?*

103. *19.09.1971—Mehmed Zahid Kotku Rh.A—Nefisle Mücadele—Hadis Sohbeti*.

104. *Kripto Paralara Yatırım Günah Mı?*

105. *PAPCİ PUBG OYNAYANLARI BEKLEYEN TEHLİKELER ABDULLAH GÜRBÜZ HOCAEFENDİ*.

106. *Kadınların Normal Zamanda Pamuk Kullanması Şart mıdır?*

107. *İnsan Cünüp Olduğunda Hemen Yıkanması Gerekir Mi?*

108. *Bir Bayandan Ibretlik Bir Soru*.

109. *Bir Bayandan Ibretlik Bir Soru*.

110. *19.05.1990—Hadis Sohbeti—Prof. Dr. Mahmud Esad Coşan Rh.A*.

111. *Ali Ramazan Efendi (k.s.)—Kadınların Araba Kullanması*...!

112. *Neden Huzuru Olmayan Bir Toplum Olduk?*

113. *Hanımlar Buyrun—Cennet Nimetleri—Rukiye Genç—Necla Nazır*.

114. *Bir Bayandan Ibretlik Bir Soru*.

115. Douglas, *Purity and Danger: An Analysis of Concepts of Pollution and Taboo*.

116. *Hanımlar Buyrun—Cennet Nimetleri—Rukiye Genç—Necla Nazır*.

CHAPTER FOUR

1. *Erdoğan'ın Sözlerini Kılıçdaroğlu Söylemiş Gibi Sorduk. Bakın AKPlilerden Ne Tepki Aldık!*

2. Johnson, *The Panthers Can't Save Us Now*, 53.

3. Marglin, "What Do Bosses Do?"

4. Braverman, *Labor and Monopoly Capital.*

5. Burawoy, "Between the Labor Process and the State."

6. See Gordon, Edwards, and Reich, *Segmented Work, Divided Workers.*

7. Foucault, *Discipline and Punish.*

8. Gonzalez and Lejano, "New Urbanism and the Barrio," 2959.

9. Begum and Barn, "Crossing Boundaries," 15.

10. Maoz, "The Mutual Gaze."

11. Zizek, *Looking Awry*; Murphy, "The Dialectical Gaze: Exploring the Subject-Object Tension in the Performances of Women Who Strip," 310.

12. Merleau-Ponty, *The Visible and the Invisible.*

13. Merleau-Ponty, *Signs.*

14. Crossley, "The Politics of the Gaze—Between Foucault and Merleau-Ponty," 411–12.

15. Durkheim, *The Elementary Forms of Religious Life.*

16. Douglas, *Purity and Danger: An Analysis of Concepts of Pollution and Taboo.*

17. Seyoum, "Ayka Addis."

18. Fortune (Addis), "DBE Repossesses Ayka Addis."

19. SODAP, "SODAP."

20. In Turkey, the hijab is now permitted for girls in middle and high school.

21. Massicard, *Street-Level Governing.*

22. The data were provided by the Bağcılar Municipality Department of Machinery and License.

23. Köklü, "Kent Merkezlerinde Suç Korkusunun İncelenmesi: Beşiktaş Örneği"; Bilen et al., "How the Fear of Crime Spatially Differs among the Districts of Istanbul?"

24. Nilson, *Michel Foucault and the Games of Truth*, 18; Foucault, *Technologies of the Self.*

25. Barth, "Introduction," in *Ethnic Groups and Boundaries.*

26. Barth.

CHAPTER FIVE

1. Avcılar, Bağcılar, Bahçelievler, Başakşehir, Bayrampaşa, Esenler, Esenyurt, Gaziosmanpaşa, Güngören, Kağıthane, Küçükçekmece, Sultangazi, and Zeytinburnu.

2. Together with five others in the Asian part of the city (Kartal, Maltepe, Sancaktepe, Sultanbeyli, Ümraniye), one in ten votes for Erdoğan in the 2023 elections

came from these two working-class districts, which make up 0.08 percent of the country's land area.

3. YSK, "Açık Veri Portalı."

4. DİE, "Genel Nüfus Sayımı—İdari Bölünüş (12.10.1980) (Census of Population By Administrative Division)"; TÜİK, "İlçelere Göre Şehir ve Köy Nüfusu, Yıllık Nüfus Artış Hızı, Yüzölçümü ve Nüfus Yoğunluğu, 2000."

5. İBB, "Mahalle Bazlı Bina Sayıları—İBB."

6. Boğazlıyan, "Hangi ilçe ne kadar yeşil?"; İBB, "İstanbul Park ve Yeşil Alan Koordinatları—İBB"; Rizzo, "New York Ranks Last for Amount of Green Space per Resident among the Major US Cities."

7. Arı, "Ekonomik ve Toplumsal Gelişmelerin Apartmanlaşma Sürecinde Konut Birimlerine Etkileri"; Yıldırım and Başkaya, "Farklı Sosyo-Ekonomik Düzeye Sahip Kullanıcıların Konut Ana Yaşama Mekanını Değerlendirmesi."

8. Dursun, "Gecekondu ve Yarı-Gecekondularda Morfolojik Analiz"; Sağlamer and Erdoğan, "A Comparative Study on Squatter Settlements and Vernacular Architecture."

9. Massey and Denton, *American Apartheid: Segregation and the Making of the Underclass.*

10. TÜİK, "1992 Genel Sanayi ve İşyerleri Sayımı—İktisadi Faaliyet Kollarına Göre İşyeri Sayısı ve İstihdam"; TÜİK, "2002 Genel Sanayi ve İşyerleri Sayımı—İstatistiki Bölge Birimleri Sınıflaması (İBBS) ve Ekonomik Faaliyet Bölümlerine Göre Yerel Birim Sayısı ve İstihdam."

11. Balaban, *A Conveyor Belt of Flesh: Urban Space and the Proliferation of Industrial Labor Practices in Istanbul's Garment Industry*; Balaban and Sarıoğlu, "Home-Based Work in Istanbul – Varieties of Organization and Patriarchy"; Balaban, "Wages and Bottlenecks: Home-Based Work and Factory System in Istanbul; Information Structures of Employment and Rigidities Embedded in the Organization of Home-Based Work."

12. Wacquant, *Urban Outcasts.*

13. Roy, "'Banana Time' Job Satisfaction and Informal Interaction."

14. Burawoy, *The Politics of Production.*

15. Burawoy, *Manufacturing Consent Changes in the Labor Process under Monopoly Capitalism.*

16. Çetin, *The Paramilitary Hero on Turkish Television.*

17. Ghazzālī, *The Remembrance of Death and the Afterlife.*

18. A pejorative pseudonym for working-class neighborhoods, possibly borrowed from Hungarian during the Ottoman times.

CHAPTER SIX

1. T.C. Cumhurbaşkanlığı, "Cumhurbaşkanı Erdoğan."

2. T.C. Cumhurbaşkanlığı, "Esnaf İle Sanatkârlarımız Bu Ülkenin ve Milletin Omurgasıdır."

3. TÜİK, "Meslek Ana Grubu ve Ekonomik Faaliyete Göre Yıllık Ortalama Brüt Kazanç, 2006"; TÜİK, "Meslek Ana Grubu ve Ekonomik Faaliyete Göre Yıllık Ortalama Brüt Kazanç (2010,2014,2018)"; TÜİK, "Meslek Ana Grubu ve Ekonomik Faaliyete Göre Yıllık Ortalama Brüt Kazanç, 2022."

4. TÜİK, "Yapı Izin Istatistikleri ve Değişim Oranları, 2002–2023 [Building Permits and Rates of Change, 2002–2023]"; TÜİK, "YAPI RUHSATI— CONSTRUCTION PERMIT Kullanma Amacına Göre Yapılacak Yeni ve Ilave Yapılar (Yeni Sınıflama)."

5. UN Stats, "National Accounts—Analysis of Main Aggregates (AMA)."

6. TÜİK, "Konut ve Çevre Problemlerine Göre Kurumsal Olmayan Nüfusun Dağılımı."

7. OECD, "Housing Prices."

8. Ceritoğlu, "Homeownership, Housing Demand, and Household Wealth Distribution in Turkey," 6.

9. WID, "World Inequality Database."

10. As discussed in chapter 2, the leader of this party, Turhan Feyzioğlu, introduced Turgut Özal, the architect of the policies that opened the path for the Islamists to power, to the military junta in 1980.

11. For example, in a content analysis commissioned by the RPP in 2017, our blind coding revealed that about 20 percent of the RPP's 711 economic promises had almost the same wording as the AKP's economic promises, while another 37 percent of the economic promises had virtually the same content.

12. CNN Türk, "Gezi'ye kaç kişi katıldı?"; Ceritoğlu, "Homeownership, Housing Demand, and Household Wealth Distribution in Turkey."

13. Atay, "The Clash of 'Nations' in Turkey," 41.

14. Göle, "Gezi—Anatomy of a Public Square Movement," 7.

15. Clark and Regan, "Mass Mobilization Protest Data."

16. Lindgaard, "It Is Too Dangerous to Be an Individual in Turkey."

17. Sözen and Yavuz, "The Gezi Protests," 147.

18. Lindgaard, "It Is Too Dangerous to Be an Individual in Turkey," 127.

19. Farro and Demirhisar, "The Gezi Park Movement," 176.

20. Carvin, "The 'Standing Man' of Turkey: Act of Quiet Protest Goes Viral."

21. Tuğal, *The Fall of the Turkish Model*, 226.

22. Gürcan and Peker, "Turkey's Gezi Park Demonstrations of 2013"; Onuş, "Ethem Sarısülük'ün otopsisi."

23. Tuğal, *The Fall of the Turkish Model*, 243.

24. Balaban, "Gezi Neydi?"

25. McDowall, *A Modern History of the Kurds*, 411.

26. Hacettepe Üniversitesi Nüfus Etütleri Enstitüsü, *Türkiye'de Göç ve Yerinden Olmuş Nüfus Araştırması*.

27. Kalkınma Bakanlığı, "Kamu Yatırımlarının Illere Göre Sektörel Dağılımı."

28. Uludağ, "7 Yıl Geçti, Ankara Gar Katliamı'nda Sorumlular Yargılanmadı."

29. TİHV, "TİHV Dokümantasyon Merkezi Verilerine Göre 16 Ağustos 2015—18 Mart 2016 Tarihleri Arasında Sokağa Çıkma Yasakları ve Yaşamlarını Yitiren Siviller."

30. TÜİK, "İl Bazında Gayrisafi Yurt İçi Hasıla, 2021."

31. En Son Haber, "TÜSİAD yönetimine giren ilk Kürt işadamı konuştu"; TÜRKONFED, "Tarkan KADOOĞLU—Yönetim Kurulu Başkanı."

32. En Son Haber, "TÜSİAD yönetimine giren ilk Kürt işadamı konuştu."

33. En Son Haber.

34. Özel, *State-Business Alliances and Economic Development*.

35. Kızılkoyun, "Turkish Police on Hunt for Top Businessman Kadooğlu on Charges of Planning Murder over Debt—Türkiye News"; Hasgül, "İşadamı Ilıcan cinayetinde Yargıtay, faillerin cezasını onadı."

36. Yüksel, Kürt Sermayesinin Siyasî Yönelimi.

37. Yüksel, 27.

38. T.C. Adalet Bakanlığı, "Tablo-2: Yatırım Projeleri Listesi"; Gelir İdaresi Başkanlığı, "Tablo 18: Merkezi Yönetim Gelirleri (2006–2022)."

39. Mills, "White Ignorance."

40. Göç İzleme Derneği, *Sokağa Çıkma Yasakları ve Zorunlu Göç Sürecinde Kadınların Yaşadıkları Hak İhlalleri ve Deneyimleri Raporu*, 9.

41. Sönmez, *AKP-Cemaat*, 25.

42. Sönmez, 25.

43. Doğan, *Political Islamists in Turkey and the Gülen Movement*, 44–47.

44. Yalçın, "AKP'nin Asıl Korkusu."

45. Çobanoğlu, *Altın Nesil'in Peşinde*, 411.

46. Çakır, *Ayet ve slogan*, 103.

47. Çakır, "Fethullah'ı kullanıp attılar"; Kasapoğlu, "Bazı ülkeler Gülen okullarını kapatmaya neden direniyor?"

48. TRT, "Kamuda FETÖ temizliği."

49. Tanyılmaz, "Chapter 3—The Deep Fracture in the Big Bourgeoisie of Turkey," 105, 107, 109.

50. TMSF, *Tasarruf Mevduatı Sigorta Fonu 2017 Faaliyet Raporu*; TMSF, "Kayyım Olunan Şirketler."

51. The representative probably misrepresented the process, which, as a bureaucrat from the agency that distributes these grants meticulously explained to me in Ankara a year ago, was so standardized that the bureaucrats' administrative autonomy was practically nil. However, this businessman was not aware of that.

52. İstanbul Sanayi Odası, "İSO—Türkiye'nin 500 Büyük Sanayi Kuruluşu."

53. This is a common practice among the Islamist and right-wing wealthy in Turkey. Students receive pocket money as a scholarship to ensure their loyalty to the movement.

54. Cumhuriyet, "Mustafa Boydak tutuklandı."

55. Özarslan, "Eski Boydak Holding Başkanı Hacı Boydak, 8 yıl sonra tahliye oldu."

56. The company originally belonged to the historically second largest industrial family, the Sabancıs, who had operated it under a different name, Pil-Sa.

57. TÜİK, "İl Bazında Gayrisafi Yurt İçi Hasıla, Iktisadi Faaliyet Kollarına (A10) Göre, Cari Fiyatlarla (Değer), 2004–2022," 2004–22.

58. Karaganis, "Delusion and Despotism"; Sayed, "The Breakdown of Erdoganomics—Michigan Journal of Economics"; Akyol, "How Erdogan's Pseudoscience Is Ruining the Turkish Economy"; Steinberg, "Analysis | Turkey's President Insists on Low Interest Rates. That Could Cost Him Politically, This Research Shows"; Shahid, "Islamonomics"; Ghitis, "Erdogan's Obsession With Low Interest Rates Could Be His Downfall."

59. Karaganis, "Delusion and Despotism"; Nakhoul, "Turkey's Erdogan, Master Campaigner, Faces Toughest Contest Yet."

60. Balaban, Türkiye'de Yoksulluk Konusunun Popülerleşmesinin Ana Nedeni, Küçük Burjuvazinin Yoksullaşması.

61. Çalışma ve Sosyal Güvenlik Bakanlığı, "Asgari Ücret."

62. TÜİK, "Ekonomik Faaliyete Göre Kurulan ve Kapanan Şirket ve Kooperatiflerin Sayı ve Sermayeleri"; TOBB, "Kurulan/Kapanan Şirket İstatistikleri."

63. Sosyal Güvenlik Kurumu, "SGK Veri Uygulaması." In December 2022, the total number of employees and self-employed persons subject to compulsory insurance amounted to 26.34 million people.

CHAPTER SEVEN

1. World Bank, "Population, Total | Data"; World Bank, "GDP (Current US$)"; World Bank, "Exports of Goods and Services (Current US$)"; World Bank, "Total Natural Resources Rents (% of GDP)."

2. Cohen, *Searching for a Different Future*; Uner and Gungordu, "The New Middle Class in Turkey"; Bello and Mascarello, "Brazil's 'New Middle Class' and the Effectiveness of Social Rights through Consumption"; Kopper, "Measuring the Middle"; Kerstenetzky et al., "The Elusive New Middle Class in Brazil"; Fernandes, *India's New Middle Class*; Varma, *The New Indian Middle Class*; Nasr, *Forces of Fortune*; Nasr, *The Rise of Islamic Capitalism*; Fernandes, "Restructuring the New Middle Class in Liberalizing India"; UDUPA, "World-Class Aspirations"; Fuller, "Modern Hinduism and the Middle Class"; Rosenfeld, *The Autocratic Middle Class*; Kurlantzick, *Democracy in Retreat*; Milanovic, *Global Inequality: A New Approach for the Age of Globalization*.

3. Masoud, *Counting Islam*; Soliman, "State and Industrial Capitalism in Egypt"; Bayat, *Street Politics*; Keshavarzian, *Bazaar and State in Iran*; Vali, *Forces of Fortune*; Vali, *The Rise of Islamic Capitalism*.

4. WID, "World Inequality Database."

5. UBS, "Global Wealth Report 2023."

6. Marx, *Capital, vol. 3*.

7. Marx, *Capital, vol. 1*, chap. 17.

8. Poulantzas, *Classes in Contemporary Capitalism*.

9. Gouldner, *The Future of Intellectuals and the Rise of the New Class*.

10. Lacan, *The Seminar of Jacques Lacan—The Ethics of Psychoanalysis 1959–1960 Book VII*, 323.

11. Pirenne, *Economic and Social History of Medieval Europe*, 43.

12. Berg, Hudson, and Sonenscher, *Manufacture in Town and Country before the Factory*; Butlin, "Early Industrialization in Europe"; Clarkson, *Proto-Industrialization*; Dunford and Perrons, *The Arena of Capital*; Kriedte, Medick, and Schlumbohm, *Industrialization before Industrialization*; Mendels, "Proto-Industrialization"; Ogilvie and Cerman, *European Proto-Industrialization*; Schön, "Proto-Industrialisation and Factories."

13. Bythell, *The Sweated Trades*; Jones, *Outcast London*; Pennington and Westover, *A Hidden Workforce*.

14. Bythell, *The Sweated Trades*.

15. Damar, "Kemalism and Hegemony: The Turkish Experience with Secularism in the Post-1990s," 48.

16. Poulantzas, *Classes in Contemporary Capitalism*, 180.

17. Wright, "Varieties of Marxist Conceptions of Class Structure," 355.

18. Braverman, *Labor and Monopoly Capital*.

19. Abbott, *The System of Professions*.

20. Jackall, *Moral Mazes*.

21. Flyvbjerg, *Making Social Science Matter*.

22. In 2009, 229.8 million rural-to-urban migrant workers were employed in China's eastern regions (ILO, "Labour Migration in China and Mongolia (ILO in China and Mongolia)"). The figure likely rose to 296 million in 2022 (Statista, "Migrant Workers in China"). In 2016, 30.5 percent of these rural migrants worked in manufacturing industries and another 19.7 percent in the construction industry (Gong, *Manufacturing Towns in China*, 1). These roughly 150 million rural migrant workers correspond to 21 percent of China's total population, 58 percent of its total industrial employment, and 14.6 percent of the global industrial workforce in 2021 (World Bank, "Employment to Population Ratio, 15+, Total (%) (Modeled ILO Estimate)"; World Bank, "Employment in Industry (% of Total Employment) (Modeled ILO Estimate)").

23. Gong, *Manufacturing Towns in China*.

24. McGee et al., *China's Urban Space*.

25. Brown, *CEO, China*.

26. Frank, *What's the Matter with Kansas?*

27. Hochschild, *Strangers in Their Own Land*.

28. Ricciardelli, "A Demographic and Legal Profile of January 6 Prosecutions."

29. Guérin, *Fascism and Big Business*; Salvatorelli, *Nazionalfascismo*; Geiger, "Panik Im Mittelstand"; Fromm, *Escape from Freedom*.

30. Gramsci, "Observations on Certain Aspects of the Structure of Political Parties in Periods of Organic Crisis," 459.

31. Neumann, "Introduction," in *The Nazi Elite*.

32. Demirkol, "2023 Yılı Milletvekili Seçimleri Üzerinden Cumhuriyetin 100. Yılında Seçmenin Siyasi Yelpazedeki Yeri."

APPENDIX A

1. Çakır, *Ayet ve slogan*; Ceyhan, *Türkiye'de Tarikatlar*; "Diyanet İşleri Başkanlığı'ndan Gizli Tarikat Raporu-1."

2. Gölpınarlı, *100 Soruda Türkiye'de Mezhepler ve Tarikatler*; Kutlu, "Diyanet İşleri Başkanlığı ve İslamiçi Dini Gruplarla (Mezhep ve Tarikatlar) İlişkileri"; Demir and Karakök, "Einige Feststellungen Über das Profilbild der Novizen der İsmailağa Gemeinde (1960–2012): Am Beispiel İstanbul"; Efe, "Kolektif Dindarlık Türü Olarak Tarikat/Cemaat Dindarlığı"; Şapolyo, *Mezhepler ve Tarikatlar Tarihi*; İnce, "Nakşîlik-Siyaset İlişkisi Bağlamında Türkiye'de Dinî Gruplar ve Milli Görüş"; Torun, "Tarikat ve Cemaatlerin Siyasetle İlişkisi"; Güner, *Tarikatlar Ansiklopedisi*; Karataş, "Tarikatlara Yönelmenin Sosyo-Kültürel ve Psikolojik Nedenleri"; Kara, *Tasavvuf ve Tarikatlar*; Eraydın, *Tasavvuf ve Tarikatlar*; Tatlılıoğlu, "Tasavvuf ve Tarikatlara Sosyolojik Bir Bakış"; Lekesiz, "Türkiye'de Cemaatler ve Tarikatler Gerçeği."

3. Bernard, *Research Methods in Anthropology: Qualitative and Quantitative Approaches*; Murdock, *Outline of Cultural Materials*.

4. Creswell, *Qualitative Inquiry and Research Design*; Saldana, *The Coding Manual for Qualitative Researchers*.

5. Bernard, *Research Methods in Anthropology: Qualitative and Quantitative Approaches*; Murdock, *Outline of Cultural Materials*.

6. Dedoose, "Home | Dedoose."

7. Trint, "Transcribe Video and Audio to Text | Content Editor | Trint."

8. Krippendorff, *Content Analysis: An Introduction to Its Methodology*.

9. Sidnell, *Conversation Analysis*.

10. Berg, *Qualitative Research Methods for the Social Sciences*.

11. Patton, *Qualitative, Research and Evaluation Methods*.

APPENDIX C

1. Marx, *Capital, vol. 2*.

2. Marx, 478–87.

3. Luxemburg and Bukharin, *Imperialism and the Accumulation of Capital*.

4. Marx, *Capital, vol. 2*, 596.

5. One caveat. This representation neither matches the sources of revenue of social classes with the composite roles of social classes in production relations nor identifies different departments of production with individual industries. For an assessment of these two issues, look at their role in the circulation process, as discuss in chapter 7.

REFERENCES

19.05.1990—Hadis Sohbeti—Prof. Dr. Mahmud Esad Coşan Rh.A, 2011. https:// www.youtube.com/watch?v=6AFeRPkfFYA.

19.09.1971—Mehmed Zahid Kotku Rh.A—Nefisle Mücadele—Hadis Sohbeti, 1971. https://www.youtube.com/watch?v=FgQfmBtL_CY.

Abbott, Andrew. *The System of Professions: An Essay on the Division of Expert Labor.* Chicago: University of Chicago Press, 1988.

Acconcia, Giuseppe. *The Uprisings in Egypt: The Mobilisation and Ban of Popular Committees and Independent Trade Unions.* Newcastle upon Tyne, UK: Cambridge Scholars, 2019.

Adaman, Fikret, and Murat Arsel, eds. *Environmentalism in Turkey: Between Democracy and Development?* New York: Routledge, 2016.

Ajl, Max, Bassam Haddad, and Zeinab Abul-Magd. "State, Market, and Class: Egypt, Syria, and Tunisia." In *A Critical Political Economy of the Middle East and North Africa*, edited by Joel Beinin, Bassam Haddad, and Shrene Seikaly, 46–67. Stanford, CA: Stanford University Press, 2021.

Aksular, Arda Deniz. "Faith Based Organizations in the Struggle against Poverty: Deniz Feneri Welfare and Solidarity Association Sample of Ankara Branch." Master's thesis, Middle East Technical University, 2008.

Akyol, Mustafa. "How Erdogan's Pseudoscience Is Ruining the Turkish Economy." Cato Institute, December 3, 2021. https://www.cato.org/blog/how -erdogans-pseudoscience-ruining-turkish-economy-1.

Al-Arian, Abdullah. *Answering the Call: Popular Islamic Activism in Sadat's Egypt.* Oxford: Oxford University Press, 2014.

Alayoğlu, Nihat. *Aile Şirketlerinde Yönetim ve Kurumsallaşma.* Yönetim Kitaplığı. İstanbul: Müsiad, 2003. https://www.musiad.org.tr/uploads/yayinlar/arastirma -raporlari/pdf/04_aile_sirketlerinde_yonetim_ve_kurumsallasma.pdf.

Alışverişin Şartları ve Yasaklanan Alışveriş Bölüm—1. Ders—Fatih Bulut, 2017. https://www.youtube.com/watch?v=akrOMfD2QKw.

Ali Ramazan Efendi (k.s.)—Kadınların Araba Kullanması . . . !, 2018. https://www .youtube.com/watch?v=34-ch4BPgEg.

Allinson, Jamie. "Class Forces, Transition and the Arab Uprisings: A Comparison of Tunisia, Egypt and Syria." *Democratization* 22, no. 2 (February 23, 2015): 294–314.

Alpagu, Hasan. "24 Ocak Kararları ve Turgut Özal Döneminin Yansımaları." In *Proceedings*, 129–33. Ankara: Turgut Özal University, 2016.

Amao, Olumuyiwa Babatunde. "A Decade of Terror: Revisiting Nigeria's Interminable Boko Haram Insurgency." In *Ten Years of Boko Haram in Nigeria: The Dynamics and Counterinsurgency Challenges*, edited by J. Tochukwu Omenma, Ike E. Onyishi, and Aloysius-Michaels Okolie, 23–41. Cham, Switzerland: Springer Nature, 2023.

Antonio, Muhammad Syafii. "Islamic Microfinance Initiatives to Enhance to Small and Medium-Sized Enterprises." In *Expressing Islam: Religious Life and Politics in Indonesia*, edited by Greg Fealy and Sally White, 251–66. Singapore: Institute of Southeast Asian Studies, 2008.

Arat, Yeşim. *Political Islam in Turkey and Women's Organizations*. İstanbul: Türkiye Ekonomik ve Sosyal Etütler Vakfı, 1999.

Arbaç, İmren. "Milli Mücadele Dönemi Rus-Türk İlişkilerinde Yeşil Ordu—Çerkez Ethem—Mustafa Suphi ve Arkadaşları Üçgeni." *Yeditepe Üniversitesi Tarih Bölümü Araştırma Dergisi* 1, no. 2 (June 13, 2017): 38–54.

Arı, Hülya. "Ekonomik ve Toplumsal Gelişmelerin Apartmanlaşma Sürecinde Konut Birimlerine Etkileri." PhD, İstanbul Teknik Üniversitesi Fen Bilimleri Enstitüsü, 1994.

Aristotle. *Aristotle's Nicomachean Ethics*. Chicago: University of Chicago Press, 2011.

ASHB. *2022 Faaliyet Raporu*. Ankara: T.C. Aile ve Sosyal Hizmetler Bakanlığı, 2023. https://www.aile.gov.tr/media/129482/ashb_2022-idare-faaliyet-raporu.pdf.

Aslan, Şükrü. *1 Mayıs Mahallesi: 1980 Öncesi Toplumsal Mücadeleler ve Kent*. Cağaloglu, İstanbul: İletişim, 2004.

Atatürk Ansiklopedisi. "Atatürk Döneminde Meydana Gelen Ayaklanmalar (1924–1938)." *Atatürk Ansiklopedisi* (blog), July 27, 2021. https://ataturkansiklopedisi .gov.tr/bilgi/ataturk-doneminde-meydana-gelen-ayaklanmalar-1924-1938/.

Atay, Tayfun. "The Clash of 'Nations' in Turkey: Reflections on the Gezi Park Incident." *Insight Turkey* 15, no. 3 (Summer 2013): 39–44.

———. *Parti, Cemaat, Tarikat: 2000'ler Türkiyesi'nin Dinbaz-Politik Seyir Defteri: İnceleme*. İstanbul: Can Sanat Yayınları, 2017.

Ayata, Sencer. "Bir Yerel Sanayi Odağı Olarak Gaziantep'te Girişimcilik." *Ekonomide Durum* 5 (1999): 85–112.

Aydınlık Gazetesi. "Diyanet İşleri Başkanlığı'ndan Gizli Tarikat Raporu." Newspaper, August 2, 2019. www.aydinlik.com.tr/diyanet-isleri-baskanligi-ndan-gizli -tarikat-raporu-i-devlet-eliyle-buyuduler-turkiye-agustos-2019#2.

Azari, Farah. "Islam's Appeal to Women in Iran: Illusion and Reality." In *Women of Iran: The Conflict with Fundamentalist Islam*, edited by Farah Azari, 1–71. London: Ithaca Press, 1983.

Balaban, Utku. *A Conveyor Belt of Flesh: Urban Space and the Proliferation of Industrial Labor Practices in Istanbul's Garment Industry*. İstanbul: Friedrich Ebert Stiftung, 2010.

———. "The Enclosure of Urban Space and Consolidation of the Capitalist Land Regime in Turkish Cities." *Urban Studies* 48, no. 10 (2011): 2162–79.

———. "Gezi Neydi?" *İnsan Hakları Okulu: Blog* (blog), July 3, 2022. https://blog .insanhaklariokulu.org/gezi-neydi/.

———. Türkiye'de Yoksulluk Konusunun Popülerleşmesinin Ana Nedeni, Küçük Burjuvazinin Yoksullaşması. İnterview by Aybars Yanık. Birikim, July 8, 2022. https://birikimdergisi.com/guncel/11067/kof-bir-yoksulluk-anlatisi-ile -sinifi-kotuler-iyiler-savasi-cercevesinden-okuyan-bir-anlati-arasinda-sikismis -durumdayiz.

———. "Wages and Bottlenecks: Home-Based Work and Factory System in Istanbul; Information Structures of Employment and Rigidities Embedded in the Organization of Home-Based Work." In *Proceedings of the International Conference on Globalization and Its Discontents*, 40–52. Cortland, NY: İzmir Economy University, 2007.

Balaban, Utku, and Esra Sarıoğlu. "Home-Based Work in Istanbul—Varieties of Organization and Patriarchy." Istanbul: The Social Policy Forum—Boğaziçi University, 2008. https://spf.bogazici.edu.tr/sites/spf.boun.edu.tr/files/1439808024 _hbw_in_istanbul_varieties_of_organization_and_patriarchy.pdf.

Balcı, Yusuf. *Halka Açık Şirket Olmak*. İş ve Yönetim Serisi. İstanbul: Müsiad, 2023. https://www.musiad.org.tr/uploads/press-400/halka-ac%CC%A7ik -s%CC%A7irket-olmak_13032023.pdf.

———. "İslam'da Çalışma İlişkileri." In *İş Hayatında İslam İnsanı (Homo Islamicus): İslami Duyarlılıkla Yönetilen Firmalarda Örgütsel Davranış Biçimleri*, edited by Hüner Şencan, 113–27. Müsiad Araştırma Raporları. İstanbul: Müsiad, 1994. https://www.musiad.org.tr/uploads/yayinlar/arastirma -raporlari/pdf/is_hayatinda_islam_insani.pdf.

Baldaro, Edoardo, and Luca Raineri. "Azawad: A Parastate between Nomads and Mujahidins?" *Nationalities Papers* 48, no. 1 (January 2020): 100–115.

Barlas, Mehmet. *Turgut Özal'ın Anıları*. İstanbul: Birey Yayıncılık, 2000.

Barth, Fredrik. "Introduction." In *Ethnic Groups and Boundaries: The Social Organization of Culture Difference*, edited by Fredrik Barth, 9–38. Long Grove, IL: Waveland Press, 1998.

Basbakanlık Devlet İstatistik Enstitüsü. *1980 genel sanayi ve işyerleri sayımı = 1980 census of industry and business establishments*. Yayın = Publication. Ankara: Basbakanlık Devlet İstatistik Enstitüsü, 1982.

Batuman, Bülent. *New Islamist Architecture and Urbanism: Negotiating Nation and Islam through Built Environment in Turkey*. New York: Routledge, 2018.

Bayat, Asef. *Street Politics: Poor People's Movements in Iran*. New York: Columbia University Press, 1997.

———. *Workers and Revolution in Iran: A Third World Experience of Workers' Control*. Illustrated edition. London: Zed Books, 1987.

BDDK. "Aylık Bankacılık Sektörü Verileri (Temel Gösterim)." Bankacılık Düzenleme ve Denetleme Kurumu, September 2023. https://www.bddk.org.tr /BultenAylik.

———. *Türk Bankacılık Sektörü Genel Görünümü*. Ankara: Bankacılık Düzenleme ve Denetleme Kurumu, 2022. https://www.bddk.org.tr/Veri/Detay/162.

Beblawi, Hazem, and Giacomo Luciani, eds. *The Rentier State*. London: Routledge, 2016.

Begum, Lipi, and Ravinder Barn. "Crossing Boundaries: Bras, Lingerie and Rape Myths in Postcolonial Urban Middle-Class India." *Gender Place and Culture* 26, no. 10 (October 3, 2019): 1324–44.

Beinin, Joel. *Workers and Thieves: Labor Movements and Popular Uprisings in Tunisia and Egypt*. Stanford, CA: Stanford Briefs, 2015.

Bello, Enzo, and Renata Piroli Mascarello. "Brazil's 'New Middle Class' and the Effectiveness of Social Rights through Consumption: A Dialectic of Inclusion and Exclusion." *Birkbeck Law Review* 2, no. 1 (January 1, 2014): 129–46.

Berg, Bruce. *Qualitative Research Methods for the Social Sciences*. Boston: Allyn and Bacon, 2001.

Berg, Maxine, Pat Hudson, and Michael Sonenscher. *Manufacture in Town and Country before the Factory*. New York: Cambridge University Press, 1984.

Bernard, H. Russell. *Research Methods in Anthropology: Qualitative and Quantitative Approaches*. Walnut Creek, CA: Altamire Press, 2006.

Bianchi, Robert. *Interest Groups and Political Development in Turkey*. Princeton Legacy Library. Princeton, NJ: Princeton University Press, 2016.

———. "Islam and Democracy in Egypt." *Current History* 88, no. 535 (1989): 93–104.

Bilen, Ömer, Öyküm Esra Aşkın, Ali Hakan Büyüklü, Ayşenur Ökten, and Mehmet Gür. "How the Fear of Crime Spatially Differs among the Districts of Istanbul?" *NWSA–Social Sciences* 8, no. 4 (2013): 153–64.

Bir Bayandan Ibretlik Bir Soru, 2011. https://www.youtube.com/watch?v=WdGyFLOSjdU.

Boğazlıyan, Esra. "Hangi ilçe ne kadar yeşil?" *Habertürk*, January 20, 2019. https://www.haberturk.com/hangi-ilce-ne-kadar-yesil-2294962.

Boratav, Korkut. *İstanbul ve Anadolu'dan Sınıf Profilleri*. Ankara: İmge Kitabevi Yayınları, 2004.

BPS-Statistics Indonesia. "Statistical Yearbook of Indonesia 2022." Jakarta: Directorate of Statistical Dissemination, 2022.

Braverman, Harry. *Labor and Monopoly Capital: The Degradation of Work in the Twentieth Century*. New York: Monthly Review Press, 1998.

Brown, Kerry. *CEO, China: The Rise of Xi Jinping*. London: I.B.Tauris, 2016.

Buğra, Ayşe. "Class, Culture, and State: An Analysis of Interest Representation by Two Turkish Business Associations." *International Journal of Middle East Studies* 30, no. 4 (November 1998): 521–39.

———. *State and Business in Modern Turkey: A Comparative Study*. Albany, NY: SUNY Press, 1994.

Buğra, Ayşe, and Çağlar Keyder. "Social Assistance in Turkey: For a Policy of Minimum Income Support Conditional on Socially Beneficial Activity." Ankara: UNDP, 2005. http://www.spf.boun.edu.tr/docs/undp%202007_sonhali.pdf.

Buğra, Ayşe, and Osman Savaşkan. *New Capitalism in Turkey: The Relationship between Politics, Religion and Business.* Northampton, MA: Edward Elgar, 2014.

Burawoy, Michael. "Between the Labor Process and the State: The Changing Face of Factory Regimes under Advanced Capitalism." *American Sociological Review* 48, no. 5 (1983): 587–605.

———. *Manufacturing Consent Changes in the Labor Process under Monopoly Capitalism.* Chicago: University of Chicago Press, 2010.

———. *The Politics of Production.* London: Verso, 1985.

Bush, Robin. "Regional Sharia Regulations in Indonesia: Anomaly or Symptom?" In *Expressing Islam: Religious Life and Politics in Indonesia*, edited by Greg Fealy and Sally White, 174–91. Singapore: Institute of Southeast Asian Studies, 2008.

Butlin, R. A. "Early Industrialization in Europe: Concepts and Problems." *The Geographical Journal* 152, no. 1 (March 1, 1986): 1–8.

Bythell, Duncan. *The Sweated Trades: Outwork in Nineteenth Century Britain.* New York: St. Martin's Press, 1978.

Cagaptay, Soner. *The New Sultan: Erdogan and the Crisis of Modern Turkey.* London: I.B. Tauris, 2017.

Çakır, Ruşen. *Ayet ve Slogan: Türkiye'de İslamcı Oluşumlar.* İstanbul: Metis, 1990.

———. "Fethullah'ı kullanıp attılar." Milliyet Gazetesi, June 26, 1999. https://www.milliyet.com.tr/siyaset/fethullahi-kullanip-attilar-5245965.

———. "Milli Görüş Hareketi." In *Modern Türkiye'de Siyasi Düşünce Cilt 6 İslamcılık*, edited by Tanıl Bora and Murat Gültenkingil, 544–603. İstanbul: İletişim, 2005.

———. *Ne Şeriat Ne Demokrasi: Refah Partisini Anlamak.* İstanbul: Siyahbeyaz, Metis Güncel, 1994.

Çalışma ve Sosyal Güvenlik Bakanlığı. "Asgari Ücret." T.C. Çalışma ve Sosyal Güvenlik Bakanlığı | Bilgi İşlem Daire Başkanlığı, İnternet Hizmetleri Şubesi, 2023. http://www.csgb.gov.tr/asgari-ucret/.

Çalmuk, Fehmi. "Necmettin Erbakan." In *Modern Türkiye'de Siyasi Düşünce Cilt 6 İslamcılık*, edited by Tanıl Bora and Murat Gültenkingil, 550–76. İstanbul: İletişim, 2005.

Carvin, Andy. "The 'Standing Man' of Turkey: Act of Quiet Protest Goes Viral." *NPR: The Two-Way*, June 18, 2013. https://www.npr.org/sections/thetwo-way/2013/06/18/193183899/the-standing-man-of-turkey-act-of-quiet-protest-goes-viral.

Çelik, Nihat, and Emre İşeri. "Islamically Oriented Humanitarian NGOs in Turkey-AKP Foreign Policy Parallelism." *Turkish Studies* 17, no. 3 (July 2, 2016): 429–48.

Cengiz, Kurtulus. *"Yav İşte Fabrikalaşak": Anadolu Sermayesinin Oluşumu: Kayseri-Hacılar Örneği.* Cağaloğlu, İstanbul: Iletisim Yayinevi, 2013.

Cenk Özbay, Maral Erol, and Ayşecan Terzioglu, eds. *The Making of Neoliberal Turkey.* Farnham, UK: Ashgate, 2016.

Ceritoğlu, Evren. "Homeownership, Housing Demand, and Household Wealth Distribution in Turkey." *Emerging Markets Finance and Trade* 56, no. 5 (April 8, 2020): 1146–65.

Çetin, Berfin Emre. *The Paramilitary Hero on Turkish Television: A Case Study on Valley of the Wolves*. Newcastle upon Tyne, UK: Cambridge Scholars, 2015.

Çetin, Ecem. "1960 darbesi sonrası Necmettin Erbakan'a hangi bakanlık teklif edildi?—Saadet Partisi Genel Başkanı Temel Karamollaoğlu ile söyleşi." Ankara Masası, April 19, 2023. http://www.ankaramasasi.com/haber/2079388/1960 -darbesi-sonrasi-necmettin-erbakana-hangi-bakanlik-teklif-edildi.

Çevik, Senem B., Efe Sevin, and Banu Baybars-Hawks. "State–Civil Society Partnerships in International Aid and Public Diplomacy: The Case of Turkey and Somalia." In *Communicating National Image through Development and Diplomacy: The Politics of Foreign Aid*, edited by James Pamment and Karin Gwinn Wilkins, 169–92. Cham, Switzerland: Springer International, 2018.

Ceyhan, Semih, ed. *Türkiye'de Tarikatlar: Tarih ve Kültür*. İstanbul: İSAM Yayınları, 2015.

Chibber, Vivek. *Locked in Place: State-Building and Late Industrialization in India*. Princeton, NJ: Princeton University Press, 2011.

Çınar, Menderes. "AKP ve İslami Hareketler: Defansif ve Dağıtıcı İktidar Kardeşliği." İn *AKP Kitabı Bir Dönüşümün Bilançosu*, edited by Bülent Duru and İlhan Uzgel, 307–15. Phoenix Yayınevi, 2013.

Clark, David, and Patrick Regan. "Mass Mobilization Protest Data." Harvard Dataverse, 2016. https://doi.org/10.7910/DVN/HTTWYL.

Clarkson, Leslie A. *Proto-Industrialization: The First Phase of Industrialization?* Houndmills, Basingstoke, UK: Macmillan, 1985.

CNN Türk. "Gezi'ye kaç kişi katıldı?" *CNN TÜRK* (blog), November 25, 2003. https://www.cnnturk.com/guncel/geziye-kac-kisi-katildi.

Çobanoğlu, Yavuz. *Altın Nesil'in Peşinde: Fethullah Gülen'de Toplum, Devlet, Ahlak, Otorite*. İstanbul: İletişim, 2012.

Cogan, Charles G. "Partners in Time: The CIA and Afghanistan since 1979." *World Policy Journal* 10, no. 2 (1993): 73–82.

Cohen, Shana. *Searching for a Different Future: The Rise of a Global Middle Class in Morocco*. Durham, NC: Duke University Press, 2004.

Creswell, John W. *Qualitative Inquiry and Research Design: Choosing among Five Approaches*. Thousand Oaks, CA: Sage, 2007.

Crossley, N. "The Politics of the Gaze—between Foucault and Merleau-Ponty." *Human Studies* 16, no. 4 (October 1993): 399–419.

Cruz, Cesi, Philip Keefer, and Carlos Scartascini. "The Database of Political Institutions 2020 (DPI2020)." Inter-American Development Bank, January 2021. https://doi.org/10.18235/0003049.

Cumhurbaşkanlığı Sarayının Harcamalarına Gösterilen Tepkiye, "İtibarda Tasarruf Olmaz" Anlayışı . . . , 2017. https://www.youtube.com/watch?v=avpxfBGt2q8.

Cumhuriyet. "AKP'li Cumhurbaşkanı Erdoğan'ın hedefindeki TÜSİAD başkanı Orhan Turan kimdir?" *Cumhuriyet*, June 16, 2022. https://www.cumhuriyet

.com.tr/turkiye/akpli-cumhurbaskani-recep-tayyip-erdoganin-hedefindeki
-tusiad-baskani-kimdir-1947680.

———. "Mustafa Boydak tutuklandı." *Cumhuriyet Gazetesi*, June 24, 2023. https://
www.cumhuriyet.com.tr/siyaset/mustafa-boydaka-gozalti-2093490.

Dal, Zülküf, and Serkan Dilek. "Comparison of Erbakan's Economic Policy Proposals with Turkey's 2002–2021 Economic Policies." *Afro Eurasian Studies* 10, no. 3 (April 18, 2022): 27–41.

Dalacoura, Katerina. "Islamism and Neoliberalism in the Aftermath of the 2011 Arab Uprisings: The Freedom and Justice Party in Egypt and Nahda in Tunisia." In *Neoliberal Governmentality and the Future of the State in the Middle East and North Africa*, edited by Emel Akçalı, 61–83. New York: Palgrave, 2016.

Damar, Erdem. "Kemalism and Hegemony: The Turkish Experience with Secularism in the Post-1990s." PhD, University of Essex, 2012.

Dedoose. "Home | Dedoose," 2023. https://www.dedoose.com/.

Delibaş, Kayhan. *The Rise of Political Islam in Turkey: Urban Poverty, Grassroots Activism and Islamic Fundamentalism*. London: I.B. Tauris, 2014.

Demir, Hüseyin, and Tunay Karakök. "Einige Feststellungen Über das Profilbild der Novizen der İsmailağa Gemeinde (1960–2012): Am Beispiel İstanbul." *Bingöl Üniversitesi İlahiyat Fakültesi Dergisi* 5, no. 9 (2017): 97–114.

Demirkol, Fırat. "2023 Yılı Milletvekili Seçimleri Üzerinden Cumhuriyetin 100. Yılında Seçmenin Siyasi Yelpazedeki Yeri." *Ekonomi İşletme Siyaset ve Uluslararası İlişkiler Dergisi* 9, no. 2–1 (2023): 131–40.

Devji, Faisal. *Muslim Zion: Pakistan as a Political Idea*. Cambridge, MA: Hurst, 2013.

Devlet İstatistik Enstitüsü. *Genel Nüfus Sayımı 24.10.1965. [Census of population, social and economic characteristics of population]*. Yayın (Devlet İstatistik Enstitüsü (Turkey)). Ankara: T.C. Başbakanlık Devlet İstatistik Enstitüsü, 1969.

Devlet İstatistik Enstitüsü (Turkey). "Sanayi ve isyerleri sayimi: imalât sanayii, 1964. Census of manufacturing industries and business establishments: manufacturing." Ankara: Devlet İstatistik Enstitüsü (Turkey), 1968.

DİE. "Genel Nüfus Sayımı—İdari Bölünüş (12.10.1980) (Census of Population by Administrative Division)." Başbakanlık Devlet İstatistik Enstitüsü—Prime Ministry, State Institute of Statistics, Turkey, 1980. https://kutuphane.tuik.gov.tr/pdf/0015840.pdf.

Diken. "Sarısülük ailesinin avukatı: Bu mahkemeden adalet beklemiyoruz." *Diken* (blog), April 6, 2014. https://www.diken.com.tr/sarisuluk-ailesinin-avukati-bu-mahkemeden-adalet-beklemiyoruz/.

Doğan, Ali Ekber. *Eğreti Kamusallık*. Cağaloğlu, İstanbul: Iletisim Yayinevi, 2007.

Doğan, Recep. *Political Islamists in Turkey and the Gülen Movement*. New York: Palgrave Macmillan, 2019.

Doğan, Sevinç. *Mahalledeki AKP: Parti İşleyişi, Taban Mobilizasyonu ve Siyasal Yabancılaşma*. İstanbul: İletişim, 2016.

Doğançay, Muharrem. "Neoliberal Kuram Bağlamında Turgut Özal ve 24 Ocak Kararları." In *Proceedings*, 150–58. Ankara: Turgut Özal University, 2016.

Dönmez, Adem. *25 Yılın Hikayesi*. İstanbul: MÜSİAD Müstakil Sanayici ve İşadamları Derneği, 2015.

Dörrbecker, Maximilian. *Map of the Districts of Istanbul*. May 31, 2020. Own work, using this base map, this orientation map and this coat of arms. https://commons.wikimedia.org/w/index.php?curid=21693300.

Douglas, Mary. *Purity and Danger: An Analysis of Concepts of Pollution and Taboo*. New York: Praeger, 1966.

Dunford, Michael, and Diane Perrons. *The Arena of Capital*. New York: St. Martin's Press, 1983.

Dünya ve Ahiret İçin Çalışmada Ölçü, 2014. https://www.youtube.com/watch?v=MqyfRFUCjPA.

Durkheim, Emile. *The Elementary Forms of Religious Life*. Edited by Mark S. Cladis. Translated by Carol Cosman. Oxford: Oxford University Press, 2008.

Dursun, Pelin. "Gecekondu ve Yarı-Gecekondularda Morfolojik Analiz." Master's thesis, İstanbul Teknik Üniversitesi Fen Bilimleri Enstitüsü, 1995.

Efe, Adem. "Kolektif Dindarlık Türü Olarak Tarikat/Cemaat Dindarlığı." *Journal of Islamic Research* 28, no. 3 (2017): 290–301.

Ekonomi Terimleri Girişimci Ajansı. "Tasarruf Bonoları." *İktisat Sözlüğü*, 2025. https://www.iktisatsozlugu.com/tr/nedir/tasarruf-bonolari/4508.

El Alami, Dawoud S. "Law No. 100 of 1985 Amending Certain Provisions of Egypt's Personal Status Laws." *Islamic Law and Society* 1, no. 1 (1994): 116–36.

Elgin, Ceyhun, M. Ayhan Köse, Fransizka Ohnsorge, and Shu Yu. "Understanding Informality." CERP Discussion Paper. London: Centre for Economic Policy Research, 2021.

Eligür, Banu. *The Mobilization of Political Islam in Turkey*. New York: Cambridge University Press, 2010.

En Son Haber. "TÜSİAD yönetimine giren ilk Kürt işadamı konuştu." *Ensonhaber*, March 2, 2013. https://www.ensonhaber.com/ekonomi/tusiad-yonetimine-giren-ilk-kurt-isadami-konustu-2013-03-02.

Eraydın, Selçuk. *Tasavvuf ve Tarikatlar*. İstanbul: Marmara Üniversitesi İlahiyat Fakültesi Vakfı, 1994.

Erbakan, Necmettin. *Adil Ekonomik Düzen*. Ankara: Refah Partisi, 1991.

———. *The Just Economic System*. Ankara: Bars Ltd. Şti., 1991.

Erder, Sema. *İstanbul'a Bir Kent Kondu Ümraniye*. Cağaloğlu, İstanbul: İletişim, 1996.

Erdoğan'ın Sözlerini Kılıçdaroğlu Söylemiş Gibi Sorduk. Bakın AKPlilerden Ne Tepki Aldık! Antalya, 2020. https://www.youtube.com/watch?v=qSSkpUrWKtc.

Ersöz, Salih Sedat. "Prof. Dr. Necmeddin Erbakan-3." Konya Yenigün Gazetesi, March 4, 2021. https://www.konyayenigun.com/prof-dr-necmeddin-erbakan-3.

Esen, Berk, and Şebnem Gümüşçü. "Rising Competitive Authoritarianism in Turkey." *Third World Quarterly* 37, no. 9 (2016): 1581–1606.

Esposito, John L. *The Future of Islam*. Oxford: Oxford University Press, 2013.

Esposito, John L., Tamara Sonn, and John O. Voll. *Islam and Democracy after the Arab Spring*. Oxford: Oxford University Press, 2015.

Eurostat. "At-Risk-of-Poverty Rate before Social Transfers (Pensions Excluded from Social Transfers) by Poverty Threshold, Age and Sex," June 12, 2024. https://ec.europa.eu/eurostat/databrowser/view/ILC_LI10__custom_6834383/default/table?lang=en.

———. "At-Risk-of-Poverty Rate by Sex," June 12, 2024. https://ec.europa.eu/eurostat/databrowser/view/tessi010/default/table?lang=en.

Evren, Kenan. *Kenan Evren'in Anılar (Cilt 2)*. İstanbul: Milliyet Yayınları, 1991.

Fakirlik Kader Midir?, 2019. https://www.youtube.com/watch?v=Yc8qWF-4kvs.

Farro, Antimo L., and Deniz Günce Demirhisar. "The Gezi Park Movement: A Turkish Experience of the Twenty-First-Century Collective Movements." *International Review of Sociology* 24, no. 1 (April 2014): 176–89.

Fernandes, Leela. *India's New Middle Class: Democratic Politics in an Era of Economic Reform*. NED-New edition. Minneapolis: University of Minnesota Press, 2006.

———. "Restructuring the New Middle Class in Liberalizing India." *Comparative Studies of South Asia, Africa and the Middle East* 20, no. 1 (2000): 88–104.

Fitne ve Fitnelerden Korunma Yolları | Nasihatler 35 | Halis Bayancuk Hoca, 2020. https://www.youtube.com/watch?v=B_XqxfiY9fo.

Flyvbjerg, Bent. *Making Social Science Matter: Why Social Inquiry Fails and How It Can Succeed Again*. Cambridge: Cambridge University Press, 2001.

Fogg, Kevin W. *Indonesia's Islamic Revolution*. Cambridge: Cambridge University Press, 2019.

Fortune (Addis). "DBE Repossesses Ayka Addis," December 27, 2018. https://addisfortune.news/dbe-repossesses-ayka-addis/.

Foucault, Michel. *Discipline and Punish: The Birth of the Prison*. New York: Vintage Books, 1977.

———. *Technologies of the Self: A Seminar with Michel Foucault*. Edited by Luther H. Martin, Huck Gutman, and Patrick H. Hutton. Amherst: University of Massachusetts Press, 1988.

Frank, Thomas. *What's the Matter with Kansas? How Conservatives Won the Heart of America*. New York: Picador, 2005.

Freer, Courtney. *Rentier Islamism: The Influence of the Muslim Brotherhood in Gulf Monarchies*. Oxford: Oxford University Press, 2018.

Fromm, Erich. *Escape from Freedom*. New York: Avon Books, 1941.

Fuller, Graham E. *The Future of Political Islam*. New York: Palgrave Macmillan, 2003.

Fuller, Jason D. "Modern Hinduism and the Middle Class: Beyond Revival in the Historiography of Colonial India." *The Journal of Hindu Studies* 2, no. 2 (November 1, 2009): 160–78.

Galal, Ahmed, ed. *Industrial Policy in the Middle East and North Africa: Rethinking the Role of the State*. Cairo: American University in Cairo Press, 2008.

Geertz, Clifford. "Thick Description: Towards an Interpretive Theory of Culture." In *The Interpretation of Cultures: Selected Essays*, 3–32. New York: Basic Books, 1973.

Geiger, Theodor. "Panik Im Mittelstand." *Die Arbeit: Zeitschrift für Gewerkschafts-politik und Wirtschaftskunde* Heft 10 (1930): 637–54.

Gelir İdaresi Başkanlığı. "Tablo 18: Merkezi Yönetim Gelirleri (2006–2022)." Bütçe Gelirleri (1923–2022), 2023. https://www.gib.gov.tr/sites/default/files/fileadmin /user_upload/VI/GBG/Tablo_18.xls.

Genç, Nurullah. *Ortaklık Kültürü*. Yönetim Kitaplığı. İstanbul: Müsiad, 2007. https://www.musiad.org.tr/uploads/yayinlar/arastirma-raporlari/pdf /ortaklik_kulturu.pdf.

Ghazzālī. *The Remembrance of Death and the Afterlife: Book 40 of The Revival of the Religious Sciences (Kitāb Dhikr al-Mawt Wa-Mā Baʿdahu: Ihyāʾ ʿUlūm al-Dīn)*. Cambridge: Islamic Texts Society, 1989.

Ghitis, Frida. "Erdogan's Obsession with Low Interest Rates Could Be His Downfall." *World Politics Review* (blog), December 2, 2021. https://www.worldpolitics review.com/in-turkey-interest-rate-gamble-could-be-erdogan-s-downfall/.

Göç İzleme Derneği. *Sokağa Çıkma Yasakları ve Zorunlu Göç Sürecinde Kadınların Yaşadıkları Hak İhlalleri ve Deneyimleri Raporu*. İstanbul: Göç İzleme Derneği, 2019. https://www.raporlar.org/wp-content/uploads/2019/01/Gocder_Yerinden _Edilen_Kadinlar_.pdf.

Gohardani, Farhad, and Zahra Tizro. *The Political Economy of Iran: Development, Revolution and Political Violence*. New York: Palgrave Macmillan, 2019.

Goldin, Claudia. "The U-Shaped Female Labor Force Function in Economic Development and Economic History." Working Paper. National Bureau of Economic Research, April 1994. http://www.nber.org/papers/w4707.

Göle, Nilüfer. "Gezi—Anatomy of a Public Square Movement." *Insight Turkey* 15, no. 3 (Summer 2013): 7–14.

Gölpınarlı, Abdülbâki. *100 Soruda Türkiye'de Mezhepler ve Tarikatler*. Cağaloglu, İstanbul: Gerçek Yayınevi, 1969.

Gong, Yue. *Manufacturing Towns in China: The Governance of Rural Migrant Workers*. Singapore: Palgrave Macmillan, 2019.

Gonzalez, Erualdo Romero, and Raul P. Lejano. "New Urbanism and the Barrio." *Environment and Planning A-Economy and Space* 41, no. 12 (December 2009): 2946–63.

Gordon, David M., Richard Edwards, and Michael Reich. *Segmented Work, Divided Workers: The Historical Transformation of Labor in the United States*. Cambridge: Cambridge University Press, 1982.

Gouldner, Alvin Ward. *The Future of Intellectuals and the Rise of the New Class*. London: Macmillan, 1979.

Gramsci, Antonio. "Observations on Certain Aspects of the Structure of Political Parties in Periods of Organic Crisis." In *Selections from the Prison Notebooks*, translated by Quentin Hoare and Geoffrey Nowell Smith, 450–62. London: Lawrence & Wishart, 1971.

Gray, Matthew. "A Theory of 'Late Rentierism' in the Arab States of the Gulf." Qatar: Center for International and Regional Studies Georgetown University School of Foreign Service in Qatar, 2011.

Green, Nile. *Global Islam: A Very Short Introduction*. Oxford: Oxford University Press, 2020.

Grütjen, Daniel. "The Turkey Welfare Regime: An Example of the Southern European Model?" *Turkish Policy Quarterly* 7, no. 1 (2008): 111–29.

Guérin, Daniel. *Fascism and Big Business*. New York: Monad Press, 1973.

Gülalp, Haldun. "Globalization and Political Islam: The Social Bases of Turkey's Welfare Party." *International Journal of Middle East Studies* 33, no. 3 (August 2001): 433–48.

Gündoğan, Mete. *Erbakan*. Nişantaşı, İstanbul: Destek Yayınları, 2019.

Güner, Ahmet. *Tarikatlar Ansiklopedisi*. İstanbul: Milliyet, 1991.

Gürakar, Esra Çeviker. *Politics of Favoritism in Public Procurement in Turkey: Reconfigurations of Dependency Networks in the AKP Era*. New York: Palgrave Macmillan, 2016.

Gürbüz, Ali Osman. "İşçi ve Halk Şirketleri Örneğinde Küçük ve Orta Büyüklükteki İşletmelerin Finansal Sorunları ve Çözüm Alternatifleri." PhD dissertation, İstanbul: Marmara University, 1987.

Gürcan, Efe Can, and Efe Peker. "Turkey's Gezi Park Demonstrations of 2013: A Marxian Analysis of the Political Moment." *Socialism & Democracy* 28, no. 1 (March 2014): 70–89.

Hacettepe Üniversitesi Nüfus Etütleri Enstitüsü. *Türkiye'de Göç ve Yerinden Olmuş Nüfus Araştırması*. Ankara: Hacettepe Üniversitesi Nüfus Etütleri Enstitüsü, 2004.

Hanımlar Buyrun—Cennet Nimetleri—Rukiye Genç—Necla Nazır, 2017. https://www.youtube.com/watch?v=VN8YlHM5ptE.

Harris, Kevan. "A Martyrs' Welfare State and Its Contradictions: Regime Resilience and Limits through the Lens of Social Policy in Iran." In *Middle East Authoritarianisms: Governance, Contestation, and Regime Resilience in Syria and Iran*, edited by Steven Heydemann and Reinoud Leenders, 61–80. Stanford, CA: Stanford University Press, 2013.

Harrison, Graham. *Developmentalism: The Normative and Transformative within Capitalism*. Critical Frontiers of Theory, Research, and Policy in International Development Studies. Oxford: Oxford University Press, 2020.

Hartshorn, Ian M. *Labor Politics in North Africa: After the Uprisings in Egypt and Tunisia*. New York: Cambridge University Press, 2019.

Harvey, David. *The Condition of Postmodernity: An Enquiry into the Origins of Cultural Change*. Cambridge, MA: Wiley-Blackwell, 1991.

Hasgül, Mevlüt. "İşadamı Ilıcan cinayetinde Yargıtay, faillerin cezasını onadı." Sabah Gazetesi, June 18, 2022. https://www.sabah.com.tr/yasam/isadami-ilican-cinayetinde-yargitay-faillerin-cezasini-onadi-6039923.

Hazine ve Maliye Bakanlığı. "2022 Merkezi Yönetim Bütçe Giderleri Ay İçi Gerçekleşmeleri Ekod4." T.C. Hazine ve Maliye Bakanlığı Muhasebat Genel Müdürlüğü, 2023. https://ms.hmb.gov.tr/uploads/sites/3/2023/07/Merkezi-Yonetim-Butce-Giderleri-Ay-Ici-Gerceklesmeleri-Ekod4-1.xls.

———. "2022 Merkezi Yönetim Bütçe Giderleri Ay İçi Gerçekleşmeleri (Program Sınıflandırması)." T.C. Hazine ve Maliye Bakanlığı Muhasebat Genel

Müdürlüğü, 2023. https://ms.hmb.gov.tr/uploads/sites/3/2023/07/Merkezi
-Yonetim-Butce-Giderleri-Ay-Ici-Gerceklesmeleri-Program-Siniflandirmasi-1.xls.

———. "Genel Yönetim Bütçe İstatistikleri—T.C. Hazine ve Maliye
Bakanlığı Muhasebat Genel Müdürlüğü." T.C. Hazine ve Maliye Bakanlığı
Muhasebat Genel Müdürlüğü, 2023. https://muhasebat.hmb.gov.tr/genel
-yonetim-butce-istatistikleri.

———. "TC Hazine ve Maliye Bakanlığı, Hazine Destekli Kefalet Sistemi
Raporları- T.C. Hazine ve Maliye Bakanlığı," December 2022. https://www
.hmb.gov.tr/finansal-piyasalar-ve-kambiyo-raporlari.

Hochschild, Arlie Russell. *Strangers in Their Own Land: Anger and Mourning on
the American Right*. New York: The New Press, 2018.

Hürriyet. "ASGARİ ÜCRET DESTEĞİ NE KADAR? 2023 asgari ücret işveren
desteği başvurusu nasıl yapılır? 6 ay süreyle çalışanlara ödenecek . . . ." Hürriyet
Gazetesi, January 7, 2023. https://www.hurriyet.com.tr/bilgi/galeri-asgari-ucret
-destegi-2023-ne-kadar-2023-asgari-ucret-isveren-destegi-basvurusu-nasil-yapilir
-6-ay-sureyle-calisanlara-odenecek-42200313/1.

———. "Hoca'nın Derneği Kavgalı Kuruldu." *Hürriyet Gazetesi*, November 8, 1998.
https://www.hurriyet.com.tr/ekonomi/hocanin-dernegi-kavgali-kuruldu-39046658.

Huzurlu Âile Hayatının Şartları—Osman Nuri Topbaş, 2016. https://www
.youtube.com/watch?v=XKwyc1bTluE.

İBB. "İstanbul Park ve Yeşil Alan Koordinatları—İBB." İstanbul Büyükşehir
Belediyesi Açık Veri Portalı, July 11, 2023. https://data.ibb.gov.tr/dataset
/parklar-ve-yesil-alanlar.

———. "Mahalle Bazlı Bina Sayıları—İBB." İstanbul Büyükşehir Belediyesi Açık Veri Portalı, January 20, 2025. https://data.ibb.gov.tr/tr/dataset
/mahalle-bazli-bina-analiz-verisi.

ILO. "Labour Migration in China and Mongolia (ILO in China and Mongolia),"
2010. https://www.ilo.org/beijing/areas-of-work/labour-migration/lang—en
/index.htm.

———. "Number of Strikes and Lockouts by Economic Activity—
Annual," November 19, 2023. https://www.ilo.org/shinyapps/bulkexplorer56
/?lang=en&id=STR_TSTR_ECO_NB_A.

———. "Trade Union Density Rate (%)—Annual," October 21, 2022. https://www
.ilo.org/shinyapps/bulkexplorer32/?lang=en&id=ILR_TUMT_NOC_RT_A.

IMF. "Datasets: Republic of Türkiye." International Monetary Fund, 2021. https://
www.imf.org/external/datamapper/profile.

———. "World Economic Outlook (October 2023)—Inflation Rate, Average
Consumer Prices." International Monetary Fund, 2023. https://www.imf.org
/external/datamapper/PCPIPCH@WEO.

İnce, Abdullah. "Nakşîlik-Siyaset İlişkisi Bağlamında Türkiye'de Dinî Gruplar ve
Milli Görüş." *Turkish Studies* 12, no. 10 (2017): 143–64.

İnce, Barış. "Bazı isimler geldi ve Erbakan'ı tehdit etti—Mehmet Bekaroğlu
ile söyleşi." Birgün Gazetesi, January 7, 2015. https://www.birgun.net/haber
/bazi-isimler-geldi-ve-erbakan-i-tehdit-etti-73631.

İnsan Cünüp Olduğunda Hemen Yıkanması Gerekir Mi?, 2020. https://www
.youtube.com/watch?v=leYNlljEStU.

International Labour Organization. *Small Matters: Global Evidence on the Contribution to Employment by the Self-Employed, Micro-Enterprises and SMEs.*
Geneva, Switzerland: International Labour Organization, 2019. https://www
.ilo.org/wcmsp5/groups/public/———dgreports/———dcomm/———publ
/documents/publication/wcms_723282.pdf.

Işık, Oğuz, and M. Melih Pınarcıoğlu. *Nöbetleşe Yoksulluk: Gecekondulaşma ve
Kent Yoksulları; Sultanbeyli Örneği.* Cağaloglu, İstanbul: İletişim, 2001.

Işık, Serap. "Turgut Özal'ın İhracat Odaklı Büyüme Politikaları ve Sonuçlarının
Değerlendirilmesi: (1983–1993 Dönemi)." In *Proceedings*, 225–33. Ankara: Turgut
Özal University, 2016.

İŞKUR. "İŞKUR İstatistikler." İŞKUR, 2023. https://www.iskur.gov.tr
/kurumsal-bilgi/istatistikler/.

İstanbul Sanayi Odası. "İSO—Türkiye'nin 500 Büyük Sanayi Kuruluşu." İstanbul
Sanayi Odası, 2023. https://www.iso500.org.tr/.

———. "İSO—Türkiye'nin İkinci 500 Büyük Sanayi Kuruluşu." İstanbul Sanayi
Odası, 2023. https://www.iso500.org.tr/ikinci-500-buyuk-sanayi-kurulusu.

ITUC. "2019 ITUC Global Rights Index: The World's Worst Countries for Workers." Brussels: International Trade Union Confederation, 2019. https://www
.ituc-csi.org/IMG/pdf/2019–06-ituc-global-rights-index-2019-report-en-2.pdf.

Jackall, Robert. *Moral Mazes: The World of Corporate Managers.* Oxford: Oxford
University Press, 2010.

Jafari, Peyman. "The Showras in the Iranian Revolution: Labour Relations and
the State in the Iranian Oil Industry, 1979–82." In *Worlds of Labour Turned
Upside Down: Revolutions and Labour Relations in Global Historical Perspectiv,*
edited by Pepjin Brandon, Peyman Jafari, and Stefan Müller, 252–85. Leiden, The
Netherlands: Brill, 2020.

Jakes, Aaron, and Ahmad Shakr. "Capitalism in Egypt, Not Egyptian Capitalism."
In *A Critical Political Economy of the Middle East and North Africa*, edited by Joel
Beinin, Bassam Haddad, and Shrene Seikaly, 123–42. Stanford, CA: Stanford
University Press, 2021.

Johnson, Cedric. *The Panthers Can't Save Us Now: Debating Left Politics and Black
Lives Matter.* New York: Verso, 2022.

Jones, Gareth Stedman. *Outcast London: A Study in the Relationship between Classes
in Victorian Society.* New York: Verso, 2013.

Joya, Angela. *The Roots of Revolt: A Political Economy of Egypt from Nasser to
Mubarak.* New York: Cambridge University Press, 2020.

*Kadınların Normal Zamanda Pamuk Kullanması Şart mıdır?—İsmailağa
NET,* 2020. https://www.ismailaga.net/video/kadinlarin-normal-zamanda
-pamuk-kullanmasi-sart-midir-19955.

Kalkınma Bakanlığı. "Kamu Yatırımlarının İllere Göre Sektörel Dağılımı."
Kamu Yatırımları Ana Sayfa, August 21, 2019. https://web.archive.org
/web/20190821171825/http://www2.kalkinma.gov.tr/kamuyat/ilozet.html.

Kandiyoti, Deniz. "Bargaining with Patriarchy." *Gender and Society* 2, no. 3 (1988): 274–90.

Kara, Mustafa. *Tasavvuf ve Tarikatlar.* İstanbul: İletişim, 1995.

Karaganis, Joe. "Delusion and Despotism: Why Erdogan's Monetary Policy Is to Blame for Turkey's Financial Crisis." *Columbia Political Review* (blog), September 21, 2022. http://www.cpreview.org/blog/2022/9/delusion-and-despotism-why-erdogans-monetary-policy-is-to-blame-for-turkeys-financial-crisis.

Karataş, Gülşen. "Tarikatlara Yönelmenin Sosyo-Kültürel ve Psikolojik Nedenleri." Marmara Üniversitesi İlahiyat Anabilim Dalı Felsefe ve Din Bilimleri Bilim Dalı, 2004.

Karaveli, Halil. *Why Turkey Is Authoritarian: From Atatürk to Erdogan.* London: Pluto Press, 2018.

Karluk, Sadık Rıdvan. "Türkiye Ekonomisini Dışa Açan 24 Ocak 1980 İstikrar Kararları: Öncesi ve Sonrasında Ekonomik Durum." In *Proceedings*, 218–24. Ankara: Turgut Özal University, 2016.

Kasapoğlu, Çağıl. "Bazı ülkeler Gülen okullarını kapatmaya neden direniyor?" *BBC News Türkçe*, August 2, 2016. https://www.bbc.com/turkce/haberler-turkiye-36950705.

Kerstenetzky, Celia Lessa, Christiane Uchôa, Nelson do Valle Silva, Celia Lessa Kerstenetzky, Christiane Uchôa, and Nelson do Valle Silva. "The Elusive New Middle Class in Brazil." *Brazilian Political Science Review* 9, no. 3 (December 2015): 21–41.

Keshavarzian, Arang. *Bazaar and State in Iran: The Politics of the Tehran Marketplace.* Cambridge: Cambridge University Press, 2007.

Kıyâmet Alâmetleri Ortaya Çıktı Mı ? Kıyâmet Alâmetleri Nelerdir ? | İsmail Hünerlice Hoca, 2020. https://www.youtube.com/watch?v=LCuUbsxuGqw.

Kızılkoyun, Fevzi. "Turkish Police on Hunt for Top Businessman Kadooğlu on Charges of Planning Murder over Debt—Türkiye News." *Hürriyet Daily News*, May 3, 2018. https://www.hurriyetdailynews.com/turkish-police-on-hunt-for-top-businessman-kadooglu-on-charges-of-planning-murder-over-debt-131267.

Kobal, Yunus. "Millî Mücadelede İç Ayaklanmalar." In *Türkler—Cilt 16*, edited by Hasan Celal Güzel, Kemal Çiçek, and Salim Koca, 78–88. Ankara: Yeni Türkiye Yayınları, 2002.

KOBİ Girişim Sermayesi Yatırım Ortaklığı A.Ş. "Ortaklık Yapımız," 2023. https://kobias.com.tr/ortaklik-yapimiz/.

Koçak, Cemil, ed. *27 Mayıs Bakanlar Kurulu Tutanakları (2 Haziran 1960—6 Kasım 1961).* İstanbul: Yapı Kredi, 2010.

Köklü, Elif. "Kent Merkezlerinde Suç Korkusunun İncelenmesi: Beşiktaş Örneği." Master's thesis, İstanbul Technical University, 2016.

Köksal, Sema. *İstanbul'daki Sosyal Demokrat Belediye Başkanları ve Gecekondu.* İstanbul: Türkiye Sosyal Ekonomik Siyasal Araştırmalar Vakfı, 1990.

Konda Araştırma. "Barometre." İstanbul: KONDA, 2017.

Kopper, Moisés. "Measuring the Middle: Technopolitics and the Making of Brazil's New Middle Class." *History of Political Economy* 52, no. 3 (June 1, 2020): 561–87.

KOSGEB. "KOBİ Tanımı Güncellendi!" Text. KOSGEB. KOSGEB, May 26, 2023. http://www.kosgeb.gov.tr/site/tr/genel/detay/8807/kobi-tanimi-guncellendi.

———. *KOSGEB 2022 Yılı Faaliyet Raporu*. Ankara: KOSGEB, 2022. https://webdosya.kosgeb.gov.tr/Content/Upload/Dosya/Kurumsal/Raporlar/KOSGEB_2022_Y%C4%Bıl%C4%Bı_%C4%B0dare_Faaliyet_Raporu.pdf.

———. Kosgeb Kobi Finansman Destek Programı Uygulama Esasları (2022). https://webdosya.kosgeb.gov.tr/Content/Upload/Dosya/KOB%C4%B0%20F%C4%B0nansman%20Destek%20Programi/1_KOB%C4%B0_Finansman_Destek_Program_Uygulama_Esaslar%C4%B1.pdf.

———. *Türkiye'deki KOBİ'lere İlişkin Bazı İstatistiki Göstergeler*. Ankara: KOSGEB, 2023. https://webdosya.kosgeb.gov.tr/Content/Upload/Dosya/Kurumsal/Raporlar/T%C3%BCrkiye'de_KOB%C4%B0'lere_%C4%B0li%C5%9Fkin_Baz%C4%B1_%C4%B0statistiki_G%C3%B6stergeler_May%C4%B1s_2023.pdf.

Kriedte, Peter, Hans Medick, and Jürgen Schlumbohm. *Industrialization before Industrialization: Rural Industry in the Genesis of Capitalism*. Cambridge: Cambridge University Press, 1981.

Krippendorff, Klaus. *Content Analysis: An Introduction to Its Methodology*. Thousand Oaks, CA: Sage, 2004.

Kripto Paralara Yatırım Günah Mı? Cübbeli Ahmet Hoca—Ertan Özyiğit Ile Kayıt Dışı—5 Mart 2021, 2021. https://www.youtube.com/watch?v=tbio3KaXyzo.

Kurlantzick, Joshua. *Democracy in Retreat: The Revolt of the Middle Class and the Worldwide Decline of Representative Government*. New Haven, CT: Yale University Press, 2014.

Kutlu, Sönmez. "Diyanet İşleri Başkanlığı ve İslamiçi Dini Gruplarla (Mezhep ve Tarikatlar) İlişkileri." *Dini Araştırmalar* 12, no. 33 (June 1, 2009): 107–27.

Lacan, Jacques. *The Seminar of Jacques Lacan—The Ethics of Psychoanalysis 1959–1960 Book VII*. Edited by Jacques-Alain Miller. Translated by Dennis Porter. New York: W.W. Norton, 1992.

Le Monde.fr. "Egypt Outlines a Vast Privatization Plan." May 24, 2022. https://www.lemonde.fr/en/international/article/2022/05/24/egypt-outlines-a-vast-privatization-plan_5984498_4.html.

Lekesiz, Ömer. "Türkiye'de Cemaatler ve Tarikatler Gerçeği." *Eskiyeni* 34 (2017): 107–18.

Lewis, Bernard. *Islamic Revival in Turkey*. London: Royal Institute of International Affairs, 1952.

Lindgaard, Jakob. "It Is Too Dangerous to Be an Individual in Turkey." In *In the Aftermath of Gezi: From Social Movement to Social Change?*, edited by Oscar Hemer and Hans-Åke Persson, 109–32. New York: Palgrave Macmillan, 2017.

Lord, Ceren. *Religious Politics in Turkey: From the Birth of the Republic to the AKP*. Cambridge: Cambridge University Press, 2018.

Luciani, Giacomo. "Allocation vs. Production States: A Theoretical Framework." In *The Rentier State*, edited by Hazem Beblawi and Giacomo Luciani, 63–82. New York: Croom Helm, 1987.

Mahdavy, Hossein. "Patterns and Problems of Economic Development in Rentier States: The Case of Iran." In *Studies in the Economic History of the Middle East: From the Rise of Islam to the Present Day*, edited by Michael A. Cook, 428–67. Oxford: Oxford University Press, 1970.

Mandaville, Peter. *Islam and Politics*. New York: Routledge, 2014.

Maoz, D. "The Mutual Gaze." *Annals of Tourism Research* 33, no. 1 (January 2006): 221–39.

Mardin, Şerif. "Center-Periphery Relations: A Key to Turkish Politics?" *Daedalus* 102, no. 1 (January 1, 1973): 169–90.

———. *Religion and Social Change in Modern Turkey: The Case of Bediuzzaman Said Nursi*. New York: SUNY Press, 1989.

Marglin, Stephen A. "What Do Bosses Do? The Origins and Functions of Hierarchy in Capitalist Production." *The Review of Radical Political Economics* 6, no. 2 (1974): 60–112.

Marx, Karl. *Capital: A Critique of Political Economy, vol. 1*. Translated by Ben Fowkes. New York: Penguin, 1976.

———. *Capital: A Critique of Political Economy, vol. 2*. Translated by David Fernbach. London: Penguin, 1992.

———. *Capital: A Critique of Political Economy, vol. 3*. Translated by David Fernbach. London: Penguin, 1993.

Masoud, Tarek E. *Counting Islam: Religion, Class, and Elections in Egypt*. New York: Cambridge University Press, 2014.

Massey, Douglas S., and Nancy A. Denton. *American Apartheid: Segregation and the Making of the Underclass*. Cambridge, MA: Harvard University Press, 1993.

Massicard, Elise. *Street-Level Governing: Negotiating the State in Urban Turkey*. Stanford, CA: Stanford University Press, 2022.

McDowall, David. *A Modern History of the Kurds*. Revised edition. London: I.B. Tauris, 2004.

McGee, T. G., George C. S. Lin, Andrew M. Marton, Mark Y. L. Wang, and Jiaping Wu. *China's Urban Space: Development under Market Socialism*. New York: Routledge, 2007.

Meder, Mehmet, and Hande Şahin. *Neo-liberal Politikaların İşçi Sınıfına Yansıması: Denizli ve Bursa Örneği*. İstanbul: Ege Yayınları, 2008.

Melvin, Jess. *The Army and the Indonesian Genocide: Mechanics of Mass Murder*. New York: Routledge, 2018.

Menchik, Jeremy. *Islam and Democracy in Indonesia: Tolerance without Liberalism*. Cambridge: Cambridge University Press, 2016.

Mendels, Franklin F. "Proto-Industrialization: The First Phase of the Industrialization Process." *The Journal of Economic History* 32, no. 1 (1972): 241–61.

Merleau-Ponty, Maurice. *Signs*. Evanston, IL: Northwestern University Press, 1964.

———. *The Visible and the Invisible*. Edited by Claude Lefort. Translated by Alphonso Lingis. Evanston, IL: Northwestern University Press, 1968.

Milanovic, Branko. *Global Inequality: A New Approach for the Age of Globalization*. Cambridge, MA: The Belknap Press of Harvard University Press, 2016.

Milli Gazete. "Tarihin ilk ayakkabılı eylemi bize ait çıktı." *Milli Gazete*, February 17, 2010. https://www.milligazete.com.tr/haber/1161133/tarihin-ilk-ayakkabili -eylemi-bize-ait-cikti.

Milli Nizam Partisi. *Milli Nizam Partisi 1. Büyük Kongresi*. Ankara: As Matbaası, 1971.

———. *Milli Nizam Partisi Kuruluş Beyannamesi*. Ankara: Nüve Matbaası, 1970.

———. *Milli Nizam Partisi Program ve Tüzük*. Ankara: As Matbaası, 1970.

Milli Selamet Partisi. *Milli Selamet Partisi 5 Haziran 1977 Seçim Beyannamesi*. Ankara: Gaye Matbaası, 1977.

———. *Milli Selamet Partisi 1973 Seçim Beyannamesi*. İstanbul: Fatih Yayınevi Matbaası, 1973.

———. *Milli Selamet Partisi Program ve Tüzük*. Ankara: Elif Matbaacılık, 1973.

Mills, Charles W. "White Ignorance." In *Race and Epistemologies of Ignorance*, edited by Shannon Sullivan and Nancy Tuana, 11–38. Albany, NY: SUNY Press, 2007.

Mitchell, Timothy. *Carbon Democracy: Political Power in the Age of Oil*. London: Verso, 2011.

Mortan, Kenan, and Osman S. Arolat. *Gaziantep Ekonomisine Bakış*. Maltepe, İstanbul: Heyamola Yayınları, 2009.

Murdock, George Peter. *Outline of Cultural Materials*. New Haven, CT: Human Relations Area Files, 2008.

Murphy, A. G. "The Dialectical Gaze: Exploring the Subject-Object Tension in the Performances of Women Who Strip." *Journal of Contemporary Ethnography* 32, no. 3 (June 2003): 305–35.

Müsiad. *İşadamlarına Kriz Dönemi Öneriler*. İstanbul: Müsiad, 2001.

———. *Yeni Ekonomi Döneminde KOBİ'ler İçin Rekabet ve Büyüme*. Cep Kitapları, İstanbul: Müsiad, 2005.

Nakhoul, Samia. "Turkey's Erdogan, Master Campaigner, Faces Toughest Contest Yet." Reuters, May 12, 2023. https://www.reuters.com/world/middle-east /turkeys-erdogan-master-campaigner-faces-toughest-contest-yet-2023-05-11/?taid =645e15358e5bed000141e87e&utm_campaign=trueAnthem:+Trending+Conte nt&utm_medium=trueAnthem&utm_source=twitter.

Nasr, Vali. *Forces of Fortune: The Rise of the New Muslim Middle Class and What It Will Mean for Our World*. New York: The Free Press, 2009.

———. *The Rise of Islamic Capitalism: Why the New Muslim Middle Class Is the Key to Defeating Extremism*. New York: The Free Press, 2010.

Neden Huzuru Olmayan Bir Toplum Olduk?—Osman Nuri Topbaş, 2018. https:// www.youtube.com/watch?v=BjUyShuLdnk.

Neumann, Franz. "Introduction." In *The Nazi Elite*, by Daniel Lerner, iii–vii. Stanford, CA: Stanford University Press, 1951.

Nilson, Herman. *Michel Foucault and the Games of Truth*. New York: Palgrave Macmillan, 1998.

Norşin Seyda Şeyh Abdulkerim Çevik / Müminlerin Vasıfları, 2016. https://www .youtube.com/watch?v=9fW_SxJuJmk.

OECD. "Data—PISA." Organisation for Economic Co-operation and Development, 2022. https://www.oecd.org/pisa/data/.

———. "Housing Prices," 2019. https://doi.org/10.1787/63008438-en.

Ogilvie, Sheilagh C., and Markus Cerman. *European Proto-Industrialization: An Introductory Handbook*. New York: Cambridge University Press, 1996.

Öniş, Ziya. "The Political Economy of Islamic Resurgence in Turkey: The Rise of the Welfare Party in Perspective." *Third World Quarterly* 18, no. 4 (1997): 743–66.

———. "Turgut Özal and His Economic Legacy: Turkish Neo-Liberalism in Critical Perspective." *Middle Eastern Studies* 40, no. 4 (2004): 113–34.

Onuş. "Ethem Sarısülük'ün otopsisi: Kurşun 9 mm. çapında." *BBC News Türkçe*, June 15, 2013. https://www.bbc.com/turkce/haberler/2013/06/130615 _ethem_sarisuluk_otopsi.

ÖSYM. "(2002-ÖSYS) Yükseköğretim Programlarına Ek Yerleştirme Ile İlgili Sayısal Bilgiler." Öğrenci Seçme ve Yerleştirme Merkezi, 2021. https://www.osym .gov.tr/TR,2190/2002-osys-yuksekogretim-programlarina-ek-yerlestirme-ile -ilgili-sayisal-bilgiler.html.

———. "2017–ÖSYS Ek Yerleştirme Sonuçlarına İlişkin Sayısal Bilgiler." Öğrenci Seçme ve Yerleştirme Merkezi, 2017. https://dokuman.osym.gov.tr/pdfdokuman /2017/OSYS/EK/Say%C4%B1salBilgiler12092017.pdf.

———. "Basın Duyurusu: 2009-ÖSYS Yükseköğretim Programlarına Ek Yerleştirme." Öğrenci Seçme ve Yerleştirme Merkezi, October 2, 2009. https:// www.osym.gov.tr/TR,1165/2009-osys-ek-yerlestirme-kontenjanlar-02102009 .html.

Özarslan, Sevinç. "Eski Boydak Holding Başkanı Hacı Boydak, 8 yıl sonra tahliye oldu." Kronos Haber, July 12, 2024. https://kronos38.news /boydak-holding-yonetim-kurulu-baskani-haci-boydak-8-yil-sonra-tahliye-oldu/.

Özbür, Sedat. *Necmettin Erbakan ve Gümüş Motor*. İstanbul: İlke Yayıncılık, 2014.

Özdemir, Mücahit, and Hakan Aslan. *Türkiye'de İslami Finansın Dönüşümünün Ekonomi Politiği*. İstanbul: SETA, 2017.

Özel, Isik. *State-Business Alliances and Economic Development: Turkey, Mexico and North Africa*. Hoboken, NJ: Routledge, 2014.

Öztürk, Murat. *Agriculture, Peasantry and Poverty in Turkey in the Neo-Liberal Age*. Wageningen, The Netherlands: Wageningen Academic, 2012.

Öztürk, Musa. "Adil Ekonomik Düzen' de Artı(k) Değerin Paylaşımı." *Journal of Turkish Studies* 12, no. 8 (October 17, 2019): 149–70.

Özuğurlu, Metin. *Anadolu'da Küresel Fabrikanın Doğuşu: Yeni İşçilik Örüntülerinin Sosyolojisi*. Ankara: Kalkedon, 2008.

PAPCİ PUBG OYNAYANLARI BEKLEYEN TEHLİKELER ABDULLAH GÜRBÜZ HOCAEFENDİ, 2020. https://www.youtube.com/watch?v =O_okvjwVYo4.

Patton, Michael Q. *Qualitative, Research and Evaluation Methods*. Thousand Oaks, CA: Sage, 2002.

Pennington, Shelley, and Belinda Westover. *A Hidden Workforce: Homeworkers in England, 1850–1985*. Basingstoke, UK: Macmillan Education, 1989.

Pepinsky, Thomas B., and R. William Liddle Mujani, Saiful. *Piety and Public Opinion: Understanding Indonesian Islam*. New York: Oxford University Press, 2018.

Pınarcıoğlu, M. Melih. "KOBİ'ler, Kolektif Verimlilik ve Sorunları." *Toplum ve Bilim* 86 (2000): 303–17.

Piore, Michael J., and Charles F. Sabel. *The Second Industrial Divide: Possibilities for Prosperity*. New York: Basic Books, 2000.

Pirenne, Henri. *Economic and Social History of Medieval Europe*. New York: Harcourt, Brace, 1937.

Poulantzas, Nicos A. *Classes in Contemporary Capitalism*. London: NLB, 1975.

Presidency of the Republic of Turkey. "Presidency of the Republic of Turkey: Biography of Recep Tayyip Erdoğan." Presidency of the Republic of Turkey, 2023. https://www.tccb.gov.tr/en/receptayyiperdogan/biography/.

Pripstein Posusney, Marsha. "Egyptian Privatization." *Middle East Report* 210 (Spring 1999). https://merip.org/1999/03/egyptian-privatization/.

Refah Partisi. *Refah Partisi 20 Ekim 1991 Genel Seçimi Beyannamesi*. Ankara, 1991. https://acikerisim.tbmm.gov.tr/xmlui/handle/11543/672.

Riaz, Ali. "Islamist Parties, Elections, and Democracy in Bangladesh." In *Islamist Parties and Political Normalization in the Muslim World*, edited by Quinn Mecham and Julie Chernov Hwang, 156–74. Philadelphia: University of Pennsylvania Press, 2014.

Ricciardelli, Michael. "A Demographic and Legal Profile of January 6 Prosecutions." Seton Hall University, June 26, 2023. https://www.shu.edu/news/a-demographic-and-legal-profile-of-january-6-prosecutions.html.

Rizzo, Alessandra. "New York Ranks Last for Amount of Green Space per Resident among the Major US Cities." *NBC New York* (blog), July 15, 2019. https://www.nbcnewyork.com/news/local/new-york-ranks-last-for-amount-of-green-space-per-resident-among-the-major-us-cities/1529935/.

Robinson, Geoffrey B. *The Killing Season: A History of the Indonesian Massacres, 1965–66*. Reprint edition. Princeton, NJ: Princeton University Press, 2018.

Robinson, Glenn E. *Global Jihad: A Brief History*. Stanford, CA: Stanford University Press, 2020.

Roccu, Roberto. "Democratization beyond Capitalist Time: Temporalities of Transition in the Middle East after the Arab Uprisings." *Middle East Critique* 28, no. 3 (July 3, 2019): 227–41.

Rosenfeld, Bryn. *The Autocratic Middle Class: How State Dependency Reduces the Demand for Democracy*. Princeton, NJ: Princeton University Press, 2020.

Ross, Michael L. "Does Oil Hinder Democracy?" *World Politics* 53, no. 3 (April 2001): 325–61.

Roy, Donald F. "'Banana Time' Job Satisfaction and Informal Interaction." *Human Organization* 18, no. 4 (1959): 158–68.

Roy, Olivier. *Globalized Islam: The Search for a New Ummah.* New York: Columbia University Press, 2004.

Sağlamer, Gülsüm, and Necmi Erdoğan. "A Comparative Study on Squatter Settlements and Vernacular Architecture." *Open House International* 18, no. 1 (1993): 41–49.

Şahinkaya, Serdar. "Devlet Sanayi ve İşçi Yatırım Bankası'ndan Türkiye Kalkınma Bankası'na: 1975–2001 Döneminde Kurumsal Yapıdaki Temel Dönüşümler Üzerine Düşünceler ve Bazı Öneriler." Ankara: ODTÜ, 2002.

Said Aly, Abdel Monem, Ayşe Öncü, Çağlar Keyder, and Saad Eddin Ibrahim. *Developmentalism and Beyond: Society and Politics in Egypt and Turkey.* Cairo: American University in Cairo Press, 1994.

Saldana, Johnny. *The Coding Manual for Qualitative Researchers.* London: Sage, 2009.

Salvatorelli, Luigi. *Nazionalfascismo.* Turin, Italy: G. Einaudi, 1977.

Sanayi ve Teknoloji Bakanlığı. "Sanayi ve Teknoloji Bakanlığı Faaliyet Raporları." T.C. Sanayi ve Teknoloji Bakanlığı, 2023. https://www.sanayi.gov.tr /plan-program-raporlar-ve-yayinlar/faaliyet-raporlari.

———. "Sanayi ve Teknoloji Bakanlığı Yatırım Teşvik İstatistikleri." T.C. Sanayi ve Teknoloji Bakanlığı, 2023. https://www.sanayi.gov.tr/istatistikler /yatirim-istatistikleri/mi1304021615.

Şapolyo, Enver Behnan. *Mezhepler ve Tarikatlar Tarihi.* İstanbul: Elif Kitabevi, 2004.

Sarıbay, Ali Yaşar. "Milli Nizam Partisi'nin Kuruluşu ve Programının İçeriği." In *Modern Türkiye'de Siyasi Düşünce Cilt 6 İslamcılık,* edited by Tanıl Bora and Murat Gültenkingil, 576–90. İstanbul: İletişim, 2005.

Savina, Gygli, Florian Haelg, Niklas Potrafke, and Jan-Egbert Sturm. "The KOF Globalisation Index—Revisited." *Review of International Organizations* 14, no. 3 (2019): 543–74.

Sayari, Sabri. "Turkey's Islamist Challenge." *Middle East Quarterly,* September 1, 1996. https://www.meforum.org/314/turkeys-islamist-challenge.

Sayed, Hadin. "The Breakdown of Erdoganomics—Michigan Journal of Economics," May 17, 2022. https://sites.lsa.umich.edu/mje/2022/05/17/the -breakdown-of-erdoganomics/.

Schneier, Edward. *Muslim Democracy: Politics, Religion and Society in Indonesia, Turkey and the Islamic World.* New York: Routledge, 2015.

Schön, Lennart. "Proto-Industrialisation and Factories: Textiles in Sweden in the Mid-nineteenth Century." *Scandinavian Economic History Review* 30, no. 1 (1982): 57–71.

Seyoum, Asrat. "Ayka Addis: A Blip in Ethiopia's Textile Vision." *The Reporter: Latest Ethiopian News Today,* November 26, 2016. https://www.thereporterethiopia .com/3101/.

Shahid, Kunwar Khuldune. "Islamonomics: How Erdogan Crashed the Turkish Economy." *The Spectator,* December 9, 2021. https://www.spectator.co.uk /article/islamonomics-how-erdogan-crashed-the-turkish-economy/.

Shils, Edward. *Center and Periphery: Essays in Macrosociology*. Chicago: University of Chicago Press, 1975.

Sidnell, Jack. *Conversation Analysis*. Malden, MA: Blackwell, 2010.

"Sigara Mevzusu," Ömer Öngüt -Kuddise Sırruh-, 1991. https://www.youtube.com /watch?v=R6ZAsOyrgCw.

SODAP. "SODAP." Sosyalist Dayanışma Platformu, 2021. https://sodap2.org/.

Soliman, Samer. "State and Industrial Capitalism in Egypt." Monograph. Cairo Papers. Cairo: American University in Cairo Press, 1998.

Sönmez, Mustafa. *AKP-Cemaat: Çatışmadan Çöküşe*. Ankara: Notabene, 2014.

Sosyal Güvenlik Kurumu. "SGK Veri Uygulaması." Sosyal Güvenlik Kurumu, 2023. https://veri.sgk.gov.tr/.

Soylu, Merve, and Harun Şencal. "Cemaatçilik ve Bireycilik Arasında Piyasa İlişkileri." *Akademik İncelemeler Dergisi* 16, no. 2 (October 15, 2021): 140–55.

Sözen, Edibe, and M. Hakan Yavuz. "The Gezi Protests: An Outburst at Turkey's Shatter-Zone." *Insight Turkey* 16, no. 1 (Winter 2014): 147–62.

Statista. "Migrant Workers in China." *Statista*, June 9, 2023. https://www.statista .com/topics/1540/migrant-workers-in-china/.

Steinberg, David A. "Analysis | Turkey's President Insists on Low Interest Rates. That Could Cost Him Politically, This Research Shows." *The Washington Post*, January 13, 2022.

Tanuwidjaja, Sunny. "Political Islam and Islamic Parties in Indonesia: Critically Assessing the Evidence of Islam's Political Decline." *Contemporary Southeast Asia* 32, no. 1 (2010): 29–49.

Tanyılmaz, Kurtar. "Chapter 3—The Deep Fracture in the Big Bourgeoisie of Turkey." In *Chapter 3—The Deep Fracture in the Big Bourgeoisie of Turkey*, 89–116. Oxford: Berghahn Books, 2015.

Tatlılıoğlu, Durmuş. "Tasavvuf ve Tarikatlara Sosyolojik Bir Bakış." *Dinbilimleri Akademik Araştırma Dergisi* 4, no. 9 (2014): 99–128.

TBB. "Türkiye'de Bankacılık Sistemi (1958'den İtibaren)—2021." Ankara: Türkiye Bankalar Birliği, 2021. https://www.tbb.org.tr/tr/banka-ve-sektor -bilgileri/istatistiki-raporlar/Turkiye%60de_Bankacilik_Sistemi_(1958% E2%80%99den_Itibaren)_/6096.

TBMM. "TBMM Ülkemizde Demokrasiye Müdahale Eden Tüm Darbe ve Muhtıralar Ile Demokrasiyi İşlevsiz Kılan Diğer Bütün Girişm ve Süreçlerin Tüm Boyutları Ile Araştırılarak Alınması Gereken Önlemlerin Belirlenmesi Amacıyla Kurulan Meclis Araştırması Komisyonu Raporu—Cilt 1." S. Sayısı: 376. Ankara: TBMM, November 2012.

T.C. Adalet Bakanlığı. "Tablo-2: Yatırım Projeleri Listesi." Ankara: T.C. Adalet Bakanlığı Strateji Geliştirme Başkanlığı, 2018. https://sgb.adalet.gov .tr/Resimler/Dokuman/2712201915062072017-yili-yatirim-toplulastirilmis -projelerin-detay-tablosu-tumu.pdf.

T.C. Cumhurbaşkanlığı. "Cumhurbaşkanı Erdoğan: 'Ahilik teşkilatı asırlarca bu topraklarda ticaretin ve dayanışmanın bel kemiği olmuştur.'" Türkiye Cumhuriyeti Cumhurbaşkanlığı İletişim Başkanlığı Resmî Sitesi, September 16, 2021.

https://www.iletisim.gov.tr/turkce/Haberler/detay/cumhurbaskani-erdogan
-ahilik-teskilati-asirlarca-bu-topraklarda-ticaretin-ve-dayanismanin-bel-kemigi
-olmustur/.

———. "Esnaf Ile Sanatkârlarımız Bu Ülkenin ve Milletin Omurgasıdır," May 25, 2015. https://www.tccb.gov.tr/haberler/410/32339/esnaf-ile
-sanatkrlarimiz-bu-ulkenin-ve-milletin-omurgasidir.

T.C. İçişleri Bakanlığı. "Mülki İdare Birimleri." Türkiye Mülki İdare Bölümleri Envanteri, 2011. https://www.e-icisleri.gov.tr/Anasayfa/MulkiIdariBolumleri
.aspx.

T.C. Kültür ve Turizm Bakanlığı. "Yeşil Ordu Cemiyeti." *Atatürk Ansik-lopedisi* (blog), March 3, 2021. https://ataturkansiklopedisi.gov.tr/bilgi
/yesil-ordu-cemiyeti/.

TCMB. "TCMB—Sektör Bilançoları—İmalat." Türkiye Cumhuriyet Merkez Bankası, 2023. https://www3.tcmb.gov.tr/sektor/#/tr/C/imalat.

———. "TCMB—Sektör Bilançoları—Metaveri." Türkiye Cumhuriyet Merkez Bankası, 2023. https://www3.tcmb.gov.tr/sektor/dosyalar/menu/metadata
_tr.pdf.

Tercan, Binali. "1948'den Bugüne İmar Afları." *Mimarlık—Mimarlar Odası* 403 (2018): 20–30.

TİHV. "TİHV Dokümantasyon Merkezi Verilerine Göre 16 Ağustos 2015—18 Mart 2016 Tarihleri Arasında Sokağa Çıkma Yasakları ve Yaşamlarını Yitiren Siviller." Ankara: Türkiye İnsan Hakları Vakfı (Human Rights Foundation of Turkey), March 22, 2016.

TİM. "History (The Union of Chambers and Commodity Exchanges of Türkiye)." Türkiye İhracatçılar Meclisi, 2022. https://www.tobb.org.tr/Sayfalar/Eng
/Tarihce.php.

———. "TİM—Türkiye İhracatçılar Meclisi—Türkiye'nin İlk 1000 İhracatçı Araştırması." Türkiye İhracatçılar Meclisi, April 6, 2023. https://www.tim.org
.tr/tr/turkiyenin-ilk-1000-ihracatci-arastirmasi.

TMSF. *Tasarruf Mevduatı Sigorta Fonu 2017 Faaliyet Raporu.* İstanbul: TMSF, 2018.

———. "Kayyım Olunan Şirketler." Tasarruf Mevduatı Sigorta Fonu, 2024. https://
www.tmsf.org.tr.

TOBB. "Kurulan/Kapanan Şirket İstatistikleri." Türkiye Odalar ve Borsalar Birliği, 2023. https://www.tobb.org.tr/BilgiErisimMudurlugu/Sayfalar/Kurulan
KapananSirketistatistikleri.php.

Topal, Aylin. "The State, Crisis and Transformation of Small and Medium-Sized Enterprise Finance in Turkey." In *The Political Economy of Financial Transforma-tion in Turkey,* edited by Galip Yalman, Thomas Marois, and Ali Rıza Güngen, 221–42. New York: Routledge, 2019.

Torun, İshak. "Tarikat ve Cemaatlerin Siyasetle İlişkisi." *Balkan Sosyal Bilimler Dergisi* 9, no. 17 (2020): 83–94.

Trint. "Transcribe Video and Audio to Text | Content Editor | Trint," 2022. https://
trint.com/.

TRT. "Kamuda FETÖ temizliği: 125 bin 678 personel ihraç edildi," July 15, 2022. https://www.trthaber.com/haber/gundem/kamuda-feto-temizligi-125-bin -678-personel-ihrac-edildi-694991.html.

Tuğal, Cihan. *The Fall of the Turkish Model: How the Arab Uprisings Brought Down Islamic Liberalism.* London: Verso, 2016.

———. "Fight or Acquiesce? Religion and Political Process in Turkey's and Egypt's Neoliberalizations." *Development and Change* 43, no. 1 (January 2012): 23–51.

———. *Passive Revolution: Absorbing the Islamic Challenge to Capitalism.* Stanford, CA: Stanford University Press, 2009.

TÜİK. "1992 Genel Sanayi ve İşyerleri Sayımı—İktisadi Faaliyet Kollarına Göre İşyeri Sayısı ve İstihdam." Nüfus ve Demografi, 2022. https://data.tuik.gov.tr /Bulten/DownloadIstatistikselTablo?p=WS6710vYGzaqvBMODPxtB1ULrR MBJu9cbWNo/RzrwwbF9TaxMfNcSIigNja9aaoc.

———. "2002 Genel Sanayi ve İşyerleri Sayımı—İstatistiki Bölge Birimleri Sınıflaması (İBBS) ve Ekonomik Faaliyet Bölümlerine Göre Yerel Birim Sayısı ve İstihdam." Türkiye İstatistik Kurumu, 2007. https://data.tuik.gov.tr/Bulten /DownloadIstatistikselTablo?p=yaoGL1BbtWjs3h7ATnptQWvTHipAHD3a2 iZzVQi3Rdpeqy465sZXAINwsMeGzIcE.

———. "Eğitim Durumuna Göre Temel Işgücü Göstergeleri." Türkiye İstatistik Kurumu, November 17, 2023. https://data.tuik.gov.tr/Bulten /DownloadIstatistikselTablo?p=BddSHyv/ZDFhtION3edIzgsgFZ /EaWuD6g9bfNFpzoKvHvkOzK3JjkQhkS6S/WBJ.

———. "Ekonomik Faaliyete Göre Kurulan ve Kapanan Şirket ve Kooperatiflerin Sayı ve Sermayeleri." Türkiye İstatistik Kurumu, May 4, 2007. https://data.tuik .gov.tr/Bulten/DownloadIstatistikselTablo?p=H44gK9h8Mz54TYEC9fTCiN 22EH6sPKneZPKe7zZUPFkBL2TxojsJPTxHLbU1rc8H.

———. "İl Bazında Gayrisafi Yurt İçi Hasıla, 2021." Türkiye İstatistik Kurumu, December 8, 2022. https://data.tuik.gov.tr/Bulten/Index?p=Il -Bazinda-Gayrisafi-Yurt-Ici-Hasila-2021-45619.

———. "İl Bazında Gayrisafi Yurt Içi Hasıla, Iktisadi Faaliyet Kollarına (A10) Göre, Cari Fiyatlarla (Değer), 2004–2022." Türkiye İstatistik Kurumu, December 8, 2022. https://data.tuik.gov.tr/Bulten/DownloadIstatistikselTablo?p=yF2U/4E /mTNce6jCP2302MDic8Bo9dC50CuGzyiaAg72K2IBVhl/rAs31w7A3yS8.

———. "İlçelere Göre Şehir ve Köy Nüfusu, Yıllık Nüfus Artış Hızı, Yüzölçümü ve Nüfus Yoğunluğu, 2000." Türkiye İstatistik Kurumu, 2022. https://data.tuik .gov.tr/Bulten/DownloadIstatistikselTablo?p=5CoZXp3xXE4PyyUwcUNbxU jXUCQ3jUmCyEQhQYq/Df548V7q2FASpUhhEw7Drw40.

———. "İstatistiklerle Çocuk, 2022." Türkiye İstatistik Kurumu, April 18, 2023. https://data.tuik.gov.tr/Bulten/Index?p=Istatistiklerle-Cocuk-2022 -49674#:~:text=ADNKS%20sonu%C3%A7lar%C4%B1na%20g%C3%B6re%20 2022%20y%C4%B1l%C4%B1nda,az%20bir%20%C3%A7ocuk%20 bulundu%C4%9Fu%20g%C3%B6r%C3%BCld%C3%BC.

———. "Konut ve Çevre Problemlerine Göre Kurumsal Olmayan Nüfusun Dağılımı." Türkiye İstatistik Kurumu, May 8, 2023. https://data.tuik.gov.tr

/Bulten/DownloadIstatistikselTablo?p=68aAdJWzA1APmU2RYPyHQG
/gbuHvh507APVPai7xazciQXf5XrZ22tUdJvAbcjcK.

———. "Küçük ve Orta Büyüklükteki Girişim İstatistikleri, 2021." Türkiye
İstatistik Kurumu, December 26, 2022. https://data.tuik.gov.tr/Bulten
/Index?p=Kucuk-ve-Orta-Buyuklukteki-Girisim-Istatistikleri-2021-45685.

———. "Meslek Ana Grubu ve Ekonomik Faaliyete Göre Yıllık Ortalama Brüt
Kazanç, 2006." Türkiye İstatistik Kurumu, December 3, 2020. https://data.tuik
.gov.tr/Bulten/DownloadIstatistikselTablo?p=d4vppYDAmHwwO75FaYo4u
byIRoG1Ye7y8zQDp18hly2qtoetpeFE2loDMDelbo2u.

———. "Meslek Ana Grubu ve Ekonomik Faaliyete Göre Yıllık Ortalama Brüt
Kazanç (2010,2014,2018)." Türkiye İstatistik Kurumu, December 3, 2020.
https://data.tuik.gov.tr/Bulten/DownloadIstatistikselTablo?p=bdAn17mAoT
9UnEH79BEpsJWriolgbUMRMO5/C3xBOZZ1fwWk1Lw11BAuJW5ZmB7V.

———. "Meslek Ana Grubu ve Ekonomik Faaliyete Göre Yıllık Ortalama
Brüt Kazanç, 2022." Kazanç Yapısı İstatistikleri, 2022, December 25, 2023.
https://data.tuik.gov.tr/Bulten/Index?p=Kazanc-Yapisi-Istatistikleri-2022
-49750#:~:text=Tablo%2D8-,Meslek,-grubuna%20gore%20y%C4%
B1ll%C4%B1k.

———. "Number of Enterprises by Size Class and Economic Activity." Small and
Medium Sized Enterprises Statistics, 2022. https://data.tuik.gov.tr/Bulten
/Index?p=49438&dil=2.

———. "Number of Persons Employed by Size Class and Economic Activity." Small
and Medium Sized Enterprises Statistics, 2022. https://data.tuik.gov.tr/Bulten
/Index?p=49438&dil=2.

———."Small and Medium Sized Enterprises Statistics, 2023." December 24,
2024. https://data.tuik.gov.tr/Bulten/Index?p=Small-and-Medium-Sized
-Enterprises-Statistics-2023-53543&dil=2.

———. "Tablo-5 Hayatta Kalma Göstergeleri (2016–2020)." Türkiye İstatistik
Kurumu, December 16, 2022. https://data.tuik.gov.tr/Bulten/Index?p
=Girisimcilik-ve-Is-Demografisi-2021-45584#:~:text=Tablo%2D5%20
Hayatta%20kalma%20g%C3%B6stergeleri%202016%2D2020.

———. "Yapı Izin Istatistikleri ve Değişim Oranları, 2002–2023 [Building Permits
and Rates of Change, 2002–2023]." Türkiye İstatistik Kurumu, November 21,
2013. https://data.tuik.gov.tr/Bulten/DownloadIstatistikselTablo?p=8u2RTT
BA4ISbtFgcbuvsYjdEMdLYtsZGlPMIY7mAgpoI6GI34N2Lf/AwmFgCQPgo.

———. "YAPI RUHSATI—CONSTRUCTION PERMIT Kullanma Amacına
Göre Yapılacak Yeni ve Ilave Yapılar (Yeni Sınıflama)." Türkiye İstatistik
Kurumu, 2016. https://web.archive.org/web/20160529035929/http://www.tuik
.gov.tr/PreIstatistikTablo.do?istab_id=609.

Tunaya, Tarık Zafer. *Türkiye'de Siyasal Partiler, Cilt 1: İkinci Meşrutiyet Dönemi.*
İstanbul: Hürriyet Vakfı Yayınları, 1988.

Turkish Statistical Institute. *Statistical Indicators (1923–2008).* Ankara: Turkish
Statistical Institute, 2008.

TÜRKONFED. "Tarkan KADOOĞLU—Yönetim Kurulu Başkanı." TÜRKON-FED, 2023. https://turkonfed.org/tr/yonetim/7/tarkan-kadooglu.

Türkün-Erendil, Asuman. "Mit ve Gerçeklik Olarak Denizli Üretim ve İşgücünün Değişen Yapısı: Eleştirel Kuram Açısından Bir Değerlendirme." *Toplum ve Bilim* 86 (2000): 91–117.

UBS. "Global Wealth Report 2023." UBS—Family Office & UHNW, 2023. https://www.ubs.com/global/en/family-office-uhnw/reports/global-wealth-report-2023.html.

UDUPA, SAHANA. "World-Class Aspirations: The New Middle Class of India." Edited by Christiane Brosius. *Economic and Political Weekly* 48, no. 15 (2013): 29–31.

Uludağ, Alican. "7 Yıl Geçti, Ankara Gar Katliamı'nda Sorumlular Yargılanmadı." *Deutsche Welle—Türkçe*, October 10, 2022. https://www.dw.com/tr/g%C3%B6z-g%C3%B6re-g%C3%B6re-gelen-bir-katliam-10-ekim-tren-gar%C4%B1-patlamas%C4%B1/a-63388031.

UN Stats. "National Accounts—Analysis of Main Aggregates (AMA)." United Nations Statistics Division, 2023. https://unstats.un.org/unsd/snaama/Basic.

Uner, Mehmet Mithat, and Aybegum Gungordu. "The New Middle Class in Turkey: A Qualitative Study in a Dynamic Economy." *International Business Review* 25, no. 3 (June 1, 2016): 668–78.

UNIDO. "UNIDO Statistics Data Portal," 2023. https://stat.unido.org/database/INDSTAT%204%202023,%20ISIC%20Revision%204.

Ünal, Recep. "Çok Ortaklı Şirketlere Genel Bakış." Expertise thesis. Ankara: Devlet Planlama Teşkilatı Müsteşarlığı, 1983.

Varma, Pavan K. *The New Indian Middle Class.* Noida, India: HarperCollins, 2015.

Varol, Çiğdem. "Entrepreneurial Networks in Local Industrial Development: A Comparative Analysis of Denizli and Gaziantep Cases." Orta Doğu Teknik Üniversitesi, Department of City and Regional Planning, 2002.

V-Dem Institute. "V-Dem Codebook—V12 March 2022." University of Gothenburg, V-Dem Institute, 2022. https://www.v-dem.net/static/website/img/refs/codebookv12.pdf.

———. "V-Dem Dataset Version 12." V-Dem Institute, University of Gothenburg, 2022. https://www.v-dem.net/.

Wacquant, Loïc J. D. *Urban Outcasts: A Comparative Sociology of Advanced Marginality.* Cambridge: Polity, 2008.

Wallerstein, Immanuel Maurice. "After Developmentalism and Globalization, What?" *Social Forces* 83, no. 3 (2005): 1263–78.

White, Jenny. *Islamist Mobilization in Turkey: A Study in Vernacular Politics.* Seattle: University of Washington Press, 2002.

WID. "World Inequality Database," 2022. https://wid.world/data/.

Wilson, Rodney. *Islam and Economic Policy: An Introduction.* Edinburgh: Edinburgh University Press, 2015.

World Bank. "Employment in Industry (% of Total Employment) (Modeled ILO Estimate)," 2022. https://data.worldbank.org/indicator/SL.IND.EMPL.ZS.

———. "Employment to Population Ratio, 15+, Total (%) (Modeled ILO Estimate)." World Bank Open Data, 2023. https://data.worldbank.org/indicator/SL.EMP.TOTL.SP.ZS.

———. "Exports of Goods and Services (Current US$)." World Bank Open Data, 2022. https://data.worldbank.org/indicator/NE.EXP.GNFS.CD.

———. "GDP (Current US$)." World Bank Open Data, 2023. https://data.worldbank.org/indicator/NY.GDP.MKTP.CD.

———. "GDP per Capita (Current US$)." World Bank Open Data, 2023. https://data.worldbank.org/indicator/NY.GDP.PCAP.CD.

———. "Labor Force Participation Rate, Female (% of Female Population Ages 15+) (Modeled ILO Estimate)." World Bank Open Data, 2024. https://data.worldbank.org/indicator/SL.TLF.CACT.FE.ZS.

———. "Population, Total | Data," 2021. https://data.worldbank.org/indicator/SP.POP.TOTL.

———. "Total Natural Resources Rents (% of GDP)." World Bank Open Data, 2021. https://data.worldbank.org/indicator/NY.GDP.TOTL.RT.ZS.

———. "Urban Population (% of Total Population) | Data," 2021. https://data.worldbank.org/indicator/SP.URB.TOTL.IN.ZS.

Wright, Erik Olin. "Varieties of Marxist Conceptions of Class Structure." *Politics & Society* 9, no. 3 (September 1, 1980): 323–70.

Yalçın, Soner. "AKP'nin Asıl Korkusu; Nurcu-Nakşibendi Kavgası!" ODATV, June 2, 2008. https://www.odatv4.com/siyaset/akpnin-asil-korkusu-nurcu-naksibendi-kavgasi-2016.

———. *Hangi Erbakan*. Yenişehir, Ankara: Başak Yayınları, 1994. http://catalog.hathitrust.org/api/volumes/oclc/30930236.html.

Yalman, Galip L. "The Neoliberal Transformation of State and Market in Turkey: An Overview of Financial Developments from 1980 to 2000." In *The Political Economy of Financial Transformation in Turkey*, edited by Galip L. Yalman, Thomas Marois, and Ali Rıza Güngen, 51–87. New York: Routledge, 2019.

Yankaya, Dilek. "28 Şubat, İslami Burjuvazinin İktidar Yolunda Bir Milat." *Birikim* 278–79 (2012): 29–37.

———. *Yeni Islâmî Burjuvazi: Türkiye Modeli*. Translated by Melike Işık Durmaz. İstanbul: İletişim, 2014.

Yaşar, M. Emin. "Dergah'tan Partiye, Vakıf'tan Şirkete Bir Kimliğin Oluşumu ve Dönüşümü: Lskenderpaşa Cemaati." In *Modern Türkiye'de Siyasi Düşünce Cilt 6 İslamcılık*, edited by Tanıl Bora and Murat Gültenkingil, 323–44. İstanbul: İletişim, 2005.

———. "Mehmet Zahid Kotku." In *Modern Türkiye'de Siyasi Düşünce Cilt 6 İslamcılık*, edited by Tanıl Bora and Murat Gültenkingil, 326–29. İstanbul: İletişim, 2005.

Yavuz, M. Hakan. *Erdoğan: The Making of an Autocrat*. Edinburgh: Edinburgh University Press, 2021.

———. "Milli Görüş Hareketi: Muhalif ve Modernist Gelenek." In *Modern Türkiye'de Siyasi Düşünce Cilt 6 İslamcılık*, edited by Tanıl Bora and Murat Gültenkingil, 591–603. İstanbul: İletişim, 2005.

———. "Political Islam and the Welfare (Refah) Party in Turkey." *Comparative Politics* 30 (1997): 63–82.

Yıldırım, Kemal, and Aysu Başkaya. "Farklı Sosyo-Ekonomik Düzeye Sahip Kullanıcıların Konut Ana Yaşama Mekanını Değerlendirmesi." *Gazi Üniversitesi Mühendislik Mimarlık Fakültesi Dergisi* 21, no. 2 (March 1, 2013): 285–91.

Yilmaz, Volkan. "The AK Party and the Politics of Healthcare in Turkey in the Last Decade," 2017.

Yilmaz, Ihsan, Mehmet Efe Caman, and Galib Bashirov. "How an Islamist Party Managed to Legitimate Its Authoritarianization in the Eyes of the Secularist Opposition: The Case of Turkey." *Democratization* 27, no. 2 (2020): 265–82.

Yilmaz, Muzaffer Ercan. "The Rise of Political Islam in Turkey: The Case of the Welfare Party." *Turkish Studies* 13, no. 3 (September 1, 2012): 363–78.

YÖK. "2020 Yılı Yükseköğretim Kurumları Sınavı Yerleştirme Sonuçları Raporu." Yükseköğretim Kurulu, 2021. https://www.yok.gov.tr/HaberBelgeleri/Basin Aciklamasi/2020/yks-yerlestirme-sonuclari-raporu-2020.pdf.

Yönder, Ayşe. "Implications of Double Standards in Housing Policy: Development of Informal Settlements in Istanbul." In *Illegal Cities: Law and Urban Change in Developing Countries*, edited by Edesio Fernandes and Ann Varley, 55–69. London: Zed Books, 1998.

YSK. "Açık Veri Portalı." Yüksek Seçim Kurulu Açık Veri Portalı (Supreme Election Council Database), 2023. https://acikveri.ysk.gov.tr/anasayfa.

"YSK Web Portal." Accessed November 18, 2023. https://www.ysk.gov.tr/.

Yüksel, Ayşe Seda. Kürt Sermayesinin Siyasî Yönelimi. Heinrich Böll Stiftung—Perspective Türkiye, 2014. https://tr.boell.org/sites/default/files /perspectives_8_tr.pdf.

Zaim, Sabahattin. "Ekonomik Hayatta Müslüman İnsanın Tutum ve Davranışları." In *İş Hayatında İslam İnsanı (Homo Islamicus): İslami Duyarlılıkla Yönetilen Firmalarda Örgütsel Davranış Biçimleri*, edited by Hüner Şencan, 101–12. Müsiad Araştırma Raporları. İstanbul: Müsiad, 1994.

Zencirci, Gizem. "Markets of Islam: Performative Charity and the Muslim Middle Classes in Turkey." *Journal of Cultural Economy* 13, no. 5 (September 2, 2020): 610–25.

Zengin, Ertuğrul. *Akıncılar Hareketi: 1970'lerde İslâmcı Gençliğin Oluşumu ve Eylemi*. İstanbul: İletişim Yayınları, 2021.

Zizek, Slavoj. *Looking Awry: An Introduction to Jacques Lacan through Popular Culture*. Revised edition. Cambridge, MA: MIT Press, 1992.

INDEX

capital: capital accumulation, 14, 18, 235;
commodity capital, 240; faubourgeoisie, 240; Gülenists, 216, 218; hydrocarbon resources, 14; international capital,
93; investment, 14; money capital, 239;
monopoly capital, 216, 239; petty bourgeoisie, 240; secularist capital, 216;
small capital, 57, 68, 216, 243; technocracy, 240. *See also* industrial capitalism;
industrialists; political economy
Cemaat, 112–13, 116, 219, 224
China, 10, 35, 68, 141, 213, 248, 250
Çiller, Tansu, 75, 215
circulation class, 13, 236, 240, 244–46,
249–50, 264
class: global middle class, 235. *See also*
bourgeoisie; proletariat
cleric, 13, 104, 110, 180, 190, 214–15
clientelism, 13, 16, 60, 117, 131, 150, 233, 247
clique, 13, 17, 63–64, 86, 104, 130, 195,
214–17, 219–20, 226, 228–29, 231, 233
coalition, 35, 43, 63, 65, 68, 80, 138, 150, 193,
195, 198, 202, 204, 225, 227
Cold War, 12–14, 18, 21, 24, 33, 46, 50–51,
55–56, 107, 191, 237, 239, 242, 249, 251
commander of jihad, 57, 64
Committee for Union and Progress, 55
commodity, 10–11, 16, 33, 61, 91, 223, 239–40
community: mosque community, 143;
phobic community, 123. *See also*
neighborhoods
competition, 9–10, 79, 88, 92, 98–99, 101–3,
107–9, 124, 148, 164, 172, 183–84,
213–14, 222, 237
comprador, 15, 59, 61, 63, 227
concentric rings, 154
confiscation, 218, 227
conflict, 18, 62, 103, 108, 112, 116, 197, 203, 208,
214, 217, 219, 224, 227, 231–32, 247, 250
conservatism: Abdülhamit, 55; cities, 61;
Ghazali, 180; government, 45; Islamism,
8; non-Islamist, 242; political elite, 62;
rural, 66; Sunni, 150
conveyor belt of flesh, 163

Davutoğlu, Ahmet, 227
demarcation, 137, 176, 185, 187, 244
Demirel, Süleyman, 61–62, 65, 67–68, 73,
75, 82, 90, 203, 215

Deniz Feneri, 75–76
Denizli, 19, 100, 102–4, 106, 108–9,
217–19, 228
department of production, 259
deskilling, 135, 236, 241, 244
developmentalism, 35, 244
dexterity, 134
dhikr, 111, 178
DHKP-C (Revolutionary People's
Liberation Party/Front), 146
dictator, 37, 44
dirt, 119–22, 140, 185–87
dirtiness, 121
discipline, 63, 77, 157, 167, 241
disenfranchisement, 37
DISIAD (Diyarbakır Industrialists and
Businessmen's Association), 208
Diyarbakır, 133, 135, 201, 204, 207–10
doctrine, 64, 81, 91, 98, 179, 214, 233
dogma, 244
drudgery, 5, 16, 140, 164, 175–77, 244
dynastic regimes, 14, 22, 28–29, 32, 34

Ecevit, Bülent, 215
ecology, 70, 110
Egypt, 22, 24, 27, 31, 35–46, 190
elite formation, 59
emic, 111, 155, 223
employment: China, 248n22; employee,
9–10, 12, 43, 88, 94, 136, 155, 168, 217;
employer, 9–11, 13, 17, 28, 89, 93, 98, 101,
111, 134, 145, 152–53, 155, 157, 162–63, 165,
167–69, 172, 187–89, 202, 213, 243;
industrial labor, 25, 28, 44–45, 70;
Kurdish employer, 157; labor force,
22–23, 26; managers, 243; piecework,
161; precarious, 16, 153; SMEs, 12, 136;
subsidies, 92; unemployment, 16, 94–95,
131, 164, 178, 244; women, 184
enclosure of urban space, 70
engineer, 15, 45, 57, 60, 64, 95, 105, 138,
221, 245
Ennahda, 43
enterprises: Gülenists, 228; industrial, 10,
49, 60, 70, 228; large, 102; multi-shareholder, 93; SMEs, 94, 134, 136; SMEs,
industrial, 12, 49, 88, 248; state-owned,
89; Township and Village-, 248;
worker-, 65

proletariat: proletarianization, 33, 97, 142,
184, 195, 198, 205, 236, 243; proletarianization, Kurds, 214; working-class
neighborhoods, 193. *See also* class;
Marx, Karl
promiscuity, 148
promissory bill, 92
proselytizer, 6–7, 9, 17, 174, 176
protectionism, 250
protest, 37, 44, 83, 183, 192–93, 198,
200–203, 208–12, 216, 222. *See also* Gezi
protoindustrialization, 242
purity, 17, 119–20, 122, 152–56, 175, 177–79,
185, 187, 189, 264; purification, 155, 240

reductionism, 230, 247
regime of domination, 13, 16, 78, 132, 152–55,
191,
religion: ideology, 22. *See also* Islam;
secularism; Alevi; Alevi Zaza
religiosity, 22–28, 33
religious: extremists, 35; government, 23, 45;
ideology, 23, 27; motifs, 12, 21–22, 149;
opposition, 22, 26, 46; orders, 16–17, 19,
43, 56–58, 63–65, 72, 77–78, 82, 87,
110–13, 116–17, 123–24, 140, 152, 174,
190, 215, 225, 234, 245, 253; revival, 34
rent: departmental disequilibrium, 264;
form of revenue, 238; proletariat, 264;
surplus value, 264
Republican People's Party, 63, 65–66, 72,
83–85, 89–90, 147, 192–94, 197–99, 225
residential, 13, 71, 79, 84, 134, 147, 157,
161–62, 194, 199, 230, 247, 250
riba, 90, 116–17
ritual, 16–17, 67, 92, 113, 117, 119–23, 143,
177–78, 188, 215, 225, 245
rızk, 112, 115
routinization, 236
rupture, 203
rural regimes, 29, 32–34

Sabancı Family, 67, 88, 206
Sadaqah, 113–14
Sadat, Anwar, 35–37, 45
Salafi, 112, 114–16, 120, 253, 255–58
salvation, 48, 63, 75, 89, 92, 111, 113, 119, 121,
123, 175, 215, 244

Salvatorelli, Luigi, 249
Santri, 35
Sarısülük, Ethem, 200
sartorial practice, 8, 122, 156–57, 178, 182
Saudi Arabia, 24, 27, 29, 31, 44
second tier of globalization, 141, 249
secularism: AKP, 197; antisecularist political spectacles, 65; authoritarian, 200;
bureaucracy, secularist, 216; capital, 222;
cosmopolitan secularist, 198; Egypt,
190; Egypt and Bangladesh, 22; Gülenists, 216; Indonesia, 36; institutions,
44; institutions, secular, 57; Islamism,
divide between Islamists and secularists, 202; Islamism, Islamist-secularist
tension, 250; Islamism, Islamists, 229,
234, 236; Islamism, Islamist–secularist
divide, 242; Kemalists, secular officers,
55; Kemalists, War of Independence, 56;
Kurds, 231; military coup, Evren,
Kenan, 67; military coup, secularist, 80;
military coup, secularist junta, 59;
Ottoman Empire, Imperial Era, 55;
petty bourgeoisie, 185; PKK, 203; political economy, 243; political establishment, secular political elites, 37; political establishment, secularist, 72;
political establishment, secularist
establishment, 14, 59; political opposition, main opposition, 130; political
opposition, secularist opposition, 147;
Republican People's Party, 197; right-
wing, 199; right-wing, Republican Trust
Party, 68; secular, 11, 15–16; secular
egalitarian country, 36; secularist, 5,
7–9, 17, 50, 194; secularist outsiders, 152;
secularist-Islamist rift, 195; social class,
247; Türkonfed, 207. *See also*
Kemalism; Islamism
Selahattin Demirtaş, 205
Selahattin Özgündüz, 144
self-made man, 139–45, 171, 187
sex, 118–22, 137, 168, 179, 253, 256
sharia, 38. *See also* Islam
Shiite, 143–44
shopkeeper, 11, 20, 57–58, 76, 86, 89, 111–12,
115–17, 153, 174–75, 189, 194, 196–97
Şirinevler, 3–5, 9–10, 12, 16, 20

owners, 205; urban population, 68;
workers, 12; working-class, 152. *See also*
Istanbul; Bağcılar
Turkmenistan, 23–24, 27, 31, 33
Tuskon (Turkish Businessmen and
Industrialists Confederation), 218
Türkonfed, 206–7, 218
Tüsiad, 83–85, 206–7, 218. *See also*
industrialists; capital

ultranationalists, 48, 66, 72–73, 199,
212, 225
Ümraniye, 75, 77–78
union of chambers, 61
urbanization, 7, 38, 40–41, 50, 64, 68:
China, 68; Egypt, 38, 41; Indonesia, 41;
Turkey, 41. *See also* cities; industrialization; migration

Vandewiele, 109
Verlagsystem, 242

wealth: billionaires, 237; distribution, 18;
distribution, middle stratum of, 235,
237; percentiles of the, 198; poverty and,
115–16; redistribution of, 10; stratum of,
239; total, 11, 237
welfare, 72, 77, 118, 146, 148, 150, 209, 215,
233, 247, 258
wildcat strike, 145, 172
woman, 120–22, 129, 168, 183–84, 187
worker: Alevi Zaza, 172; female, 156; garment, 166; guest, 149; Kurdish, 213;
turnover, 145; unionization, 46;
unskilled, 19

Xiaoping, Deng, 248

Yenimahalle, 145–46, 149–51, 160

zakat, 98, 114
Zaza, 150, 160, 172
Zeytinburnu, 75, 139, 149, 171